Fruzsina Gárdos-Orosz

Constitutional Justice under Populism

The Transformation of Constitutional Jurisprudence in Hungary since 2010

1828
AKADÉMIAI KIADÓ
Wolters Kluwer

Published by:
Kluwer Law International B.V.
PO Box 316
2400 AH Alphen aan den Rijn
The Netherlands
E-mail: lrs-sales@wolterskluwer.com
Website: www.wolterskluwer.com/en/solutions/kluwerlawinternational

Sold and distributed by:
Wolters Kluwer Legal & Regulatory U.S.
920 Links Avenue
Landisville, PA 17538
United States of America
E-mail: customer.service@wolterskluwer.com

and

Published by:
Akadémiai Kiadó, Budafoki út 187-189. A/3 III. floor, Budapest
E-mail: info@akademiai.hu
Website: www.akademiai.hu

1st edition, 2024, 244 pages
Printed: Serifa®
Printed on acid-free paper

ISBN 9789403520285 (Kluwer Law International)
ISBN 9789403520384 (e-book, Kluwer Law International)
ISBN 9789403520483 (web-PDF, Kluwer Law International)
ISBN 9789634549727 (Akadémiai Kiadó)
ISBN 9789634549710 (e-book, Akadémiai Kiadó)

The publication is based on the author's Hungarian book: 'Az alkotmánybíráskodás átalakulása Magyarországon 2010 után' (The transformation of Hungarian constitutional jurisdiction after 2010), published by Akadémiai Kiadó in 2023.

The publication was supported by the framework of projects PID2021-126765NB-I00 of the MICIN and AICO/2021/099 of the GVA Spain, the HUN-REN Centre for Social Sciences and the ELTE Law School.

GOBIERNO DE ESPAÑA MINISTERIO DE CIENCIA E INNOVACIÓN GENERALITAT VALENCIANA HUN REN CENTRE FOR SOCIAL SCIENCES ELTE LAW

CONTENT

Constitutional Justice under Populism

The Transformation of Constitutional Jurisprudence in Hungary since 2010

INTRODUCTION

In the 2010 parliamentary elections, the former opposition party Fidesz – Hungarian Civic Alliance (Fidesz – Magyar Polgári Szövetség) and its coalition partner, the Christian Democratic Party (Kereszténydemokrata Néppárt or KDNP), won a landslide victory, and the new government won a two-thirds parliamentary majority. In the spring of 2011, in the absence of two opposition parties (which had withdrawn from the constitutional procedure in protest against the "destruction of the rule of law"), the National Assembly adopted Hungary's new Fundamental Law, which has since been amended eleven times in its first ten years.

The transformation of Hungarian constitutional jurisprudence can be followed in chronological order in this book. I start from what we learned at university about the concept of constitutional courts and constitutional adjudication, then I review the events of the past twelve years, and finally review what we know about the in stitution's many functions in order to summarise how the experiences of the twelve years, summarised in this book, compare to the ideal. The book provides a timeline of how we saw the changes in Hungarian constitutional adjudication between 2010 and 2022.

The first chapter of the book presents basic concepts of constitutional review in a historical and theoretical-dogmatic approach. The second chapter describes the changes in the law governing the Hungarian Constitutional Court (AB). The third chapter focuses on the key issues in the redefinition of constitutional review and related jurisprudence in the period between 2010 and 2022. The fourth chapter examines the nature and experience of the new trend in constitutional adjudication, the German-type constitutional complaint procedure. The fifth chapter asks how constitutional review of legislation and judicial decisions have evolved in major and politically sensitive cases such as the economic crisis, the terrorist threat or the pandemic, in which a two-thirds government majority has settled conflicting socio-economic relations through crisis legislation. This is not only the case in Hungary, but also elsewhere in Europe, which is why in this chapter I present the results of collaborative studies of the practice of the constitutional courts of some EU member states and of the Strasbourg and Luxembourg courts. This is in order to understand more fully in which respects and in which cases Hungarian constitutional court practice has been unique.

I will conclude in the volume by returning to what is meant by constitutional review in the classical sense as the basis of the Kelsen-type constitutional adjudication. I will try to justify my conclusion that the nature of today's Hungarian Constitutional Court – due to the constraints of the changed political and constitutional environment – is closer to a constitutional advisory body orienting the jurisprudence of the ordinary courts than to a Kelsen-type constitutional court with effective constitutional review of the legislation.

Several of the studies that form the starting point, and in some cases the basis, of the book were written together with my colleagues. I started my analysis of the new jurisprudence of the Constitutional Court in 2011 as a staff member of the Constitutional Court, former law clerk of judge István Kukorelli, my distinguished professor at ELTE Law School, when we were preparing *Az alkotmányjogi panasz kézikönyve [The Handbook of the Constitutional Complaint]* (published in 2015) under the guidance of Secretary General Botond Bitskey. In this undertaking, Johanna Fröhlich was my partner in providing our readers with a thorough introduction to the practice of the admissibility of the constitutional complaint, while considering the function and legitimacy of this legal instrument in the new constitutional order. Johanna and I also looked at the practice of other countries in relation to the admissibility of *amparo, Verfassungsbeschwerde* or *Question Prioritaire de Constitutionnalité* (QPC). We were able to take part in the new venture of introducing the constitutional complaint. After the publication of *Az alkotmányjogi panasz kézikönyve [The Handbook of the Constitutional Complaint]*, I was asked by András Jakab to write a chapter on the Constitutional Court for the volume *A magyar jogrendszer állapota [The State of the Hungarian Legal System]* (2015). In the framework of the research cooperation between the Curia (Supreme Court of Hungary) and the Constitutional Court, the Institute for Legal Studies of the Hungarian Academy of Sciences, Centre for Social Sciences (CSS Institute for Legal Studies), under my coordination, carried out a large-scale, book-length undertaking of empirical, quantitative and qualitative analysis of the relationship between the ordinary courts and the Constitutional Court in relation to the protection of specific rights. The material was eventually published as a study in a four-volume work edited by Péter Darák, President of the Curia, and Tamás Sulyok, President of the Constitutional Court, and is also available in one volume published by the CSS Institute for Legal Studies. In collaboration with Zsolt Ződi and Viktor Olivér Lőrincz, we have tried to explore the significance of the constitutional complaint in the system of legal remedies. Subsequently, my doctoral student Renáta Bedő and I examined how the enforcement of the Fundamental Law is evolving in private relations in the practice after 2012, i.e. how the new framework of constitutional complaints affects ordinary judicial practice. This line of investigation for me was particularly interesting, since the main thesis of my PhD published in 2011 was that the introduction of a German-type constitutional complaint in Hungary could be well suited to the structure of Hungarian constitutional democracy, and that it would be necessary to establish the indirect horizontal effect of the former Constitution in constitutional law.

My suggestions have come true, but the problem is that the constitutional environment surrounding these conceptions has fundamentally changed from liberal to populist constitutionalism. I had already considered it important in my PhD thesis, which I completed in 2010, to start from the complex functioning of the constitutional system, in which we situate this legal institution and the constitutional normative concepts and observations on the related jurisprudence. This is why I wrote in my study for the *Alkotmánybírósági Szemle [Constitutional Court Review]*, some of these analytical elements are also part of the related book chapter, that it is important to pay attention to whether certain classical legal institutions, while retaining their classical regulation in the new constitutional system, still fulfil their original constitutional role, i.e. whether they contribute to the functioning of an open society based on equal human dignity, to the protection of individual rights, to the limitation of the exercise of public power, and to the common good in the pluralistic sense.

Péter Gárdos helped me in understanding the group of foreign currency loan cases, which also concerned the indirect private law enforcement of the Fundamental Law. I published two papers with him in the journal *Jogesetek Magyarázata [Explanation of Legal Cases]*, prior to my own constitutional law-focused investigation, and their summarizing observations are also included in the present volume. I learned about the concept of the Constitution and the Constitutional Court from András Bragyova, former judge of the Constitutional Court during the months of discussions that accompanied the preparation of our study. Herewith, I would like to commemorate him after his decease with respect and affection.

The most intensive collaboration I have had over the last eight years has been with Zoltán Szente. The products of this work are two edited volumes in Hungarian and two in English, as well as numerous collaborative articles. The results and lessons learned from this research are also part of this book; the original version of the last, comparative chapter was jointly prepared with him. He was, furthermore, the academic reader of the Hungarian version of the present volume.

I would like to thank my colleagues (teachers, friends and family) for researching and working with me on these topics, and for their permission to use some of the results of our common reflections for the purposes of this book as indicated in the text.

1. CONSTITUTIONAL REVIEW, CONSTITUTIONAL COURTS AND THE INSTITUTIONAL CHALLENGES OF THE 21ST CENTURY IN EUROPE

Although there has been a long tradition of judicial review in the United States since the famous Marbury v. Madison case[1] of 1803, it was only after the Second World War that it became widespread in Europe – and later around the world – for states to set up constitutional courts to enforce and control the application of their constitutions.[2] Constitutional courts were in most cases established by the constitutions themselves, and also defined the powers which the constitutional court was empowered to exercise in order to verify – and possibly enforce – the application of the constitution.

The Austrian jurist Hans Kelsen is regarded as the father of European-style constitutional jurisprudence and the independent institution that underpins it, the constitutional court, which is separate from other constitutional institutions.[3] It is true that a state body with similar powers to enforce the constitution had already been conceived in Czech law, but the first functioning institution was created in Austria.[4] According to the Kelsen approach, constitutional review is a necessary and indispensable corollary of a constitutional democracy, since it is only in this way that the constitution, which defines the scope of the normative legal order, can become alive and applicable. According to Kelsen, the constitution is the supreme norm *(Grundnorm)* to which all lower legislation must conform.[5] In Kelsen's thought, normativity, the prescriptive character, is associated with sanction. In his

---

1 *Marbury v. Madison,* 5 U.S. (1 Cranch) 137 (1803).

2 Cappelletti, Mauro – Adams, John Clarke: "Judicial Review of Legislation: European Antecedents and Adaptations", *Harvard Law Review,* 1966/6, 1207–1224; Favoreu, Louis: *Les Cours Constitutionnelles,* Paris, Presses Universitaires de France, 1986, 16–31; Rousseau, Dominique: *La justice constitutionnelle en Europe,* Paris, Montchrestien, 1998; Schwarze, Jürgen: *Verfassungsrecht und Verfassungsgerichtsbarkeit im Zeichen Europas,* Baden-Baden, Nomos, 1998.

3 Bragyova, András: *Az alkotmánybíráskodás elmélete,* Budapest, Közgazdasági és Jogi Könyvkiadó – MTA Állam- és Jogtudományi Intézet, 1994; Paczolay, Péter: "Hans Kelsen és az alkotmánybíráskodás európai modelljének fejlődése », in Cs. Kiss, Lajos (ed.): *Hans Kelsen jogtudománya,* Budapest, Gondolat, 2007, 447; Kelemen, Katalin – Steuer, Max: "Constitutional Court of Hungary", in Grote, Rainer – Lachenmann, Frauke – Wolfrum, Rüdiger (eds.): *Max Planck Encyclopedia of Comparative Constitutional Law,* Oxford University Press, 2019.

4 Halmai, Gábor: "Hans Kelsen és a magyar Alkotmánybíróság", *Világosság,* 2005/II, 3–14.

5 Kelsen, Hans: *Tiszta jogtan,* Budapest, ELTE Állam- és Jogtudományi Kar, Bibó István Szakkollégium, 1988, 47.

view, constitutional review only makes sense if it is able to filter out the unconstitutional norm from the legal system, which is only possible if the constitutional court is given the power by the constitution to annul legislation.[6] The characteristic feature of a Kelsen-type constitutional court is therefore that it can annul an unconstitutional norm, and become a negative legislator, so to speak. Kelsen, as a famous politician of his time as well as being a legal theorist, also accepted that the constitutional court, which is given this role to ensure constitutional law and order, is not only – and not necessarily – composed of judges. The constitutional court is thus based, as originally conceived, on the premise that political decision-making in a constitutional state is determined by law, within the framework of the constitution.[7] It is therefore acceptable that members of parliament and other democratically elected public figures (politicians) should have the right to petition the constitutional court, and it is also acceptable that the constitutional court, like the state legislature, should ultimately have a say as a "negative legislator", by identifying the constitutional limits to the realisation of political objectives by law. The constitutional court operates at the border between law and politics; it is now common to acknowledge this when examining the functioning of one or other constitutional court.[8] However, the constitutional court, as originally conceived, is both a legal and a political institution in the system of state organisation: its function is political in the sense that its findings relate to politics and identify the limits of political action,[9] but legal in the sense that it is a state institution for the interpretation and enforcement of the constitution, which carries out its interpretation of constitutional law according to a predefined set of procedures and legal methodological criteria. It takes decisions with public justification on the constitution as a legal document, in a way that is transparent and comprehensible to all.

The power of the Constitutional Court to review the constitutional validity of legislation, i.e. its conformity with the constitution, either before or after its entry into force, in the context of an abstract review procedure, guarantees a decision which is of general application and *erga omnes*, i.e. with the same effect for everyone. This means that the Constitutional Court, according to the Kelsen concept, examines whether a law or a legislative provision fits into the legal system, i.e. within the constitutional framework, completely independently of a specific case or cases. The abstract test conceived by Kelsen, and which is thus prevalent, presupposes that the constitutional court interprets both the constitution and the statute or legislative provision that is the subject of the constitutionality inquiry. The image of

6 Kelsen, Hans: "Ki legyen az alkotmány őre?", in Takács, Péter (ed.): *Államtan. Írások a XX. századi általános államtudomány köréből,* Budapest, Szent István Társulat, 2003, 289–332.

7 Kelsen, Hans: "Wesen und Entwicklung der Staatsgerichtsbarkeit", in Häberle, Peter (ed.): *Verfassungsgerichtsbarkeit,* Darmstadt, Wissenschaftliche Buchgesellschaft, 1976, 98–144.

8 Gárdos-Orosz, Fruzsina – Szente, Zoltán (eds.): *Jog és politika határán. Alkotmánybíráskodás Magyarországon 2010 után,* Budapest, HVG-ORAC, 2015.

9 Győrfi, Tamás: *Az alkotmánybíráskodás politikai karaktere. Értekezés a magyar alkotmánybíráskodás első tíz évéről,* Budapest, Indok, 2001.

constitutional courts is therefore very much determined by the way in which they define their own interpretative activity or by the way in which the Constitution prescribes this interpretative activity. The majority of constitutions do not provide for the manner in which and the rules according to which the constitutional court should carry out its interpretative task, although some constitutions, including the Hungarian one, contain some provisions on this basic activity. Since the interpretative principles and methods are mostly developed by the constitutional courts themselves as a result of judicial work, they contribute to a greater or lesser extent – depending on their activity in the field of interpretation – to the determination of the substantive content of the constitution.

The abstractly formulated normative text of the constitution as a written word cannot, according to our current linguistic philosophical knowledge, in itself as a text, prescribe the procedural and substantive conditions under which a law can be valid. Indeed, a constitutional provision determines the conditions of validity for hundreds and thousands of legal acts. In the process of human, constitutional-judicial and legal-applicative contributions, in the operation of the constitutional court as a constitutional institution, it is therefore necessary to carry out the process of deduction, i.e. to derive from the abstract norm, legal principle or more concrete constitutional rule the decision that describes whether a specific legal provision is in conformity with the constitution or not. The operation of the constitution cannot therefore be imagined without legal and constitutional interpretation.[10] According to the Kelsen approach, the decision on the constitutionality of a law, which is generally binding on all, can be taken most effectively and legitimately by a specialised body with a mandate from the political constitution-making authorities.[11] The literature also refers to what is known collectively as the new constitutionalism, a constitutional system which no longer truly believes in the sovereignty of the people or of parliament, but which, by relativising the concept of sovereignty, has arrived at the ideal of self-limiting power, which entails a constitutional court with the power to annul laws.[12] The majority of states that are ostensibly or actually constitutional democracies now have a constitution with a catalogue of fundamental rights, which is defended by a constitutional court.[13]

When we look at the constitutional review, the functioning of constitutional courts and the higher courts that also perform constitutional review functions, we see that both the constitutional review of legislation and the constitutional review of court decisions raise a number of fundamental questions that provide basic di-

---

10 Zippelius, Reinhold: *Juristische Methodenlehre,* München, C. H. Beck, 1994; Alexy, Robert: *Theorie der juristischen Argumentation,* Frankfurt am Main, Suhrkamp, 1991; Bobbitt, Philip: "Methods of Constitutional Argument", *University of British Columbia Law Review,* 1989/3, 449–458.

11 Kelsen, Hans: "Ki legyen az alkotmány őre?", in Takács, Péter (ed.): *Államtan. Írások a XX. századi általános államtudomány köréből,* Budapest, Szent István Társulat, 2003, 289–332.

12 Stone Sweet, Alec: "Constitutional Court", in Rosenfeld, Michel – Sajó, András (eds.): *Oxford Handbook of Comparative Constitutional Law,* Oxford, Oxford University Press, 2012, 821.

13 Law, David – Versteeg, Mila: "The Evolution and Ideology of Global Constitutionalism", *California Law Review,* 2011/5, 1163.

lemmas about the organisation of the state. Perhaps this is why research into constitutional review is so popular today.

Today, in a constitutional democracy, the final decision on questions of interpretation of the law is often taken by the constitutional courts, which is binding on all, and thus has a direct impact on the legal system as a whole. Its role is very different from that of the traditional judiciary, and its activity is decisive in the exercise of public power.[14]

In a constitutional democracy, the conception of public law tends to regard constitutional review as a legal function; in America, for example, John Marshall, the first Chief Justice of the Supreme Court, said almost two hundred years ago, "Judicial power, as contradistinguished from the power of the laws, has no existence. Courts are the mere instruments of the law, and can will nothing. When they are said to exercise a discretion, it is a mere legal discretion, a discretion to be exercised in discerning the course prescribed by law; and, when that is discerned, it is the duty of the court to follow it. Judicial power is never exercised for the purpose of giving effect to the will of the judge, always for the purpose of giving effect to the will of the legislature [...]."[15]

This notion has prevailed consistently in the United States: "When an act of Congress is appropriately challenged in the courts as not conforming to the constitutional mandate, the judicial branch of the Government has only one duty – to lay the article of the Constitution which is invoked beside the statute which is challenged and to decide whether the latter squares with the former."[16] Until today it remains the case that, "to declare a state act unconstitutional is not to declare that we (the court) prohibit it, but that the constitution prohibits it".[17]

In Germany, the Federal Constitutional Court *(Bundesverfassungsgericht)* began its work in 1951. As one author of an authoritative article concludes, the German Federal Constitutional Court has probably never been seriously attacked for its politically relevant activities.[18] This is true even if it is undoubtedly the case that

---

14 Stone Sweet, Alec: "Constitutional Court", in Rosenfeld, Michel – Sajó, András (eds.): *Oxford Handbook of Comparative Constitutional Law*, Oxford, Oxford University Press, 2012, 821.

15 *Osborn v. Bank of the United States*, 9 Wheaton 738 (1824), 866, cited in Szente, Zoltán: "Jog és politika határán: az alkotmánybíróságok és az alkotmánybíráskodás jellegéről", in Gárdos-Orosz, Fruzsina – Szente, Zoltán (eds.): *Jog és politika határán. Alkotmánybíráskodás Magyarországon 2010 után*, Budapest, HVG-ORAC, 2015, 13.

16 Judge Owen Roberts' reasoning in *United States v. Butler*, 297 U.S. 1 (1936), 62, cited in Szente, Zoltán: "Jog és politika határán: az alkotmánybíróságok és az alkotmánybíráskodás jellegéről", in Gárdos-Orosz, Fruzsina – Szente, Zoltán (eds.): *Jog és politika határán. Alkotmánybíráskodás Magyarországon 2010 után*, Budapest, HVG-ORAC, 2015, 14.

17 See Antonin Scalia's opinion, *American Trucking Assns. v. Smith*, 110 L Ed 2d 148 (1990), 174, cited in Szente, Zoltán: "Jog és politika határán: az alkotmánybíróságok és az alkotmánybíráskodás jellegéről", in Gárdos-Orosz, Fruzsina – Szente, Zoltán (eds.): *Jog és politika határán. Alkotmánybíráskodás Magyarországon 2010 után*, Budapest, HVG-ORAC, 2015, 14.

18 Möllers, Christoph: "Scope and Legitimacy of Judicial Review in German Constitutional Law – the Court versus the Political Process", in Hermann, Pünder – Waldhoff, Christian (eds.): *Debates in German Public Law*, Oxford – Portland, Hart, 2014, 4, 14.

both types of constitutional review courts, which are models of American and European-style constitutional adjudication, are engaged in law-related (legal) politics, i.e. their decisions influence other actors in the exercise of public power, such as the legislature, the executive and the judiciary. Their activities (because of their effects) are therefore sometimes in its effect not of a purely legal nature.[19]

In Hungary, the literature on constitutional justice is rich, and the political and/or legal character of the institution has been a much debated issue since the change of regime of 1989.[20] After 2010, radical changes in the constitution and the regulation of the Constitutional Court led to even more intense debates. According to Gábor Halmai, for example, since the spring of 2013, when only the ruling parties nominated a majority of constitutional judges, the Constitutional Court has largely decided politically sensitive issues according to the ideas of the political majority.[21] Zoltán Szente has shown that there is a correlation between the position of the political majority electing the Constitutional Court judge and the vote of the judge in support of the Government case,[22] and therefore, in order to establish a balanced Constitutional Court with a pluralistic approach to values, it would be necessary to elect candidates from different political forces in order to ensure that the Court functions according to the rules of deliberative plural democracy.

The role and function of the constitutional court decision-making has long been considered of legal nature, in Hungarian literature, Zoltán Szente calls this the "legal model".[23] According to this theory, the Constitutional Court must apply legal criteria and methodology in its decision-making. The decisions of the courts are based solely on the relevant legislation and the constitution, the original intentions of the framers or precedents, or possibly on the weighing of social interests.[24] The normative concept of constitutional adjudication was based on the idea that legal activity is different from political activity in its goals, function and methodology, and that while the political branches of power – the legislature and the executive –

---

[19] Some authors interpret this experience as calling into question the *countermajoritarian* nature of constitutionalism. Mazmanyan, Armen: "Majoritarianism, Deliberation and Accountability as Institutional Instincts of Constitutional Courts", in Popelier, Patricia – Mazmanyan, Armen – Vandenbruwaene, Werner (eds.): *The Role of Constitutional Courts in Multilevel Governance,* Cambridge – Antwerp – Portland, Intersentia, 2013, 169.

[20] E.g. Győrfi, Tamás: *Az alkotmánybíráskodás politikai karaktere. Értekezés a magyar alkotmánybíráskodás első tíz évéről,* Budapest, INDOK, 2001; Sólyom, Péter: "Kelsen köpönyegéből. A magyar Alkotmánybíróság keletkezéstörténetéhez", *Közjogi Szemle,* 2021/2, 1–17.

[21] Halmai, Gábor: "In memoriam magyar alkotmánybíráskodás. A pártos alkotmánybíráskodás első éve", *Fundamentum,* 2014/1–2, 56–57.

[22] Szente, Zoltán: "Az alkotmánybírák politikai orientációi Magyarországon 2010 és 2014 között", *Politikatudományi Szemle,* 2015/1, 31–57.

[23] Szente, Zoltán: "Jog és politika határán: az alkotmánybíróságok és az alkotmánybíráskodás jellegéről", in Gárdos-Orosz, Fruzsina – Szente, Zoltán (eds.): *Jog és politika határán. Alkotmánybíráskodás Magyarországon 2010 után,* Budapest, HVG-ORAC, 2015, 13.

[24] Pacelle, Richard L. Jr. – Curry, Brett W. – Marshall, Bryan W.: *Decision Making by the Modern Supreme Court,* New York, Cambridge University Press, 2011, 32.

carry out political activity, the courts carry out legal activity. The activity of the constitutional court is more akin to the latter because of its legal nature even if the decisions have a political impact.[25] Constitutional adjudication is essentially an application of law, not policy-making.[26] This means that the interpretation of the law is a legal activity even if it is carried out in a politically charged environment, where the consideration of this environment and the taking into account of social needs also becomes a criterion for the court's discretion.[27]

Thus, according to Szente, the study of constitutional adjudication according to the legal model deals with traditional jurisprudential approaches and theories of interpretation, and is based on the assumption that constitutional judges apply these (or one of them) as a judicial philosophy in constitutional disputes.[28]

The constitutional court as an institutional construct is most strikingly characterised by the fact that it is a guarantee of constitutional functioning, but in such a way that the constituent power, and often even a qualified legislative majority, cannot be constrained in a way that would prevent it from functioning in the long term and fundamentally against its intent.[29] The constitutional court is thus inherently limited, because the electoral or appointment process, the number and composition of its members, the definition of its competencies and the provision of its procedures are all made by the constitution-maker or legislature in such a way that the constitutional court stands alongside the legislative and executive institutions of the state bodies that make the laws, as the supreme guardian and the supreme constitutional interpreting power. Its influence is, however, in fact limited by law only as far as is desirable for the political power. It is precisely because of this specificity that some authors have argued that the constitutional court cannot, *by definition*, be an institution truly independent of politics in its existence, since its scope for action depends on the political forces in power. Some authors have even gone so far as to argue that it is therefore seen as a particularly harmful institution for constitutional democracy, causing imbalances in political competition between parties, because, according to this view, constitutional courts always compromise with the dominant political forces in order to maintain their existence.[30]

---

25 For example, Wechsler, Herbert: "Toward Neutral Principles of Constitutional Law", *Harvard Law Review*, 1959, 1–35, esp. 10, 19, 25.

26 Pritchett, Herman C.: "The Development of Judicial Research", in Grossman, Joel B. – Tanenhaus, Joseph (eds.): *Frontiers of Judicial Research*, New York, Wiley, 1969, 49.

27 Szente, Zoltán: "Jog és politika határán: az alkotmánybíróságok és az alkotmánybíráskodás jellegéről", in Gárdos-Orosz, Fruzsina – Szente, Zoltán (eds.): *Jog és politika határán. Alkotmánybíráskodás Magyarországon 2010 után*, Budapest, HVG-ORAC, 2015, 14.

28 *Ibid.*

29 Dahl, Robert A.: "Decision Making in a Democracy: The Supreme Court as a National Policy Maker", *Journal of Public Law*, 1957, 279–295.

30 Hirschl, Ran: *Towards Juristocracy. The Origins and Consequences of New Constitutionalism*, Cambridge, Harvard University Press, 2007.

But others, such as Tom Ginsburg, have formulated the essence of the constitutional court's functioning as operating on the logic of insurance.[31] Alec Stone Sweet argues that the constitution itself is a contract between members of the political community. If we imagine that the members of the political community have to agree on the content of the constitution, we can easily imagine a compromise whereby all the rights and entitlements that the parties consider important are included in the constitution, and of course that these rights can be limited. The constitution must also provide for how these rights will be guaranteed by the state. This brings us easily to the idea/necessity of constitutional enforcement, because in this way the constitution also demonstrates that a constitutional institution is responsible for enforcing the constitution, i.e. for enforcing rights.[32] The more incomplete and questionable the treaty – i.e. the constitution – between the members of the political community is, the less it will settle any disputes that arise, the greater the competence of the constitutional court becomes, since its task is to decide constitutional disputes on the basis of the written text.

In Alec Stone Sweet's summary of the constitutional court's function, many argue that issues that are not settled by the constitution are not within the jurisdiction of the constitutional court, as they are not actually agreed by the political community. Another argument is that the political community has laid down the rights, the principles and rules for the reconciliation of rights and the functioning of the state that it could agree on at the level of the treaty at the time of the constitution-making process, and has also provided for the constitutional court to decide on constitutional disputes, and in part on legal disputes. The constitutional court was thus empowered by the constitutional treaty to decide – by rooting its reasoning in the constitution – on questions which are not answered in the constitution. Indeed, the intention of the political community that established the constitutional court was precisely to ensure the rule of law even in the case of an imperfect or incomplete treaty and to find a way of ensuring that the constitution could function even when it was not desirable or possible to start over and over again with new constitution drafting or repeated constitutional amendments to resolve new and emerging issues. The constitutional court, according to this argument, is thus precisely an institution that has the power to decide cases that the constituent power did not contemplate when it drafted the constitution. It is a kind of general insurance for all damage, not just that which could have been foreseen.[33] The constitutional court will even have the competence to review the constitutional amendment in a particular case, a power which is not explicitly conferred on the

[31] Ginsburg, Tom: *Judicial Review in New Democracies. Constitutional Courts in Asian Cases,* Cambridge, Cambridge University Press, 2003.

[32] Stone Sweet, Alec: "Constitutional Court", in Rosenfeld, Michel – Sajó, András (eds.): *Oxford Handbook of Comparative Constitutional Law,* Oxford, Oxford University Press, 2012, 821.

[33] *Ibid.* 823–826.

constitutional court by the constitution, but may be derived by the constitutional court itself.[34]

This is why many argue that the constitutional court is not simply a constitutional institution within the organisation of the state, but has a general mandate to defend the constitution.[35]

If we assume that the constitutional court has general powers, its jurisdiction may include not only the review of the constitutionality of laws and regulations, but also, for example, the review of elections, the review of the legality of municipal regulations or the review of the violation of international treaties in domestic law. It is also a legitimate question within this interpretative framework how certain classical constitutional protection tasks of the ordinary courts can be outsourced to the constitutional courts in order to better protect constitutionality. This will lead us to the procedure of the constitutional complaint, the very new procedure in constitutional adjudication. The constitutional court is thus given powers which the constitutional authority would not entrust to the ordinary courts. Some of these powers are politically sensitive issues, such as criminal prosecutions of presidents, heads of state or other high-ranking officials. Constitutional courts, on the other hand, cannot become political bodies at the boundary between law and politics, and therefore develop doctrines and methodology in interpreting their jurisdiction in order to avoid political decision-making.

Although the powers of constitutional courts are not the same in all states, it can be said that in the centralised model, a significant number of constitutional courts carry out abstract review of norms, which can be *ex ante*, i.e. a constitutional review carried out after the adoption of the law but before its promulgation, or *ex post,* i.e. a review after its promulgation. The essence of the abstract review procedure is that the constitutional court examines whether the (challenged) law or provision of law indicated by the petitioner is contrary to the article of the constitution indicated by the petitioner.[36]

In many cases, however, the constitutional courts also carry out a specific constitutional review. There are two main ways of doing this. One is known as a judicial initiative, judicial referral in Hungarian law, but this is also the case in other countries. A judge, in the course of a case pending before him or her, finds that the applicable law or legal provision is contrary to one or more provisions of the constitution. This is called a concrete constitutional review because the specific case, the specific legal conflict, is visible behind the norm being checked. In the event that the constitutional court finds an unconstitutionality, it will have an impact on the pending concrete case, since it will be finally decided by the ordinary court in the

[34] Gárdos-Orosz, Fruzsina: "Unamendability as a judicial discovery", in Albert, Richard – Oder, Bertil Emrah (eds.): *Unamendability,* Cham, Springer, 2018, 231–258.

[35] Stone Sweet, Alec – Mathews, Jud: "Proportionality Balancing and Global Constitutionalism", *Columbia Journal of Transnational Law,* 2008, 68–149.

[36] Stone Sweet, Alec: "Constitutional Court", in Rosenfeld, Michel – Sajó, András (eds.): *Oxford Handbook of Comparative Constitutional Law,* Oxford, Oxford University Press, 2012, 821.

new legal context, cleansed of the unconstitutional norm. However, the examination and possible annulment of the constitutionality of a legal norm may have an impact on other pending cases, depending on the provisions of the acts on the constitutional courts or of other procedural acts: annulment may, for example, apply to all cases pending before the ordinary court.

The other type of case-specific examination of legislation, i.e. the concrete review of a piece of legislation, occurs when an individual constitutional complaint may be lodged with the constitutional court to examine the constitutionality of a provision of law which was applied in the specific case. In this case, the laws governing the constitutional courts generally require the complainant to exhaust the remedies available before the public administrative authorities and the ordinary courts and then to indicate the unconstitutionality in the form of a petition. In this case, too, the review of the norm is linked to the specific case and controversy.

In the case of concrete norm control, the question arises to what extent it is linked to the specific case, i.e. is the nature of norm control different from that of abstract norm control. Is the interpretative function of the constitutional court limited to the examination of constitutionality issues, such that it cannot act as a super-judicial body in the adjudication of concrete disputes, or does the constitutional court have specific concerns in this particular case related to the legal dispute and the controversy itself? In either case, in effect the outcome of the concrete case will be fundamentally influenced by the decision of the constitutional court.

The nature of constitutional adjudication is also essentially determined in all countries by the question of who can be petitioners in constitutional court proceedings. In most cases, the petitioners can only be certain public dignitaries, such as the Ombudsman or a defined majority of the Parliament, or possibly the President of the Republic or the Government. The fact that not anyone can initiate proceedings before the constitutional court *(actio popularis)* also leads to a limited constitutional jurisdiction, since political actors often only initiate proceedings when it is in their interest to do so. The direct contribution to the democratic legitimacy of the institution is therefore undoubtedly reduced when it is distanced from the people, when a citizen cannot initiate public interest proceedings, but the constitutional court will reliably deal only with issues that are raised by and acceptable to the main political branches and public actors. The constitutional court will therefore not expand its jurisprudence into areas where it could be an undesirable actor. The definition of the scope of the petitioners is therefore very important in defining the nature and evaluating the relevance of the constitutional court.

Constitutional judges are usually elected for a fixed term, usually from nine to twelve years. Although the way in which constitutional judges are elected varies from country to country, depending on the constitutional system, the rules typically seek to ensure that there is political consensus on the appointment of constitutional judges, i.e. that there is no partisan constitutionalism. In the Czech Republic, for example, this is achieved by requiring the Parliament and the President to agree on the nomination of a constitutional judge, while in Germany both chambers of the Parliament have a say in the choice of the constitutional judge, and in France the choice is made or delegated by a one-third to one-third ratio of other major actors and institutions of state power.[37] In Hungary, nominations used to be made by a parliamentary committee under a composition system called parity, with an equal number of government and opposition politicians sitting in the committee which is chaired by the opposition. Constitutional courts are also characterised by the fact that they operate in a collegial form, and in addition to sitting in plenary session, they may also take decisions in councils of five or three judges, or even as individual judges. The size of constitutional courts is not very large, usually between 5 and 15 people, which means that a small body, carefully selected by consensus, is responsible for guarding the constitution.[38]

In relation to the functioning of the individual constitutional courts, it is also necessary to examine whether they actually have an impact on the development of the legal system.[39] In Hungary, a major political science research project has recently attempted to measure the actual influence of the Visegrád countries' constitutional courts and councils on the functioning of the legislature.[40]

The impact of the practice of the constitutional court on the practice of the ordinary courts is of particular importance, since the practice of the ordinary courts is of primary importance in the field of fundamental rights protection. Constitutional culture is best shaped when ordinary courts take account of fundamental rights in their judgments. It has been mentioned on several occasions that constitutional courts have played a significant role in shaping the constitutional environment in many states.

In many cases, the constitutional court has used its power to interpret the constitution to reach conclusions, such as when the French Constitutional Council ruled in 1971 that, although the text of the 1958 Constitution did not include human rights, they should be considered part of the Constitution.[41] Or some constitutional courts, including the Hungarian one, have deduced rights from the Constitution that were not explicitly included, such as the right to a name.[42]

In the event that constitutional justice in a constitutional state operates in such a way that the constitutional court is the depository of constitutional protection, the effect of the operation of the body will be that political decision-making

37 Stone Sweet, Alec: "Constitutional Court", in Rosenfeld, Michel – Sajó, András (eds.): *Oxford Handbook of Comparative Constitutional Law,* Oxford, Oxford University Press, 2012, 825. See more details Harding, Andrew – Leyland, Peter (eds.): *Constitutional Courts: A Comparative Study,* London, Wildy, Simmonds & Hill, 2009.

38 Stone Sweet, Alec: "Constitutional Court", in Rosenfeld, Michel – Sajó, András (eds.): *Oxford Handbook of Comparative Constitutional Law,* Oxford, Oxford University Press, 2012, 825.

39 *Ibid.*

40 Pócza, Kálmán (ed.): *Constitutional Politics and the Judiciary: Decision-making in Central and Eastern Europe,* London – New York, Routledge, 2018.

41 Decision No. 11–44. DC du 16 Jillet 1971. Conseil Constitutionnel.

42 Decision 58/2001. (XII. 7.) AB.

will be shaped in accordance with the decisions of the constitutional court, and that ordinary judicial jurisprudence will also take into account the decisions of the constitutional court on particular issues and generally adopt the approach that the constitutional court takes. A dialogue will thus be established between the constitutional court and the legislative and executive branches of government, resulting in the judicialization of politics.[43] The increasing practice of constitutional courts to shift the path of legal interpretation from negative legislation to positive legislation is also due to the emergence of a horizontal effect of fundamental rights in practice and theory. This means that the provisions of the constitution apply in private law relationships, either directly or, in most states, indirectly. Thus, ordinary courts, in interpreting the applicable law, take into account the relevant constitutional provisions and interpret the law in accordance with them. In those states where such enforcement of the constitution is expected, the complainant can usually challenge a decision of the ordinary court that does not comply with the constitution by lodging a constitutional complaint with the constitutional court.[44]

In Hungary, the so-called negative legislation[45] is a well-established – albeit from a linguistic perspective not correct – term in constitutional law, which appears especially in the context of constitutional control of the legislative power, since if the constitutional court annuls a law, which is an indispensable part of European-style constitutional adjudication, it actually shapes the legal system.

In addition, some constitutional courts besides rejecting of accepting the petitioner's claims, holding effective or annulling the projected piece of legislation even have the power to declare a constitutional omission or a so-called constitutional requirement. In the case of a declaration of constitutional failure to act, the constitutional court calls on the legislator to restore the legal environment in conformity with the constitution by enacting a new law with constitutional content. In ordering a so-called constitutional requirement, the constitutional court gives an interpretation of the law which is binding on all and which the legislature and the courts must accept in order to uphold the constitutionality of the legal system and the specific piece of legislation.

Taking these attributes into account a library of literature has been written on the legitimacy of the constitutional court, the constitutional judiciary, as a constitutional institution which is empowered to review legislation made by a legislator who has won a mandate in a democratic election. The constitutional court is not itself composed of persons elected by the people; moreover, it is usually a body of

43 Stone Sweet, Alec: *Governing with Judges. Constitutional Politics in Europe,* Oxford, Oxford University Press, 2000.

44 Gárdos-Orosz, Fruzsina: *Alkotmányos polgári jog? Az alapvető jogok alkalmazása a magánjogi jogvitákban,* Budapest – Pécs, Dialóg Campus, 2011.

45 The established term was also recently used by the President of the Constitutional Court to describe the activities of the Constitutional Court in a conference presentation, Sulyok, Tamás: *Az alkotmányos önazonosság az Alkotmánybíróság döntéseiben,* https://alkotmanybirosag.hu

lawyers, possibly former ordinary judges, and members of the academic community, so in most states in the world it is not only not democratically elected by the people, but is a body of persons of high social status, socialized according to other types of legal decision-making processes. In other words, as the critics put it, a kind of legal elite which, under the new system of constitutionalism, is entitled to decide whether a law enacted by a parliament legitimately representing all social strata can be considered constitutional. This is usually decided on the basis of the methods of interpretation laid down by the constitutional court or the supreme court itself, according to the constitutional content established by constitutional interpretation. The concepts of juristocracy,[46] and legal constitutionalism[47] were both coined to describe and explain the role of the courts in the final, politically relevant decision-making, the resolution of disputes through the legal process and ultimately the constitutional courts that determine constitutional disputes at the highest level. Tamás Győrfi argues in his book against the new constitutionalism that there is no legitimate explanation for the role of constitutional adjudication in constitutional democracies in this way; it is an outsourcing of political decision-making that cannot work well in the long run because the most empowered and appropriate representative bodies do not make democratic decisions in the governance of society.[48]

In the case of the constitutional court, the fact that we are not talking about a judicial body in the classical sense is an additional problem of legitimacy. Although the constitutional court is usually composed of lawyers, the task it carries out – especially in the case of the abstract review of norms – is not a classical judicial one. The judicial function is also commonly understood, particularly in continental law, as a function connected with the implementation and enforcement of the law. This function, whether or not we understand it in a Montesquieuian sense, as the mouth of the law, is not one which involves shaping constitutional politics in an autonomous and proactive way. In contrast, the actual activity of constitutional courts moves away from this role and becomes an institution that actively shapes constitutional policy, but is bound by the rules of legal reasoning. The judicialization of politics, as mentioned above, also occurs because constitutional interpretation takes place in the light of legal principles and norms, which then have a policy-shaping effect.[49]

The American legal realism movement (e.g. Karl Llewellyn, Jerome Frank) questioned the validity and enforceability of this normative approach as early as the

[46] The latest in the debate, *Jogelméleti Szemle,* 2015/4, http://jesz.ajk.elte.hu/2015_4.pdf

[47] "Politikai konstitucionalizmus – jogi konstitucionalizmus vita", *Fundamentum,* 2015/2–3, https://fundamentum.hu/politikai-alkotmanyossag

[48] Győrfi, Tamás: *Az alkotmánybíráskodás politikai karaktere. Értekezés a magyar alkotmánybíráskodás első tíz évéről,* Budapest, INDOK, 2001.

[49] Stone Sweet, Alec: *Governing with Judges. Constitutional Politics in Europe,* Oxford, Oxford University Press, 2000.

early 20th century,[50] claiming that in reality judges follow their own preferences in the guise of legal reasoning. More recent criticisms have mainly focused on the fact that the legal model is merely a set of normative ideas, which is not suitable for exploring and explaining constitutional court decision-making. The legal approach cannot be empirically justified.[51]

At the very end of the 20th century, during the constitutional changes in Central and Eastern Europe, in the main stage of European integration, the legal model of constitutionalism spread in Europe, despite the criticisms already voiced.[52] The regime-changing states introduced the legal institution of constitutional adjudication in constitutional democracies in the belief that it was an institution with a legal function.[53] The clearest example of this from Hungary is that, under *Act XXXII of 1989 on the Constitutional Court,* only a person with a law degree and at least 20 years' legal experience or an outstanding legal scholar could be elected as a constitutional judge. In the 1990s, in the constitutional democracies, a new era of prosperity seemed to be dawning in an almost fully unified Europe; in the Western world, the concept of the rational regulatory state was winning out, as in the information society all the necessary information was available to make rational policy decisions, followed by effective regulation and law enforcement. The legal model of constitutional review fits perfectly into this concept.

Today, however, it is widely held that the functioning of European societies, including political decision-making, cannot always be described by rational arguments. The problems of the economic crisis, the migration crisis, terrorism, the pandemic etc., have often been met with responses that were incomprehensible to those who consistently thought in Enlightenment terms. The fact is that governments and public regulatory systems in the 21st century face a number of challenges in the global information society that may require innovative solutions. However, the big question for state organisation – and the constitutionalism that guides it – is whether governments will imagine state organisation still along the lines of the classic values of liberal democracy, or whether other

50 In fact, even Marbury v. Madison raised the question of how much of a possible overstepping of competence was a political act on the part of the Supreme Court. See Marshall, William P.: "Constitutional Law as Political Spoils", *Cardozo Law Review,* 2005, 527.

51 For a summary of these critiques, see Pacelle, Richard L. Jr. – Curry, Brett W. – Marshall, Bryan W.: *Decision Making by the Modern Supreme Court,* New York, Cambridge University Press, 2011, 32–33.

52 Schwartz, Herman: *The Struggle for Constitutional Justice in Post-Communist Europe,* Chicago, University of Chicago Press, 2000; Sadurski, Wojciech (ed.): *Constitutional Justice, East and West. Democratic Legitimacy and Constitutional Courts in Post-Communist Europe in a Comparative Perspective,* Hague – London, Kluwer Law International, 2002; Ismayr, Wolfgang: "Die politischen Systeme Osteuropas im Vergleich", in Ismayr, Wolfgang (ed.): *Die politischen Systeme Osteuropas,* Opladen, Leske und Budrich, 2002, 15-19.

53 Bragyova, András: *Az új alkotmány egy koncepciója,* Budapest, KJK – MTA Állam- és Jogtudományi Intézet, 1995; Sajó, András: *Önkorlátozó hatalom,* Budapest, KJK – MTA Állam- és Jogtudományi Intézet, 1995.

standards will emerge in response to new challenges. As we see, populism, the so-called populist constitutionalism, is on the rise in more and more states as a global phenomenon.

I will examine the functioning of the Hungarian Constitutional Court within this interpretative framework, focusing primarily on how its activities are aligned with the concept of the legal model after 2010 when the populist Orbán Government gained two thirds constitution making majority in Parliament. The constitutional law literature in other countries has also focused on this issue in recent years, with numerous papers on the practice of the Constitutional Court in the context of the financial crisis,[54] the migration crisis,[55] the fight against terrorism,[56] or constitutional concerns about new technologies,[57] as well as on the legitimacy crisis and conflicts of jurisdiction in constitutional adjudication.

In our volumes co-edited with Zoltán Szente, we have examined how constitutional courts react to political decisions made in this challenging new climate, often under the influence of populist power. This has included considering whether the activity and character of constitutional courts in Europe is changing, and whether their practice is changing. In broad terms, all European constitutional courts follow the legal model described above in their creed. They insist on carrying out legal activity, judging their own activities and their decisions on the basis of predefined normative benchmarks and past practice. In our book we have attempted to group together the practice of the ten constitutional courts under review, the European Court of Human Rights (ECtHR) in Strasbourg and the Court of Justice of the European Union (CJEU), and to place at one end of the scale those constitutional courts whose practice and position in the constitutional order has not changed much in recent years, despite the global or European and domestic populist challenges mentioned above, and at the other end of the scale those bodies whose practice and position has changed a lot. Hungary is one of the countries at the latter end of the scale: since the early 1990s, the Constitutional Court's position in public law, its functions and powers, and its substantive inter-

54 Contiades, Xenophon (ed.): *Constitutions in the Global Financial Crisis. A Comparative Analysis,* Farnham, Ashgate, 2013; Iglesias-Rodriguez, Pablo – Triandafyllidou, Anna – Gropas, Ruby (eds.): *After the Financial Crisis. Shifting Legal, Economic and Political Paradigms,* London, Palgrave Macmillan, 2016; Morrison, Fred L. (ed.): *Fiscal Rules – Limits on Governmental Deficits and Debt,* Berlin, Springer, 2016.

55 Bilgic, Ali: *Rethinking Security in the Age of Migration: Trust and Emancipation in Europe,* London, Routledge, 2013.

56 Akhgar, Babak – Brewster, Ben (eds.): *Combatting Cybercrime and Cyberterrorism,* Cham, Springer, 2016; Kaunert, Christian – Léonard, Sarah (eds.): *European Security, Terrorism and Intelligence. Tackling New Security Challenges in Europe,* London, Palgrave Macmillan, 2013; Richards, Anthony: *Conceptualizing Terrorism,* Oxford, Oxford University Press, 2015.

57 Noonan, Norma – Nadkarni, Vidya (eds.): *Challenge and Change. Global Threats and the State in Twenty-first Century International Politics,* London, Palgrave Macmillan, 2016, 2.

pretative practice have changed a great deal.[58] In the 21st century, every constitutional court must answer three questions:

(1) whether it will continue to adhere to previously established standards, normative constructs and interpretative methods in a changed social, economic, technological and political environment,

(2) whether it will adapt them in order to answer novel questions in an often challenging environment,

(3) or whether it will abandon its previous judicial philosophy, by which I mean adapting to certain trends in interpretative theory and not opting for a new judicial philosophy or a different attitude.

Of course, these are not categories into which the entire, uniform practice of one or another constitutional court can be classified, but it is clear from the decisions of the constitutional courts that the practice of one or another body tends to point in one direction or another, or more in one than the other. Comparative constitutional law is experiencing a renaissance,[59] and within this field one of the most researched areas is constitutional adjudication,[60] and in this context methodological issues[61] and comparative studies. Although these are issues which I have spent much time examining in recent years (and I will refer to the results of these studies in this book), in this monograph I will focus on understanding the functioning of the Hungarian Constitutional Court since 2010 in one of the most visible populist political regimes of the world. I will explain below a Hungarian step-by-step transformation of a classical constitutional court.

---

58 Szente, Zoltán – Gárdos-Orosz, Fruzsina (eds.): *New Challenges to Constitutional Adjudication in Europe*, London, Routledge, 2018; Szente, Zoltán – Gárdos-Orosz, Fruzsina (eds.): *Populist Challenges to Constitutional Interpretation in Europe and Beyond*, London, Routledge, 2021.

59 See the new wave of comparative constitutional law literature Hirschl, Ran: *Comparative Matters – The Renaissance of Comparative Constitutional Law*, Oxford, Oxford University Press, 2013; Tushnet, Mark: *Advanced Introduction to Comparative Constitutional Law*, Cheltenham, Edward Elgar, 2014.

60 Harding, Andrew – Leyland, Peter (eds.): *Constitutional Courts: A Comparative Study*, London, Wildy, Simmonds & Hill, 2009; Comella, Víctor Ferreres: *Constitutional Courts and Democratic Values*, New Haven – London, Yale University Press, 2009; Brewer-Carías, Allan R. (ed.): *Constitutional Courts as Positive Legislators. A Comparative Law Study*, Cambridge, Cambridge University Press, 2011; Popelier, Patricia – Mazmanyan, Armen – Vandenbruwaene, Werner (eds.): *The Role of Constitutional Courts in Multilevel Governance*, Cambridge – Antwerp – Portland, Intersentia, 2013; Hübner Mendes, Conrado: *Constitutional Courts and Deliberative Democracy*, Oxford, Oxford University Press, 2013; De Visser, Maartje: *Constitutional Review in Europe. A Comparative Analysis*, Oxford, Hart, 2014.

61 Kapiszewski, Diana – Silverstein, Gordon – Kagan, Robert A. (eds.): *Consequential Courts: Judicial Roles in Global Perspectives*, Cambridge, Cambridge University Press, 2013; Groppi, Tania – Ponthoreau, Marie Claire (eds.): *The Use of Foreign Precedents by Constitutional Judges*, Oxford, Hart, 2013.

2. THE CONSTITUTIONAL COURT OF THE FUNDAMENTAL LAW. THE BEGINNINGS[1]

When the commentary[2] of the regime-changing Constitution[3] was published in 2009, the authors outlined the role played by the Constitutional Court in the system of constitutional institutions during its nearly twenty years of operation.[4] They presented a significant institution which, despite valid criticisms, was able to serve as an adequate safeguard in Hungary against the emergence or resurgence of dictatorship and managed to explain and enforce the new democratic rules of the Constitution.[5] History has shown that the regime-changing states of the region had been able to stabilise their new institutions in the two decades after 1990. There have been attempts in Hungary to have a constituent majority decide on some fundamental issues of democracy, constitutionalism or fundamental rights, but these efforts have been mostly unsuccessful.[6] However, the decisions

---

1 This chapter was originally published in Gárdos-Orosz, Fruzsina: "Alkotmánybíróság 2010–2015", in Jakab, András – Gajduschek, György (eds.): *A magyar jogrendszer állapota 2010–2015,* Budapest, MTA TK Jogtudományi Intézet, 2016, 442–479.

2 Jakab, András (ed.): *Az Alkotmány kommentárja I–II.*, Budapest, Századvég, 2009.

3 The *Act XX of 1949 on the Constitution of the Republic of Hungary,* which was first and fundamentally amended by *Act XXXI of 1989* in accordance with the requirements of constitutional democracy.

4 After the change of regime, the Constitutional Court started its operation on 1 January 1990.

5 Vincze, Attila – Csuhány, Péter – Sonnevend, Pál – Jakab, András: "Az Alkotmánybíróság", in Jakab András (ed.): *Az Alkotmány kommentárja I–II.*, Budapest, Századvég, 2009, 1099–1172.

6 This is documented, for example, in Sólyom, László: "Az alkotmány őrei", in Sólyom, László: *Documenta, Alkotmányjog,* Budapest, HVG-ORAC, 2019; Bragyova, András: *Az új alkotmány egy koncepciója,* Budapest, KJK – MTA Állam- és Jogtudományi Intézet, 1995; Sajó, András: Önkorlátozó hatalom, Budapest, KJK – MTA Állam- és Jogtudományi Intézet, 1995. See also e.g. Pokol, Béla: *A magyar parlamentarizmus,* Budapest, Cserépfalvi, 1994; Sajó, András: "A »láthatatlan alkotmány« apróbetűi. A magyar Alkotmánybíróság első ezerkétszáz napja", *Állam- és Jogtudomány,* 1993/1–2, 37–96; Kis János: "Alkotmánybíráskodás a mérlegen", in Kis János: *Alkotmányos demokrácia. Három tanulmány,* Budapest, INDOK, 2000. Comprehensive and summary critical analysis until 2010 Szente, Zoltán: "Az Alkotmánybíróság értelmezési gyakorlata 1990–2010", in Deli, Gergely – Szoboszlay-Kiss, Katalin (eds.): *Tanulmányok a 70 éves Bihari Mihály tiszteletére,* Győr, Universitas, 2013, 505; Holló, András: *Az alkotmányjognak asztalánál,* Budapest, HVG-ORAC, 2015.

of the Kelsen-type Constitutional Court[7] were mostly accepted by the constitutional institutions,[8] and the Court enjoyed broad support in society.[9] In the field of legal development, even with its inconsistencies, it arguably marked out an approach that broadly corresponded to the mainstream expectations of liberal (constitutional) democracy.[10] However, by the time of the 2011 constitution-making process, some important changes were already in the making, with the constitutional majority setting the direction for a repositioning of the institution.[11] The new arrangements for the Constitutional Court were developed in several steps, the first of which date back in 2010. Shortly after its inaugural session, the Parliament elected in 2010 adopted the "Amendment of the Constitution of 5 July 2010", which abolished the parity committee nomination of the constitutional court judges by amending Article 32/A (4) of the Constitution, replacing it with a committee based on the standard representation of the MPs in Parliament.[12] The functional restructuring of the Constitutional Court had already begun in the context of the preparations for the new Fundamental Law (the new constitution).

The parliamentary majority with constitution-amending powers also decided in 2010 to reduce the influence of the Constitutional Court by limiting its competencies. The aim of the related constitutional amendment was to ensure that the Constitutional Court would not scrutinise the content of laws on central financial

[7] Sólyom, László: "A magyar Alkotmánybíróság önértelmezése és Hans Kelsen", in Cs. Kiss, Lajos (ed.): *Hans Kelsen jogtudománya*, Budapest, Gondolat, 2007.

[8] Of course, even before 2010 there were conflicts between the legislature and the Constitutional Court, some elements of the annulled "Zétényi-Takács Law" were said to be unconstitutional and appeared unnoticed as part of a new legislative product, or we could read on the website of the National Assembly the numerous unconstitutional omissions that the legislator failed to comply within the deadline or at all. For more information on the first Sólyom era, see Győrfi, Tamás – Kazai, Viktor Zoltán – Orbán, Endre: *Kontextus által világosan. A Sólyom-bíróság antiformalista elemzése*, Budapest, L'Harmattan, 2022.

[9] In 2010, in a survey measuring trust in institutions, the Constitutional Court ranked second after the Public Health and Medical Officer Service (ÁNTSZ), http://www.median.hu/object.9521ea4b-830b-470e-ad59-ffc591bc6ac3.ivy. In opinion polls, the Constitutional Court's position in 2014 is more average, see, e.g., Szabó I., László: „Az intézményi, szervezeti bizalom helyzete Magyarországon 2014 elején", *Nemzet és Biztonság*, 2014/3, 133–139.

[10] Kukorelli, István: "A magyar alkotmánybíráskodás előzményei, létrejötte és jellemzői", in Kukorelli, István – Tóth, Károly: *A rendszerváltoztatás államszervezeti kompromisszumai*, Lakitelek, Antológia, 2016, 398–407.

[11] On the political position and the political considerations behind the transformation, see Pócza, Kálmán: "Az Alkotmánybíróság", in Körössényi, András (ed.): *A magyar politikai rendszer – negyedszázad után*, Budapest, Osiris, 2014, 161–184.

[12] For more detailed information on the rules and significance of the committee nomination procedure, see Erdős, Csaba: "Az alkotmánybíróság kontrollmechanizmusainak változásai", in Kecskés, Gábor (ed.): *Doktori műhelytanulmányok*, Győr, Széchenyi István Egyetem Állam- és Jogtudományi Doktori Iskola, 2013, 137–141.

matters that are essential for governance.[13] (The restrictive provision survives in Article 37 (4) and (5) of the Fundamental Law,[14] and with one or two striking exceptions[15] the Constitutional Court has rejected petitions to that effect on the grounds of lack of competence.[16])

On 6 June 2011, Parliament adopted *Act LXI of 2011 amending Act XX of 1949 on the Constitution of the Republic of Hungary,* which was published in the *Magyar Közlöny [Hungarian Gazette]* (the official platform of the publication of legislation in Hungary) on 14 June 2011. According to Article 5 of the Act, "Parliament shall, by 31 July 2011, elect a President of the Constitutional Court from among the members of the Constitutional Court by a two-thirds majority of the members of National Assembly". Previously, the Constitutional Court itself elected its President from among its members for a three-year term, but under the new rules, the President is elected by a two-thirds majority of the National Assembly from among the judges of the Constitutional Court, and his or her term of office lasts until the end of the judge's term of office.[17] The President's position is traditionally strong, since, for example, in the event of a tie, his vote is decisive and the President signs

---

13 *Act CXIX of 2010* on the amendment of the Constitution was published in the *Magyar Közlöny [Hungarian Gazette]* No. 177 of 2010. For a detailed analysis of the restriction, see Bánkuti, Miklós et al.: "Vélemény Magyarország új alkotmányos rendjéről", *Fundamentum,* 2012/1, 5–34; Tilk, Péter: "Gondolatok az Alkotmánybíróság vizsgálati lehetőségeinek szűkítéséről", in Trócsányi, László (ed.): *Dikaiosz Logosz. Tanulmányok Kovács István emlékére,* Szeged, Pólay Elemér Alapítvány, 2012, 145–153; Tordai, Csaba: "Az első év tapasztalatairól", *Alkotmánybírósági Szemle,* 2012/2, 131–133; Tóth, Gábor Attila: "Mi van és mi legyen a magyar alkotmányjogban?", *Közjogi Szemle,* 2011/2, 2–3.

14 "As long as government debt exceeds half of the total gross domestic product, the Constitutional Court may, within its powers set out in Article 24 (2) *b)* to *e),* review the Acts on the central budget, the implementation of the central budget, central taxes, duties and contributions, customs duties and the central conditions for local taxes for conformity with the Fundamental Law exclusively in connection with the rights to life and human dignity, to the protection of personal data, to freedom of thought, conscience and religion, or the rights related to Hungarian citizenship, and it may annul these Acts only for the violation of these rights. The Constitutional Court shall have the unrestricted right to annul Acts having the above subject matters as well, if the procedural requirements laid down in the Fundamental Law for making and promulgating those Acts have not been met." This limitation shall apply until the condition of Article 37 (4) is met, i.e. until the public debt falls below half the amount of GDP. This condition is unlikely to be met in the near future, based on financial and economic analyses.

15 Decision 184/2010. (X. 28.) AB and Decision 37/2011. (V. 10.) AB on the unconstitutionality of the 98% tax.

16 On the examination of sectoral special taxes and the limitation of powers, see Chronowski, Nóra – Drinóczi, Tímea – Zeller, Judit: "Túl az Alkotmányon", *Közjogi Szemle,* 2010/4, 1–12.

17 According to the wording introduced by the Fourth Amendment to the Fundamental Law, "[t]he Constitutional Court shall be a body composed of fifteen members, each elected for twelve years with the votes of two thirds of the Members of the National Assembly. The National Assembly shall, with the votes of two thirds of the Members of the National Assembly, elect a member of the Constitutional Court to serve as its President until the expiry of his or her term of office as judge of the Constitutional Court. Members of the Constitutional Court may not be members of political parties or engage in political activities."

the cases, determining who will be the judge rapporteur. The judge rapporteur has a particularly strong influence on the way the decision takes shape and on the final content of the decision. Among the many tasks of the President, it should also be pointed out that he/she sets the agenda, i.e. decides which cases are to be heard by the Constitutional Court and when. This is also of strategic importance.[18]

With the entry into force of the constitutional amendment, the number of constitutional judges increased from 11 to 15, and the new judges were elected by the two-thirds majority in Parliament.[19] At the same time, the term of office of judges was increased from nine to twelve years and the possibility of re-election was abolished.[20]

The position of the constitutional judges elected by the two thirds majority was strengthened by the fact that the amendment of *Act CLI of 2011 on the Constitutional Court* (Act on the Constitutional Court or Abtv.) removed the provision that the mandate of the constitutional judge shall expire upon reaching the age of 70.[21] The former Constitution and the Act on the Constitutional Court had already set a new framework before the adoption of the Fundamental Law for the operation of the Constitutional Court.[22]

2.1. Concerning the transformation

In Hungary, the Constitutional Court has played a major role in shaping the public and private legal order – even in ways of activism that can be criticised – in the post-1990 period, especially in the years following the change of regime. This is perhaps

18 The powers of the President of the Constitutional Court are set out in Article 17 (1) of the Act on the Constitutional Court.

19 The Fidesz–KDNP party coalition won an absolute two-thirds majority in the National Assembly in both 2010, which allowed them to act as a constituent power under the former Constitution. According to Article S) (2) of the Fundamental Law, the consent of a two-thirds majority of the Members of Parliament is also sufficient to amend the Fundamental Law and to adopt a new constitution.

20 The legislator has also provided in the new Article 15 (3) of the new Act on the Constitutional Court that the twelve-year term of office of a judge who is serving his or her term of office shall be extended if a new judge has not been elected in due time. However, this provision was repealed by Article 42 (3) of *Act CCVII of 2013*, due to the contradiction with Article 24 (8) of the Fundamental Law.

21 The rule was repealed by Article 42 (1) of *Act CCVII of 2013*, which entered into force on 11 December 2013. By the end of 2014, a total of six Acts had amended the Abtv. on 55 points: *Act CCI of 2011, Act CXXXI of 2013, Act CXXXIII of 2013, Act CCVII* of *2013, Act CCXXIII of 2013* and *Act CCXXXVIII of 2013*.

22 The explanatory memorandum of the constitutional amendment bill submitted in October 2010 clearly set out the constituent power's vision: according to it, the Constitutional Court's broad powers of norm control were justified during the period of regime change after 1989, but "with the consolidation of the rule of law, such a broad scope of constitutional review has become unjustified". Explanatory memorandum to Bill T/1445.

the reason why the constitution-making and constitution-amending two-thirds Fidesz–Christian Democrats (Orbán Government) majority did not undertake a complete reform of the Constitutional Court in 2011. The Constitutional Court remained as an important constitutional institution[23] in the new regime, and its considerable competencies were reserved, as was the idea of the Constitutional Court having the final say on the content of the Constitution/Fundamental Law from 2012. The Constitutional Court continued to interpret the scope of protection, rights and entitlements granted by the Fundamental Law, i.e. the foundations of the state organisation, with binding effect for all decisions. The organisationally independent and separate (from ordinary judiciary) Constitutional Court can annul legislation. However, with a two-thirds constituent majority, neither the constitution making majority itself nor the newly elected constitutional judges could responsibly believe that they were the autonomous interpreters of the Fundamental Law, since between 2010 and 2013 the constitution making and amending two thirds majority in Parliament overruled the Constitutional Court's decisions on many occasions by constitutional amendments.[24] Although in other European states the relationship between the government majority and the constitutional court has also been characterised by strained relations,[25] the Hungarian situation is special because before 2010 the Constitutional Court not only proved capable of setting the "standard" by establishing the basis for the legal argumentation that is to be followed, but also had already acquired a general and stable legitimacy. Several studies have shown, however, that the decisions of the Constitutional Court or the reasoning behind them have rarely been reflected in the case law of the judiciary, the legal doctrine evolved quite independently from the Constitutional Court decisions in most of the cases.[26] The Constitutional Court had greater influence on the political branches of power.

The details of the full reorganisation of competencies which unfolded during the constitution making process are the following. Under Article 24 of the Fundamental Law, the Constitutional Court is the supreme body for the protection of the Fundamental Law. The Constitutional Court examines laws adopted but not promulgated for conformity with the Fundamental Law. It reviews the conformity with the Fundamental Law of the legislation applicable to a specific judicial case, at

23 Tóth, Gábor Attila: "Folytatja-e az Alkotmánybíróság?", in Tóth, Gábor Attila: *Életfogytig szabadláb. Alkotmányjogi karcolatok*, Budapest, Élet- és Irodalom, 2011, 26.

24 For an analysis of the constitutional amendments before 2012, see, e.g., Stumpf, István: "Rule of Law, Division of Powers, Constitutionalism", *Acta Juridica Hungarica*, 2014/4, 299–317. Calls the result "limited constitutionalism", see Chronowski, Nóra: "Az alkotmánybíráskodás sarkalatos átalakítása", *MTA Law Working Papers*, 2014/8, 4, 1–16, https://jog.tk.mta.hu/uploads/files/mtalwp/2014_08_Chronowski.pdf

25 As an example, the initial difficulties of political acceptance of the German Constitutional Court are usually cited, see Pócza, Kálmán: "Politika és Alkotmánybíróság: a Bundesverfassungsgericht létrejötte", *Külügyi Szemle*, 2014/1, 111–131.

26 For a summary and a review of the relevant research, see Gárdos-Orosz, Fruzsina: *Alkotmányos polgári jog? Az alapvető jogok alkalmazása a magánjogi jogvitákban*, Budapest – Pécs, Dialóg Campus, 2011.

the referral of the ordinary court, it examines the judicial referrals within 90 days at the latest. On the basis of a constitutional complaint, it reviews the conformity with the Fundamental Law of the legislation applied in the individual judicial case and the conformity with the Fundamental Law of the judicial decision as such. At the initiative of the Government, a quarter of the Members of Parliament, the President of the Curia, the Prosecutor General or the Commissioner for Fundamental Rights, the Constitutional Court reviews the conformity of legislation with the Fundamental Law in ex-postex-post abstract norm control procedure. The Constitutional Court also examines whether legislation is in conflict with international treaties and whether an international treaty is in conformity with the provisions of the Fundamental Law. The Constitutional Court may review constitutional amendments on procedural grounds. The Fundamental Law itself allows the Constitutional Court to exercise additional functions and powers defined in a cardinal act.

In addition to the ex-post abstract review procedure, the ex-post concrete review procedure, the ex-ante review procedure and the constitutional complaint procedure, the Constitutional Court has the competence to interpret the Fundamental Law in the abstract, to examine any conflict of laws with international treaties both ex-ante and ex-post, to examine the constitutionality of municipal ordinances, judicial decisions, to examine conflicts of jurisdiction between public bodies. The Constitutional Court is charged with the removal of the President of the Republic from office, to provide an opinion in connection with the unconstitutional operation of a religious community, to examine a decision of the Parliament in connection with the recognition of an organisation carrying out religious activities, to examine a decision of the Parliament related to the ordering of a referendum, and to provide an opinion if the body of local government representatives is operating unconstitutionally.[27] The competences remained exceptionally vague also after 2012.

Prior to 2012, the Constitutional Court had a greater caseload in reviewing the decisions of the National Electoral Commission (NEC) and examining the violation of the legislative acts by municipal regulations. The legislator has therefore transferred these decisions of an administrative adjudicative nature to the Municipal Council of the Curia (supreme court), which was partly created specifically for this purpose. In the course of the following analysis, due to limitations of its scope, I will not deal with the other competences defined in the cardinal act on the competencies of the Constitutional Court, including abstract constitutional interpretation, nor will I deal with the preliminary and ex-post examination of the conflict with international treaties, because these and such procedures, due to their insignificant number, do not contribute largely to defining the nature and character of domestic constitutional adjudication.[28] However, it is worth noting that, by European standards, the Constitutional Court's tasks and powers are extremely complex.

---

27 Act on the Constitutional Court, Chapter II.

28 Constitutional Court statistical data, www.mkab.hu/statisztika

With the new rules on competencies, the composition of cases has changed completely before the Court. The so-called *actio popularis* that anyone could turn to the Constitutional Court to submit a petition ceased to exist with the Fundamental Law. There is no longer any ex-post abstract review of the law initiated by people acting of public interest, which previously accounted for the lion's share of cases. The range of petitioners in abstract review proceedings has therefore been radically reduced. In addition, a new set of constitutional complaints, which can also be used to review judicial decisions, is now available to persons whose rights under the Fundamental Law have been infringed, even if they wish to challenge the norm on which the judicial decision is based. If the constitutionality of the rule needs to be reviewed because the application or the effect of the law has directly infringed a fundamental right, the aggrieved person may also have recourse to the possibility of lodging a constitutional complaint.[29]

Table 1: Changes in competencies of the Constitutional Court, 2009–2014[30]

Scope	*2009*	*2010*	*2011*	*2012*	*2013*	*2014*
Number of cases Received	1452	1994	1825	1100	714	952
Signed for the Rapporteur Judge	757	1284	983	445*	264	390
Abstract ex-post analysis of unconstitutionality	466	1058	918	25	13	3
Of which judicial initiative	98	440	556	65	49	54
Of which Ombudsman initiative	9	5	13	23	13	2
Of which actio popularis	359	613	349			
Constitutional complaint [pursuant to Article 26 (1) of the Abtv., former Article 48 of the Abtv.]	51	144	91	80	36	30
Constitutional complaint pursuant to Article 26 (2) of the Abtv.				353	38	42
Constitutional complaint pursuant to Article 27 of the Abtv.				**295**	**125**	**161**

* The figure includes 353 cases reserved as constitutional complaints among the previous post-constitutional abstract review petitions.

29 The detailed rules and experiences of the old and new powers are discussed in the next chapter.

30 Source: www.mkab.hu/statisztika, and for data before 2012, Botond Bitskey, Secretary General of the Constitutional Court.

The table does not include mass motions (hundreds, sometimes thousands) with essentially identical wording, with the exception of the 2011 judicial referrals, which include a large number of motions in parking ban cases.

Although the comparison of the figures before and after 2012 is difficult and imprecise due to the change in the registration system, the different scope of the data available, the data cleaning carried out for the data after 2012, and the mass of petitions received in some specific cases with identical or almost identical content, it can be concluded that the new legislation has clearly modified the rules of interaction between the constitutional institutions and the function of the Constitutional Court. Whereas previously the relationship between the executive and the legislature, i.e. between the legislature and the Constitutional Court, was more intense, the new rules provide for a steady deepening of the relationship between the ordinary courts and the Constitutional Court.

As a result of the reform, by 2015 the norm control related to individual judicial cases was predominantly conducted in the field of judicial initiatives (referrals), with some cases of constitutional complaints under Article 26 (1) (known before 2012 as well by the former Constitution and Constitutional Court Act) and (2) (which can be initiated even in the absence of the possibility of court proceedings, by the direct application of the law) generating the substantive norm control review procedure. The number of abstract ex-post norm control cases decreased significantly.

The vast majority of cases, however, are still constitutional complaints under Article 27 of the Act on the Constitutional Court, in which the Constitutional Court examines the procedure and ultimately the decision of the ordinary court. As a legal consequence, in addition to the small number of annulments and prohibitions of application, there are an increasing number of cases in which the operative ruling part of a Constitutional Court decision contains a so-called constitutional requirement which gives *erga omnes* effect to the constitutional interpretation of the law formulated by the Constitutional Court, with the aim of guiding the practice of the courts.

Prior to 2012, anyone could apply to the Constitutional Court under the *actio popularis,* the posteriori abstract review procedure, without any interest and without prior judicial proceedings. Of course, as the text of the petitions shows, in most cases, individual interests, supposed rights and/or interests violations were behind the individual petitions, but the procedural order did not require the prior enforcement of rights in the form of administrative and judicial procedures as it did after 2012, so it was easy to go directly to the Constitutional Court. Since the Fundamental Law decided to abolish the *actio popularis,* after 1 January 2012, persons and organisations acting in defence of the constitutional order and not directly concerned by a specific individual case can only bring their constitutional position to the attention of the Constitutional Court in the form of an *amicus curiae* in connection with a specific pending case, without the right to submit a petition. Whereas in 2010, 545 *actio popularis* petitions were pending before the Constitutional Court, in 2013, 74 constitutional complaints, including those for review of the norms, and 198 constitutional complaints against judicial decisions were submitted to the Constitutional Court by the persons and organisations concerned. As can be seen from the table above, the number of petitions has not generally decreased significantly since 2012, but their distribution and filtering has changed.

The essence of the transformation between 2010 and 2013 is therefore that the order in which constitutional institutions and individuals interacted with the Constitutional Court has fundamentally changed. This change is not exclusively in the dimension of individual legal protection and general objective legal protection, since general objective legal protection can also indirectly achieve individual legal protection. Rather, the change is that the emphasis in the current system is on the control of the constitutionality of the application of the law rather than on the control of the legislation. Although the number of decisions on the merits in relation to judicial decisions under Article 27 of the Act on the Constitutional Court is half the number of decisions on the merits in the various procedures ultimately concerned with the control of norms,[31] it can hardly be denied, given the direction and significance of the individual decisions, that decisions on the merits in the procedure for the control of norms in 2015 represent a significant constraint for the legislator.[32] And since 2012, the importance of effective and efficient constitutional review of the legislature and the constitution amending power has often been stressed in the literature.[33] Indeed, the two directions of the two-way constitutional protection do not represent alternatives, but complement each other, both being a guarantee of the constitutional ideal of self-limiting power.

At the time when the idea of the new Constitutional Court (Court with new competencies) was born, the role of the body was clearly reflected in its statement of 28 October 2010: "The Constitutional Court of the Republic of Hungary is an important institution and guarantee of the democratic rule of law, its main task being to protect the Constitution, constitutionality and the fundamental rights of citizens. [...] In the ex-post review of legislation, the Constitutional Court has two main requirements. The first is that constitutional review must cover all legislation, irrespective of the subject matter of the legislation, and the second is that the Constitutional Court must be able to annul legislation which has been declared uncon-

[31] As of 30 September 2015, 20 substantive inquiries in the merits of judicial decisions had been completed, while 43 substantive review proceedings had been completed, including the review of the constitutional complaint procedure.

[32] In 2015, up to 30 September, the Constitutional Court annulled three legislative provisions and declared omissions in five cases. On the identification with the public interest, see, e.g., Balázs, Zoltán: "A közérdek az alkotmánybíráskodásban (2012–2014)", in Gárdos-Orosz, Fruzsina – Szente, Zoltán (eds.): *Jog és politika határán. Alkotmánybíráskodás Magyarországon 2010 után,* Budapest, HVG-ORAC, 2015, 75–104.

[33] Gárdos-Orosz, Fruzsina – Szente, Zoltán (eds.): *Jog és politika határán. Alkotmánybíráskodás Magyarországon 2010 után,* Budapest, HVG-ORAC, 2015.

stitutional."[34] The Declaration of the Constitutional Court stresses the permanence of the functions and tasks of constitutional jurisdiction in Hungary in spite of the changes. In contrast, the attitude of the Constitutional Court since 2015 has been characterised by a more adaptive approach to changing circumstances, as illustrated by the words of Barnabás Lenkovics, President of the Constitutional Court, in an interview: "The Constitutional Court must keep pace with changing circumstances. The same standards that the Constitutional Court developed and applied to the legislator in stable or at least such perceived circumstances cannot be applied unchanged in significantly changed historical circumstances. This would result in certain standards becoming dogma, paralysing the functioning of the legislature, governance and even the rule of law, making it impossible to tackle a crisis. This explains the restructuring of the content and conditions of fundamental rights in the Fundamental Law, as well as the significant restructuring of the powers of the Constitutional Court, shifting them towards the protection of individual fundamental rights."[35]

2.2. The experience of competences

The procedure of the Constitutional Court is essentially subject to a motion.[36] Even under the previous legislation, the Court could only act *ex officio* in a very narrow range of cases, and it developed the doctrine of the so-called "close relation" itself to determine the cases in which it could turn to the examination of a legal provision not mentioned in the petition. Nevertheless, the Fourth Amendment to the Fundamental Law adopted on 25 March 2013 has narrowed the scope of the Constitutional Court's discretion in this matter by emphasising in detail the elements of the requirement to submit a valid petition and the strictly connected scope of the constitutional review. The rule expressly stated that "Those provisions of a legislative act that were not requested to be reviewed may be reviewed and annulled by the Constitutional Court only if there is a close substantive connection between them and the provisions requested to be reviewed." Thus, the Constitutional Court is now not only bound by its own practice in this issue, which obviously gives it

[34] Position of the Constitutional Court on the draft constitutional amendment bill amending its powers, October 28, 2010, https://alkotmanybirosag.hu/kozlemeny/az-alkotmanybirosag-allasfoglalasa-a-hataskorenek-modositasara-iranyulo-alkotmanymodositasi-torvenyjavaslattal-kapcsolatban

[35] Interview with Barnabás Lenkovics in *Jogi Fórum*, http://www.jogiforum.hu/interju/122. Contrary to this view, see Sólyom, László: "Ezen a lejtőn nehéz lesz megállni!", *Iustum Aequum Salutare*, 2010/4, 5–9.

[36] An exception is that after 2012, the Constitutional Court can only declare an unconstitutional omission as a legal consequence *ex officio*, it cannot be initiated. The Constitutional Court may initiate an examination of an international treaty violation *ex officio*, the interesting aspects of which are discussed later in the main text.

greater discretion, but is also bound by this specific legislation not to be able to widen its competence in this regard. The role and responsibility of the petitioner is therefore more pronounced in determining what will be subject to constitutional review in Hungary, however it is not necessary to submit the motion by an advocate or other legal representative. In the following, I will therefore not only present the substantive outcome of the Constitutional Court proceedings, but also try to assess the input side as well, assessing the number of petitions.

A significant proportion of the motions, in particular the constitutional complaints, are not suitable for consideration on the merits, and are not admissible. As regards the organisation and functioning of the Constitutional Court, the previous practice has been changed by the introduction of a single judge, who can reject motions with formal defects by a one-person decision if the petitioner has not accepted the information provided by the Secretary General, and the single judge considers that the motion is not suitable to form the basis for further proceedings.

In accordance with Article 50 (1) of the Act on the Constitutional Court, the typical forum for the adjudication of cases has become the five-member council, a 5-member panel of judges. In the vast majority of cases, the admissibility of constitutional complaints is examined by a five-member chamber, and thus decisions on the refusal of admission, which are not decisions on the merits, are also taken in this forum. The five-member panel may act under Article 50 (2), unless the case falls within the exclusive competence of the full panel of 15 judges. The Council of five judges may not annul a law, but it may annul a judicial decision and may also declare an omission or a constitutional requirement.[37]

It is therefore much less possible than in the past to judge the substantive work of the Constitutional Court solely on the basis of the decisions of the whole session. This fact leads to interesting conclusions, since the Constitutional Court's constant practice in most matters was previously determined by the plenary session. It is true that the Constitutional Court still generally discusses significant legal consequences in plenary session and pronounces them in a decision taken in plenary session, but this practice is uncertain, as it depends to a large extent on the caseload, and on the fact that the President and the judges of the Constitutional Court decide whether it can be maintained in the future. No legislative or judicial solution has yet been found to ensure unity of the judicial practice between the five-member panels, but under the current rules the President may order a case to be heard in plenary session in order to ensure unity of jurisprudence, a power which, if properly exercised, may be able to address the problem.

[37] On the rules of the procedure of the Secretary General, the single judge procedure and the procedure of the five-member chambers in relation to the constitutional complaint procedures, which represent a significant part of the caseload, see Bitskey, Botond – Fröhlich, Johanna – Gárdos-Orosz, Fruzsina – Rajos, Krisztina: "Az alkotmányjogi panaszeljárás általános szabályai", in Bitskey, Botond – Török, Bernát (eds.): *Az alkotmányjogi panasz kézikönyve*, Budapest, HVG-ORAC, 2015, 59–216; Kelemen, Katalin: *Judicial dissent in European constitutional courts: A comparative and legal perspective*, Routledge, 2018.

2.2.1. The constitutional complaint

According to the explanatory memorandum of the Fundamental Law, the constitutional complaint under Article 27 of the Act on the Constitutional Court, which is a completely new constitutional review competence in Hungary "opens a new era of fundamental rights protection", as it "provides an additional special remedy for the complainant who has already exhausted his or her effective ordinary remedies, which in the case of the most serious – constitutional – violations of rights provides an opportunity to make a decision in accordance with the Fundamental Law".

In what follows, I will show the difficulties encountered in achieving the legitimate legislative objective in the period 2012–2015 before the stabilisation of the jurisprudence[38] and how the new competence compares with the other two old-new types of constitutional complaint.

Pursuant to Article 24 (2) *c)* of the Fundamental Law, the Constitutional Court shall review the conformity of the law applied in an individual case with the Fundamental Law on the basis of a constitutional complaint. Pursuant to Article 24 (2) *d)* of the Fundamental Law, the Constitutional Court shall also review the conformity of a judicial decision with the Fundamental Law on the basis of a constitutional complaint. The Act on the Constitutional Court has established three categories of constitutional complaints, detailing the rules of the Fundamental Law.

Pursuant to Article 26 (1) of the Act on the Constitutional Court, "In accordance with Article 24 (2) *c)* of the Fundamental Law, person or organisation affected by a concrete case may submit a constitutional complaint to the Constitutional Court if, due to the application of a legal regulation contrary to the Fundamental Law in their judicial proceedings a) their rights enshrined in the Fundamental Law were violated, and b) the possibilities for legal remedy have already been exhausted or no possibility for legal remedy is available." This type of constitutional complaint was already a living legal institution in Hungarian law before 2012.

According to Article 26 (2) of the Act on the Constitutional Court, unlike in the previous case, the procedure of the Constitutional Court may also be initiated by way of exception if the petitioner has suffered a direct legal injury as a result of the application or enforcement of a provision of a statute that is contrary to the Fundamental Law, without a judicial decision, and there is no legal remedy procedure to remedy this legal injury, or the petitioner has already exhausted his/her legal rem-

[38] The findings of the study on constitutional complaints are largely based, in many places textually identical, on my earlier research conducted jointly with Johanna Fröhlich; published in Bitskey, Botond – Fröhlich, Johanna – Gárdos-Orosz, Fruzsina – Rajos, Krisztina: "Az alkotmányjogi panasz eljárások tapasztalatai az indítvány beérkezésétől az érdemi elbírálásig", in Bitskey, Botond – Török, Bernát (eds.): *Az alkotmányjogi panasz kézikönyve,* Budapest, HVG-ORAC, 2015, 102–225, extended form Gárdos-Orosz, Fruzsina: "A bírói döntések ellen benyújtott alkotmányjogi panaszok befogadhatósága I. Az Abtv. 26. § (1) bekezdése", *Alkotmánybírósági Szemle,* 2013/4, 74–81; Gárdos-Orosz, Fruzsina: "A bírói döntések ellen benyújtott alkotmányjogi panaszok befogadhatósága II. Az Abtv. 27. §-a", *Alkotmánybírósági Szemle,* 2014/1, 82–89.

edy options. This type of complaint is often referred to in the literature as a direct constitutional complaint.

Pursuant to Article 27 of the Act on the Constitutional Court, the person or organisation concerned may lodge a constitutional complaint with the Constitutional Court against a judicial decision that is contrary to the Fundamental Law, based on Article 24 (2) *d)* of the Fundamental Law, if the decision on the merits of the case or any other decision ending the court proceedings violates the petitioner's right guaranteed by the Fundamental Law, and the petitioner has already exhausted his/her legal remedies or no legal remedies are available to him/her. This competence to review the constitutionality of judicial decisions is often referred to in the jargon as a "genuine" or "German-type" constitutional complaint.[39] This initial provision has been supplemented by the possibility for an organisation or public body to appeal to the Constitutional Court if its powers under the Fundamental Law are infringed. This amendment caused great controversy, as many interpreted the opening of the possibility to lodge a constitutional complaint as implying that the right of the public body under the Fundamental Law could be violated and remedied by the Constitutional Court. In my opinion, if the provision were to be interpreted along German lines, the Constitutional Court could accept constitutional complaints from public institutions that allege a breach of competence, i.e. a breach of their right under the Fundamental Law, since the previously established and common-sense doctrine is that public bodies (with the exception of the rights of self-government) do not have a right under the Fundamental Law, and conceptually cannot have fundamental rights.[40]

The Constitutional Court may also conduct a joint procedure under Articles 26 (1) and 27 of the Act on the Constitutional Court, if the constitutionality of the judicial application of law and the constitutionality of the norm on which it is based is doubtful from the point of view of the assessment of the underlying constitutional problem.[41]

The introduction of the new competencies was probably a consolation prize for the abolition of the *actio popularis*. In proceedings with an individual rights focus, however, procedural law sets high standards of admissibility and standing. The primary aim of these types of constitutional complaints is to remedy the violation of rights by annulling the court decision and the unconstitutional norm. In these procedures, the unconstitutional norm is removed from the legal system as

39 For technical reasons, I will not use the adjective "real", in the rest of this paper; in certain contexts I will refer to the legal institution as a constitutional complaint against judicial decisions or as a complaint under Article 27 of the Act on the Constitutional Court.

40 This is later interpreted differently by the Constitutional Court, which has ruled that it is the task of the Constitutional Court to remedy the violation of the right to a fair trial by public bodies, as provided for in the Fundamental Law. This interpretation is dogmatically problematic and runs counter to the correct interpretation of the law.

41 On the problem of a confirmatory application and interpenetrability, see Decision 3/2013. (II. 14.) AB, Reasoning's [20]–[23].

a peripheral legal effect or, as in Hungarian law, the declaration of a constitutional requirement binding on all has a law-forming effect. The annulment of a judicial decision will also have an impact on subsequent judicial practice in general, but the individual nature of the remedy means that the criteria for admissibility in constitutional court proceedings can be tailored to this specificity.[42]

The examination of the admissibility of constitutional complaints has become a new procedure in the competence of the Constitutional Court – a formal and substantive examination of the admissibility of the merits of the petition. In Hungary, the new Act on the Constitutional Court – similar to the rules of procedure of the constitutional courts in the region following the German model[43] – put the principle of equality above all and primarily and explicitly enforce the principle of screening, i.e. in the course of the admissibility procedure the Constitutional Court only examines the observation of the formal and substantive criteria set out in the Abtv. for the individual petitions, and in principle cannot consider other aspects, cannot select cases from the pool of petitions. The Constitutional Court should decide all valid petitions. However, the criteria for quasi selection are also found in Article 29 of the Act on the Constitutional Court, according to which the admissibility of a petition is, however, conditional on the proof of an infringement of fundamental right affecting the merits of the case or on the presentation of a question of fundamental constitutional importance in relation to a specific case.[44] Similar criteria with a filtering role for questions of fundamental constitutional importance exist in other countries, such as Germany[45] or Spain.[46]

The Constitutional Court has stated in several cases that the purpose of a constitutional complaint is generally to remedy a violation of rights[47], ultimately this distinguishes this competence from the former abstract review of norms in *actio popularis*. However, it also recognised that a constitutional complaint for the an-

[42] These issues have also been intensively addressed in the literature. See, e.g., Tóth J., Zoltán: "Az egyéni alapjogvédelem az Alkotmányban és az Alaptörvényben I–II.", *Közjogi Szemle*, 2012/3–4, 11–19; Vissy, Beatrix: "Az individuális alapjogvédelem kilátásai az alkotmánybíráskodásban. Merre mutat az alkotmányjogi panasz iránytűje?", *Magyar Közigazgatás*, 2012/2, 199–211.

[43] [No author:] "A »valódi alkotmányjogi panasz« és elbírálásának főbb jellemzői – nemzetközi kitekintés", *Alkotmánybírósági Szemle*, 2011/2, 64–74.

[44] Decision 28/2015. (IX. 24.) AB on the unconstitutionality of the decision of the Curia on the referendum initiative on the equal retirement age for men and women.

[45] "Specifisches Verfassungsrecht". See for more on this in Hungarian, Zakariás, Kinga: "A rendes bíróságok határozatainak felülvizsgálata a Német Szövetségi Alkotmánybíróság gyakorlatában", *Jogtudományi Közlöny*, 2010/2, 98–104.

[46] In Spain, the Organic Law 2/1979 on the Constitutional Court (Ley Orgánica 2/1979, de 3 de octubre, del Tribunal Constitucional; LOTC) introduced the institution of *amparo*. Organic Law No 6/2007 amending the LOTC provided for, among other things, a major change to the rules on admission. It introduced an additional condition, similar to that of a question of fundamental constitutional importance, which allowed only petitions of constitutional importance to be admitted to the Constitutional Court. This criterion was elaborated in detail by the Constitutional Court in STC 155/2009 (Constitutional Court Decision).

[47] Order 3367/2012. (XII. 15.) AB, Reasoning [11], [13]; Decision 6/2013. (III. 1.) AB, Reasoning [214].

nulment of a norm has an objective, general constitutional protection function as well, as a result of which the legal consequences are determined in a way that go beyond the individual case.

2.2.1.1. Against a judicial decision. Review of the constitutionality of the law applied

In constitutional complaint procedures initiated under Article 26 (1) of the Act on the Constitutional Court, the person or organisation concerned in an individual case may challenge a decision made in an individual court procedure on the grounds that the court applied a piece of legislation that is contrary to the Fundamental Law, and thus the decision violated her fundamental right. The requirement of being affected is also specifically laid down in the text of the Abtv. In practice, the test of relevance is generally and essentially limited to determining whether or not the complainant is a party to the judicial case he or she is challenging.

However, according to the explanatory memorandum to Articles 26–31 of the Act on the Constitutional Court, "[t]he use of the concept of involvement (being affected) is a broader framework for the protection of fundamental rights than if the possibility were open only for the party to the case".[48] This type of complaint has been part of Hungarian law since the fall of the communist regime, and it seems that even without the admissibility procedure, it was not suitable for a large-scale review of unconstitutional norms. The criteria set out as part of the admissibility procedure have further narrowed the pool of successful petitioners. Individual rights can be redressed if an unconstitutional law has been applied in a given case, and the Constitutional Court can even impose a general ban on its application, but the statistics here show that this mechanism is working with little effectiveness.

2.2.1.2. Review of legislation where the application directly infringes fundamental rights

Complaints under Article 26 (2) of the Act on the Constitutional Court may be filed by a person or organisation directly affected by the application or entry into force of a provision of a statute that is contrary to the Fundamental Law.

The constitutional complaint regulated by Article 26 (2) of the Act on the Constitutional Court is special and exceptional in several respects. Studies on the new competencies of the Constitutional Court[49] have critically examined the legitimacy of the "exceptional nature" of this power, i.e. the relationship between the "exceptional nature" of the law and the remedial nature of constitutional review.

---

48 The Constitutional Court has already dealt with the question – admittedly, on the basis of a complaint under Article 27 of the Act on the Constitutional Court – whether, for example, in a criminal case the victim may file a constitutional complaint in addition to the accused. Decision 1/2015. (I. 16.) AB.

49 See, e.g., Naszladi, Georgina: "Az alkotmányjogi panasz első fél éve", *Közjogi Szemle*, 2012/4, 41–42.

As regards the practice of Article 26 (2) of the Act on the Constitutional Court, the Constitutional Court has interpreted the admissibility criteria in a very strict manner, and the application of the provisions on time limits and the scope of the right to be heard has led to the fact that only a very narrow range of constitutional complaints submitted under Article 26 (2) of the Act have passed through the admissibility procedure.[50] According to the interpretation of the Constitutional Court, the complaint can only be lodged within 180 days of the entry into force of the act causing the infringement, but in many cases the infringement does not occur within this period in real life.

The practice of admission of constitutional complaints under Article 26 (2) of the Act on the Constitutional Court illustrates the dilemmas that arise when comparing and distinguishing this type of constitutional complaint and the subsequent abstract review procedure that could be initiated by anyone *(actio popularis)* before the entry into force of the Fundamental Law. At one end of the spectrum of scholarly opinions is that this constitutional complaint is a new form of the former *actio popularis* based on a well-defined concern, so the admissibility should be defined in a vague manner, while at the other end of the spectrum of opinions is a strict competence restriction vis-à-vis the *actio popularis*, requiring the personal, direct and actual concern of the petitioners to be proven for admissibility.[51]

Between these two extremes, there may be several alternative solutions and directions according to the different admissibility criteria, which are influenced by different judicial perceptions and different ideas about the function of the constitutional complaint. The subjective legal protection function of the constitutional complaint may be most closely intertwined with the function of protecting objective constitutionality, the objective order of constitutional values. In a decision, the Constitutional Court formulated this dichotomy as follows: "The primary aim is individual, subjective legal protection: to remedy the legal injury caused by the unconstitutional legislation or unconstitutional judicial decision that has actually caused the legal injury. The secondary objective of constitutional complaints concerning the review of legislation is to prevent similar infringements in the future and thus to objectively protect the constitutional legal order."[52] Thus, the Constitutional Court has the possibility of both cleansing the

50 The statistics on the website of the Constitutional Court show that 77 cases were still pending in this procedure as of 31 December 2014. Between 1 January and 31 December 2014, a total of 40 proceedings under Article 26 (2) of the Act on the Constitutional Court were concluded at the level of the Secretary General or single judge, and 19 cases were concluded by consolidation. In the same period, a further 22 cases were dismissed by the Council of the Constitutional Court.

51 Zakariás, Kinga: "A bírósági határozatok ellen irányuló alkotmányjogi panasz a Német Szövetségi Alkotmánybíróság Esra-határozatának tükrében", *Alkotmánybírósági Szemle*, 2011/2, 92.

52 Order 3367/2012. (XII. 15.) AB, Reasoning's [13]–[14]. Confirmed by Decision 6/2013. (III. 1.) AB, Reasoning [214].

legal system of unconstitutional norms and providing a remedy for the specific complainant.

Individualised redress for this type of complaint can often cause difficulties in the absence of a judicial procedure. In addition to a statute annulled in a procedure under Article 26 (2) of the Act on the Constitutional Court, a further adoption of a proper constitutional act is often required to remedy the legal infringements caused by the unconstitutional statute. This can be facilitated, for example, by the definition of constitutional requirements or omission, but the Constitutional Court cannot guarantee the remedy of the infringements by these means alone.

2.2.1.3. Against a judicial decision: Review of the constitutionality of a judicial decision

Pursuant to Article 27 of the Act on the Constitutional Court, under Article 24 (2) *d)* of the Fundamental Law, the person or organisation affected in an individual case may appeal to the Constitutional Court to challenge a judicial decision that is contrary to the Fundamental Law.

With regard to the admissibility of constitutional complaints against judicial decisions under Article 27 of the Act on the Constitutional Court, the Constitutional Court follows a very strict practice when examining the admissibility criteria set out in the Constitutional Court Act. In the first months of the new case law, the Constitutional Court had to clarify that, pursuant to Article 71 (3) of the Act on the Constitutional Court, motions for ex-post review of norms filed before 1 January 2012 could only be converted into constitutional complaints under Article 26 (2) of the Act on the Constitutional Court.[53]

Looking at the statistics for the first five years from 2012 to 2016, there is a clear shift from the numerical dominance of the first year of an Article 26 "old type" complaint to the clear dominance of an Article 27 "German-type" complaint. While in 2012, the majority of complaints were based on norm-review, in 2013 and 2014 the majority of complaints were clearly based on Article 27 of the Abtv.[54] This can be explained, on the one hand, by the fact that in the first year the cases brought back

[53] This requirement appeared for the first time in Decision 3023/2012. (VI. 21.) AB, according to which Article 71 (3) of the Act on the Constitutional Court does not contain such a restriction, and the submitted complaint otherwise complied with the statutory requirements. Reasoning's [10]–[14].

[54] Of the total number of cases pending on 1 January 2012 and opened by 31 December 2012, approximately 700 were under Article 26 of the Act on the Constitutional Court [of which 354 under Article 26 (1) and 353 under Article 26 (2)], while under Article 27 there were 300. The same proportion in 2013 was as follows: only 68 cases were opened or pending under Article 26 (1), 128 under Article 26 (2), but a total of 198 under Article 27. In 2014, the same figures are 64 [Article 26 (1)], 77 [Article 26 (2)] and 220 (Article 27). It is also noticeable that the other two types of constitutional complaints under Article 26 of the Act on the Constitutional Court have started to balance out in terms of the number of cases, i.e. the initial dominance of Article 26 (2) complaints has steadily declined.

from before 2012 increased the number of complaint procedures under Article 26 and, on the other hand, by the fact that the possibility to challenge court judgments under Article 27 was completely unknown due to the unexpected introduction of the German-type constitutional complaint. Furthermore, the Constitutional Court has taken a markedly cautious approach to the use of the complaint instrument under Article 27 of the Fundamental Law. The most common ground for refusal was the absence of a question of fundamental constitutional importance. The difficulties of separating the issues of interpretation of the law to be resolved in the ordinary course of judicial interpretation and the interpretation of the Fundamental Law were outstanding. The adjudication of complaints under Article 27 of the Act on the Constitutional Court would often require new expertise and an approach different from that of the abstract review of norms, both from the constitutional judge and from the law clerks in addition to each branch of the ordinary judiciary. In contrast to the norm-control procedure, it is an orientation of the ordinary courts towards the constitutional review practice.

By 2015, the most popular type of constitutional complaint among petitioners was the German type under Article 27 of the Act on the Constitutional Court. Apart from a few exceptional cases,[55] petitioners mainly complained about the procedure of the ordinary courts on the grounds of a violation of their right to a fair trial[56] and their right to legal remedy[57] under Article XXVIII of the Fundamental Law. However, it was also common to claim violation of the right to property. Less frequently, motions and major decisions were made on the right of public access to data of public interest[58] or freedom of expression.[59]

In the proceedings initiated on the basis of Article 27, a separate question also arose concerning the extent to which the previous practice of the Constitutional Court could be applied, since it had been developed in the course of the norm control proceedings. In the Constitutional Court's view, "[t]he Constitutional Court has made it its task to review the constitutionality of judicial decisions, but in exercising this power it continues to act to remedy violations of the rights guaranteed by the Fundamental Law and ultimately to protect the Fundamental Law itself. It follows that the constitutional rules of the system of requirements of the right to a fair trial are now the constitutional yardstick not only for legislation but also for individual judicial decisions as well."[60] In sum, the Court believes that the constitutional standards are interchangeably applicable in all procedures, no matter in which procedure they were introduced.

[55] Decision 3/2013. (II. 14.) AB – violation of the right of assembly.

[56] Decision 21/2014. (VII. 15.) AB; Decision 3174/2014. (VI. 18.) AB; Decision 34/2013. (XI. 22.) AB; Decision 25/2013. (X. 4.) AB; Decision 8/2013. (III. 1.) AB.

[57] Decision 3064/2014. (III. 26.) AB.

[58] Decision 25/2014. (VII. 22.) AB; Decision 5/2014. (II. 14.) AB; Decision 21/2013. (VII. 19.) AB.

[59] Decision 19/2014. (V. 30.) AB; Decision 13/2014. (IV. 18.) AB; Decision 1/2014. (I. 21.) AB.

[60] Decision 7/2013. (III. 1.) AB, Reasoning's [25]–[27].

The Constitutional Court distances itself in principle from the review of discretionary judicial decisions, fearing of the charge of being the fourth instance court in ordinary judicial case.[61] In several of its decisions, the Court has ruled that in order to declare a constitutional complaint against a judicial decision admissible, it is not sufficient to merely criticise the court decision and the court procedure,[62] the complaint must also address the constitutional aspect of the criticism, i.e. how and why the petitioner's rights under the Fundamental Law were violated by the court decision.[63]

In several decisions, the Constitutional Court has stated that the courts must interpret the law, and that the Constitutional Court can only define the constitutional limits of the scope of this interpretation: "However, the Constitutional Court cannot interfere in the activity of the courts in all cases where, in the petitioner's view, the law has been applied in violation of the Fundamental Law and no further remedy is open. Neither the abstract principle of the rule of law, nor the fundamental right to a fair trial in general, nor the prohibition of discrimination in general terms can provide alone a basis for the Constitutional Court to act without becoming a 'super-court' in the case."[64] The Constitutional Court will uphold a constitutional complaint under Article 27 of the Act on the Constitutional Court if the error in the interpretation and application of the law by the court is such that it results in the violation of a specific right guaranteed by the Fundamental Law.[65] However, the above sentences, which are often cited as a benchmark, do not mean that the Constitutional Court, which is also vested with the power of annulment laws and judicial decisions, does not carry out a special appellate function in the matter of the constitutional application of the law and the interpretation of law in conformity with the Fundamental Law. The difficulty arises precisely from the fact that the scope of ordinary judicial remedies and that of constitutional court remedies can hardly be separated from each other regarding the scope of constitutionality issues and regarding certain substantive issues of fundamental rights adjudication.

The Constitutional Court is increasingly formulating the so-called constitutional requirements instead of annulling the piece of legislation or the judicial decision in the case of constitutional complaints challenging a judicial decision. In its view, in cases involving a fundamental right, the courts will act in accordance with the Fundamental Law if, in their interpretation, they take into account the constitutional requirements aimed at determining the content of the fundamen-

61 Decision 3037/2014. (III. 13.) AB.

62 In one case, for example, the Constitutional Court stressed that "the task of ensuring the unity of judicial jurisprudence is not the task of the Constitutional Court, but of the courts, and in particular the Curia". Order 3297/2012. (X. 19.) AB, Reasoning [8].

63 Order 3103/2012. (VII. 26.) AB, Reasoning [5]; Order 3117/2012. (VII. 26.) AB, Reasoning [5]; Order 3118/2012. (VII. 26.) AB; Order 3379/2012. (XII. 15.) AB.

64 Order 3325/2012. (XI. 12.) AB, Reasoning's [14]–[15].

65 Decision 3265/2014. (XI. 4.) AB, Reasoning [45].

tal right concerned.[66] "The Constitutional Court's role in proceedings based on a constitutional complaint is primarily judicial protection. Under Article 27, its task is to enforce the rights guaranteed by the Fundamental Law. Consequently, the Constitutional Court's task also includes answering the question of which interpretation of a given piece of legislation meets certain requirements inherent in the rights recognised in the Fundamental Law. The Constitutional Court itself, as the final domestic legal forum, ultimately guarantees the application of the system of fundamental rights through the constitutional review of judicial decisions. At the same time, the Constitutional Court ensures that the decisions of the judiciary be also in conformity with the international human rights obligations as well."[67]

However, in practice, after the formulation and articulation of the desirable principles, in many cases it is questionable whether the concerns of legal interpretation and application of law formulated in relation with the challenged court decision can be validly rephrased as constitutional concerns. In the absence of a transparent and uniform set of criteria, decisions often appear arbitrary. In many disputed cases, some judges do not recognise a constitutionally assessable relation between the fundamental rights provision of the Fundamental Law and the interpretation of the law which is considered to be in breach of fundamental rights, while for others the relation is obvious.[68] In other cases, there is disagreement as to how the law applied in the judicial decision should be interpreted in order to satisfy the requirement of constitutional interpretation.[69] The Constitutional Court stresses that "in accordance with the nature of the complaints provided for in Article 27 of the Act on the Constitutional Court, the Constitutional Court decides on questions of constitutionality concerning the merits of the specific case, but the consequences of this for the specific case must be drawn by the ordinary court. In this way, the complainant can guarantee an effective remedy against the infringements of rights in court decisions."[70]

The decisions completed in the first few years show that the Constitutional Court's rulings have in some cases contributed to the ordinary judicial enforcement (in the form of highly divided decisions) of the constitutional content of the right

---

66 Decision 28/2014. (IX. 29.) AB, Reasoning [28]. See also Decision 8/2014. (III. 20.) AB on the indirect horizontal scope of the Constitution.

67 Decision 30/2014. (IX. 30.) AB, Reasoning [22].

68 E.g. Decision 3243/2014. (X. 3.) AB, Andás Bragyova's dissenting opinion: "Therefore, in my opinion, there is a constitutional standard for the legal norms regulating the termination of employment; which also means that the termination of employment may violate the employee's constitutional right to employment, as well as, of course, other constitutional right" [66].

69 "The Constitutional Court thus examined whether the interpretation of the law in court decisions constitutes an unconstitutional restriction on the freedom of the press and freedom of expression (opinions in comments)" Decision 19/2014. (V. 30.) AB, Reasoning [45] (internet moderation). Decision 13/2014. (IV. 18.) AB (the ability to criticise public figures).

70 Decision 21/2013. (VII. 19.) AB, Reasoning [53].

to a fair trial, the right to a remedy, the right to access to public data, the right to assembly or to freedom of expression. The problem is, however, that the number of decisions in the merits is negligible compared to the entire number of petition submissions, which means that very few rights-seekers obtain directly legal protection through the constitutional complaints procedure.

With regard to the legal consequences of a complaint under Article 27 of the Act on the Constitutional Court, the fundamental question was whether it is possible to establish a failure to act, a judicial omission, or whether this is contrary to the competence of the Constitutional Court [e.g. Decision 19/2015. (VI. 15.) AB]. Another question is what expectations Article 28 of the Fundamental Law sets out for this procedure, when can a judicial decision be annulled because of the negligence towards observing the compulsory methods of interpretation set out by Art. 28 of the Fundamental Law. According to the original wording of Article 28 of the Fundamental Law, "in the application of the law, the courts shall interpret the text of the law [...] in accordance with the Fundamental Law".

2.2.2. Judicial referral – concrete norm control

The judicial initiative (judicial referral) is not a new legal institution in Hungarian constitutional law; the Constitutional Court has been exercising this competence since 1990. A judge hearing a case may submit a motion to the Constitutional Court if he or she finds that an unconstitutional piece of legislation should be applied in a case pending before him or her. In such a case, the judicial proceedings are suspended and the matter is referred to the Constitutional Court.

In 2015, the largest volume of ex-post control of norms in Hungary was the number of judicial referrals that were later converted into substantive decisions in the merits. In addition to the drying up of ex-post abstract review procedures, judges have been given a special responsibility for the thorough constitutional monitoring of the applicable legislation, since from the state side only the judges acting in individual cases have maintained their activity in initiating constitutional court proceedings compared to other state institutions which became more deferential to the constitution-making two thirds parliamentary majority such as the ombudsman. This means that every year, as shown in Table 1, the Constitutional Court receives judicial initiatives for review of the norms in around 60-70 cases per year, in a constant curve. In the last decade, many important cases have been brought before the Constitutional Court on judicial referral, such as the constitutionality of the so-called nullity act,[71] the constitutionality of the reorganisation of consumer loan contracts (the "foreign currency loan cases") or the provisions on the aggravation of cumulative penalties (three strikes).[72]

[71] Decision 24/2013. (X. 4.) AB.

[72] Decision 23/2014. (VII. 15.) AB.

2.2.3. Ex-post abstract norm control

In 2011, there were 969 cases pending before the Constitutional Court, of which 558 were ex-post abstract review. Of these, 545 were *actio popularis* and 13 were ombudsman motions. As of 1 January 2012, cases initiated on the basis of an *actio popularis* motion were discontinued if they could not be converted into a constitutional complaint under Article 26 of the Act on the Constitutional Court and the petitioner did not expressly request this by means of a supplement to the motion submitted on the basis of the criteria of the quasi-new Act on the Constitutional Court and the Rules of Procedure of the Constitutional Court. In terms of proportions, the number of cases pending as constitutional complaints was insignificant.

According to the new legislation, only the Government, a quarter of the members of Parliament, the President of the Curia, the Prosecutor General or the Commissioner for Fundamental Rights may initiate an ex-post abstract review of a norm, i.e. an examination of the constitutionality of an act after its promulgation, but which is not related to a violation of an individual right contained in the Fundamental Law, or to a specific case.

In 2011, 58 percent of ex-post review procedures were ex-post abstract review, 37 percent were judicial initiatives and only 5 percent were constitutional complaints. After 2012, however, posteriori abstract norm control was initiated almost exclusively by the Commissioner for Fundamental Rights (ombudsman) among dedicated petitioners,[73] and in terms of volume, this competence remained at the same level in 2012.[74] On the basis of these reviews, several important decisions were born, such as Articles 7 and 8 of *Act CCXI of 2011 on the right of succession of registered partners, Act CCXI of 2011 on the protection of families,* where the parallel reasoning annexed to the decision is very important. The Constitutional Court has often been often divided, as was the case in the decisions on the declaration of the unconstitutionality and annulment of Article 3 (3) *c)* of *Act LXXX of 2003 on legal aid in judicial proceedings,*[75] the case on the unconstitutionality and annulment of certain articles of the Transitional Provisions of the Fundamental Law.[76]

In 2013, some important decisions were taken on the basis of an ombudsman proposal. For example, the decision to examine the Fourth Amendment to the Fundamental Law[77] has fundamentally shaped the character of constitutional adjudication. While the case involving the size of prison cells and the decision on the

[73] The right of petition of the Prosecutor General and the President of the Curia only came later, in 2013, due to international pressure. Lápossy, Attila: "Populáris akcióból ombudsmani akciók?", *Magyar Közigazgatás,* 2011/3, 120–131; Lápossy, Attila: "Közvetve és közvetlenül: az alapvető jogok biztosának indítványozási jogköre az alkotmánybíráskodás és alapjogvédelem szemszögéből", *Kodifikáció és Közigazgatás,* 2012/2, 39–52.

[74] In 2012, 25 ombudsman petitions were received.

[75] Decision 42/2012. (XII. 20.) AB.

[76] Decision 45/2012. (XII. 29.) AB.

[77] Decision 12/2013. (V. 24.) AB.

declaration and annulment of certain provisions of the *Decree 5/1998. (III. 6.) IM on the health care of prisoners,* which found certain provisions of this decree to be unconstitutional, undoubtedly advanced the enforcement of the rights of prisoners, while the decision on the detention of juveniles for offences[78] represented a step backwards in the protection of fundamental rights, because it defined the content of the fundamental right under examination more narrowly than in previous practice.

Three significant cases from 2014 are worth mentioning in the field of ex-post abstract norm control: the Decision 7/2014. (III. 7.) AB on the criticism of public figures, the decision of the Court on the declaration of the unconstitutionality of the wording "in the justifiable public interest" of Article 2:44 of *Act V of 2013 on the Civil Code* and its annulment, which avoided, however, a confrontation with the Curia. The case of the continuous national security checks of civil servants[79] was also referred to the Constitutional Court on the Ombudsman's motion and was annulled. The decision, handed down on 27 May, ruled that the wording of Article 65 (5) of *Act I of 2012 on the Labour Code,* which states that a woman who is pregnant or has undergone a human reproductive procedure is entitled to protection against dismissal only if she has informed her employer of her condition before the notice of dismissal, is unconstitutional and was annulled by the Constitutional Court.[80]

However, in the first half of 2015, the output of ex-post abstract review procedures fell to only two decisions.[81] A quarter of the MPs filed an ex-post abstract review motion in relation to the election of members of the Metropolitan Assembly of the Metropolitan Self-Government, which had already been decided.[82] In 2015, five new motions were also filed by opposition MPs, all on politically sensitive issues.[83] The Government also requested a constitutional review of certain provisions of the 2011 judicial reform, which were criticised in the second opinion of the Venice Commission on the subject.[84] Among the dedicated petitioners, the President of the Curia referred to the Constitutional Court the case of national security checks on judges,[85] and the Prosecutor General also submitted a petition once, in December 2015.[86] Apart from exceptions such as those mentioned above, the Government has an interest in initiating a posteriori abstract review proceedings only if it seeks the annulment of a two-thirds legislative act passed in a previous term. In other

[78] Decision 3142/2013. (VII. 16.) AB.

[79] Decision 9/2014. (III. 21.) AB on the declaration of the unconstitutionality of *Act LXXII of 2013 on the amendment of certain acts necessary to establish new rules for national security control and Act CXXV of 1995 on national security services and the annulment of certain provisions of the Act.*

[80] Decision 17/2014. (V. 30.) AB.

[81] Decision 3023/2015. (II. 9.) AB.

[82] Decision 26/2014. (VII. 23.) AB.

[83] Cases II/00861/2015, II/0292/2015, 2/3093/2015, II/03094/2015, II/03285/2015.

[84] Decision 13/2013. (VI. 17.) AB.

[85] Case II/01063/2015. AB.

[86] Case II/03423/2015 on the maintenance of a legal relationship on the basis of a national security clearance in the event of a risk to national security is pending.

cases, it can correct the breach of the Fundamental Law within its own powers and by means of a legislative act of Parliament, which represents the same majority as the Government. In the case of a conflict of interest with regard to regulations, the President of the National Bank of Hungary, the president of an independent regulatory body, or a local government regulation may be questioned as well from the point of view of its constitutionality before the Court.

The Ombudsman would be the authentic petitioner in general fundamental rights cases affecting many people, but it can be seen that the Commissioner cannot be said to be active in petitioning. The personal role of the petitioner thus plays a major role in influencing the functioning of the Constitutional Court. In order to preserve public participation after abolishing the *actio popularis,* when the right of social organisations to petition had been rejected by the Constituent Majority, a specific system could have been envisaged which would have allowed a limited number of citizens to petition the Constitutional Court or make the dedicated institutions more concerned in this matter.

Analyses of the case law of the Constitutional Court show that even among the decisions in the merits issued under the competence of ex-post abstract norm control, there were very few cases in which the Constitutional Court actually and ultimately imposed a constitutional limit on the will of the legislature or the Government by declaring an annulment, an omission or a constitutional requirement ruling unconstitutionality.[87]

2.2.4. Preliminary abstract norm control

The role of ex-ante norm control was particularly significant during László Sólyom's term as President of the Republic. Neither before nor after 2010 was it typical for the Constitutional Court to receive a large number of applications for preliminary review of norms.[88] As the President of the Republic is free to decide, at least in practice, whether to use the political veto or the constitutional veto, he may also decide to order Parliament to discuss and decide again on the new law, taking into consideration the constitutional concerns in the context of a political veto before the law is promulgated.[89]

According to Article 24 (2) *a)* of the Fundamental Law, the Constitutional Court shall examine laws adopted but not promulgated, for their conformity with the

87 Halmai, Gábor: "Pártos alkotmánybíráskodás (2010–2014)", in Gárdos-Orosz, Fruzsina – Szente, Zoltán (eds.): *Jog és politika határán. Alkotmánybíráskodás Magyarországon 2010 után,* Budapest, HVG-ORAC, 2015, 105–150.

88 Kovács, Virág: "A ki nem hirdetett törvények Alaptörvénnyel való összhangjának vizsgálatáról", *Alkotmánybírósági Szemle,* 2012/2, 78–91.

89 Article 9 (3) *i)* of the Fundamental Law states – among the powers of the President of the Republic – that the Head of State may send adopted Acts to the Constitutional Court for an examination of their conformity with the Fundamental Law or may return them to the National Assembly for reconsideration.

Fundamental Law. In addition, the Act on the Constitutional Court allows for the possibility of a preliminary examination of other acts, thus allowing for a preliminary examination of the conformity of certain provisions of an international treaty with the Fundamental Law and a preliminary examination of the provisions of the statutory act contained in a normative decision. The Constitutional Court must decide on the motion in the short term, and within 30 days at the latest.[90]

The Fundamental Law differs from the text of the former Constitution on several points. According to Article 6 (2) of the Fundamental Law, not only the President of the Republic, but also the Parliament may initiate a preliminary review procedure. In this way, the Constitutional Court may in fact be forced into the position of an advisory body.

Since 1 January 2012, two decisions have been adopted on the motion of the President of the Republic: the Decision 16/2015. (VI. 5.) AB on the unconstitutionality of the Act amending certain laws related to the management of state land property and the Decision 1/2013. (I. 7.) AB on the examination of certain provisions of the Act on Electoral Procedure (electoral registration). According to these numbers, we can qualify this competence as non-central to the Hungarian constitutional adjudication.

2.3. The approach to the pre-Fundamental Law case law

On 25 March 2013, with the Fourth Amendment to the Fundamental Law, the Parliament, by a two-thirds majority, established the following rule as point 5 of the Final and Miscellaneous Provisions of the Fundamental Law (Transitory Provisions): "The decisions of the Constitutional Court made prior to the entry into force of the Fundamental Law are repealed. This provision shall be without influence to the legal effects produced by those decisions."

However, the period prior to 1 January 2012, the date of entry into force of the Fundamental Law, remained still relevant for a while from a substantive point of view, because the Constitutional Court first more explicitly,[91] and then in its 2013 decision less explicitly, considered that the practice of interpreting the Fundamental Law established on the basis of the former Constitution as one that should be

---

90 Article 40 (4) of the Act on the Constitutional Court.

91 Decision 22/2012. (V. 11.) AB. Naszladi, Georgina: „Alkotmánymódosítások alkotmányosságáról döntött az Alkotmánybíróság", *Közjogi Szemle,* 2011/3, 65–66; Erdős, Csaba: „Az 1989-es Alkotmányon nyugvó alkotmánybírósági határozatok hatályon kívül helyezésének egyes aspektusai", in Gárdos-Orosz, Fruzsina – Szente, Zoltán (eds.): *Alkotmányozás és alkotmányjogi változások Európában és Magyarországon,* Budapest, Nemzeti Közszolgálati és Tankönyv Kiadó Zrt., 2014, 297–315.

followed, provides that former decisions of the Constitutional Court do not contradict the rules of the Fundamental Law.[92]

The external perceptions and self-perceptions of constitutional judges are categorised in many ways in social science. Analyses show that there are partisan and non-partisan, right-wing and left-wing judges,[93] that there are judges who are active in the defence of fundamental rights but abstain from deciding questions of state organisation, there are textualist and activist judges, conservative and liberal, dogmatic, etc.[94] In Hungary, all these classifications, which are certainly not without foundation in their various nuances, must be supplemented by two very important categories. At the time of the entry into force of the new Fundamental Law, there were judges who represented continuity, i.e. who considered the previous practice of the Constitutional Court to be maximally authoritative in the new system, while others did not consider it authoritative in the least, and what is more, they considered it to be explicitly and fundamentally wrong on many issues. A further important observation from the point of view of the assessment of domestic constitutional court practice is that some judges explicitly considered the acquis of international and EU legal development to be the standard, while others emphasised the specificities of the "Hungarian way" and in many cases did not wish to adopt the interpretation of international law by international courts without reservations, even taking into account Articles E) and Q) of the Fundamental Law.[95]

As regards the attitude towards the old Constitutional Court decisions, different attitudes can be observed. In several cases, the Constitutional Court referred to Decision 13/2013. (VI. 17.) AB, but only one of the criteria – textual consistency – was taken into account in the reasoning. On this basis, it accepted, without further reasoning, that since the Constitution and the Fundamental Law regulate the fundamental right in question with the same content, the Constitutional Court may take into account the statements of its previous decisions in its proceedings.[96]

This approach has been consistently challenged by the position that it is unacceptable for the Constitutional Court to simply declare the requirements of Deci-

---

92 Decision 13/2013. (VI. 17.) AB. See more on the evaluation Erdős, Csaba: "Az 1989-es Alkotmányon nyugvó alkotmánybírósági határozatok hatályon kívül helyezésének egyes aspektusai", in Gárdos-Orosz, Fruzsina – Szente, Zoltán (eds.): *Alkotmányozás és alkotmányjogi változások Európában és Magyarországon,* Budapest, Nemzeti Közszolgálati és Tankönyv Kiadó Zrt., 2014, 297–315.

93 Szente, Zoltán: "Az alkotmánybírák politikai orientációi Magyarországon 2010 és 2014 között", in Gárdos-Orosz, Fruzsina – Szente, Zoltán (eds.): *Jog és politika határán. Alkotmánybíráskodás Magyarországon 2010 után,* Budapest, HVG-ORAC, 2015, 151–184; Chronowski, Nóra – Drinóczi, Tímea: "Alkotmánybírói függetlenség Európában. És Magyarországon?", *Közjogi Szemle,* 2010/3, 26–32.

94 The most detailed argumentation see: Halmai, Gábor: "Pártos alkotmánybíráskodás (2010–2014)", in Gárdos-Orosz, Fruzsina – Szente, Zoltán (eds.): *Jog és politika határán. Alkotmánybíráskodás Magyarországon 2010 után,* Budapest, HVG-ORAC, 2015, 105–150.

95 I will come back to the debate in the next chapter.

96 See, e.g., Decision 36/2013. (XII. 5.) AB, Reasoning [24].

sion 13/2013. (VI. 17.) AB as a precondition for the transposition of old Constitutional Court decisions, and then, without checking any of the conditions, declare that "on the basis of the specific case, the Court has considered that there is no obstacle to the applicability of the arguments, legal principles and constitutional context developed in the previous decisions of the Constitutional Court".[97] For example, Béla Pokol, a member of the Constitutional Court, argues that the adoption of old arguments and formulas in such decisions directly renders the decision invalid under the Fundamental Law and that, in his view, the formulas thus adopted, which are based on the previous Constitution, cannot be invoked again in the course of constitutional adjudication.[98]

András Téglási sums up well the observations on the use of the previous Constitutional Court practice. He calls the adoption of practice based on the previous Constitution a derivative interpretation. He further breaks it down into three parts: automatic transposition, which means transposition without any further examination,[99] transposition according to the criteria of Decision 22/2012. (V. 11.) AB,[100] and transposition according to the criteria of Decision 13/2013. (VI. 17.) AB.[101]

Adoption under the above-mentioned decisions of Constitutional Court can be further broken down into conceptions following a formal or actual substantive examination of the criteria to be adopted. In the former case, reference was made only *pro forma* to Decision 22/2012. (V. 11.) AB[102] or Decision 13/2013. (VI. 17.) AB,[103] while in the latter case, the examination was carried out in accordance with the criteria given.[104]

Within this, it can also be observed that in some cases the Constitutional Court referred directly to the arguments of a decision made before 1 January 2012,[105] but

97 Dissenting opinion of the Constitutional Judge Béla Pokol to the Decision 20/2013 (VII. 19.) AB.

98 Dissenting opinion of the Constitutional Judge Béla Pokol to the Decision 20/2013. (VII. 19.) AB, [69].

99 See, e.g., the adoption of the previous practice regarding the general obligation of the legislative bodies to consult, Decision 44/2012 (XII. 20.) AB, Reasoning's [13]–[15].

100 According to Decision 22/2012 (V. 11.) AB, the arguments contained in the old Constitutional Court decisions can be used if "the specific provisions and rules of interpretation of the Fundamental Law – with the same or similar content as the previous Constitution – allow it". Reasoning [40].

101 In the Decision 13/2013. (VI. 17.) AB, the Constitutional Court interpreted the term "ceasing to have effect" as follows: "If the substantive conformity of the given section of the Fundamental Law with the Constitution, the contextual conformity of the Fundamental Law as a whole, the consideration of the rules of interpretation of the Fundamental Law and the applicability of the findings on the basis of the specific case do not prevent the application of the findings." This decision states, as a fourth condition, that "the use of arguments contained in decisions taken before the entry into force of the Fundamental Law must be justified in sufficient detail". Reasoning's [31]–[32].

102 See, e.g., Decision 3380/2012. (XII. 30.) AB, Reasoning's [12]–[13].

103 See, e.g., Decision 36/2013. (XII. 5.) AB, Reasoning [24].

104 See, e.g., with regard to the right of assembly, Decision 3/2013. (II. 14.) AB, Reasoning [38].

105 See, e.g., Decision 36/2013. (XII. 5.) AB, Reasoning's [31], [38]–[39], [41].

then in several cases it referred to the arguments of a decision made before 1 January 2012 through a decision made after 2012.[106]

In contrast, Téglási uses the term 'original interpretation' for cases in which the Constitutional Court does not refer to its previous case law, but interprets certain provisions of the Fundamental Law in an original way. He points out, however, that in many cases the Court actually adopts its reasoning based on the earlier Constitution (it would be difficult to do otherwise), but does not mention the earlier decision[107] or, separately, there are cases in which the relevant earlier decision based on the Constitution does not actually appear in the decision.[108]

The dilemma needs to be highlighted because the post-2012 constitutional review has been fundamentally determined by the path the Court has consistently chosen and the extent to which it builds its practice on pre-2012 foundations. As the detailed analysis of Csaba Erdős and András Téglási cited above shows, the practice in the first years was volatile and uncertain, and there was clearly no consensus among the members of the Court on the issue, as can be seen from the separate and parallel opinions.[109] The real problem, of course, is obviously not why point 5 of the Final and Miscellaneous Provisions of the Fundamental Law is not consistently applied by the Constitutional Court, but why such an unmanageable provision for legal interpretation can be found in the Fundamental Law, which is certainly also incongruous with the Fundamental Law of 18 April 2011, which recognises the continuity of the rule of law. This problem is reflected in the sceptical, hesitant and largely dismissive practice of the Constitutional Court. Nevertheless, the view has subsequently prevailed, apparently also as a result of the proliferation of new post-2012 decisions, that the Constitutional Court's practice can be a secure point

[106] Thus, for example, the decisions taken after the Fourth Amendment of the Fundamental Law with regard to Article 70/A of the Constitution and Article XV of the Fundamental Law also refer back to the analysis carried out in Decision 42/2012. (XII. 20.) AB. See, e.g., Decision 23/2013. (IX. 25.) AB, Reasoning [87]; Decision 26/2013. (X. 4.) AB, Reasoning [182]; Decision 3214/2013. (XII. 2.) AB, Reasoning [34].

[107] See, e.g., with regard to the right of association, Decision 3114/2013. (VI. 4.) AB, Reasoning [21].

[108] See the constitutional requirement for the right of assembly as set out in Decision 3/2013. (II. 14.) AB. For an analysis of the decision, see Tóth J., Zoltán: "A »valódi« alkotmányjogi panasz használatba vétele: az Abtv. 27. §-a szerinti panasz első két éve az Alkotmánybíróság gyakorlatában", *Jogtudományi Közlöny*, 2014/5, 224–238.

[109] With regard to the role of judges, it is worth noting the dissenting opinions on the Decision 20/2013. (VII. 19.) AB. Imre Juhász and Béla Pokol, for example, emphasise the difference in the content of Article 70/B (1) of the Constitution (right to work) and Article XII of the Fundamental Law (right to free choice of occupation), although the Constitutional Court of the time derived the right to free choice of occupation from the Constitution. According to the dissenting opinions, the slight changes in the text of the norm must be interpreted in the light of the sharply different philosophies of the two documents. It is true that the wording of some provisions may be similar, but the taxonomy of the Constitution, the message of the chapter on "Freedom and Responsibility" and, in this case, Article O) of the Constitution, which states that "[e]veryone is responsible for himself and must contribute to the performance of the functions of the State and the community according to his ability and means", must also be taken into account.

of reference in the argumentation and that, following the eleven amendments so far introduced, the text, spirit and requirements for interpretation of the Fundamental Law differ from the former Constitution on most issues. The debate has thus settled down over time.

2.4. The role of international law and EU law

The applicability of international legal standards and their authoritative nature has been particularly controversial in the post-2010 Constitutional Court practice.[110] Although Article E)[111] and Article Q)[112] of the Fundamental Law did not bring about fundamental changes, fundamental dilemmas of approach did arise after its entry into force.[113] Theoretically, the debate could have been provoked by the fact that the regulation on the constitutionality of public finance laws did not cover the examination of the infringement of international treaties that could be examined *ex officio* by the Constitutional Court. This would mean that the Constitutional Court could also examine public finance laws *ex officio* if there were a suspicion of an international treaty violation. In this way, the international treaty in question would replace the Fundamental Law, if necessary, and would quasi supersede it.[114]

Apart from this, the extent to which the Constitutional Court takes into account the decisions of international conventions and international judicial forums that interpret them in a binding manner, in particular the Strasbourg-based ECtHR, also influences its practice in the protection of fundamental rights. After 2012, the interpretation emerging from the majority of decisions is that, under Article Q) of the Fundamental Law, the Constitutional Court interprets domestic legislation in accordance with the generally recognised rules of international law and, in the case of other sources of international law, in accordance with the international legal obligations promulgated in the legislation, and thus enforces it as long as this interpretation is compatible with the values of the Fundamental Law.[115]

---

110 More generally, on how international law can be applied in various constitutional court proceedings, see Blutman, László: "A nemzetközi jog joghatásai az alkotmánybírósági eljárásokban", *Jogelméleti Szemle,* 2013/4, 2–32.

111 Gárdos-Orosz, Fruzsina: "Újabb áttekintés az uniós jog alkalmazásának magyarországi alkotmányos kereteiről", *Közjogi Szemle,* 2013/4, 44–53.

112 Sulyok, Gábor: "Újabb visszatérés a nemzetközi jog és a belső jog viszonyának alaptörvényi szabályozásához", in Fekete, Balázs – Horváthy, Balázs – Kreisz, Brigitta (eds.): *A világ mi magunk vagyunk... Liber Amicorum Imre Vörös,* Budapest, HVG-ORAC, 2014.

113 Téglási, András: "Az Alkotmánybíróság alapjogvédelmi gyakorlata az Alaptörvény hatálybalépése után", in Gárdos-Orosz, Fruzsina – Szente, Zoltán (eds.): *Alkotmányozás és alkotmányjogi változások Európában és Magyarországon,* Budapest, Nemzeti Közszolgálati és Tankönyv Kiadó Zrt., 2014, 327.

114 Jakab, András: *Az új Alaptörvény keletkezése és gyakorlati következményei,* Budapest, HVG-ORAC, 2011, 282.

115 Decision 34/2013. (XI. 22.) AB, Reasoning [25].

In the case where the Fundamental Law formulates the substantive content of a fundamental right in the same way as an international treaty, "the level of protection of fundamental rights provided by the Constitutional Court can in no case be lower than the level of international protection (typically as developed by the Strasbourg Court of Human Rights)".[116] The majority position has been widely disputed in the Court, with the spokesman for the concurring and dissenting opinions usually being Béla Pokol. The position was that direct acceptance of the general rules of international law can only be interpreted in a manner compatible with Hungarian state sovereignty if it is merely a framework for the international treaty-making activities of the Hungarian state.[117]

In contrast, the consistent representative of the other position, former Constitutional Judge Péter Kovács, argues that the question is not whether the Constitutional Court has a legal obligation to follow Strasbourg case law, but rather whether a deviation from the international level of legal protection raises the responsibility of the state under international law. In his view, it does and the Constitutional Court is therefore obliged to enforce these standards of legal protection.[118] Constitutional Judge Béla Pokol, however, argues that Hungary's obligation to comply with the practice of the Strasbourg ECtHR – apart from the fact that Hungary accepts any fine imposed in its individual judgments – cannot mean that the Constitutional Court of Hungary is bound by the interpretation of the law given by the ECtHR's case-law when interpreting the Fundamental Law.[119]

The emergence of such an open debate is new in the practice of the Constitutional Court, and it is obviously essential for the further development of jurisprudence how this debate will be finally decided in the Constitutional Court. Ten years after the entry into force of the Fundamental Law, Béla Pokol's position seems to remain a minority one, and the Court refers to international law and EU practice in its arguments. However, since 2016 as I will discuss in the next chapter, the debates on the protection of the constitutional identity led to an interpretation which is reserved towards EU law requirement of the rule of law.

---

[116] Decision 36/2013. (XII. 5.) AB, Reasoning [26], which in this respect refers back to, *inter alia*, Decision 61/2011. (VII. 13.) AB, ABH 2011, 290, 321, Decision 166/2011. (XII. 20.) AB, ABH 2011, 545, and Decision 43/2012. (XII. 20.) AB, Reasoning [67].

[117] Dissenting Opinion to Decision 34/2013. (XI. 22.) AB.

[118] Kovács, Péter: "Az Emberi Jogok Európai Bírósága ítéletére való hivatkozás újabb formulái és technikái a magyar Alkotmánybíróság, valamint néhány más európai alkotmánybíróság mai gyakorlatában", *Alkotmánybírósági Szemle,* 2013/2, 84.

[119] Dissenting opinion of the Constitutional Judge Béla Pokol to the Decision 34/2013. (XI. 22.) AB.

3. AFTER THE BEGINNING – NEW CHALLENGES – NEW RESPONSES

The following chapter is divided into three parts, in which I discuss the main problems affecting constitutional adjudication in Hungary. Following the adoption of the Fundamental Law, the main concern in the literature has been the impact on constitutional justice of the mandatory principles of constitutional interpretation that the constituent power has laid down in the text of the Fundamental Law. This is the subject of the first chapter. Not entirely unrelated to this is the focus of the second chapter, which concentrates on the significance of the constitutional traditions, and in particular the historical constitutional acquis (the achievements of the historical constitution) and examines the role of the Constitutional Court in the development of the specific foundations of the new Hungarian constitutionalism. In the third chapter, I cannot avoid discussing the experience of the Constitutional Court in reviewing the constitutionality of unconstitutional constitutional amendments. This was a crucial dilemma after the entry into force of the Fundamental Law. The competence of the constitutional judiciary to review constitutional amendments in the merits was finally hold *ultra vires* by the Constitutional Court, and this unstable conclusion was fast reinforced by the constitution making majority by provisions in the Fourth Amendment to the Fundamental Law. In this chapter, I will also address the question of whether it makes sense to speak of a genuine, classical *countermajoritarian* difficulty when there is a two-thirds constitution making and amending Government majority in Parliament, i.e. whether a constitutional court that should be a real limit to legislative power can operate in such a constitutional environment with the original function. In the last part of the chapter, I will also briefly discuss the essential characteristics of constitutional activism or, in other words from the other direction, of deferential behaviour towards the political branches of power in the new constitutional environment.

3.1. The principles of interpretation[1]

Unlike the former Constitution (1949/1989), the 2011 Fundamental Law sets out the main methods of constitutional interpretation. The relevant guidelines are scattered throughout the constitutional text without specifying a hierarchy of the different principles of interpretation to be applied.

The Fundamental Law sets out principles of interpretation on how the Fundamental Law itself should be interpreted, and on how legislation should be interpreted. The fact that principles of interpretation appear in the text of the Fundamental Law may at first sight seem to limit the Constitutional Court's freedom to formulate the constitutionality yardsticks, tests and principles of interpretation.[2] This is a novelty, since in the pre-2012 constitutional jurisprudence no such constraints applied, the Constitutional Court itself having set the standards of interpretative practice.[3]

According to Article R) (3) of the Fundamental Law, "[t]he provisions of the Fundamental Law shall be interpreted in accordance with their purposes, the National Avowal contained therein and the achievements of our historic constitution". The National Avowal (or National Creed) is part of the Preamble to the Fundamental Law. The spirit of the Preamble has also determined the interpretation of the provisions of the Fundamental Law, although the normative nature of the Preamble has always been a matter of debate in Hungarian constitutional law.[4] After the 2012 transformation, the Constitutional Court initially emphasised that the interpretation of other provisions of the Fundamental Law should be in line with the spirit of the Avowal, but in the first period it did not attribute normative binding force to the Avowal. The new spirit, which is also reflected in the Avowal, may have a law-forming force in the case of a specific decision, as can be seen when examining individual decisions.[5]

---

1 The original publication details of the extended version of the following chapter are given in GÁRDOS-OROSZ, Fruzsina: "Constitutional interpretation under the Fundamental Law of Hungary", in SZENTE, Zoltán – GÁRDOS-OROSZ, Fruzsina (eds.): *Populist Challenges to Constitutional Interpretation in Europe and Beyond*, London, Routledge, 2021, 143–159.

2 For the rules of interpretation see, e.g., JAKAB, András: *Az új Alaptörvény keletkezése és gyakorlati következményei*, Budapest, HVG-ORAC, 2011, 198; CHRONOWSKI, Nóra – DRINÓCZI, Tímea – Kocsis, Miklós: "Mozaikok, azaz milyen értelmezési kérdéseket vethet fel az alaptörvény?", Új Magyar Közigazgatás, 2011/6–7, 11–13.

3 POZSÁR-SZENTMIKLÓSY, Zoltán: *Alapjogok mérlegen. Az általános alapjogi tesztek dogmatikája*, Budapest, HVG-ORAC, 2016.

4 Fekete, Balázs: "Történeti elemek az EU-tagállamok alkotmány-preambulumaiban", in LAMM, VANDA – MAJTÉNYI, Balázs – PAP, András László (eds.): *Preambulum az alkotmányokban*, Budapest, Complex, 2011, 33–45.

5 On the Constitutional Court's interpretative practice on the preamble, see in particular Decision 34/2014. (XI. 14.) AB, Reasoning [51]; Decision 29/2014. (IX. 30.) AB, Reasoning [35]; Decision 21/2014. (VII. 15.) AB, Reasoning's [37], [56].

The analysis of the historical constitutional acquis (the achievements of the historical constitution) was also sporadic in the practice of the Constitutional Court at the beginning. It first dealt with the issue in Decision 3/2012. (VII. 17.) AB. According to its opinion, "[i]t is for the Constitutional Court to determine what of the historical constitution is included in the acquis as an achievement under the Fundamental Law. [...] In this new situation, the Constitutional Court's responsibility is extraordinary, one might say historic: when examining concrete cases, it must necessarily include in its critical horizon the relevant sources of the history of legal institutions." The real impact of the interpretative principle is thus also here shaped by the Constitutional Court on a case-by-case basis, so that we can examine the issue on a case-by-case basis, instead of an abstract normative conceptual approach.

The principles of interpretation of the Fundamental Law include taking into account the purpose of the provisions of the Fundamental Law. In the case of a completely new constitution, an objective teleological interpretation of the constitution naturally easily turns into an originalist or subjective teleological interpretation, since the purpose of the constitutional provision is not only stated in the explanatory memorandum of the constitution, but the intention of the constitution making power is also well known from parliamentary minutes or mass media. The constitutional judge inevitably takes this into account. This means that, although the Constitutional Court examines the purpose of the Fundamental Law provision, it is difficult for it to ignore its personal view of the purpose of the recent provision in the legal and political context in force, and also of the intention of the constituent power.

The Constitutional Explanatory Memorandum to the provisions on the interpretation of the Fundamental Law does not help much in understanding the provision, but it draws attention to the fact that the purpose of the Fundamental Law cannot be defeated by interpretation of the Fundamental Law. However, a key question, which can only be decided on a case-by-case basis, may be whether the Constitutional Court attaches any significance to this interpretative rule beyond this formal and general interpretation standard.[6]

According to the explanatory memorandum of the Fundamental Law, although the principles of interpretation listed above are primary, they do not exclude the application by the Constitutional Court of other established forms of interpretation of the law.[7]

Article N) (1) of the Fundamental Law sets out a further interpretative principle: "Hungary shall observe the principle of balanced, transparent and sustainable budget management." Paragraph (2) states that the National Assembly and the Government shall have primary responsibility for the observance of this principle, while paragraph (3) states that the Constitutional Court, courts, local governments and other state organs shall be obliged to respect this principle in the performance of their duties.

---

6 Szente, Zoltán: *Érvelés és értelmezés az alkotmányjogban*, Budapest, Dialóg Campus, 2013.

7 Bill T/2627, http://www.parlament.hu/irom39/02627/02627.pdf

Although in 2014–2015 the Constitutional Court examined issues affecting the national economy, for example in the foreign currency loan decisions[8] or in the case of the victims of Quaestor Financial Advisory Ltd.[9], the public reasoning did not contain any argument that the relevant provision of the Fundamental Law requires the Constitutional Court to take into account budgetary aspects in its interpretation. Presumably, the reason why Article N) of the Fundamental Law has not been invoked in practice is that its application would constitute a fundamental limitation on the exercise of the Constitutional Court's powers in the same way as the limitation of competencies contained in Article 37 (4) of the Fundamental Law (exclusion of the review of the central budget related laws). In the event that the prohibition of review of central budget laws is not affected by the legislation challenged before the Constitutional Court, the Constitutional Court would be in breach of the limits on the exercise of its jurisdiction because of the rules on constitutional interpretation. This would certainly be contrary to the classical conception of constitutional adjudication.[10]

In addition to Articles R) and N) of the constitution, Article 28 also set out a principle of interpretation, although primarily in relation to ordinary judicial practice. According to the text as originally adopted, "In the course of the application of law, courts shall interpret the text of laws primarily in accordance with their purpose and with the Fundamental Law. When interpreting the Fundamental Law or laws, it shall be presumed that they serve moral and economic purposes which are in accordance with common sense and the public good." Following the constitutional change, judge Tamás Lábady argued, referring to the horizontal effect of the Fundamental Law, that damages in cases of trivial injury cannot be awarded in litigation relating to personal injury because such an interpretation would be contrary to Article 28 of the Fundamental Law.[11] Today, as I will show in the fourth part of this volume, this Article is of great importance, and the basic question in constitutional complaint proceedings is whether the ordinary court has enforced the requirements of Article 28 of the Fundamental Law. In the Seventh Amendment to the Fundamental Law adopted in 2018, the text of the norm in force in 2022 was supplemented by a further requirement: "In the course of ascertaining the purpose of a law, consideration shall be given primarily to the preamble of that law and the official explanatory justification of the bill is adopting to the amending, the law." According to the original text of the Fundamental Law, in reviewing the constitutionality of judicial decisions, the Constitutional Court essentially verifies whether the court had properly considered the objective purpose of the legal norms applicable to the case at hand. By this "objective purpose", the Constitutional Court first understood the social or economic purpose that the legislator intended to achieve

---

8 E.g. Decision 14/2014. (V. 13.) AB.

9 Decision 32/2015. (XI. 19.) AB.

10 Bragyova, András: *Az alkotmánybíráskodás elmélete*, Budapest, KJK – MTA Állam- és Jogtudományi Intézet, 1994, esp. 149–208.

11 Lábady, Tamás: "Sérelemdíj *versus* nem vagyoni kártérítés", *Állam- és Jogtudomány*, 2016/1, 40–45.

by the legislation. The new wording of the law, which sought to change the previous practice, also raises the question of taking account of the subjective and original intentions of the legislator involved in the adaptation of the law.

Initially, the practice of the Constitutional Court was uncertain as to whether this provision also applies to the Constitutional Court as a court, and how, with respect to the case law of ordinary courts, with what interpretation and to what extent the Constitutional Court should enforce compliance with this provision in the course of constitutional complaint procedures. If so, how can it do so without becoming a super-judicial court itself, which would be required to reinterpret the law under Article 28 of the Fundamental Law?[12] The problem is not so glaring because the Constitutional Court has interpreted that a constitutional complaint based on the violation of Article 25 (3) or Article 28 of the Fundamental Law is not admissible, as these provisions do not name individual rights under the Fundamental Law.[13] Article 28 of the Fundamental Law is located in the chapter of the Fundamental Law on ordinary courts, so that, on the basis of the contextual interpretation, this provision is only binding on the courts. However, it is interesting to observe how the Constitutional Court enforces these provisions when examining the application of Article 28 in relation to the interpretation of the law by the courts, and I will return to this in the fourth part of the volume, when I will analyse the case law in the context of the relationship between the ordinary courts and the Constitutional Court.

Another interesting point about the application of Article 28 and its review is that the Fourth Amendment to the Fundamental Law prohibits the Constitutional Court from going beyond the scope of the petition. This cannot happen even if the Court sees a close link between a constitutional provision not identified by the petitioner and the violation of rights under examination, and it is increasingly rare in constitutional court proceedings because of the principle of the petition's restrictive nature and the duty of the narrow interpretation of the elaborative competence of the Constitutional Court related to it (the principle of close relation as discussed above).[14] Nevertheless, there is no reason in principle why, in the case of an admissible petition, the Court should examine whether the challenged judicial decision is in general in conformity with the Fundamental Law, so that the interpretation requirements of Article 28 have been complied with by the ordinary court, and this is therefore increasingly the case

12 Tilk, Péter – Naszladi, Georgina: "Az Alkotmánybíróságra vonatkozó szabályozás átalakulása 2010 után", in Gárdos-Orosz, Fruzsina – Szente, Zoltán (eds.): *Jog és politika határán. Alkotmánybíráskodás Magyarországon 2010 után*, Budapest, HVG-ORAC, 2015, 41–74.

13 Order 3231/2012. (IX. 28.) AB; Order 3363/2012. (XII. 15.) AB.

14 The wording inserted into Article 24 (4) of the Fundamental Law by the Fourth Amendment to the Fundamental Law is presumably a reaction (in the form of a so-called revision) to the fact that the Constitutional Court in a previous decision extended the motion by reference to a close connection in its Decision 1/2013. (I. 7.) AB on the first version of the new Electoral Procedure Act. In a broad interpretation of the criterion of "close connection" – as is often the case in previous Constitutional Court practice – the institution of registration on request was comprehensively examined by the Constitutional Court in the preliminary review procedure (on the basis of a motion of the President of the Republic).

in the practice of the Constitutional Court. It is difficult for the Constitutional Court to avoid in its daily practice that Article 28 has an impact on its own interpretation of the law. But it is equally true that the ordinary courts must also take into account the principles of interpretation of the Fundamental Law when interpreting it e.g. in a constitutional compliant procedure, because constitutional interpretation is not the prerogative of the Constitutional Court, but an everyday practice.

According to Article R) (3), the provisions of the Fundamental Law must therefore be interpreted in accordance with (a) its "purposes", (b) "the National Avowal" and (c) "the achievements of our historical constitution". Paragraph (4) of the same Article states that "the protection of the constitutional identity and Christian culture of Hungary shall be an obligation of every organ of the State".

Although the general fundamental rights limitation test is not a method of interpretation, but a measure of interpretation, it is important to mention it here because it was not previously included in the Fundamental Law and has a significant impact on the interpretation practice of the Constitutional Court. Article I (3), the Fundamental Law codified the basic rules for the resolution of conflicts of fundamental rights, the fundamental rights balancing test, according to which the rules governing fundamental rights and obligations must be laid down by statutory act. A fundamental right may be restricted only to the extent strictly necessary to enable another fundamental right to be exercised effectively or to protect a constitutional value, in proportion to the aim pursued and with due regard for the essential content of the fundamental right.

In addition to the prescription of binding interpretative principles and methods, the Fourth Amendment of the Fundamental Law of March 2013 repealed all Constitutional Court decisions issued before the entry into force of the Fundamental Law, which had a major impact on constitutional interpretation, as I discussed the related jurisprudential dilemmas above. The purpose of this amendment was clearly to oblige the Constitutional Court to adopt a new jurisprudence in line with the values of the Fundamental Law.

Given that there are theoretically many different methods of constitutional interpretation, the Fundamental Law cannot provide a closed list of methods. It merely provides a list of preferred methods of interpretation to be taken into account when reaching a decision.

In what follows, I will examine whether the role of constitutional interpretation, the process of giving the text of the constitution an *erga omnes* meaning in relation to an abstract or concrete constitutional issue, is different in the constitutional system[15] that has been in operation since 2010. My question is whether or not the new

[15] Arato, Andrew: "How We Got Here? Transition Failures, Their Causes and the Populist Interest in the Constitution", *SSRN Electronic Journal,* 2017 January, 1108 (or *Philosophy and Social Criticism,* 2019/9–10, 1108); Bugarič, Bojan: "The Two Faces of Populism: Between Authoritarian and Democratic Populism", *German Law Journal,* 2019/3, 392–393; Bugarič, Bojan – Kuhelj, Alenka: "Varieties of Populism in Europe: Is the Rule of Law in Danger?", *Hague Journal on the Rule of Law,* 2018 March, 22; Anselmi, Manuel: *Populism. An Introduction,* Oxfordshire, Routledge, 2018, 87.

principles of interpretation have been applied in the case-law of the Constitutional Court in general, and in particular in those decisions which, in their final result, have favoured the new legal and political programme formulated by the Government, in terms of the merits of the decision.

I will argue that, although the text of the Fundamental Law introduces new constitutional interpretative requirements, a significant part of these can be translated into the language of classical constitutional doctrine. If not entirely – such as the reference to the acquis of the historical constitution or the National Avowal – then these have so far (except in a few controversial cases) perhaps not had a fundamental impact on constitutional interpretation precisely because of their conceptual indeterminacy. From another point of view, my hypothesis is that the specific formulation of classical methods of interpretation and the codification of vague legal concepts do not necessarily lead to a radical change in the practice of law, because they can be dogmatically accommodated within the classical, established framework, as the legal practitioner wishes. If, however, the jurisprudence on the principles of interpretation does change fundamentally, and new concepts open up new approaches, this is not only due to the text and context of the Fundamental Law, but also to the intention of the legislator, which is inextricably linked with the constituent power.

3.1.1. A new set of interpretative methods or a reformulation of classic interpretative methods?

By way of introduction, let me briefly review the methods that have become important and recognisable in the jurisprudence of the Hungarian Constitutional Court following the democratic transition.[16] These methods are compared below with the new rules listed earlier in the Fundamental Law in order to understand the nature of the new constitutional requirements.

(a) Interpretation according to grammatical meaning *(textualism)* is the most common method of legal interpretation around the world. It is the discovery of the *plain meaning* of a text. This is the leading method of interpretation in the practice of the Hungarian Constitutional Court, and is almost always present, explicitly or implicitly, in the decisions of the Constitutional Court.

(b) The original intent, or originalist, interpretation seeks to identify the original intent of the framers and/or the original meaning of the text, which, according to this approach, is reflected in the text. Two further basic cases can be distinguished when exploring the original meaning of the text. The first is that constitutional interpretation must determine the original meaning of the constitutional provision, i.e. how the text could have been understood according to the interpretation meth-

[16] Jakab, András – Dyevre, Arthur – Itzcovich, Giulo (eds.): *Comparative Constitutional Reasoning*, Cambridge, Cambridge University Press, 2017; Szente, Zoltán: "The Interpretive Practice of the Hungarian Constitutional Court: A Critical View", *German Law Journal*, 2013, 1591–1614.

ods in use at the time of its adoption, and the second is to consider how the text was understood by the constitution-making authority.

Legal-historical values and constitutional interpretations based on them always reflect a more conservative, traditional conception of law than a progressive interpretation of the text that is not at all bound to the past. If we assume that the achievements of the historical constitution are constitutional values that certain theories and non-positivist legal approaches consider to be the roots of the current legal order, we may come to assume that Article R) of the Fundamental Law necessarily leads constitutional judges towards such historical legal content which is in their original environment is based on less open, less progressive and less inclusive interpretation of the law.

(c) The teleological (purposive) interpretation seeks to reveal the purpose of the rule, the *ratio legis*. This is also reflected in Article R) of the Fundamental Law, according to which constitutional provisions must be interpreted in accordance with their purpose. One would think that this provision in itself gives the Constitutional Court a wide margin of discretion, but the next sentence in paragraph (4), on the protection of constitutional identity and Christian culture, limits this freedom.

(d) A pragmatic interpretation is when the judge takes into account the social, economic, technological, political, etc. consequences of his decision, i.e. the possible extra-legal effects of the decision.

In Hungarian law, Article N) of the Fundamental Law requires a pragmatic interpretation, because it requires all state bodies to act in a manner that respects the financial and economic objectives of the state. So far, this provision has not been of great practical significance, as the Constitutional Court, according to Article 37 (4) of the Fundamental Law, is essentially not (or only to a very limited extent) allowed to examine constitutionally controversial issues related to central budget legislation. However, from a doctrinal point of view, this power of pragmatic interpretation is of great importance.

(e) Contextual interpretation is when the individual provisions of the Fundamental Law are interpreted in the context of the text as a whole, taking into account the other provisions of the text in order to preserve the integrity of the Fundamental Law.

In Hungary, Article R) of the Fundamental Law stipulates that the preamble and the achievement of the historical constitution are of particular importance, since they must be taken into account in the interpretation of all other provisions. Contextual interpretation is a simpler task in the case of a constitutional text where there are provisions which are normatively equivalent to each other in a specific structure, in a logical order, with the preamble retaining its purely preambular character, i.e. without normative provisions as in the rest of the Fundamental Law. In the case of Hungary, it is interesting to note that, based on the text of the Fundamental Law, the contextual interpretation also takes into account elements that are not defined in the Fundamental Law, such as Christian culture.

(f) Moral interpretation is based on the assumption that behind the text of the constitution there is a political philosophy from which case-by-case moral judgments follow. Thus, the manifestation of moral interpretation is the individual, morally based judgment of a judge, which goes beyond the textual interpretation of the Fundamental Law, but is based on the text, and can be considered legitimate because it conveys the philosophy and values of the Fundamental Law in the interpretation of it.

Constitutional identity also appears in the text of the Fundamental Law since the Seventh Amendment to the Fundamental Law, and the Constitutional Court has given content to this concept on a case-by-case basis. The role of moral interpretation can be enhanced in the practice of the Constitutional Court through this provision. Constitutional identity is a symbol of a kind of community morality which, as the core of the Fundamental Law, is given special importance over individual moral considerations.

In conclusion, although we can associate each new interpretative principle or method formulated in the Fundamental Law with a classical approach, the Fundamental Law also represents many novelties in terms of interpretative methods. The methods also leave room for the constitutional institution to simply relate them back to the classic methods, but the differently worded prescriptions also leave room for the Constitutional Court to depart from previous practice by referring to them. It is not typical for the constituent power to tie the hand of the interpreter to such an extent, nor is it typical to link the past to the present and the future with such strong textual conceptual guidance as a prescription for constitutional interpretation in the light of the historical constitution of Hungary of before the Second World War. But behind the newness, the old is still apparent: originalist, historical, moral, textual, contextual, etc. interpretation.

My next question is whether these methods are really relevant in the case law of the Constitutional Court, or whether the concerns about the principles of interpretation, which have been expressed by several authors since 2010, are not confirmed by the case law.

3.1.2. Application of mandatory interpretation methods in the practice of the Constitutional Court

Although the constitution-making power has tried to limit the Constitutional Court's free and loose choice of interpretative methods, this was not clearly effective at first. Following the entry into force of the new Fundamental Law, the Constitutional Court ruled in 2012 that it could continue to use in its new decisions constitutional theorems from previous Constitutional Court decisions that it had developed before the entry into force of the Fundamental Law. This is subject to the condition that the Fundamental Law contains identical or similar provisions to the former Constitution in most of the substantive constitutional issues.[17]

[17] Decision 22/2012. (V. 11.) AB.

3.1.2.1. Application of the new mandatory interpretation methods

When the Fourth Amendment to the Fundamental Law in 2013 *expressis verbis* provided for the annulment of all Constitutional Court decisions made before 2012, the Constitutional Court apparently maintained its previous position that it could rely on previous practice. In this case, however, it had to provide reasons for the validity of the reference. This means that although the Constitutional Court has refused, in principle, to build its new constitutional practice without its previous case law, and in particular in the first years following 2012, it referred in a number of cases to its previous case law and confirmed the pre-2012 jurisprudence, it had to develop a justification for this. Thus, despite the appearance of binding interpretative principles or methods in the constitutional text, the change in post-2012 jurisprudence has not been striking in the first years of the new jurisprudence. It was also typical that the Court tended to avoid applying provisions that were still unclear in the Fundamental Law. The first references were made to the achievements of the historical constitution in 2013[18] but there was no dogmatic clarification of its application, the new set of concepts were being used by the Court rather as a decorative element in its first decisions.[19] The Court's interpretative practice was initially consistent only in the sense, it stated that the constitutionality of a legal rule could not be challenged solely on the basis of the violation of Article R) (3).[20] Although the constitutional provision on respect for the achievements of the historic constitution is certainly flexible enough to be used in almost any argument, it is less useful when it comes to providing convincing arguments for a definitive interpretative result.

The content of the historical constitution has by its nature been subject to constant change in the past, and there are no guidelines for determining which period or state of affairs should be taken as the benchmark for constitutional interpretation. The Fundamental Law only states that the Hungarian state's self-determination ended on 19 March 1944, when Nazi Germany invaded the country. Presumably, this date is the end point of the historical constitution. In reality, the Constitutional Court occasionally selects certain rules or customs of historical Hungarian law, i.e. it considers the historical constitution as a sort of menu from which to choose.

We must also highlight the difficulty of the provisions relating to the taking into account of the National Avowal, which contains abstract values, objectives, solemn declarations and historical references, with a rather limited real impact on the practice of law. In practice, therefore, the reference to the Preamble is more of a

18 Szente, Zoltán: "The Interpretive Practice of the Hungarian Constitutional Court: A Critical View", *German Law Journal*, 2013, 1591–1614; Tóth, Gábor Attila: "Historicism or Art Nouveau in Constitutional Interpretation? A comment on Zoltán Szente's The Interpretive Practice of the Hungarian Constitutional Court – A Critical View", *German Law Journal*, 2013/8, 1615–1626.

19 Vörös, Imre: "A történeti alkotmány az Alkotmánybíróság gyakorlatában", *Közjogi Szemle*, 2016/4, 44–57.

20 Szente, Zoltán: "The Interpretive Practice of the Hungarian Constitutional Court: A Critical View", *German Law Journal*, 2013, 1591–1614.

decorative element that reinforces or rhetorically complements the argument, but has not yet modified or clarified the interpretation of the specific provision of the Fundamental Law that is being applied.

Furthermore, the Constitutional Court has undoubtedly given a prominent role to purposive interpretation in Article R) in order to explore the interpretation of the constitutional text, but this intention is rather implicit in practice. The Constitutional Court rarely refers explicitly to the purpose of the legislation and hardly ever refers to this specific guidance of the Fundamental Law. The purposive intention can rather be inferred from the fact that in several cases the Constitutional Court has consulted the legislator, in particular the Minister of Justice.[21]

Article N), which obliges the Constitutional Court to take account of budgetary considerations, raises the question of which constitutional requirements should be preferred when the question of constitutionality is pitted against economic rationality (for example, the requirement of balanced budget management). This interpretative requirement would in itself be an extremely difficult task to apply, as the possibilities for constitutional review of central budgetary legislation are severely limited and the protection of the rights enshrined in the Fundamental Law and respect for balanced budget management would be two difficult-to-reconcile sets of considerations in constitutional interpretation. This provision was therefore not applied by the Constitutional Court in this sense.

To sum up, although the introduction of the new interpretative principles and methods was undoubtedly intended to orient the interpretative practice of the Constitutional Court, these requirements, because of their vagueness and their non-systematic nature, seemed in the short term rather unlikely to bring about any meaningful changes in the interpreters' thinking. In the long term, it is conceivable that, with the right efforts, some of them could be integrated into the new Hungarian constitutional system, but the practice of the last ten to twelve years does not yet show such a trend. However, as I emphasised in the introduction to this chapter, this does not mean that there have not been substantive changes in the practice of law. My observation is that these substantive changes – such as the fundamental change in the concept of human dignity or the introduction of the concept of constitutional identity – have not been caused by new interpretative principles.

3.1.2.2. Politically sensitive cases

In the following, I will examine how the Constitutional Court's practice of constitutional interpretation has evolved in so-called politically sensitive cases. I believe that the characteristics of constitutional adjudication are revealed to us not only by the everyday defence of the Fundamental Law, which I will examine in the fourth chapter of this volume, but also by the role and decisions of the Constitutional Court in cases of great importance. In this sub-analysis, I have paid particular at-

[21] Sebők, Miklós – Gárdos-Orosz, Fruzsina – Kiss, Rebeka – Járay, István: "How to quantify constitutional reasoning – a text mining approach" (forthcoming).

tention to how interpretation evolves. For the purpose of the analysis, I will consider as politically sensitive those cases that, according to the relevant political science and constitutional law literature, are well representative of Hungarian constitutionalism after 2010:[22] (a) the construction of a constitutional identity, (b) the issue of legal borrowing, (c) the invocation of crisis management as a source of legitimacy for the introduction of new measures that deviate from previous rule of law requirements, (d) the restriction of certain fundamental rights, and (e) intolerance or discrimination against certain minorities.

Below I briefly examine five Constitutional Court decisions that provide practical examples of the features mentioned here. In doing so, I will argue that the characteristics given to describe the erosion of classical constitutional jurisprudence can be found in the practice of the Hungarian Constitutional Court.

(a) In Decision 22/2016. (XII. 5.) AB, the Commissioner for Fundamental Rights requested that the court interpret the Fundamental Law in an abstract interpretation procedure. As explained in the petition, the specific constitutionality issue is related to the Council of the European Union Decision (EU) 2015/1601 of 22 September 2015 on migration. The Ombudsman requested an authentic interpretation of Article E) of the Fundamental Law in relation to accession to and cooperation with the EU. In this decision – which is discussed in more detail in the following chapter on constitutional identity – the Constitutional Court based its decision on the concept of constitutional identity, which was not yet included in any domestic legal text at the time. The case was decided after the Government had failed to get a similar constitutional amendment passed by Parliament because it did not have a two-thirds majority in Parliament at the time, and an attempt to introduce such a rule by referendum failed because the referendum was invalid.[23]

The Constitutional Court held that, although the EU provides adequate protection for fundamental rights, the Constitutional Court cannot waive the protection of fundamental rights, and the exercise of joint powers with the EU cannot result in the infringement of human dignity or the essential content of other fundamental rights protected by the Hungarian Fundamental Law. In the context of this question, the Constitutional Court has established two main limits to the extent to which the exercise of joint competences with the EU exceeds the limits of the Government's assessment of the *ultra vires* acts of the European Union, namely, first, that the exercise of joint competences must not infringe Hungary's sovereignty and, second, that it must not lead to a violation of constitutional identity. The Constitutional Court stressed that the protection of constitutional identity must

22 Szente, Zoltán: "Populist Constitutionalism in Populist challenges to Constitutional Interpretation in Europe and Beyond", in Szente, Zoltán – Gárdos-Orosz, Fruzsina (eds.): *Populist Challenges to Constitutional Interpretation in Europe and Beyond*, London, Routledge, 2021.

23 Szente, Zoltán: "The Controversial Anti-Migrant Referendum in Hungary is Invalid", https://constitutional-change.com/tag/invalid-referendum

take the form of a constitutional dialogue based on the principles of equality and collegiality, with mutual respect for each other.[24]

The new concept of constitutional identity has been developed in line with the Government's political objectives, in opposition to EU legislation.[25] This is confirmed by the fact that as soon as the Government regained its two-thirds majority in Parliament, Parliament incorporated the concept of identity into the text of the Fundamental Law by means of the Seventh Amendment to the Fundamental Law. In the reasoning of the Constitutional Court, the reference to the National Avowal is purely decorative, and the historical constitution is not part of it either: "The Constitutional Court of Hungary interprets the concept of constitutional identity as Hungary's self-identity, and it shall expand the content of this concept on a case-by-case basis on the basis of the Fundamental Law as a whole and its individual provisions, in accordance with the National Avowal and the achievements of our historical constitution, as provided for in Article R) (3) of the Fundamental Law."[26]

This decision foreshadows an uncertain, case-by-case interpretation of the central substantive legal concept in the context of the interpretation of all other provisions of the Fundamental Law.

(b) Constitutional dialogue. The issue of constitutional dialogue is presented through the problem of the constitutionality review of the parliamentary act on NGOs and the constitutionality review of the act on higher education related to the case of the Central European University. The amendments to the act to be reviewed by the Constitutional Court in the constitutional complaint and ex-post review procedures were adopted by the Parliament in 2016. They introduced unfavourable measures on the financial accounting of NGOs, in particular on the issue of funds arriving from abroad, and imposed serious and hardly practical requirements for the authorisation of CEU's teaching activities in the country which led in fact to the resettlement of the university in Vienna.

The Constitutional Court did not rule on the sensitive issues. It could have considered initiating a preliminary ruling procedure before the Court of Justice of the European Union, but it did not do so because the Constitutional Court was dealing with a purely domestic constitutional issue, despite the fact that the case was already before the CJEU under EU law. The Constitutional Court had never before initiated a preliminary ruling procedure, but in this case it cited the importance of EU dialogue in favour of suspending the case. In these cases, the Constitutional Court suspended its proceedings pending until the decision of the Court of Justice of the European Union and then terminated the proceedings on the grounds of the non-effectiveness of the rule. This is how the Constitutional

---

24 This decision was supported by the AB with even more extreme reasoning in Decision 32/2021. (XII. 30.) AB, which I will discuss later.

25 Chronowski, Nóra – Vincze, Attila: "Önazonosság és európai integráció", *Jogtudományi Közlöny,* 2017/3, 117–132.

26 Decision 22/2016. (XII. 5.) AB.

Court avoided the necessary annulment of the act because of the open violation of the Fundamental Law.

The Venice Commission also criticised several aspects of the amended act on NGOs because, although on paper some of the provisions on transparency of foreign funding may appear to be in line with European standards, the circumstances surrounding the adoption of the law, in particular the campaign launched by some public authorities against NGOs receiving foreign funding, have made these provisions problematic.[27] The amendment of the national law on higher education has been criticised as well, not only in Hungary, but also by the Parliamentary Assembly of the Council of Europe and the Venice Commission, which have also severely criticised the Hungarian legislation.[28]

In the decisions of the Constitutional Court on the suspention of proceedings, the dissenting opinions warned that the dogmatic approach borrowed from the practice of other European constitutional courts, i.e. the emphasis on "constitutional dialogue", in the decision as a reason for the suspention order, is flawed. In the system of multi-level constitutionalism, "constitutional dialogue" emphasises cooperation and the denial of the hierarchy of decision-making, but in this case the Constitutional Court used this reference to make a purely domestic legal decision dependent on the EU legal response of EU law in the spirit of "dialogue". The reasoning of the decision, using the concept of "constitutional dialogue" borrowed from the practice of other constitutional courts and mainstream literature, may have been used rather to delay a politically sensitive decision by the Constitutional Court.

(c) Good examples of references to the crisis situation in shaping constitutional practice are the decisions of the Constitutional Court in 2014 and 2015 on the credit crisis. These decisions have underpinned the crisis management legislation of the two-thirds majority Parliament and confirmed the constitutionality of the exceptional measures introduced to intervene in contractual relations.

The law adopted by the Parliament in 2011 to resolve the foreign currency loan crisis in Hungary made fundamental changes in two areas: it declared the exchange rate margin null and void and the unilateral modification of the contract unfair. The law established a very specific and strict procedural regime for financial institutions to rebut the presumption of unfairness.[29] In the relevant decision[30], the

---

27 CDL-AD(2017)015-e, Hungary – Opinion on the Draft Law on the Transparency of Organisations receiving support from abroad, http://www.venice.coe.int/webforms/documents/?pdf=CDL-AD(2017)015-e

28 CDL-AD(2017)022-e, Hungary – Opinion on Article XXV of 4 April 2017 on the Amendment of Act CCIV of 2011 on National Tertiary Education, endorsed by the Venice Commission at its 112th Plenary Session (Venice, 6–7 October 2017), http://www.venice.coe.int/webforms/documents/?pdf=CDL-AD(2017)022-e

29 For a detailed analysis of the law and this decision, see Gárdos-Orosz, Fruzsina: "Constitutional Justice in Credit Crisis. The Hungarian Case", *Südosteuropa*, 2018/1, 94–118.

30 Decision 34/2014. (XII. 4.) AB.

AB, responding to the Government's crisis argument, established a new standard of retroactivity, the right to a fair trial and the right to property that is unusual in Hungarian constitutional law, but did not refer to the fact that it is obliged to apply these new interpretation methods in the future, when there is no financial crisis.[31] In another decision on the same issue,[32] the Constitutional Court underlined that the global financial crisis of 2008–2009 had made the debtor's autonomy of action and self-determination impossible, thus violating the right to human dignity of the persons concerned.

This broad interpretation of the financial and material basis for autonomy of action was also disputed by many within the Court, as the parallel and dissenting opinions of the decision show. The Constitutional Court returned to the unorthodox interpretation of the right to human dignity later,[33] although this was not only contrary to the earlier interpretation of the right to human dignity,[34] but was not a clear definition per se. (Similar reasoning appeared later, for example, in Decision 32/2021. (XII. 30.) AB, which stated that a change in the social composition of the residential environment caused by illegal migration could lead to a violation of human dignity.)

It seems that the constitutional limits of state intervention in crisis situations have changed, and the new understanding of the protection of human dignity has contributed to this. The only reference to Article R) as an interpretative tool in the decision is in support of a specific interpretation of Article M) on consumer protection. The Constitutional Court stated that, in accordance with the National Avowal, "We hold that we have a general duty to help the vulnerable and the poor". The interpretation of Article M) of the Fundamental Law and, in this context, the interpretation of the right to human dignity has thus been changed by the fact that the Constitutional Court, in its reasoning, referred to the Preamble of the Fundamental Law by way of the reference to Article R).

(d) The judgments in politically sensitive cases relating to the right of assembly also provide an excellent illustration of how in these situations the Constitutional Court has changed its interpretation of the right to human dignity in order to transform constitutional practice. In the case of a demonstration in front of the Prime Minister's house,[35] the Constitutional Court referred to the protection of the family

31 Gárdos-Orosz, Fruzsina: "Rendhagyó alkotmányossági mércék az Alkotmánybíróság »devizahiteles« határozataiban", in Gárdos-Orosz, Fruzsina – Szente, Zoltán (eds.): *Jog és politika határán. Alkotmánybíráskodás Magyarországon 2010 után*, Budapest, HVG-ORAC, 2015, 373–409.

32 Decision 2/2015. (II. 2.) AB.

33 Deli, Gergely – Kukorelli, István: "Az emberi méltóság alapjoga Magyarországon", *Jogtudományi Közlöny*, 2015/7–8, 337–347; Zakariás, Kinga: *Az emberi méltóság*, Budapest, Pázmány Press, 2019, esp. 68–97.

34 Dupré, Catherine: *The Age of Dignity: Human Rights and Constitutionalism in Europe*, Oxford, Hart, 2015, 82–112.

35 Decision 13/2016. (VII. 18.) AB.

and the home as rights deriving from the protection of human dignity and already mentioned in the Fundamental Law, which may constitute a limit to the right to assembly. The concept of home, which was introduced in Article L) of the Fundamental Law by the Seventh Amendment, was not previously a legal concept and was not included in the Fundamental Law or in legislation, but now appears as a right in the context of the protection of privacy and is protected against the classical freedoms, including the right to assembly. The decision of the Constitutional Court found an unconstitutional omission and the National Assembly consequently enacted a new law on assembly in 2018, which, in line with the new constitutional requirements, now gave greater importance to the protection of privacy at the expense of freedom of assembly. It is interesting from the perspective of our topic that the fundamental change in the content of the law did not occur as a result of the application of a new interpretative principle or method, but was developed independently of it, and was undoubtedly transformative for the protection of fundamental rights in Hungary.

(e) Decision 2/2019. (III. 5.) AB was related to the Government's anti-immigration, anti-pluralism and maintaining social homogeneity policy. The amendment to the Fundamental Law that triggered the legal dispute between the European Union and the Hungarian Government read as follows: [Article XIV (1)] "No alien population shall be settled in Hungary. A foreign national, not including persons who have the right to free movement and residence, may only live in the territory of Hungary if their application is individually examined by the Hungarian authorities."

The Government asked the Constitutional Court for an abstract interpretation of Article XIV (1) and (4) of the Fundamental Law, in particular its new provision on the right of asylum, in the light of the Seventh Amendment to the Fundamental Law. The background to the motion was thus a dispute between the Government and the European Commission on the compatibility of the new Hungarian asylum legislation (including the Seventh Amendment to the Fundamental Law) with EU law.

Here, the Constitutional Court (in complete contrast to its position in the CEU case described earlier) ruled that the Hungarian Fundamental Law can only be interpreted in final terms by Hungarian constitutional institutions, and ultimately by the Constitutional Court. In the case of the new provision of the Fundamental Law on the right of asylum, the Constitutional Court reached a conclusion contrary to the textual interpretation and the European institutional interpretations based on the textual approach, and following a completely eclectic interpretation it arrived to the conclusion that the plain meaning understanding of the text is not valid. On the basis of a contextual interpretation, the provision means according to the Court, that the right of asylum in disputed cases must not be understood as a subjective fundamental right, and therefore its denial cannot be a violation of fundamental rights. The provision as interpreted should be understood as the principle of non-refoulement, respect of which requires the State to receive the asylum seeker in accordance with Hungarian law (i.e. it may only return him to the country of departure or transit if the legal conditions for this are met). The reasoning of the decision was noteworthy because it is quite rare – especially in the case of a new amendment to the Fundamental Law – that the Constitutional Court does not interpret the text according to the grammatical interpretation, but nuances its ordinary meaning by means of other interpretative principles. In this case, the decision reacted to an interpretative conflict between the EU and Hungary by reinterpreting a conflicting rule of the Fundamental Law.

3.1.3. Conclusions

Despite the fact that the Constitutional Court is the authentic interpreter of the constitutional text and is bound by the methods laid down in the Fundamental Law, the Court would in principle have considerable leeway to apply the new interpretative principles and methods, since the constitutional power has not established a hierarchy between the provisions, nor has it declared an obligation to apply them exclusively.

I found that, although the practice of the Constitutional Court had changed greatly, especially in politically sensitive cases, I considered that the change was not specifically due to the new constitutional interpretation rules. Although they are often referred to by the Constitutional Court, they are more rhetorical flourishes than the reasons for the actual changes.

3.2. Constitutional protection of the identity of the Fundamental Law[36]

3.2.1. Populist constitutionalism

According to Jan-Werner Müller, the central element of populist politics is the *"Volksgeist" (people's spirit).* Identity and common culture are more important than the actual will of the political majority.[37] Blocker takes this line of thought further, arguing that for this politics, 'the people' is not an existential entity, the concept of the people is not focused on society, but rather has a transcendent, metaphysical content: the people is itself a 'collective subject' based on tradition, shared suffering in the past and a history that unites the people.[38] In Hungary, it was with such an ideology in mind that the Fundamental Law was adopted and amended, and it was this ideology that fundamentally determined the construction of constitutional

[36] The original publication source of parts of the following chapter is Gárdos-Orosz, Fruzsina: "Reference to constitutional traditions in populist constitutionalism – the case of Hungary", *Acta Juridica Hungarica,* 2020/1, 23–51.

[37] Müller, Jan-Werner: *Contesting Democracy: Political Ideas in Twentieth-Century Europe,* New Haven, Yale University Press, 2013, 53.

[38] Blokker, Paul: "Populism as a constitutional project", *International Journal of Constitutional Law,* 2019/2, 542.

identity. In the next chapter, I will examine the role of the Constitutional Court in the construction of constitutional identity and, in particular, in giving meaning to the concept of the historical constitution enshrined in the Fundamental Law.

Although the use of the term "constitutional populism" or "populist constitutionalism" is relatively widespread in political science literature and has been adopted in legal literature, there is no generally accepted definition of the term.[39] The phenomenon of the crisis of liberal constitutional democracy has been described in the literature in various ways, among others as "authoritarian constitutionalism"[40], "autocratic legalism"[41], "hybrid constitutionalism"[42] or "illiberal constitutionalism", with no consistent literature position on the issue.[43]

In Europe, populist constitutional demands often appear in constitutional democracies. In legal terms, populist constitutionalism cannot be considered a new construction of state organisation. Populist political aspirations usually transform the legal system step by step. In Hungary, we have already reviewed the legislative changes concerning the constitutional judiciary in this volume, so we have looked at how new political ideas have shaped the tasks of constitutional review. The process is a two-way one: populist political ideas have transformed the regulation of the Constitutional Court, and the functioning and practice of the Constitutional Court has contributed to the legal meaning and therefore to the applicability of the new constitutionalist vision and the new constitutional identity.[44]

Zoltán Szente identifies the elements that are commonly referred to as the characteristics of "populist constitutionalism" on the basis of an extensive review of the legal and political science literature. In our joint paper, we show that these elements prevail to different degrees in different European constitutional democracies, and that some of them, according to the literature, are not present in populist states either.[45] In any case, in my opinion, the new Hungarian constitutional identity is

---

39 The term is also used in a positive sense, e.g., in Batt, John: "American Legal Populism: A Jurisprudential and Historical Narrative, Including Reflections on Critical Legal Studies", *Northern Kentucky Law Review,* 1995, 651–762.

40 Tushnet, Mark: "Authoritarian Constitutionalism", *Cornell Law Review,* 2015, 391–462.

41 Scheppele, Kim Lane: "Autocratic Legalism", *University of Chicago Law Review,* 2018/2, 545–583.

42 Verschraegen, Gert: "Hybrid Constitutionalism, Fundamental Rights and the State", *Rechtsfilosofie en Rechtstheorie,* 2011, 216–229.

43 Drinóczi, Tímea: "A 22/2016. (XII. 5.) AB határozat: mit (nem) tartalmaz, és mi következik belőle. Az identitásvizsgálat és az ultra vires közös hatáskörgyakorlás összehasonlító elemzésben", *MTA Law Working Papers,* 2017/1, https://jog.tk.hu/mtalwp/a-222016-xii-5-ab-hatarozat-mit-nem-tartalmaz-es-mi-kovetkezik-belole-az-identitasvizsgalat-es-az-ultra-vires-kozos-hataskor-gyakorlas-osszehasonlito-elemzesben

44 Tushnet, Mark – Bugaric, Bojan: "Populism and Constitutionalism: An Essay on Definitions and Their Implications", *Cardozo Law Review,* 2020/6, 2345–2393.

45 Szente, Zoltán – Gárdos-Orosz, Fruzsina: "Constitutional effects of populism on EU Member States", in Andreu, Josep Maria Castellà – Simonelli, Marco Antonio (eds.): *Populism and Contemporary Democracy in Europe. Old Problems and New Challenges,* Cham, Palgrave Macmillan, 2022, 113–135.

built up from such and similar elements. These are: the critique of the separation of law and politics, according to which populists reject the limitation of political power by legal norms and the policy-neutral conception of law in liberal democracy, because it undermines the representation of national interests. The opposition to elitism, the contrast between a virtuous people and the old corrupt, cosmopolitan elite, and the reference to a united people (nation, community) as opposed to this elite (i.e. international organisations or EU institutions or NGOs) that protects the rights of LGBTQ communities or immigrants, alternative churches or other minorities that do not represent the interests of the majority. Anti-institutionalism and anti-pluralism can also be an important element of populist political aspirations, as can the desire to prioritise the public interest and the general will of the people over individual and particular interests.[46] The public interest and the general popular will, on the other hand, are shaped by the public power of the state alongside the political parties; the more pronounced the public power is, the stronger its presence in the everyday life of a country. This presence depends to a large extent on the concentration of resources.

The populist interpretation of the constituent power, according to the relevant literature, seems to place the rule of the people above the rule of law; the "collective subject", shaped by tradition, common suffering and destiny, is therefore given greater importance in the construction of constitutional rules. Populist constitutionalism is characterised by the absolutisation of the principle of majority rule, insofar as populist parties have won elections. The instrumentalisation of law in regimes such as Hungary means that the constitution can provide an effective toolkit for preserving power and breaking down checks and balances while respecting the formalities of the rule of law; therefore, these populist regimes are characterised by active constitutional review where possible.[47]

However, in the words of Francisco Balaguer Callejón, there seems to be an unresolvable tension between populist political ideas and constitutionalism, since constitutionalism is based on the idea of a plural conception of the nation (the people) and the inherent limitation of majority power, while populists generally demand the victory of the will of the majority, and if populists gain power over the state, they implement this popular will according to their own convictions in the form of constitutions, constitutional amendments and other legal norms.[48] He cites the example of Spain, where the Catalan secessionists accept the constitutional

46 Szente, Zoltán: "Populism and populist constitutionalism", in Szente, Zoltán – Gárdos-Orosz, Fruzsina (eds.): *Populist Challenges to Constitutional Interpretation in Europe and Beyond*, London, Routledge, 2021, 3–28.

47 *Ibid.*

48 Callejón, Francisco Balaguer: "Interpretación constitucional y populismo", *Revista de Derecho Constitucional Europeo*, 2020, https://www.ugr.es/~redce/REDCE33/articulos/04_BALAGUER.htm; Callejón, Francisco Balaguer: "Constitutional Interpretation and Populism in Contemporary Spain", in Szente, Zoltán – Gárdos-Orosz, Fruzsina (eds.): *Populist Challenges to Constitutional Interpretation in Europe and Beyond*, London, Routledge, 2021, 217–232.

framework, but when it contradicts their aims, they invoke the superior will of the 'people', which they alone represent, and no longer consider it desirable to abide by the constitutional norms as originally understood. However, this is no longer the will of the people, which expresses its will through the democratic institutions of the rule of law, but the will of the 'people', which adopts populist policies and is thus constituted by itself, from which a significant proportion of citizens, political and social groups are excluded.[49]

The reinterpretation of general ideas of constitutionalism, with particular reference to popular sovereignty, is often referred to as a populist phenomenon. National populism, which is also characteristic of Hungary, emphasises the nation as a cultural entity whose history we can be proud of.[50] According to Eatwell and Goodwin, national populism is a movement that is increasingly challenging the mainstream of Western politics in the early years of the 21st century. National populism focuses on the culture and tradition that belongs to the nation, emphasising the promise that politics will give a voice to a united people. Kaltwasser and Mudde also argue that this form of populism emphasises that the ultimate source of popular will is a collective unity, the nation. The 'common people' is a central concept that explicitly or implicitly refers to a class concept "combining socio-economic status with specific constitutional traditions and popular values".[51] In contrast to liberal democracy, where the word 'people' refers to an integrative and inclusive political community (political nation), in the populist lexicon the people as a source of political power is more likely to be an exclusive and well-defined community, often based on common cultural, historical and religious grounds. Tradition, especially constitutional tradition, can be an important element in this new theorisation of the people, the cultural nation.

In the following, I will examine how the issue of constitutional tradition is being addressed in the post-2012 Hungarian constitutional context, and how the Constitutional Court has contributed to the interpretation of the new constitutional identity based on a unified nation. To this end, I will introduce the new constitutional environment from the point of view of populism theories[52] and identify the reference to constitutional traditions in the practice of the Constitutional Court, with a particular focus on the role of the historical constitution (achievements of the historical constitution) in the construction of constitutional identity.

---

49 Callejón, Francisco Balaguer: "Constitutional Interpretation and Populism in Contemporary Spain", in Szente, Zoltán – Gárdos-Orosz, Fruzsina (eds.): *Populist Challenges to Constitutional Interpretation in Europe and Beyond,* London, Routledge, 2021, 217–232.

50 Eatwell, Roger – Goodwin, Matthew: *National Populism: The Revolt against Liberal Democracy,* London, Pelican, 2018, 32.

51 Mudde, Cas – Kaltwasser, Cristóbal Rovira: *Populism. A Very Short Introduction,* Oxford, Oxford University Press, 2017, 10–11.

52 See the interviews in Ablonczy, Bálint: *Az alkotmány nyomában. Beszélgetések Szájer Józseffel és Gulyás Gergellyel,* Budapest, Elektromédia, 2011; Tóth, Péter – Molnár, Benedek – Németh, Márton (eds.): *Mérlegen az Alaptörvény. Interjúkötet hazánk új alkotmányáról,* Budapest, HVG-ORAC, 2013; Vízkelety, Mariann (editor-in-chief): *5 éves az Alaptörvény. Válogatás az ünnepi konferenciasorozat beszédeiből,* Budapest, Magyar Közlöny Lap- és Könyvkiadó, 2017.

3.2.2. The role of the "constitutional tradition" in the identity of the Fundamental Law

The Constitutional Court's interpretative practice is primarily shaped by the text of the Fundamental Law. The new Fundamental Law, which entered into force on 1 January 2012 refers to constitutional traditions in a number of places; we have seen this in the case of the principles of interpretation. In Hungary, after the establishment of the Constitutional Court on 1 January 1990, the most important yardstick developed by the Constitutional Court and adopted from foreign and international constitutional judicial practice was the so-called necessity-proportionality test, with which the Constitutional Court constantly examined the constitutionality of legal restrictions on rights, more or less along the lines of the case law of the German Federal Constitutional Court. This approach was codified in the Fundamental Law in Article I (3) of the Fundamental Law.[53] However, the other important general rule on constitutional interpretation is Article R) (3) of the Fundamental Law, which provides that the provisions of the Fundamental Law shall be interpreted in a manner consistent with, inter alia, the National Avowal and the achievements of our historic constitution. Paragraph (4) of the same Article states that "the protection of the constitutional identity and Christian culture of Hungary shall be an obligation of every organ of the State".[54]

The Fourth Amendment of the Fundamental Law of March 2013, with the obvious aim of forcing the Constitutional Court to change its interpretative practice, repealed all the decisions of the Constitutional Court taken before the entry into force of the Fundamental Law (1 January 2012).[55]

The preamble of the Fundamental Law, the National Avowal, states that "[w]e honour the achievements of our historical constitution and we honour the Holy Crown, which embodies the constitutional continuity of Hungary's statehood and the unity of the nation".

---

[53] Article I (3) of the Fundamental Law: "The rules for fundamental rights and obligations shall be laid down in an Act. A fundamental right may only be restricted to allow the effective use of another fundamental right or to protect a constitutional value, to the extent absolutely necessary, proportionate to the objective pursued and with full respect for the essential content of that fundamental right."

[54] Drinóczi, Tímea – Chronowski, Nóra – Kocsis, Miklós: "What Questions of Interpretation may be Raised by the New Hungarian Constitution?", *Vienna Journal on International Constitutional Law,* 2012, 41–64.

[55] Sonnevend, Pál – Jakab, András – Csink, Lóránt: "The constitution as an instrument of everyday party politics: the basic law of Hungary", in von Bogdandy, Armin – Sonnevend, Pál (eds.): *Constitutional Crisis in the European Constitutional Area. Theory, Law and Politics in Hungary and Romania,* Oxford, Hart, 2015, 46–123; Uitz, Renáta: "The Illusion of a Constitution in Europe: the Hungarian Constitutional Court after the Fifth Amendment of the Fundamental Law", in Bell, John – Paris, Marie-Luce (eds.): *Rights-Based Constitutional Review. Constitutional Courts in a Changing Landscape,* Cheltenham, Edward Elgar, 2016, 374–405.

Although the Holy Crown was already recognised as a state symbol by law in 2010,[56] it only acquired real constitutional significance with the Fundamental Law. However, the significance and role of the doctrine of the Holy Crown, which is linked to the kingdom, in the constitutional identity of the republic remains unclear.[57] There is also a question as to the normative implications of certain elements of the Preamble in constitutional law. More than twelve years after the adoption of the Fundamental Law, the acquis of the historical constitution is part of the constitutional identity, a construction intended to confirm the essence and basis of the Fundamental Law. However, the question is how the past relates to the essence of the constitution in constitutional practice.

According to some estimates, Hungary has a thousand-year constitutional tradition,[58] dating back to the founding of the state, i.e. the coronation of Stephen I as king. However, Hungary's thousand-year constitutionality is very different from that of England, for example, because we are talking about a legal history that has been interrupted many times in its development, often under foreign influence, and which has restarted from new points.[59]

Before the adoption of Hungary's first written constitution in 1946 (Act I of 1946, the so-called Small Constitution, it could not enter into force due to the historical circumstances), a so-called historical or historic constitution was in force.[60] The Fundamental Law states that the continuity of the historical constitution was interrupted only by the Nazi invasion of 1944. Scholarly critics of such a revival of the historical constitution at first argued that the historical constitution can only be the subject of legal-historical research, or serve as a solemn reference to the historical past in the preamble of a country's constitution, but cannot be meaningfully linked to the law in force.[61]

References to constitutional history are not alien to the interpretative practice of the Hungarian Constitutional Court, but they have rarely appeared as arguments in decisions explicitly limiting the will of the legislature.[62] The reference to constitutional traditions was part of the Savigny-type historical interpretation,

---

[56] See *Act LXXXIII of 1995 on the Use of the National Symbols of the Republic of Hungary and the Names of the Republic of Hungary*, and *Act I of 2000 on the Commemoration of the Founding of the State of Saint Stephen and the Holy Crown.*

[57] Szente, Zoltán: "The Doctrine of the Holy Crown in the Hungarian Historical Constitution", *Journal of the History of Law*, 2013/4, 109–115.

[58] Zétényi, Zsolt (ed.): *A történeti alkotmány – Magyarország ősi alkotmánya*, Budapest, Magyarországért Kulturális Egyesület, 2010.

[59] Szente, Zoltán: "Az angol és a magyar párhuzamos alkotmányfejlődés mítosza", *Közjogi Szemle*, 2016/2, 23–32.

[60] Szente, Zoltán: "The Doctrine of the Holy Crown in the Hungarian Historical Constitution", *Journal of the History of Law*, 2013/4, 109–115.

[61] Schweitzer, Gábor: *A magyar királyi köztársaságtól a magyar köztársaságig*, Budapest, Publikon, 2017, 153.

[62] Vörös, Imre: "A történeti alkotmány az alkotmánybíróság gyakorlatában", *Közjogi Szemle*, 2016/4, 44–57.

which was a traditional interpretative approach seeking additional legal arguments to support the *ratio decidendi* of the decision to discover the meaning of the text.

According to the dictionary of the Hungarian language, tradition is "a custom, morality, taste or conception that has long been preserved in written or unwritten form, handed down from generation to generation and applied".[63] The reference to the continuity of law, the procedural or substantive continuity of the historical constitution, has often played a significant role in legitimising the various constitutional systems. However, constitutional development in Hungary, characterised by the rule of law, the protection of fundamental rights by law or the separation of powers, was often the result of external influences on the state, as Hungary was often dependent on other countries in the organisation of the state. Constitutional norms, if not always created out of necessity, often depended on alliances, external interests, coexistence and cooperation. In the case of the Central European states, it seems almost impossible to refer to individual, unique, autochthonous constitutional traditions, and thus to identify "typically Hungarian" traditions.

The word tradition is used only twice in the Fundamental Law, but never in the context of constitutional tradition. In Article U) of the Fundamental Law, the text condemns the former communist order: "The state structure based on the rule of law, established in accordance with the will of the nation through the first free elections held in 1990, and the previous communist dictatorship are incompatible. The Hungarian Socialist Workers' Party and its legal predecessors and the other political organisations established to serve them in the spirit of communist ideology were criminal organisations, and their leaders shall have responsibility without statute of limitations for", among other things, "systematically devastating the traditional values of European civilisation." As I will explain, traditional values in this context are not values of liberal constitutionalism, but the general demands of humanity. The word tradition appears again in another provision as a religious tradition in the text of the National Avowal: "We recognise the role of Christianity in preserving nationhood. We value the various religious traditions of our country." No other reference is made in the text of the Fundamental Law.

Within the concept of constitutional tradition, Hungary's Fundamental Law emphasises the achievements of the historical constitution.[64] This legal approach to certain elements of constitutional tradition is very far from the legal positivist, legalistic approach to law, which was not only characteristic of the socialist system that influenced Hungarian law, jurisprudence and legal thinking for a long time, but is a typical feature of the constitutional jurisprudence also later, after the regime

63 "Hagyomány" [Tradition] in the dictionary of the Hungarian language.

64 RIXER, Ádám: "Hungary's Fundamental Law and the concept of the historical constitution", *European Journal of European History of Law*, 2013/4, 8; "A történeti alkotmányunk is jogforrás!" Attila Horváth to Mandiner, 15 December 2016, https://jog.mandiner.hu/cikk/20161214_a_torteneti_alkotmanyunk_is_jogforras_horvath_attila_a_mandinernek

change.[65] When the Constitutional Court first referred to the historical constitution, it was presumably because of this attitude, that the Court referred rather to certain specific positive legal norms (legislation of constitutional value) and classical principles that were in force at a particular period in history. The Constitutional Court rarely referred to conventions or customary law, even though they largely determined the approach to the historical constitution.[66]

Critics of the role of the historical constitution in the Fundamental Law stress that the historical constitution is incompatible with the existing democratic constitutional order if we interpret the elements of the positive law of a certain historical period as still valid for the sake of the interpretation of the Fundamental Law.[67]

So what is then a constitutional tradition in Hungary under the Fundamental Law? The problem inherent in the hybrid concept of constitutionalism is uncertainty. The legacy of the 1989 democratic transition is liberal constitutionalism, based on the limitation of state power, the rule of law, the separation of powers and the protection of human rights. The Fundamental Law was adopted explicitly in accordance with the provisions of the 1989 Constitution of the democratic transition based on its Preamble as indicated in Article 2 of the Closing Provisions in the Fundamental Law,[68] while it differs from this document mainly in that its provisions go far back into historical times, to the old constitutional traditions. The indeterminacy of these earlier traditions, however, also means that the current content of constitutionalism remains uncertain.[69] It could also be said that the constitutional tradition chosen by the two-thirds parliamentary majority that created the constitution builds the current constitutional order on uncertain depths rather than on solid foundations.

It may seem surprising, but the introduction of the German-type constitutional complaint in the 2011 Fundamental Law is a very interesting new legal institution in this respect. The German-type constitutional complaint mechanism under Article 27 of Act on the Constitutional Court is a good instrument for forcing the incor-

---

65 Jakab, András: "A szocializmus dogmatikai hagyatéka", *Jogelméleti Szemle,* 2003/4, http://jesz.ajk.elte.hu/jakab15.html

66 Szakály, Zsuzsa: "A történeti alkotmány és az alkotmányos identitás az Alaptörvény tükrében", *Pro Publico Bono – Magyar Közigazgatás,* 2015/3, 24–38, http://uni-nke.hu/uploads/media_items/szakaly-zsuzsaa-torteneti-alkotmany-es-az-alkotmanyos-identitas-az-alaptorveny-tukreben.original.pdf. See also the almost complete collection of references to the historical constitution by the Constitutional Court, Rixer, Ádám: *A vívmány-teszt,* Budapest, Ludovika Egyetemi Kiadó, 2018.

67 Szente, Zoltán: "A 2011. évi Alaptörvény és a történeti alkotmány összekapcsolásának mítosza", *Közjogi Szemle,* 2019/1, 1–8.

68 Closing provisions of the Fundamental Law, point 2.

69 As the legal historian Ferenc Eckhart wrote, many of the articles of the *Golden Bull* were invalid a hundred years after its adoption. Eckhart, Ferenc: "Jog és alkotmánytörténet", in Hóman, Bálint (ed.): *A magyar történetírás új útjai,* Budapest, Magyar Szemle Társaság, 1932, 316. The most famous Article 31 of the Golden Bull, which contained the *ius resistendi* of the nobles, was abolished in 1687.

poration of constitutional traditions into the interpretation of the law, because ordinary courts have become accountable for taking them into account. The problem is, however, that if the interpretation of the Fundamental Law by the Constitutional Court is uncertain because of the mandatory interpretation methods provided for in Article R) of the Fundamental Law, this uncertainty also has an impact on the ordinary judicial practice.[70] In an optimal case, however, the practice of the ordinary courts could crystallise what the Hungarian courts consider to be the achievements of the historical constitution.

In the following, I will show how the "acquis (achievements) of the historical constitution" as a legal construct is put into practice.

3.2.3. The revival of the historical constitution?

For constitutional lawyers who were socialised after 1990 and who dealt with positive law, the concept of a historical constitution seemed completely alien to the system of the Fundamental Law. The Fundamental Law is Europe's newest written constitution, alongside the Constitution of the Vatican 2020, and its adoption was based on the constitution of the 1989 democratic transition. The first obvious idea might have been that the new provision of the Fundamental Law was linked to one of the classic methods of interpretation, the historical interpretation (which was used by the Hungarian Constitutional Court anyway).[71] After initial hesitation, the Constitutional Court sought to give substance to the new provision of the Fundamental Law, and over the years case law has also turned towards the elaboration of a new concept of specific constitutional value.[72] The reference in Article R), the historical constitution (the achievements of the historical constitution), has become a constitutional yardstick. [73]

The website of the Constitutional Court lists 79 decisions between 2012 and 2020 that mention the achievements of the historical constitution or Article R) per se, but in this context. Of these 76 mentions relate to the substance of the decisions. In the majority, parallel and dissenting opinions, there were a total of 92 references, a significant number of which referred to Article R) or the historical constitution, but did not contain a related argument. In only 30 cases did the

70 Gárdos-Orosz, Fruzsina: Challenges to Constitutional Adjudication in Hungary since 2010", in Belov, Martin (ed.): *The Role of Courts in Contemporary Legal Orders,* The Hague, Eleven Publishing, 2019, 321–340.

71 Ádám Rixer identifies four approaches to the interpretation of the Fundamental Law: rejectionist, learning, applicationist and centring. Rixer, Ádám: *A vívmány-teszt,* Budapest, Ludovika Egyetemi Kiadó, 2018, 107–117.

72 Gábor Schweitzer discusses the absurdity of this hybridity, while András Varga Zs. argues that it is a progressive legal solution to strengthen constitutionality by linking past, present and future. Varga Zs., András: "Történeti alkotmányunk vívmányai az Alaptörvény kógens rendelkezésében", *Iustum Aequum Salutare,* 2016/4, 83–89.

73 Rixer, Ádám: *A vívmány-teszt,* Budapest, Ludovika Egyetemi Kiadó, 2018.

Constitutional Court use the achievements of the historical constitution as a substantive part of the argument.[74] Among the references to legal history, although not part of the historical constitution, the *Act I of 1946 on the Constitution* (the so-called Small Constitution), which is an essential element of our legal history was a popular choice. However, as this last example shows, the references to legal history often refer to legislation that would have been part of the historical constitution at the time. Examples of the principles referred to are equality,[75] or the need to protect forests,[76] or the principle of maternity support,[77] but these are also part of the Fundamental Law in force, the references do not mean an additional value.

In some cases, the Constitutional Court has referred to the historical constitution in a way that is not clear as to the role of the reference in the reasoning.[78] In other cases, one can read a related historical account without being able to identify the achievements of the historical constitution.[79] There have been only few cases in this period in which the Constitutional Court has carried out a thorough historical analysis.[80]

In most cases, the identified achievements of the historical constitution, such as freedom of the press, are fully in line with the content of the Fundamental Law, so their mention is rather illustrative, because the reference does not contribute to the interpretation of the provision of the Fundamental Law.[81] There have been only few cases where the recognition as a constitutional convention has been challenged by the Court, where there was disagreement among the constitutional judges which appeared in parallel and dissenting opinions.[82]

From the outset, the Constitutional Court has agreed that a decision cannot be based solely on the historical constitutional acquis without specifying the constitutional legal basis in positive law in effect. The weight of the reference depends on the specific case, but the reference to the historical constitution is always an additional element in the argument.[83] A dissenting opinion focuses in decision 22/2019. (VII. 26.) AB on the role of the historical reference when the decision can be derived from the Fundamental Law and the historical approach does not add to this.[84] The decision stated that our sovereign statehood is an

74 Gera, Anna: "Dsuang Dszi álma az alkotmánybíróságról", *MTA Law Working Papers,* 2021/6, https://jog.tk.hu/mtalwp/torteneti-alkotmanyunk-vivmanyai-az-alaptorveny-specialis-alkotmanyos-rendszereben

75 Decision 22/2016. (XII. 5.) AB.

76 Decision 14/2020. (VII. 6.) AB.

77 Decision 3023/2016. (XI. 18.) AB.

78 Decision 45/2012. (XII. 29.) AB; Decision 5/2013. (II. 21.) AB.

79 Decision 4/2013. (II. 21.) AB; Decision 6/2013. (III. 1.) AB t.

80 E.g. Decision 22/2019. (VII. 26.) AB.

81 E.g. Decision 28/2014. (IX. 29.) AB.

82 Decision 34/2017. (XII. 11.) AB.

83 Decision 25/2018. (XIII. 28.) AB; Decision 22/2019. (VII. 5.) AB; Decision 3001/2019. (I. 7.) AB.

84 See *Act CIV of 2010* and *Act CLXXXV of 2010.*

achievement of the historical constitution, and the dissenting opinion stressed that thinking about sovereignty in the EU and international legal space today requires quite different approaches than may have prevailed at the time of the historical constitution.

Despite all these uncertainties, the Constitutional Court stressed the importance of historical arguments, stating that without such knowledge "our present public law and our legal culture in general would be rootless".[85] Whereas in the first years of the application of the Fundamental Law, the Constitutional Court stressed, in rather formal statements, that the body had "taken into account" that certain rights and principles had historical roots embedded in the historical constitution, later on it made a more serious effort to actually find the origins of certain rights or institutions in the historical constitution. One such example was freedom of the press, which was underpinned by Article XVIII of the *Act of 1848*.[86] This specific example also illustrates the problem of the limitations of Savigny's historical interpretation and the importance of the elaborate conditions of application of the classical method of interpretation. In this case, for example, the 1848 law was a major step forward for the freedom of the press in the 19th century, but would be a major step backwards in its protection today. Some elements of past legislation, even those with positive constitutional value for the extension of the rights, cannot be applied literally – they require further contextual and historical interpretation. Without this framework of legal interpretation, a reference of the Constitutional Court is arbitrary. Another good example is the derivation of certain guarantees of judicial independence from *Act IV of 1869*. The new legislation on the judiciary adopted in the same year as the Fundamental Law *(Act CLXII of 2011 on the legal status and remuneration of judges)* show that judicial independence is undoubtedly one of the stable values of classical liberal development, the guarantees of independent operation of the judiciary stated in *Act IV of 1869* and *Act CLXII of 2011* as well, but the provisions of guarantee were still very different in 1869 from what we require today.[87]

There are other reasons why it is problematic to refer to past sources of law as sources of the law in force. In many cases, past provisions served as principles rather than rules because of the nature of the historical constitution, but this distinction is not clear from the text of the legislation. In a given case, therefore, there is no contradiction between the old and the current text of the law, but there may be a contradiction in their meaning. If a piece of legislation from the past were to be regarded as still applicable today, one could, for example, argue for a reduction in the level of protection of fundamental rights, which is certainly not the aim. This highlights the dogmatic difficulties of the idea.

---

85 Decision 33/2012. (VII. 17.) AB.

86 Decision 28/2014. (IX. 29.) AB; Decision 3002/2018. (I. 10.) AB.

87 Szente, Zoltán: "A 2011. évi Alaptörvény és a történeti alkotmány összekapcsolásának mítosza", *Közjogi Szemle*, 2019/1, 1–8.

In addition to the dogmatic, i.e. conceptual-logical, interdisciplinary nature of the undertaking also causes difficulties in the practice of Constitutional Court. For example, Decision 16/2016. (X. 20.) AB refers to the preamble of *Act I of 1946* (Small Constitution) as the acquis of the historical constitution, despite the fact that this Act deliberately broke continuity with the historical constitution in all its essential elements, such as the form of government, the question of sovereignty or the structure of the legislative power.[88] It therefore relativizes the historical constitution, separating it from the legal-historical approach.

This line of interpretation was also followed by László Sólyom, the first President of the Constitutional Court between 1990 and 1999, and later President of the Republic, when he stated that when interpreting the provisions of the Fundamental Law in question, the constitutional achievements between 1989 and 2010, the law-making and law-enforcing achievements of democratic constitutional law making should also be assessed as the achievements of the historical constitution.[89] Both the interpretation of the Constitutional Court in connection with the Small Constitution and László Sólyom's approach are interpretations that break with the conceptual construction of the historical constitution in Hungarian legal history. The debate points to the fact that the acquis of the historical constitution as a construction of the current Fundamental Law is not necessarily identical with the elements of the historical constitution according to legal history. This might be a decision of contemporary constitutional interpretation of the Fundamental Law.

In a dissenting opinion, András Varga Zs., a judge of the Constitutional Court, referred to the *Golden Bull* of 1222 as one of the achievements of the historical constitution and thus the source of the current constitutional provisions in the context of the protection of human rights and limited public power. He also referred to the respect for "public autonomies", in the context of the *Tripartitum* of 1517, religious freedom in the context of the *Edict of Torda* of 1568, the *Pragmatica Sanctio* of 1723, the principle of parliamentary government and equality before the law in relation to the revolutionary laws of 1848, and the principle of separation of powers, recognition of judicial independence and protection of national minorities in relation to the laws of the Austro-Hungarian Compromise of 1867.[90]

The example shows that if it searches, the Constitutional Court may find a related rule in the law in force at the time of the historical constitution and may refer to it as a constitutional acquis, an achievement of the historical constitution, but it is

---

88 See the above examples and more in Szente, Zoltán: "A historizáló alkotmányozás problémái – a történeti alkotmány és a Szent Korona az új Alaptörvényben", *Közjogi Szemle,* 2011/4, 1–13.

89 Reference to the interview with László Sólyom, Szakály, Zsuzsa: "A történeti alkotmány és az alkotmányos identitás az Alaptörvény tükrében", *Pro Publico Bono – Magyar Közigazgatás,* 2015/3, http://uni-nke.hu/uploads/media_items/szakaly-zsuzsaa-torteneti-alkotmany-es-az-alkotmanyos-identitas-az-alaptorveny-tukreben.original.pdf

90 See the concurring opinion in Decision 22/2016. (XII. 5.) AB.

not clear what its significance is for constitutional interpretation beyond rhetorical aspects, especially if, as shown above, its content necessarily differs from modern expectations, whether it is about the exercise of public power or the protection of rights by the state.[91] On the other hand judges may not be historians, therefore it is a question of contemporary legal interpretation how far the judges must respect the results of history science in this regard.

Péter Paczolay, who was the President of the Constitutional Court when the Fundamental Law was adopted, wrote about the impossibility of the present use of the historical constitution, proposing a flexible interpretation of the existing legal construction therefore to give meaning to it. In his view, the most important constitutional tradition is that the law in effect should be applied, i.e. today's domestic, international and EU law should be applied, using methods of interpretation developed and evaluated by legislations, courts and legal scholars.[92] The Constitutional Court, in this spirit, but reflecting to the new provisions of the Fundamental Law as well, has in many cases applied an essentially historical interpretation, although it has referred to Article R) of the Fundamental Law and the achievements of the historical constitution.[93] However, a methodological problem is that the classical method, i.e. historical interpretation, is often transformed into a kind of test in jurisprudence in order to comply with the Fundamental Law. The Constitutional Court, by forcibly referring to the related provision of the Fundamental Law and some elements of our legal history without real argumentative force seems to desire to prove that it interprets the Fundamental Law according to the constituent imaginary. In doing so, however, the aim of the interpretative activity is reversed, as if the Constitutional Court were seeking to find the relevant legal norms and principles in the past. In the interpretation of law, given that law is a social subsystem, the past, the present and the future are interconnected, and it is natural to look to the past for clues to the future. However, the normative force of this past for the present is questionable also for concerns of intergenerational justice. Another possible justification for the introduction of this new concept is that the constituent power sought to stabilise the new constitutional system by developing constitutional constructions that reach back into the past and are bound by the past. It has been explained above that the official purpose of making the Fundamental Law even stronger by applying the achievements of the historical constitution cannot be achieved by applying such a conceptual construction, which is legally uncertain.

91 See this opinion and other examples by Szente, Zoltán: "Az angol és a magyar párhuzamos alkotmányfejlődés mítosza", *Közjogi Szemle,* 2016/2, 23–32.

92 Paczolay, Péter: "A történeti alkotmány és a konzervatív jogi gondolkodás", in Tőkéczki, László (ed.): *Magyar konzervatizmus. Hagyomány és jelenkor,* Budapest, Batthyány Lajos Alapítvány 1994, 29–36.

93 Gera, Anna: "Dsuang Dszi álma az alkotmánybíróságról", *MTA Law Working Papers,* 2021/6, https://jog.tk.hu/mtalwp/torteneti-alkotmanyunk-vivmanyai-az-alaptorveny-specialis-alkotmanyos-rendszereben

Decision 22/2016. (XII. 5.) AB states that the exact content of the constitutional identity, based in part on the historical constitution, will be elaborated by the Constitutional Court on a case-by-case basis.[94] In the following chapter, I will examine how, on these uncertain foundations, the Constitutional Court has begun to unpack the elements of constitutional identity.

3.2.4. The protection of constitutional identity by the Constitutional Court

The legal concept of constitutional identity in Hungary was born in the political context of the migration crisis, when the Hungarian Government wanted to express its rejection of the EU's migration policy.[95] The elements of national identity[96] formulated in opposition to EU policies and legislation were quickly constitutionalised in the form of constitutional identity.[97] The Constitutional Court played a decisive role in this process, as the Government did not have a two-thirds majority in Parliament for several months, and was therefore unable to get the relevant amendment to the fundamental Law it had proposed passed, and the referendum initiated by the Government was also invalid.[98]

The Constitutional Court ruled in Decision 22/2016. (XII. 5.) AB on the interpretation of Article E) of the Fundamental Law, which regulates the relationship between EU and domestic law, in favour of the Government's objectives. The abstract constitutional interpretation procedure was proposed by the Commissioner for Fundamental Rights, who argued that the EU rule violates the right to human dignity enshrined in the Fundamental Law by treating refugees arriving in the EU as a group in the asylum procedure, and that the proposed quota system does not provide them with individualised procedural protection. The specific constitutional issue, as explained in the application, therefore related to the European Union Council Decision 2015/1601 of 22 September 2015 on migration. The Ombudsman raised the need for an interpretation of Article E)

94 Szente, Zoltán – Gárdos-Orosz, Fruzsina: "Judicial deference or political loyalty?", in Szente, Zoltán – Gárdos-Orosz, Fruzsina (eds.): *New Challenges to Constitutional Adjudication in Europe*, London, Routledge, 2018, 99.

95 Drinóczi, Tímea: "A 22/2016. (XII. 5.) AB határozat: mit (nem) tartalmaz, és mi következik belőle. Az identitásvizsgálat és az ultra vires közös hatáskörgyakorlás összehasonlító elemzésben", *MTA Law Working Papers*, 2017/1, https://jog.tk.hu/mtalwp/a-222016-xii-5-ab-hatarozat-mit-nem-tartalmaz-es-mi-kovetkezik-belole-az-identitasvizsgalat-es-az-ultra-vires-kozos-hataskorgyakorlas-osszehasonlito-elemzesben

96 Sulyok, Tamás – Deli, Gergely: "A magyar nemzeti identitás az Alkotmánybíróság gyakorlatában", *Alkotmánybírósági Szemle*, 2019/1, 57–59.

97 Rixer, Ádám: *Features of the Hungarian Legal System after 2010*, Budapest, Patrocinium, 2012.

98 Halmai, Gábor: "Abuse of Constitutional Identity. The Hungarian Constitutional Court on Interpretation of Article E) (2) of the Fundamental Law", *Review of Central and East European Law*, 2018, 23–42.

of the Fundamental Law in relation to the issue at hand, as in his view it was not clear whether Hungary had to comply with an EU rule that violated the Fundamental Law.[99]

The Constitutional Court has ruled that the EU generally provides adequate protection for fundamental rights. This does not, however, exempt the Constitutional Court from enforcing the rights enshrined in the Fundamental Law, since the provisions of the Fundamental Law must also apply in the exercise of common competences. The Constitutional Court must therefore ensure that the exercise of joint competences with the European Union does not infringe human dignity or the essential content of other fundamental rights which, according to the Constitutional Court's interpretation of the Fundamental Law, form part of the constitutional identity. The Constitutional Court is responsible for protecting the identity of the Fundamental Law based on the historical constitution and the sovereignty of Hungary.

The Constitutional Court stressed that the protection of constitutional identity must take the form of a constitutional dialogue based on the principles of the equality and collegiality of the partners in the European dialogue, with mutual respect for each other.[100]

In point III.7.2. of the reasoning of the decision, the Constitutional Court stated that "Hungary's constitutional identity is a fundamental value that is not created by the Fundamental Law, but is merely recognised by it. Consequently, constitutional self-identity cannot be renounced by an international treaty – Hungary can only be deprived of its constitutional self-identity by the definitive cessation of its sovereignty, its independent statehood. The protection of constitutional identity therefore remains the task of the Constitutional Court as long as Hungary remains a sovereign state."[101]

However uncertain the scope of constitutional traditions and the related acquis of the historical constitution and their role in the current constitutional order may be, the Constitutional Court has reasoned that they form part of the constitutional identity and thus constitute a core of constitutionality that is protected against EU law.

We would assume that tradition and identity represent a kind of stability and continuity in the life of the state. The problem in Hungary, however, is that the constituent power and the Constitutional Court shape its content on a case-by-case basis, and thus the identity based on the historical constitution is not an organic, natural construct of state life, which is fed by constitutional practice, but an

---

[99] Orbán, Endre: "Quo vadis, »alkotmányos identitás»?", *Közjogi Szemle*, 2018/3, 1–13.

[100] Lásd még elemzésünket: Bodnár, Eszter – Gárdos-Orosz, Fruzsina –Pozsár-Szentmiklósy, Zoltán: "Developments in Hungarian Constitutional Law", in Albert, Richard – Landau, David –Faraguna, Pietro – Drugda, Šimon (eds.): *2016 Global Review of Constitutional Law,* Boston, ICONnect-Clough Center, 2017, 77–81.

[101] Decision 22/2016. (XII. 5.), Reasoning [67].

artificial concept, defined without precedent and quickly introduced, which aims to make the framework of domestic and acceptable EU legislation dependent on individual decisions. This introduction and interpretation of the concept of constitutional identity by the Constitutional Court has thus led to unpredictability rather than stability, and this decision and the Seventh Amendment to the Fundamental Law, which was intended to confirm it, have led to the loss of the specific framework for constitutional interpretation rather than to its being rendered imprecise. Among the many examples that have emerged since 2016, I will now mention one to support my claim.

On behalf of the Government, the Minister of Justice applied to the Constitutional Court in 2021 for an interpretation of Article E) (2) and Article XIV (4) of the Fundamental Law, because, in his opinion, the implementation of the judgment of the CJEU delivered on 17 December 2020 in Case C-808/18 raised a constitutional problem that required an interpretation of the Fundamental Law.

According to the petitioner, the implementation of the judgment of the Court of Justice of the European Union in Case C-808/18 raised the specific constitutional issue of whether "Hungary may enforce an obligation under European Union law which may lead to a foreign national illegally staying in Hungary staying in the territory of the Member State (Hungary) for an indeterminable period of time and thus becoming a *de facto* part of the population of the country".

The Constitutional Court ruled in Decision 32/2021. (XII. 20.) AB that if the exercise of joint competences with the European Union is incomplete, Hungary is entitled to exercise non-exclusive competences in accordance with the presumption of sovereignty, as long as the institutions of the Union do not take the necessary measures to effectively exercise joint competences. The Constitutional Court did not examine the specific case again, but stressed that abstract domestic constitutional interpretation cannot be the subject of a review by a CJEU judgment. The procedure in the present case did not extend to an examination of the primacy of EU law. The Constitutional Court reiterated that the protection of Hungary's inalienable right to determine its territorial unity, population, form of government and state organisation is part of its constitutional identity. If the lack of exercise of shared competence leads to consequences which may infringe the right to self-identity, and thus the human dignity of persons living on the territory of Hungary, the Hungarian State must exercise its constitutional duty to protect the right to self-identity. In this case, it is necessary for the Hungarian State to ensure, by means of Hungarian legislation based on the Hungarian Fundamental Law, the exercise of the right to human dignity and all the conditions necessary for the protection of constitutional identity. According to the AB, it is not for the Constitutional Court, but for the legislature and the legislator, to determine whether, in the present case, the composition of the population is specifically altered where persons who do not have a residence permit reside in Hungary for an indefinite period. Even though the Constitutional Court did not in this case answer the specific constitutional problem for the admissibility of an abstract constitutional interpretation, it did state, as a completely novel and unprecedented idea, that human dignity may be violated when the social environment of a person changes significantly, and that illegal immigration is related to a question of composition of the population which may be linked to the constitutional identity protected against EU law.

The decision is an excellent support for the above conclusion that the definition of constitutional identity in Decision 22/2016. (XII. 5.) AB is perfectly open, and the Court can add new elements to the Fundamental Law in the protection of constitutional identity, since its content is completely uncertain, primarily as it is bound to the uncertain notion of the historical constitution.

3.2.5. Conclusions

In this chapter, I have shown that quasi-legal concepts – such as the achievements of the historical constitution or constitutional identity – are easily instrumentalised in the Hungarian populist state, in this case becoming tools of politics, because they have no predetermined legal content; they are not organic in law. This is problematic because, in a democracy governed by the rule of law, constitutional texts must have a recognisable legal meaning and function as legal texts in order to be a limit on public power. The Constitutional Court's task is to interpret an abstract normative text according to the established methods of constitutional interpretation, but the Constitutional Court also becomes vulnerable if it has to interpret a text with an uncertain legal meaning by unknown methods. Constitutional Court decisions on the achievements of the historical constitution and on constitutional identity have shown that the interpretation of new concepts is in their result uncertain as well. The Constitutional Court is bound only by the Fundamental Law, but if this has no identifiable content, decision-making may become arbitrary. This is also the case with the formulation of the constitutional identity.

According to the American legal philosopher Robert Cover, legal texts are surrounded by a rich narrative universe *(Nomos)* – different stories of identity and meaning.[102] As Michel Rosenfeld writes in one of his works, the construction of a constitutional identity is based on a kind of selection from these different identities.[103] This selection is clearly reflected in Hungary's Fundamental Law. The question is, however, whether *Nomos* is the result of an organic constitutional development with the participation of all state institutions and society, or whether it is merely a sudden political idea that has to be imposed on society through state institutions, the Constitutional Court and the courts. The construction of

102 Cover, Robert: "The Supreme Court 1982 Term. Foreword: Nomos and Narrative", *Harvard Law Review*, 1982, 4–68.

103 Rosenfeld, Michel: *The Identity of the Constitutional Subject: Selfhood, Citizenship and Community*, London, Routledge, 2009, 344.

a narrative – a process of individual identity formation – is by its very nature an autonomous process if it is to be a sustainable and reproducible narrative in the long term. In this chapter, I have argued that in the case of Hungarian national populist constitutionalism, the understanding of constitutional tradition in the construction of constitutional identity and the interpretation of other elements of law is not the result of an autonomous constitutional development, but rather of a completely new constitutional interpretation offered by the two thirds Government majority, in the development of which the Constitutional Court has taken a significant role.

3.3. Some classic dilemmas of constitutional adjudication in a new light

The next chapter will show that the classical dilemmas of constitutional adjudication in the post-2010 Hungarian constitutional space, in the legal system established by the two-thirds constitution making majority, are placed in a particular light. The almost continuous constitution making majority of the party coalition elected in 2010, 2014, 2018 and 2022 has created an unfavourable, suboptimal situation for democratic separation of powers, because a constitution that can be changed by the government majority at any time, by definition, can hardly be suitable for limiting public power. It could have been considered that the constituent power could have been self-restricted by establishing a stricter rule on constitution-making and constitutional amendment, but this was not done. The opposite has been the case, with constitution-making and constitutional amendment becoming a tool of daily politics, with one new constitution having been written quickly in 2011 and eleven amendments added to it in the past 12 years. The 2011, let us say, consolidated version of the former Constitution became a completely new one by amendments and by interpretation in the past 12 years responding to the needs of the daily party politics. The question is what role the Constitutional Court can play in this political system: can we still talk about constitutional review as a limit to the elected majority, what does constitutional activism mean in this constitutional environment, and can we question the review of constitutional amendments when they violate the fundamental principles and values of constitutionalism? Can that Constitutional Court, that operates in the current political environment with a permanent two-thirds constitution-making majority, have any chance of retaining its classic constitutional function?

3.3.1. A "countermajoritarian difficulty"

A library of literature has been written on the legitimacy of constitutional adjudication worldwide,[104] because the constitutional court is a modern constitutional institution, empowered to review legislation made by a legislator who has won a legislative mandate in a democratic election. The Constitutional Court on the other hand is not itself composed of members directly elected by the people. In the event of unconstitutionality, constitutional courts, however, annul legislation. Furthermore, the judges not only lack direct electorate support, but in most countries around the world, the Court is composed of members of an elite, run by people of high social status, operating according to a legal type decision-making procedure.[105] Constitutional courts uphold the separation of powers, the democratic functioning of the state and are responsible for the protection of human rights against mostly directly elected public power.[106] In sum, although they are not themselves organised through direct democratic procedures, they can review legislation adopted by the supreme representative body.[107] The question is how the dilemma of the exercise of constitutional review power against the majority power is presented in Hungary.[108]

The Hungarian Constitutional Court was established in 1990, just after the democratic transition from Socialism. In the first period after the regime change, the Constitutional Court played a significant role in the development of constitutional

[104] Waldron, Jeremy: "The core of the case against judicial review", *Yale Law Journal,* 2006/115, 1346–1407; Stone Sweet, Alec: "Constitutional Courts", in Rosenfeld, Michel – Sajó, András (eds.): *The Oxford handbook of comparative constitutional law,* Oxford, Oxford University Press, 2012, 816–830; Bickel, Alexander: *The Least Dangerous Branch: The Supreme Court at the Bar of American Politics,* New Haven, Yale University Press, 1986; Ely, John Hart: *Democracy and Distrust: A Theory of Judicial Review,* Cambridge – London, Harvard University Press, 1980; Lemieux, Scott E. –Watkins, David J.: *Judicial Review and Contemporary Democratic Theory: Power, Domination, and the Courts,* New York – London, Routledge, 2018.

[105] Kapiszewski, Diana – Silverstein, Gordon – Kagan, Robert A. (eds.): *Consequential Courts: Judicial Roles in Global Perspective,* Cambridge, Cambridge University Press, 2013.

[106] Zurn, Christopher F.: *Deliberative Democracy and the Institutions of Judicial Review,* Cambridge, Cambridge University Press, 2007.

[107] Bragyova, András: "Demokrácia és alkotmánybíráskodás", in Tóth, Károly (ed.): *Emlékkönyv dr. Szentpéteri István egyetemi tanár születésének 70. évfordulójára,* Szeged, JATE ÁJK Tudományos Bizottság, 1996, 135–159. Bragyova refers to the following recent publications: Ely, John Hart: *Democracy and Distrust: A Theory of Judicial Review,* Cambridge – London, Harvard University Press, 1980; Michael J. Perry: *The Constitution, the Courts, and Human Rights: An Inquiry into the Legitimacy of Constitutional Policymaking by the Judiciary,* New Haven, Yale University Press, 1982, 78. We should also mention Dworkin, Ronald: "The Forum of Principle", *New York University Law Review,* 1981/56, 469–518; Dworkin, Ronald: *A Matter of Principle,* Cambridge, Harvard University Press, 1985, 33.

[108] In the American literature, this is the so-called *countermajoritarian difficulty.* Ely, John Hart: *Democracy and Distrust: A Theory of Judicial Review,* Cambridge – London, Harvard University Press, 1980.

democracy in Hungary.[109] Hungary's new constitution, adopted as the *Fundamental Law,* which replaced the previous Constitution[110] and entered into force on 1 January 2012, has given the Constitutional Court a new role.[111] The new rules on the Constitutional Court were adopted in several steps, with the first changes being made in 2010, when the Orbán Government won a two-thirds constitution-making parliamentary majority. According to the official explanatory memorandum to *Act CLI of 2011 on the Constitutional Court,* the aim of the reform was to give greater weight to the subjective protection of fundamental rights in individual complaints and to eliminate the possibility of *actio popularis,* the procedure by which anyone could apply to the Constitutional Court to have a law annulled without having suffered a concrete personal violation of his or her rights. At the level of constitutional and statutory regulation, i.e. at the level of substantive law, the Constitutional Court has retained its considerable powers and it is still a living law that the Constitutional Court is the institution that has the final say on the interpretation of the content of the Fundamental Law and can annul a legislative provision in the event of unconstitutionality.

However, as I have explained above in detail, two warning signs about the constitutional function were evident immediately after 2010: firstly, the Government initiated a constitutional amendment that limited the powers of the Constitutional Court in cases involving central budgetary issues, and secondly, they increased the number of judges from 11 to 15, and changed the procedure for electing constitutional judges to the majority government's candidates in Parliament instead of the previous procedure of seeking consensus between the parliamentary parties.

With the adoption of the Fundamental Law, the two-thirds majority of the Constitutional Court began to develop its own interpretation of the Fundamental Law by establishing binding methods of interpretation, which apply not only to the Constitutional Court but also to the ordinary courts.

Some theories of democracy argue that the possibility of constitutional review is not sufficiently justified in the face of parliamentary constitutional protection, and some theories of democracy have also been increasingly critical of the growing importance of constitutional court decisions.[112]

---

109 Vincze, Attila – Csuhány, Péter – Sonnevend, Pál – Jakab, András: "Az Alkotmánybíróság", in Jakab, András (ed.): *Az Alkotmány kommentárja I–II.*, Budapest, Századvég, 2009, 1099–1172.

110 The *Act XX of 1949 on the Constitution of the Republic of Hungary* was essentially recreated in 1989 with a general amendment of the socialist constitution and further amendments during the democratic transition.

111 Paczolay, Péter: "Megváltozott hangsúlyok az Alkotmánybíróság hatásköreiben", *Alkotmánybírósági Szemle,* 2012/1, 67.

112 Hirschl, Ran: *Towards Juristocracy: The Origins and Consequences of the New Constitutionalism,* Cambridge, Harvard University Press, 2004; Gyorfi, Tamas: *Against the New Constitutionalism,* Cheltenham, Edward Elgar, 2016; Gardbaum, Stephen: *The New Commonwealth Model of Constitutionalism: Theory and Practice,* Cambridge, Cambridge University Press, 2013.

This was also the case in Hungary, after the lively debates on political and legal constitutionalism, and judicial and parliamentary constitutional protection, already described in chapter two, which in a critical atmosphere led to the limitation of the powers of the Constitutional Court.

However, the classic legitimacy debates quietened down after 2013, because the constituent power moved the genotype of the constitutional court to a different constitutional environment, and the genotype took on a different phenotypical appearance. In Hungary, despite the significant change in the powers of the Constitutional Court, the main problem is that it has sworn to defend a constitution whose provisions are in conflict with the classical values of constitutionalism. The early legitimacy debates have made the real possibility of a contradiction fade in the shadow of an institutional threat, both on the theoretical-dogmatic and practical levels.[113] The adaptation of the institution to the new political system is very high and its resistance is very low, so that the *countermajoritarian* difficulty will be lost along with the *countermajoritarian* character of the Constitutional Court. Dealing with the political majority by enforcing constitutional limits also seems an impossible undertaking because constitutional practice has shown that the majority will overrule the Constitutional Court's opinion on constitutionality, even by means of a constitutional amendment. In my view, the Constitutional Court faces serious constraints in its daily functioning, but it enjoys the freedom to decide whether it wishes to contribute actively to the implementation of the new constitutional policy or chooses to resist.

3.3.2. Activism and/or deference

Another great classic question of constitutional jurisprudence, which has been on the agenda in Hungarian constitutional law since 1990, is the extent to which the text of the constitution can be separated from its linguistic meaning obtained through textual interpretation. Judicial restraint and judicial minimalism[114] are the opposite of judicial activism. Some approaches contrast formal interpretative practice with transformative practice. Even before the term "judicial activism" was coined, constitutional judges were often criticised for asserting principles that they themselves had revealed in interpreting the constitution. In the United States, for example, Thomas Jefferson criticised Chief Justice John Marshall for

---

113 Landau, David E.: "Political institutions and judicial role in comparative constitutional law", *Harvard International Law Journal*, 2010/51, 319–378. For the ideal from the German tradition, which has perhaps had the greatest influence in Europe, see Vanberg, Georg: *The Politics of Constitutional Review in Germany*, Cambridge, Cambridge University Press, 2005; Stern, Klaus: *Verfassungsgerichtsbarkeit zwischen Recht und Politik*, Düsseldorf, Westdeutscher, 1979.

114 Perry, Michael J.: "An Originalist Understanding of Minimalism", *Northwestern University Law Review*, 1993/88, 84–164; Sunstein, Cass S.: *One Case at a Time: Judicial Minimalism on the Supreme Court*, Cambridge, Harvard University Press, 2001.

this.[115] Some people speak of activism when a judge decides a case before him according to his own judgement, without departing from the grammatical interpretation of the text but explaining it, while others say that excessive activism is when a judge completely breaks with the law.[116]

The practice of the early years of the Hungarian Constitutional Court was also described by many scholars as activist, with some authors describing it positively and others negatively.[117] Whether we are in India, Israel or Hungary, activism means that the court goes beyond the positivist approach of interpreting the text and decides on issues not clearly settled by the constituent power.[118] The problem of judicial legislation or judicial constitution-making also arises in the context of activism,[119] and this is usually contrasted with the so-called negative legislator status. The latter implies that decisions nullify unconstitutional norms, while excessive activism implies that the body examining the constitutionality of a constitution adds new criteria of constitutionality to the constitutional legal system in a proactive manner.[120] The issue of judicial activism leads us to the controversial field of judicial supremacy,[121] which examines the role of the constitutional court in liberal constitutional democracies in the context of constitutional adjudication in originally political matters.[122] Since, as mentioned above, parliamentary constitutional protection was paramount at the birth of the modern idea of the constitution, it was only later that the role of the courts in the formulation of fundamental constitutional questions grew and judicial constitutional protection spread.[123] In Hungary, too, there has been intense debate about the role of the

115 Zoldan, Evan: "Targeted Judicial Activism", *16 Green Bag,* 2d 465, 2013.

116 Canon, Bradley C.: "Defining The Dimensions Of Judicial Activism", *Judicature,* 1983/6, 236.

117 Pokol, Béla: "Az alapjogok és az »alapjogi« bíráskodás", *Társadalmi Szemle,* 1991/5, 55–64; Pokol, Béla: "Aktivista alapjogász vagy parlamenti törvénybarát? A magyar alkotmánybíráskodásról", *Társadalmi Szemle,* 1992/5, 67–78; Takács, Albert: "Az alkotmányosság dilemmái és az Alkotmánybíróság ítéletei", *Acta Humana,* 1990/1, 38–56.

118 Scharpf, Fritz Wilhelm: *Die Grenzen der richterlichen Verantwortung. Die political-question-Doktrin in der Rechtsprechung des amerikanischen Supreme Court,* Karlsruhe, C. F. Müller, 1965.

119 Claus, Laurence P. – Kay, Richard S.: "Constitutional Courts as »Positive Legislators«, in the United States", *American Journal of Comparative Law,* 2010/1, 479–504.

120 Brewer-Carías, Allan-R.: *Constitutional Courts as Positive Legislators. A Comparative Law Study,* Cambridge, Cambridge University Press, 2011.

121 For basic works on this, see, e.g., Whittington, Keith E.: "The Political Foundations of Judicial Supremacy", in Barber, Sotirios A. – George, Robert P. (eds.): *Constitutional Politics,* Princeton, Princeton University Press, 2002, 261–297; Gardbaum, Stephen: "What is judicial supremacy?", in Jacobsohn, Gary – Schor, Miguel (eds.): *Comparative Constitutional Theory,* Cheltenham, Edward Elgar, 2018, 21–44.

122 All before Marcic, René: *Vom Gesetzesstaat zum Richterstaat. Recht als Mass der Macht / Gedanken über den demokratischen Rechts- und Sozialstaat. Der Weg zwischen Sicherheit und Freiheit. Wien,* Springer, 1957; Marcic, René: *Verfassung und Verfassungsgericht,* Wien, Springer Verlag, 1963.

123 Weiner, Greg: *The Case against Judicial Supremacy,* Lawrence Kansas, University Press of Kansas, 2019.

Constitutional Court in shaping the constitutional system in 1989 democratic transition.[124]

However, in Hungary, under its populist government, activism of constitutional judges in the above sense is a rare phenomenon, and when it is observed in jurisprudence, the decisions, the interpretations do not aim at developing specific legal-constitutional arguments and principles to explain values of constitutionalism, but rather at providing legal support for political ideas, i.e. the activist decisions support the political goals of the government and provide new constitutional arguments in the building of the new constitutional regime.

An example of this phenomenon is the definition of identity already analysed.[125] After the democratic change of regime, the Constitutional Court was severely criticised for its activism. In this 2016 Decision the Constitutional Court on constitutional identity, the Court was no less activist, but this activism was already aimed at expressing the nature of the Fundamental Law being different from the former Constitution in its identity. The Fundamental Law did not include a constitutional identity in its text and did not establish a hierarchy of rights, which would have meant that some provisions have a priority over others. Here, activism emerged in the context of the invalid referendum on the protection of constitutional identity and the failed constitutional amendment in the context of the regulation of migration issues, as I have described above in other contexts.[126] In the early 1990s, when the so-called Sólyom Court after 1990 handed down a number of landmark decisions in which the court effectively formulated new constitutional requirements or rights,[127] these activist approaches usually appeared in the context of fundamental rights issues. In this case, however, it is not a question of fundamental rights, but the Constitutional Court has activistically created a national review jurisdiction in EU relations by constructing a concept of identity that, instead of protecting fundamental rights, has contributed

124 Issue 4/2015 of *Jogelméleti Szemle [Legal Theory Review]* was the first to open the debate among Hungarian constitutional lawyers.

125 For a critique of the decision and questions of legal interpretation affecting several levels of constitutionality in the relationship between the Constitution and EU law, see Drinóczi, Tímea: "A 22/2016. (XII. 5.) AB határozat: mit (nem) tartalmaz, és mi következik belőle. Az identitásvizsgálat és az ultra vires közös hatáskörgyakorlás összehasonlító elemzésben", *MTA Law Working Papers*, 2017/1, https://jog.tk.hu/mtalwp/a-222016-xii-5-ab-hatarozat-mit-nem-tartalmaz-es-mi-kovetkezik-belole-az-identitasvizsgalat-es-az-ultra-vires-kozos-hataskorgyakorlas-osszehasonlito-elemzesben; Chronowski, Nóra – Vincze, Attila: "Önazonosság és európai integráció", *Jogtudományi Közlöny*, 2017/3, 117–132.

126 Gárdos-Orosz, Fruzsina: "Reference to constitutional traditions in populist constitutionalism – the case of Hungary", *Acta Juridica Hungarica*, 2020/1, 23–51.

127 Drinóczi, Tímea – Gárdos-Orosz, Fruzsina – Pozsár-Szentmiklósy, Zoltán: "Formal and Informal Constitutional Amendment in Hungary", *MTA Law Working Papers*, 2019/18, https://jog.tk.hu/mtalwp/formal-and-informal-constitutional-amendment-in-hungary

to the adjudication of a sovereignty policy issue which was later adopted through constitutional arguments.[128]

The opposite of activism, judicial restraint and a narrow interpretation of constitutional review are also an evergreen dilemma of constitutional jurisprudence.[129] Constitutional Court decisions are in principle legal in nature, but often political in effect, so the Constitutional Court can be a significant player in the political space.[130] This is not a problem, but a specific feature of constitutional adjudication.[131] Institutions at the interface between law and politics can play a significant role in the institutional exercise of public power and in the shaping of public policy,[132] even if their decisions are taken strictly on the basis of legal constitutionalism.

The dilemmas of restraint, of refusing to be politically involved, are again being seen in a special light in Hungary. Here I will illustrate how this is reflected in the practice of the Constitutional Court with just one example, already described in more detail above.

As I will explain in detail in chapter five of this volume, following the global financial crisis, the first Decision of the Hungarian Constitutional Court on the right to unilateral contract modification in consumer loan contracts of financial institutions, with its new, different interpretation of the Fundamental Law, set new constitutional standards in the broad sense of constitutional consumer protection, primarily with regard to the rule of law and legal certainty, the right to a fair trial, its sub-legal powers and the prohibition of retroactive legislation (judicial activism). All these innovations, however, were aimed at justifying the constitutional approval of the crisis management legislation by the parliamentary majority and demonstrated a non-interfering attitude of abstention against the government's ideas.

Barnabás Lenkovics, the judge who drafted the decision, said in an interview that in the event of a national emergency, it is better for the Constitutional Court to

---

128 Scharpf, Fritz W.: "A Functional Analysis", *The Yale Law Journal,* 1966/4, 517–597; Henkin, Louis: "Is There a »Political Question« Doctrine?", *The Yale Law Journal,* 1976/5, 597–625; Redish, Martin H.: "Judicial Review and the »Political Question«", *Northwestern University Law Review,* 1985, 1031–1061.

129 Scharpf, Fritz W.: "A Functional Analysis", *The Yale Law Journal,* 1966/4, 517–597; Henkin, Louis: "Is There a »Political Question« Doctrine?", *The Yale Law Journal,* 1976/5, 597–625; Redish, Martin H.: "Judicial Review and the »Political Question«", *Northwestern University Law Review,* 1985, 1031–1061.

130 Perry, Michael J.: *The Constitution, the courts, and human right: an inquiry in the legitimacy of constitutional policymaking by the judiciary,* New Haven, Yale University Press, 1982; Hönnige, Christoph: *Verfassungsgericht, Regierung, und Opposition: Die vergleichende Analyse eines Spannungsdreiecks,* Wiesbaden, VS Verlag, 2007; Lamprecht, Rolf – Malanowski, Wolfgang: *Richter machen Politik,* Frankfurt am Main, Fischer, 1979.

131 Peretti, Terri Jennings: *In Defense of a Political Court,* Princeton, Princeton University Press, 1999.

132 For Germany see, e.g., Lamprecht, Rolf – Malanowski, Wolfgang: *Richter machen Politik,* Frankfurt am Main, Fischer, 1979.

interpret its powers more narrowly and leave more room for government action.[133] This attitude, as shown above, was also the case in the context of the promulgation of the special legal order caused by the pandemic.

The issue of judicial activism in Hungary and the question of upholding politically controversial laws are interesting because we can see that in many cases the two go together, with the Constitutional Court deferring to the government in cases where this requires an explicitly activist interpretation and the other was around. The goal is in both cases to support the Government initiatives.

In US constitutional law, the political question doctrine[134] is used to determine what is not subject to constitutional review because it is not a question of law, among other issues before the Supreme Court. In creating this doctrine, the U.S. Supreme Court has held that political questions are not for the court and are not litigable. Constitutional jurisprudence operates at the intersection of law and politics,[135] but in the United States, courts decline to decide political questions, while in the Hungarian jurisprudence the preference of the Court primarily is to decide in the case of valid petition.

However, sometimes the Constitutional Court decides differently, as an example of how the classic U.S. doctrine, which is not adapted at the theoretical-dogmatic level, is applied still in the practice of the Hungarian Constitutional Court, I would like to mention the constitutional complaint procedure of the Central European University (CEU), which has also been discussed in another context. It is true that, in general, the Constitutional Court interprets its jurisdiction as meaning that it must decide on the motions that come before it, that have been submitted in due process and are in due form, and that it does not therefore select among cases, but in some cases the Constitutional Court has nevertheless found a procedural solution not to decide on the case in question. This was done with striking inconsistency in the politically sensitive case of the CEU that attracted a lot of press coverage.

In our 2018 ICON report[136] we explained that the Decision 3199/2018. (VI. 21.) AB and Decision 3200/2018. (VI. 21.) AB – the suspension of the proceedings on the so-called lex CEU (on the impossibility of the operation of the Central European University in Hungary, originally financed by George Soros) – were a clear depar-

133 *Jogi Fórum [Legal Forum]*, 19 May 2014.

134 Scharpf, Fritz W.: "A Functional Analysis", *The Yale Law Journal*, 1966/4, 517–597; Henkin, Louis: "Is There a »Political Question« Doctrine?", *The Yale Law Journal*, 1976/5, 597–625; Redish, Martin H.: "Judicial Review and the »Political Question«" *Northwestern University Law Review*, 1985, 1031–1061.

135 Stone Sweet, Alec: *Governing with Judges. Constitutional Politics in Europe*, Oxford, Oxford University Press, 2000; Henkin, Louis: "Is There a »Political Question« Doctrine?", *The Yale Law Journal*, 1976/5, 597–625.

136 Bodnár, Eszter – Gárdos-Orosz, Fruzsina – Pozsár-Szentmiklósy, Zoltán: "Hungary", in Albert, Richard – Landau, David – Faraguna, Pietro – Drugda, Simon (eds.): *2018 Global Review of Constitutional Law*, Boston, ICONnect-Clough Center, 2019, 138–142. Here I follow and quote our comments on this case published in the volume.

ture from previous jurisprudence, in order to avoid a decision by the Constitutional Court on this politically sensitive issue.

The problem of "nothing is what it appears to be" is the one we have to deal with here, as we move towards a summary of the lessons of the book. Using examples from case law, I argue that in cases where the political and the constitutional environment of an institution changes, the function of the institution is transformed even if its powers and procedures remain apparently unchanged.

In Hungary, the Constitutional Court's task is to defend the Fundamental Law, which, with the eleven amendments, has been shaped by the independent position of the same two-thirds political majority, the same governing coalition under the same leader, which has not only changed some important rules on the Constitutional Court in its Fundamental Law, but also gives the jurisprudence a narrower margin of interpretation. The lessons drawn from a general observation of the functioning of the legal system[137] also suggest that the Constitutional Court operates in a political environment that offers the possibility of both abolishing the institution and of a two-thirds majority in Parliament amending the Fundamental Law by changing the content of certain decisions by means of a constitutional amendment.

If constitution-making is the prerogative of the current political majority, then the Constitutional Court can hardly be an effective constraint on public power in the context of this sort of populist governmental behaviour I described in chapter 3.2 in relation to the literature on national populism. The literature cited highlights the concentration of public power as a characteristic feature of this system, and also emphasizes the attempt to achieve this concentration even better, the ideal of the effective unity of strong state power is ruling. My examples have shown that the counterweight function of the institution of the Constitutional Court fades in such a political system, and therefore the classical dilemmas and the concrete and contemporary questions we generally raise can only be understood in a different light.

3.3.3. Constitutional review of the amendment of the Fundamental Law[138]

Although the Constitutional Court is not competent to examine the constitutionality of the amendment to the Fundamental Law, the question deserves special mention. The limits of the constitutional jurisdiction in this matter are essentially determined by whether the Fundamental Law contains any guidance on this issue

[137] Gárdos-Orosz, Fruzsina (ed.): *A magyar jogrendszer rezilienciája 2010–2020*, Budapest, HVG-ORAC – Társadalomtudományi Kutatóközpont, 2022.

[138] For a more detailed discussion of this topic see Gárdos-Orosz, Fruzsina: "Az alkotmánymódosítások alkotmányossági felülvizsgálata: elméleti koncepciók, nemzetközi trendek és magyar kérdések", in Gárdos-Orosz, Fruzsina – Szente, Zoltán (eds.): *Alkotmányozás és alkotmányjogi változások Európában és Magyarországon*, Budapest, Nemzeti Közszolgálati és Tankönyv Kiadó Zrt., 2014, 167–184.

and by the position taken by the Constitutional Court in its decisions. The relevance of this competence in Hungary – especially in the period between 2010 and 2013, a period of intense constitutional amendment debates – is well illustrated by the rich literature on the subject, the relevant Constitutional Court practice and the Fourth Amendment to the Fundamental Law.[139]

According to the Fourth Amendment to the Fundamental Law, the Government, a quarter of the Members of Parliament, the President of the Curia, the Prosecutor General or the Commissioner for Fundamental Rights may initiate a procedural review of the drafting and amendment of the Fundamental Law within 30 days of its promulgation. The Constitutional Court must decide on the motion in urgency, but within 30 days at the latest. If the Constitutional Court finds that the Fundamental Law or the amendment to the Fundamental Law did not comply with the procedural requirements, it shall annul the Fundamental Law or the amendment to the Fundamental Law with retroactive effect from the date of its promulgation.

The Fourth Amendment to the Fundamental Law thus added a new paragraph to it in order to confirm its own position on the question of the reviewability of the constitutional amendment, in response to an earlier Constitutional Court controversy and the Constitutional Court decision that revealed it. In justifying the Fourth Amendment, the parliamentary majority referred to the codification of the consequent practice of the Constitutional Court.

However, this is nuanced by Decision 61/2011. (VII. 12.) AB[140] and Decision 45/2012. (XII. 29.) AB,[141] which assessed the constitutionality of the Transitional Provisions of the Fundamental Law. Although the Constitutional Court has never reviewed a constitutional amendment since 1990 and it was clear that its competence was limited to the constitutional review of legislation, in 2011, in the light of the major restructuring of the legal system after 2010, the Constitutional Court was already considering the establishment of a constitutional review test for constitutional amendments. Because of these two decisions, the possibility of a (activist) constitutional interpretation of substantive review hung like the sword of Damocles

139 For interpretations and assessments of this competence, see Gárdos-Orosz, Fruzsina – Szente, Zoltán (eds.): *Alkotmányozás és alkotmányjogi változások Európában és Magyarországon*, Budapest, Nemzeti Közszolgálati Egyetem, 2014, 145–241. More recently and for a summary, see Erdős, Csaba: "Az Alkotmánybíróság gyakorlata az alkotmánymódosítások felülvizsgálatának és alkotmányi szabályok közti kollízió feloldásának területein", in Gárdos-Orosz, Fruzsina – Szente, Zoltán (eds.): *Jog és politika határán. Alkotmánybíráskodás Magyarországon 2010 után*, Budapest, HVG-ORAC, 2015, 317–348.

140 Drinóczi, Tímea: "Gondolatok az Alkotmánybíróság 61/2011. (VII. 12.) AB határozatával kapcsolatban", *Jura*, 2012/1, 37–46.

141 For a detailed analysis of the decision, see Szente, Zoltán: "Az Alkotmánybíróság döntése Magyarország Alaptörvényének Átmeneti rendelkezései alkotmányosságáról. Az Alaptörvény integritása és az alkotmányozó hatalom korlátai", *Jogesetek Magyarázata*, 2013/2, 11–21.

over the constitutional majority, which responded to this situation in the Fourth Amendment to the Fundamental Law.[142]

Following this, in its Decision 12/2013. (V. 24.) AB, the Constitutional Court also emphasised that, although the review of the content of constitutional amendments falls outside the competence of the Constitutional Court in view of the prohibition laid down in the Fourth Amendment to the Fundamental Law adopted by the Parliament, the Constitutional Court – as the supreme body for the protection of the constitution – continues to interpret and apply the Fundamental Law as a coherent system and takes into account all its provisions relevant to the case in question when making its decisions.[143] However, following the Fourth Amendment to the Fundamental Law, the field of interpretation within which the Constitutional Court can operate in the context of the review of the constitutionality of constitutional amendments is still extremely narrow.

This position raises a number of theoretical questions about the role and powers of the constitution making power, the purpose of constitutions and constitutional decisions, and the limits of constitutional interpretation and review of such constitutional rules, constitutional acts and constitutional decisions. In some countries where the possibility of judicial review of constitutional amendments has been explicitly recognised, the supreme apex courts (constitutional courts) often consider the revised amendments as constitutive acts outside the scope of the original constitution-making power. Some of these states' constitutions contain a so-called eternity clause, which facilitates the justification of decisions to review constitutional amendments. Even in systems without an eternity clause, however, there may be arrangements whereby supreme courts (constitutional courts), in order to improve the interpretation of civil and political rights, or to preserve the constitutional 'basic structure', 'identity' or 'integrity', even annul amendments which they consider to be 'unconstitutional'.

In theory, there could be a constitution that excludes the possibility of amendment. There are none in Europe. In the United States of America, the text of the constitution cannot be amended, but amendments can be made to it, so that one amendment can override another. In essence, this is also an amendment.[144] In Hungarian constitutional law thinking, the eternity clauses of the German Constitution are an important reference point. Articles 1 and 20 of the German Basic Law and

142 On the constitutional amendment and legislative reactions to certain Constitutional Court decisions and on the transformation of the Constitutional Court and constitutional adjudication in general, see Chronowski, Nóra: "Az alkotmánybíráskodás sarkalatos átalakítása", *MTA Law Working Papers*, 2014/8, 4, https://jog.tk.mta.hu/uploads/files/mtalwp/2014_08_Chronowski.pdf

143 For a more detailed justification of the decision, see Vincze Attila: "Az Alkotmánybíróság határozata az Alaptörvény negyedik módosításáról. Az alkotmánymódosítás alkotmánybírósági kontrollja", *Jogesetek Magyarázata*, 2013/3, 12.

144 The Twenty-first Amendment, for example, repealed the Eighteenth.

the substance of the principles they contain cannot be amended.[145] The French,[146] the Italian,[147] the Greek,[148] the Cypriot[149] and the Romanian constitutions also contain eternity clauses. These clauses mostly deal with the democratic system, the rule of law, the form of government, the territory of the state and the most important human rights (human dignity, equality). The Romanian constitution went furthest, enshrining the principles of judicial independence and political pluralism, as well as the official language of the state, in the form of immutable (eternity) constitutional requirements.[150] If a constitution has eternity or sunset clause, it is also easier to approach the dilemma of the possibility of constitutional review of constitutional amendments.

However, there is no eternity clause in the Hungarian Constitution, and it is debatable whether there are any implicitly unchangeable rules.[151] In contrast to the constitutions of Switzerland[152] or Norway[153], the Fundamental Law has not codified whether there are any substantive limits to constitutional amendment.[154] The Constitutional Court, in its Decision 12/2013. (V. 24.) AB, in its ruling on the ombudsman's petition for review of the Fourth Amendment to the Fundamental Law, referred to the European and international legal order, the permissible and exemplary practice of other states and the doctrine of coherence as a theoretical explanation of the limitation of the constitution making power.

Unlike the constitutions of many other countries, Hungary's Fundamental Law does not distinguish between the original and the derivative constitution-making power. In states where, for example, a special constitutional amendment procedure is available which narrows the scope of those entitled to initiate an amendment[155] (Poland), where the people may also initiate a constitutional amendment[156] (Lithuania), or where an amendment requires a referendum to be confirmed before it can

145 This means that the provisions establishing the right to human dignity, the inviolability of human rights, the social and democratic rule of law *(Rechtsstaat),* the federal state system, popular sovereignty, the subordination of state organs and the right of resistance cannot be change.

146 Article 89 of the French Constitution.

147 Article 138 of the Italian Constitution.

148 Chapter II Part IV of the Greek Constitution.

149 Article 182 of the Cyprus Constitution.

150 Article 18 of the Romanian Constitution.

151 Bragyova, András – Gárdos-Orosz, Fruzsina: "Vannak-e megváltoztathatatlan normák az Alaptörvényben?", *Állam- és Jogtudomány,* 2016/3, 35–63.

152 Articles 193 (4) and 194 (2) of the Swiss Constitution state that the amendment of the Constitution may not conflict with international law.

153 Article 112 of the Norwegian Constitution stipulates that constitutional amendments must not violate the spirit of the Constitution.

154 In Switzerland and Norway, there is no constitutional review, so the eternity clauses are clearly preserved by parliament.

155 Article 118 (1) of the Polish Constitution.

156 Article 147 of the Lithuanian Constitution.

enter into force[157] (Ireland), the procedural solution may allow certain conclusions to be drawn about the eternity of a constitutional provision.[158]

In Hungary, too, it would be simpler to define the constitution-making power in a way that separates it from the legislative power. In Hungary, however, it has never been the case that constitutions have actually been adopted by the political community by direct expression of will, and therefore the people appear not only in theory but also in fact as an abstract concept in Hungarian constitutionalism in this context.

It was only in the fourth year after the change of regime that the Hungarian Constitutional Court encountered the issue of judicial review of constitutional amendments, and found that it was only possible on procedural grounds.[159] Neither the former Constitution nor the Fundamental Law made a distinction between a new constitution and an amendment to the existing constitution, both being subject to the same procedure. Since the change of regime, the Constitutional Court has consistently held that it is not competent to examine the substance of constitutional amendments, as they do not constitute legislation which it is competent to review.[160] The Constitutional Court has stressed that the Constitution does not contain any provision declaring a provision to be unamendable or irrepealable.[161] The Constitutional Court further stated that the amendment of the Constitution falls within the competence of the constituent power and that the amendment becomes part of the Constitution.[162] In general, the Constitutional Court has approached the question of the ascertainability and reviewability of an unconstitutional amendment as a classic problem of separation of powers.

The main problem with the possibility of reviewing constitutional amendments in Hungary is that the Parliament has often amended the Fundamental Law in cases where it disagreed with the Constitutional Court's former decision. The Constitutional Court's Decision 61/2011. (VII. 13.) AB was the first decision to be taken after the Parliament had included in the Constitution the possibility to impose a tax that the Constitutional Court had previously declared unconstitutional. The Constitutional Court indicated that it was extremely concerned that the Parliament is using the Constitution to promote current political interests. It considered this method unacceptable from the point of view of the rule of law, the stability of the legal order and the constitutional order. The Constitutional Court also criticised this behaviour because it considered that it weakened the democratic legitimacy of

[157] Article 46.2 of the Irish Constitution.

[158] Further examples of procedural differences can be found in Erdős, Csaba: *Az Országgyűlés döntési autonómiájának aktustani megközelítése*, Győr, Széchenyi István Egyetem Állam- és Jogtudományi Doktori Iskola, 2014, 189–190.

[159] Order 293/B/1994. AB, ABH 1994, 362.

[160] In summary, Decision 1260/B/1997. AB, ABH 1998, 816, 819–826.

[161] Decision 39/1996. (IX. 25.) AB, ABH 1996, 134, 138.

[162] Order 293/B/1994. AB, ABH 1994, 362.

the Constitution, as it did not ensure a broad social consensus behind all its provisions.[163] Despite these strong statements, the Constitutional Court maintained its previous view that it was not entitled to review the substance of amendments to the constitution. A minor novelty of the decision was that the Constitutional Court explicitly stated that it had the power to examine whether the Parliament had respected procedural requirements.[164]

The reasoning of the decision also confirms that the constituent power is also bound by the coherent norms of international law, the general principles of *ius cogens* and the international law accepted by the Hungarian state. In the same part of the decision, the Constitutional Court concluded that the principle of separation of powers prevails and that the Court must respect the limits that apply to it and cannot replace of the legislative or constituent power.[165]

The next significant decision regarding the assessment of constitutional amendments by the Constitutional Court was Decision 45/2012. (XII. 29.) AB. The Decision of the Constitutional Court ruled that the first part (preamble) and several articles of the Transitional Provisions of the Fundamental Law of Hungary (31 December 2011) were unconstitutional and therefore annulled them with retroactive effect to their promulgation. The Constitutional Court stated that the Fundamental Law cannot be amended by legislation other than the Fundamental Law, even if the legislator declares it to be part of the Fundamental Law. Thus, the legislator in the Transitory Provisions takes over the powers of the constituent power, violates the principle of separation of powers and makes it impossible for the Constitutional Court to review the constitutionality of the legislation in question from a substantive point of view. However, the Decision of the Constitutional Court remained within the limits of the justification of procedural, formal unconstitutionality, and the Parliament, following the decision, made it clear once again that the political decision of the constituent power cannot be reviewed, i.e. the two thirds majority is free to amend the Fundamental Law in the ordinary procedure.

The Constitutional Court, in its aforementioned Decision 12/2013. (V. 24.) AB on the Fourth Amendment to the Fundamental Law, declared that, as the supreme body of the protection of the Fundamental Law, it does not have the power to review the content of the amendment, but in the future it will interpret and apply the Fundamental Law as a coherent system, taking into account all its provisions relevant to the case at hand and interpreting them in a consistent manner.

---

163 Decision 61/2011. (VII. 13.) AB, Reasoning, point V/1.

164 Erdős, Csaba: "Rubiconon innen… és túl? Az Alkotmánybíróság gyakorlata az alkotmánymódosítások felülvizsgálatának és az alkotmányi szabályok közti kollízió feloldásának területein", in Gárdos-Orosz, Fruzsina – Szente, Zoltán (eds.): *Jog és politika határán. Alkotmánybíráskodás Magyarországon 2010 után*, Budapest, HVG-ORAC, 2015, 321–324.

165 For a detailed analysis of the decision, see Szente, Zoltán: "Az Alkotmánybíróság döntése Magyarország Alaptörvényének Átmeneti rendelkezései alkotmányosságáról: az Alaptörvény integritása és az alkotmányozó hatalom korlátai", *Jogesetek Magyarázata*, 2013/2, 11–21, www.jema.hu/article.php?c=231

The Commissioner for Fundamental Rights asked the Constitutional Court to declare that certain provisions of the Fourth Amendment to the Fundamental Law of Hungary are unconstitutional. The Ombudsman referred primarily to formal, procedural unconstitutionality, but argued that, in addition to the public law invalidity in the narrow sense, in his view, the public law invalidity also arises in a broader sense if an internal contradiction arises in the Fundamental Law as a result of an amendment. Amendments that disrupt the unity of the Fundamental Law and create internal contradictions cannot be considered to be incorporated into the Fundamental Law. The petitioner considered the violation of the unity, the integrity of the Fundamental Law to be obvious, since the fourth constitutional amendment was contrary to the content of the previous decisions of the Constitutional Court.

According to the Decision of the Constitutional Court, under Article 24 (5) of the Fundamental Law, the Constitutional Court may only review the Fundamental Law and the amendment of the Fundamental Law with regard to the procedural requirements (in case of procedural errors). The wording of the Fundamental Law includes, by analogy, the circle of the proposers, the adaptation procedure, the two-thirds majority, the provisions on marking, the rules on signature and promulgation, i.e. it requires compliance with the provisions of the Fundamental Law for a valid constitutional amendment. The Constitutional Court drew attention to the limits of its power to review constitutional amendments and the principle of separation of powers, and stated that it would not extend its competencies to the examination of the Fundamental Law and new norms amending it without express authorisation. Accordingly, it has decided that it can only examine the constitutionality of the Fundamental Law and its amendments to a limited extent.

The Constitutional Court added to this reasoning by stating that when interpreting the Fundamental Law, it will in future take into account Hungary's obligations under international law, which go hand in hand with EU membership, as well as the generally recognised rules of international law and the fundamental principles and values they embody. All these rules constitute a single set of values which cannot be ignored either in the constitution-making process or in the legislative process, or in the course of constitutional review.

Similar to other Hungarian authors,[166] I feel that in this decision the Constitutional Court intended to leave open a loophole to extend the scope of its powers. This loophole could have led to a solution which, if the requirement of coherent interpretation had been considered further, would have emptied the content of the unconstitutional constitutional norm in a given case. By retaining the power of

[166] Erdős, Csaba: "Rubiconon innen... és túl? Az Alkotmánybíróság gyakorlata az alkotmánymódosítások felülvizsgálatának és az alkotmányi szabályok közti kollízió feloldásának területein", in Gárdos-Orosz, Fruzsina – Szente, Zoltán (eds.): *Jog és politika határán. Alkotmánybíráskodás Magyarországon 2010 után*, Budapest, HVG-ORAC, 2015, 321–324.

'coherent interpretation' of the Fundamental Law, the Constitutional Court treated interpretation at least partly as an act of will, in so far as it considered that its task was not merely to discover and enforce the original intention of the constituent power, but also to interpret and apply the provisions of the Constitution together and autonomously. If the constitutional authority adopts constitutional elements that appear to disrupt the integrity of the Fundamental Law (which are, for example, incompatible with international *ius cogens*, our international commitments), the constitutional review must decide in a proper and publicly justifiable manner, in the course of a well-founded procedure, which interpretation or conflict in the case before it is compatible with the validity of the constitutional provisions.

Although the constitutional power quickly put an end to creative thinking in this direction with the Fourth Amendment to the Fundamental Law, the Decision 22/2016. (XII. 5.) AB returned to this line of thought, the argument of coherence. The Constitutional Court discovered the constitutional identity as a new, substantive constitutional concept, which could possibly be the yardstick for a substantive constitutional review of a contrary constitutional amendment in the future, since the Constitutional Court also referred to the coherence of the constitution.[167] However, this understanding is contrary to the grammatical interpretation of the Fourth Amendment to the Fundamental Law.

In Hungary, therefore, it would be unrealistic to predict that the Constitutional Court will define the "fundamental structure or constitutional identity" of the Fundamental Law as an explicit eternity clause,[168] nor can we take as a model the example of the French *Conseil Constitutionnel,* which has always completely rejected the possibility of reviewing the content of constitutional amendments, emphasising the sovereignty of the French people. (The *Conseil* has, moreover, taken this position strongly, despite the eternity clause, although if we assume that the French Constitution inherently limits the possibility of amending the Constitution and contains an eternity provision that the republican form of government cannot be changed,[169] we could also conclude that the *Conseil* could be more permissive in reviewing constitutional amendment in respect of other provisions.)

It is interesting that in Europe, the Constitutional Court often does not even use its power to annul an unconstitutional constitutional amendment in states

167 Halász, Iván: "Alkotmányos identitás", in Gárdos-Orosz, Fruzsina – Halász, Iván (eds.): *Alkotmányjogi alapok,* Budapest, Dialóg Campus, 2019; Drinóczi, Tímea: "A tagállami identitás védelme", in Jakab, András – Fekete, Balázs (eds.): *Internetes Jogtudományi Enciklopédia* (EU law column, column editors: Varju, Márton – Horváthy, Balázs), 2018, http://ijoten.hu/szocikk/a-tagallami-identitas-vedelme

168 Kesavananda Bharati Sripadagalvaru and Ors. v. State of Kerala and Anr. (AIR 1973 SC 1461). For more on Indian jurisprudence on constitutional amendments, see Halmai, Gábor: *Alkotmányjog, emberi jogok, globalizáció: az alkotmányos eszmék migrációja,* Budapest, L'Harmattan, 2013, 31–47.

169 Baranger, Denis: "The language of Eternity: Judicial Review of the Amending Power in France (or the Absence Thereof)", *Israel Law Review,* 2011/3, 389–428.

where it would otherwise have the power to do so. The German Federal Constitutional Court, for example, has ruled that constitutional amendments not covered by the eternity clause are reviewable, but even when it has carried out such a review, it has refrained from annulling the provisions, when it had the possibility to do so on the merits (in the 1960s and 1970s). The German Federal Constitutional Court has also stressed that the most important task of the constitutional body in reviewing constitutional amendments is interpretation. Interpretation means that it must determine the meaning of the new text in the light of the Constitution as a whole, its structure and the fundamental order of constitutional values. By contrast, in Austrian and Czech constitutional jurisprudence, as in India, we find cases of constitutional courts declaring substantive unconstitutionality, but of course in much less contentious cases and with much less activist interpretation than in India.[170]

In Europe, the possibility of reviewing constitutional amendments in the context of ex-ante review procedures is quite rare. However, the Romanian Constitution allows for this in the context of *ex officio* procedures. The Turkish constitution[171] explicitly allows ex-post review of constitutional amendments, but only from a procedural point of view. Under the Russian[172] and the Bosnian-Herzegovinian[173] constitutions, the constitutions of the Member States may be reviewed for consistency with the federal constitution. However, this case law is specific to the federal states and does not concern the theoretical basis for the reviewability of constitutional amendments discussed in this thesis.

Of more interest for the present chapter is the practice of states where judicial review of constitutional amendments is possible, but this power is not laid down in the constitution with a precise description, but has been developed by the constitutional courts themselves through their decisions. In France, Spain, Austria, Cyprus and Germany, for example, it is possible to examine whether the constitution-making power has complied with the procedural rules in adopting the amendment.[174] The Austrian, Cypriot and German constitutional courts, however, were rather uncertain in their practice as to whether their jurisdiction could include a substantive review of constitutional amendments in addition to a formal review. According to the relevant Austrian decision, constitutional amendments that do not concern fundamental issues and are of a more technical nature are a separate category. Such amendments are not subject to review by the Austrian Constitutional Court. However, if the amendment results in fundamental changes to the constitution, the

170 Pfersmann, Otto: "Unconstitutional constitutional amendments: a normativist approach", *Zeitschrift für öffentliches Recht*, 2012/1, 98–103.

171 Article 148 (1) of the Turkish Constitution.

172 Article 125 (2) *b)* of the Russian Constitution.

173 Article 6 (3) *a)* of the Constitution of Bosnia and Herzegovina.

174 Gözler, Kemal: *A judicial review of constitutional amendments: a comparative study,* Bursa, Ekin, 2008.

Constitutional Court should provide greater scope for review of the constitutional amendment. [175]

There have been very few cases in Europe where a constitutional court has declared a constitutional amendment unconstitutional. In a constitutional democracy, this does not usually happen even where the constitutional court has the competence to do so on the basis of an explicit mandate or an interpretation of the constitutional court's powers.[176] However, this tendency is rather indicative of the fact that in stable democracies this need is not so strongly expressed.[177]

However, political factors also influence the way constitutional ideas are put into practice on a day-to-day basis, and the position of each constitutional court is also a factor in the development of the rules of judicial review.[178] Judicial activism is no longer a clearly negative concept, even if the trend towards 'soft' judicial review in other parts of the world (e.g. Canada, New Zealand) suggests this.[179]

The comparison of the Constitutional Court's practices in relation to the review of the constitutionality of constitutional amendments and the analysis of the literature show that in Hungary the Constitutional Court has made only one feeble attempt to examine the content of unconstitutional constitutional amendments, and after that, following the Fourth Amendment to the Fundamental Law, the Constitutional Court, with the express will of the constituent power, has no competence to examine the content of constitutional amendments, but can only examine them on a procedural basis. However, in a somewhat different spirit from the provision of the Fundamental Law, the Constitutional Court in its Decision 22/2016. (XII. 5.) AB, nevertheless made doctrinal statements on constitutional identity, from which at least an attempt to justify the possibility of future review may be inferred. To sum up, in this respect, the Hungarian Constitutional Court was not an effective check or counterweight to the constitution-amending activity of the two-thirds parliamentary majority in the period after 2010.

---

175 Austrian Constitutional Court decisions G-12/00 and G 48-51/00 of 10 March 2010.

176 Such was the case with the Turkish Constitutional Court's decision in a major case concerning democracy, Islam, secularisation and headscarves. Decisions E.2008/16 and K.2008/116.

177 Troper, Michael: "The logic of justification of judicial review", *International Journal of Constitutional Law,* 2003/1, 105–107.

178 Stone Sweet, Alec: *Governing with judges: constitutional politics in Europe,* Oxford, Oxford University Press, 2000, I.

179 See Kovács, Ágnes: "New trend in the debate on justifying judicial review: Considering the benefits of judicial reasoning", in Cserne, Péter – Könczöl, Miklós – Soniewicka, Marta (eds.): *The Rule of Law and Challenges to Jurisprudence,* Frankfurt am Main, PL Academic Research – Peter Lang, 2014.

4. THE RELATIONSHIP BETWEEN THE CONSTITUTIONAL COURT AND THE ORDINARY COURTS IN THE PROTECTION OF FUNDAMENTAL RIGHTS

In this chapter, I report on the results of the research, which was carried out under my supervision and coordination by the CSS Institute of Legal Studies, in response to a call of the Constitutional Court and the Curia.[1]

4.1. Constitutional presumptions

Article I of the Fundamental Law establishes the protection of fundamental rights as the primary duty of the state. Fundamental rights are the fundamental values of the legal system, and constitutional considerations concerning the effectiveness of the organisation of the State are secondary to their protection.

It is a constant refrain of the Constitutional Court's decisions that the state must create the legal conditions necessary for the protection of certain fundamental rights in such a way as to comply with the Fundamental Law. This also serves to establish and preserve the rule of law as enshrined in Article B) of the Fundamental Law. The Constitutional Court has deduced from the provision on the rule of law that the State must enable the most favourable exercise of fundamental rights.[2] If this is the case, the primary duty of all state institutions is to carry out their work in

[1] The edited volume was finally published in its original form only later, with the book chapters originally presented in three separate volumes, as conceived by the managers who launched the competition. The studies used for the habilitation thesis, in their original form and with the significant contributions of the co-authors, are. Gárdos-Orosz, Fruzsina – Lőrincz, Viktor Olivér – Ződi, Zsolt: "Egy új alkotmányjogi panaszeljárás (Abtv. 27. §) jelentőségének mérhetősége a bírósági és az alkotmánybírósági alapjogvédelem rendszerében", in *Az Alaptörvény érvényesülése a bírói gyakorlatban II. Alkotmányjogi panasz: a hatáskörrel kapcsolatos kérdések,* Budapest, HVG-ORAC, 2019, 363–385; Gárdos-Orosz, Fruzsina: "A rendes bíróságok és az Alkotmánybíróság kapcsolata az alapjog-érvényesítésben", in *Az Alaptörvény érvényesülése a bírói gyakorlatban III. Alkotmányjogi panasz: az alapjog-érvényesítés gyakorlata,* Budapest, HVG-ORAC, 2019, 11–18; Vadász, Vanda – Gárdos-Orosz, Fruzsina: "Alkotmányértelmezés a rendes bíróságok és az alkotmánybíróság gyakorlatában a bírói kezdeményezések tükrében", in *Az Alaptörvény érvényesülése a bírói gyakorlatban IV. A bírói kezdeményezések gyakorlati tapasztalata,* Budapest, HVG-ORAC, 2019, 237–318.

[2] Decision 34/1992. (VI. 1.) AB, ABH 1992, 192, 201.

the spirit of the fundamental rights approach. What does this mean for the courts? The principles and practice of applying the fundamental rights enshrined in the constitution and their interpretative practice of the Constitutional Court in ordinary courts jurisprudence have long been shaped in Hungarian law.[3] However, the introduction of the new constitutional complaints procedures was a turning point in this development.

In the 2011 publication *Alkotmányos polgári jog? (Constitutional Civil Law?)* I also argued that further promotion of fundamental rights based on the interpretation of the constitutional text is necessary to ensure that the primacy of fundamental rights is upheld in the interpretation of the ordinary court's judicial practice. The constitutional objective at the level of principle was to ensure that the State provides the strongest possible protection of fundamental rights for natural persons and legal persons. The system of fundamental rights is dynamic: fundamental rights protection is an intrinsic value, but the content of certain fundamental rights in relation to specific legal disputes cannot be described in advance in an abstract way and precisely. However, decisions formulated in the course of judicial law-making have the same limits as formal law-making, so that, among many other requirements, the necessity-proportionality test or the guarantee of essential content of the right, for example, also apply to the application of the law. When judging fundamental rights, the task of the ordinary court is to interpret and apply the law in such a way as to avoid an unconstitutional violation of a fundamental right by interpreting it in accordance with the constitution. In principle, the ordinary court must refer to the Fundamental Law and the relevant Constitutional Court decisions to demonstrate that it has complied with these constitutional requirements.[4]

According to Article I (3) of the Fundamental Law, the ordinary court may not restrict a fundamental right, because this can only be done by a legislative act, and therefore the judicial application of the constitution is only possible within the framework indicated by the legislator and the Constitutional Court. The role of the courts in the system of enforcement of fundamental rights is indisputable. The Constitutional Court has ruled that respect for fundamental rights cannot be confined to the State in the abstract, but that each of its organs, each person exercising public authority, must comply with and enforce the constitutional obligations relating to fundamental rights. According to Decision 36/1992. (VI. 10.) AB, it is through these organs that the State carries out its constitutional task.

Article 28 and Article R) of the Fundamental Law also confirms that in Hungary the fundamental rights adjudication is essentially the task of the ordinary courts.

---

[3] For details, see Gárdos-Orosz, Fruzsina: *Alkotmányos polgári jog? Az alapvető jogok alkalmazása a magánjogi jogvitákban*, Budapest – Pécs, Dialóg Campus, 2011.

[4] Gárdos-Orosz, Fruzsina: "Az alapjogok korlátozása", in Jakab, András – Könczöl, Miklós – Menyhárd, Attila – Sulyok, Gábor (eds.): Internetes Jogtudományi Enciklopédia (Constitutional Law column, column editors: Bodnár, Eszter – Jakab, András), 2020, http://ijoten.hu/szocikk/az-alapjogok-korlatozasa

Moreover, according to the provisions of our Civil and Criminal Procedure Code, in the case of a successful constitutional complaint, the decision of the Constitutional Court is followed by ordinary court procedure to settle the case. In the case of a judicial referral, it is ultimately the "ordinary" judge who also makes the final decision on the dispute, in which the judge complies with the *erga omnes* binding decision of the Constitutional Court. In the new procedure, the judge will, of course, no longer apply the annulled legislation, but she will nevertheless decide on the outcome of the specific dispute.

In Hungary, the Curia may issue a uniformity decision, in which it may rule on the interpretation of a statute and its application in a binding way for lower courts, if the practice of the courts is not uniform or if the Curia wishes to change its own practice. The Fundamental Law already expressly provides for the Constitutional Court's right to examine the constitutionality of such decisions of the Curia. This is not a specific legal remedy, as it does not concern closed individual cases, but it can nevertheless be seen as a step forward in that the state recognises that the court is developing law which may be of a similar weight to legislation in certain specific individual cases. The framework for this legal development is different from the legislative mandate of the legislator, but it is given a role in judicial practice similar to that of the Constitutional Court decisions. This means that while uniformity decision is binding on all courts and is applied as quasi-legislation by ordinary courts, constitutional court decisions with *erga omnes* effect can also play a similar role in law, especially if they were of particular importance in the development of an ordinary court decision that was published by the Curia in the Collection of Court Decisions and thus became a quasi-precedent in the Hungarian legal system. Decisions made in the context of Article 27 constitutional complaint procedure of the Act on the Constitutional Court or constitutional requirements made in proceedings under Article 26 (1) constitutional complaint procedure of the Act on the Constitutional Court may be suitable for being treated by the ordinary court as a source of law in the course of proceedings in a manner similar to decisions of uniformity of the Curia and legislation. However, it is questionable whether such a uniform treatment of legal sources is forward-looking from the point of view of the protection of fundamental rights.

At the time of our research, it could be observed that references to decisions of the Constitutional Court in abstract review proceedings prior to 2012 are as prevalent in judicial practice as more recent decisions on constitutional complaints. This trend is changing over time. At the level of legal interpretation, it is worthwhile to deal with the two groups of cases separately, with the role that decisions taken in abstract review proceedings can play in the protection of fundamental rights implemented by the ordinary court, with the role that they can and do play in the justification of the court's decisions, and with the role that they can play in the objective protection of fundamental rights under the effect of the Constitutional Court's decisions. These groups of cases should be considered in the context of

Articles 27 and 26 (2), their operative parts and reasoning's, and the constitutional requirements for the application of the law laid down therein.

In Hungary, the Fundamental Law states that fundamental rights may only be limited by legislative act. Judicial legal development must be assessed in the light of this constitutional provision. It is primarily this rule that also defines the framework for the courts to apply the Fundamental Law and the decisions of the Constitutional Court, since the court must always bear in mind that the restriction of a fundamental right can only be provided for by legislative act. It follows that the judiciary cannot determine the content of a fundamental right independently of the practice of the legislature and the Constitutional Court, which has to judge the constitutionality of the law.

However, the court has the power to determine the content of the fundamental right in the specific case and to rule on it; if there is no relevant constitutional court decision, it does so by its own interpretation of the constitution. With the entry into force of the Fundamental Law in January 2012, the Constitutional Court was given the possibility to review this ordinary judicial interpretation of the constitution before the Constitutional Court in the form of the German-type constitutional complaint.

Separation of powers means that each branch of power has its own specific function in the enforcement of fundamental rights. According to some conceptions, the court is the sole enforcer of the norm. According to the opposite view, the development of law is *de facto* effected by means of the law created by the judge, since it is the judge's task to derive a rule from the words of the law and to decide on the basis of that rule. It is the judge who turns the text of the law into a norm. When examining judicial decisions, it must be assumed that the Fundamental Law and the decisions of the Constitutional Court have a guiding character in the application of the law. Ultimately, it is the court that determines the content of valid law. The Constitutional Court has repeatedly stressed the classic principle that, unlike the other two branches of power, which are political in nature, the judicial branch is permanent and neutral.[5] The courts interpret laws and administrative norms independently. The judiciary is in principle independent of political changes, and its coherence is facilitated by its continuity, its tradition and its close links with theory.[6] In principle, it is precisely because of this constitutional function and nature that the courts and the Constitutional Court must make a concerted effort to ensure a high and constant level of protection of fundamental rights, despite the battles of political power.

Within this theoretical framework, we examined the experience of the complaint procedure under Article 26 (1) of the Act on the Constitutional Court and the complaint procedure under Article 27 of the Act on the Constitutional Court in the period 2012–2016. We paid particular attention to the assessment of whether, in the

[5] Montesquieu: *A törvények szelleméről,* Bukarest, Kriterion, 1987.

[6] Decision 38/1993. (VI. 11.) AB, ABH 1993, 256.

context of judicial protection, the constitutional complaint is an effective tool for redressing individual rights violations, or whether the new legislative environment may rather bring about a strengthening of the objective, institutional side of fundamental rights protection. Our assumption was that there is probably very little that the constitutional court procedure can do at the level of individual legal protection, since a large volume of fundamental rights protection has to be dealt with in the courts. This is also shown by the comparative figures for review and substantive constitutional complaint procedures. The old and the new constitutional court powers are therefore more suited to the objective, institutional protection function, and this responsibility is also illustrated by the fact that since 2012, the reference to the Fundamental Law in the decisions of the constitutional court has been steadily increasing in the practice of ordinary courts.

Our hypothesis was partly confirmed and partly refuted by the results of the research. As explained below, it has become clear that since 2012, the practice of the ordinary courts has changed; more attention is paid to the fundamental rights approach, and in some decisions, in addition to the doctrinal aspects of the case law, the consideration of constitutional law aspects is also raised. More often in this area, the reference to the Fundamental Law or to certain decisions of the Constitutional Court is only a decorative element in the judgment or order, but is not of major importance for the *ratio decidendi* in the reasons for the decision. Our results clearly show that the principles of interpretation set out in Articles R) and 28 of the Fundamental Law, play a major role in shaping judicial practice. Although the research has primarily aimed at examining the changes in the cooperation between the Constitutional Court and the Curia in the protection of fundamental rights, it is perhaps not without reason to recognise and articulate that some of the partial results of the research show that the change has not been primarily in the protection of fundamental rights, but rather in the general approach to the interpretation of legislation under the Fundamental Law. The Constitutional Court can assess unconstitutionality in the context of a fundamental rights violation much more easily than complaints regarding the principles of interpretation of the Fundamental Law, and according to its constant practice, it prefers not to deal with them, rejecting the petition if it considers the deficiencies of the constitutional interpretation as unconstitutional in itself.

Our assumption was that the courts and the Constitutional Court, and in particular the members of the two high courts, have different attitudes towards constitutional review, different definitions of their tasks and different judicial identities. The Constitutional Court is not a court in the sense that it is called upon to decide individual disputes. It is a court in the sense that it interprets and applies the law within a normative constitutional order. The ordinary court's task is to adjudicate on fundamental rights, and in doing so it must take account of the protection of fundamental rights. It is helpful to clarify the constitutional function of the constitutional complaint or the judicial initiative and to take stock of the practical implementation of certain issues in order to answer such dilemmas. The research was based on the findings of the case-law analysis group of the Curia and on publications in the literature.

The quantitative analysis showed how the reference to the Constitutional Court's practice has changed in ordinary court practice since 2010, broken down by year. Frequency is not only a question of the absolute number of references, but also of the number of times pre-2012 and post-2012 Constitutional Court practice was referred to. We also examined which "basic decisions" were the most frequently cited. A further question may be how these are perceived in jurisprudence.

An examination of the quality of the references showed whether the assumption that the introduction of the German-type complaint under Article 27 of the Act on the Constitutional Court increased the importance of the fundamental rights protection aspects and the reference to the practice of the Constitutional Court in the ordinary court practice is justified. A further question was whether, if there was a reference to the provision of the Fundamental Law, international or EU human rights aspects or specific piece of the Constitutional Court practice, this influenced the interpretation of the law, i.e. whether it was a substantive, influential reference. Where it was found that the interpretation of the law was shaped by the reference to the Decision of the Constitutional Court, a further question was whether the interpretation of the legal issue in question had changed from the previous interpretation. Is the reference to fundamental rights included as confirmation or as an argument justifying a change in case law? In the research analysing each fundamental right, we have examined cases where the previous case law has changed by reference to fundamental rights under the same normative text.[7]

The quantitative and qualitative studies carried out by the research team on the basis of these questions showed the impact of the introduction of the constitutional complaint on judicial practice in Hungary, how it changed the interpretive approach of judges, which rights changed and which rights did not. A hypothesis that has been frequently put forward in the literature is that the introduction of a constitutional complaint theoretically increases the enforcement of fundamental rights in judicial practice even if no specific case is quashed by the Constitutional Court, because judges are more vigilant in these aspects due to the threat of being

---

7 Szilágyi, Emese: "A kommunikációs alapjogok általános értelmezése és alkalmazása a rendes bírósági és az alkotmánybírósági gyakorlatban – a bírói kezdeményezések és az alkotmányjogi panaszos ügyek tapasztalatai", in *Az Alaptörvény érvényesülése a bírói gyakorlatban III. Alkotmányjogi panasz: az alapjog-érvényesítés gyakorlata*, Budapest, HVG-ORAC, 2019, 98–121; Hollán, Miklós: „Büntetőbírói döntések az Alkotmánybíróság ítélőszéke előtt a *nullum crimen et nulla poena sine lege* elv tükrében", in *ibid.* 64–97; Tordai Csaba: "Az alkotmánybírósági esetjog hatása a rendes bírói ítéletekre az információszabadság és a képmáshoz való jog területén", in *ibid.* 245–259; Sepsi, Tibor: "Az Alaptörvény személyes adatok védelméhez való joggal összefüggő rendelkezéseinek érvényesülése – az alkotmánybírósági gyakorlat a rendes bíróságok eljárásában az Alaptörvény hatálybalépése óta", in *ibid.* 260–276; Drinóczi, Tímea: "A tulajdonhoz való alapjog értelmezésének eltérései a rendes bírósági és az alkotmánybírósági gyakorlatban: a bírói kezdeményezések és az alkotmányjogi panaszok tapasztalatai", in *ibid.* 277–312.

challenged by a constitutional complaint. The research has shown that the first five years prove this hypothesis, but the change is rather partial: for some fundamental rights there has been a marked change, while for others there has been only a slight confusion.[8]

4.2. The significance of the constitutional complaint

4.2.1. Subject of the inquiry

In recent years, the literature has devoted much attention to the legal institution of constitutional complaints, both on the level of practical knowledge and theoretical background, and even comparative studies have been published on the subject. Nevertheless, it is difficult to judge on the basis of all these studies what kind of remedy, beyond the ordinary judicial remedy, the constitutional complaint provides and how effective it is.

The law does, of course, distinguish between constitutional complaints against a judicial decision on the basis of whether the petitioner has raised a complaint about the constitutionality of the law applied in his case or about the judicial decision-making process, procedure or interpretation of the law itself. However, it is common ground that in the constitutional complaint procedure the petitioner seeks the annulment of the ordinary court decision. If the complaint is successful, the result of the procedure will be the annulment of the court decision. The legal instrument of the constitutional complaint is therefore unique in that it leads to the annulment of the court decision, but it is not a completely individual decision, because according to the newer concepts, which have been confirmed by the Constitutional Court, the grounds of the decision of the Constitutional Court have *erga omnes* effect, alongside the operative part of the decision.

Although the theoretical significance of the constitutional complaint has been much discussed in the literature, the question of how to measure its significance in domestic law has not been asked. Analyses have shown how the findings of the Constitutional Court can be assessed in specific cases, and what role can be attributed to them in improving or destroying the legal doctrine. We have also devoted much attention to the question of how the subjective protection of fundamental rights and the objective constitutional protection of the legal order function can be assessed in the course of constitutional complaint procedures. We have also considered the balance of inclusion. However, we have not been able to assess the effectiveness with which this legal instrument operates in the current institutional order, in the current legislative environment.

8 See *ibid.*

4.2.2. Constitutional complaint pursuant to Article 27 of the Act on the Constitutional Court[9]

"In accordance with Article 24 (2) *d)* of the Fundamental Law, persons or organisations affected by judicial decisions contrary to the Fundamental law may submit a constitutional complaint to the Constitutional Court if the decision made regarding the merits of the case or other decision terminating the judicial proceedings a) violates their rights laid down in the Fundamental Law, and b) the possibilities for legal remedy have already been exhausted by the petitioner or no possibility for legal remedy is available for him or her."

Since the entry into force of the Fundamental Law, i.e. since 1 January 2012, the vast majority of cases before the Constitutional Court are constitutional complaint proceedings under Article 27 of the Constitutional Court Act, in which the Constitutional Court examines the proceedings and ultimately the decision of the ordinary court. In the operative part of the decision of the Constitutional Court, as a legal consequence, in addition to a small number of annulments and prohibitions of application, there are an increasing number of cases where a constitutional requirement is stated which gives *erga omnes* effect to the constitutional interpretation of the law, with the aim of guiding the practice of the courts.

From the point of view of the constitutionality of the application of the law, the Constitutional Court has become a forum for appeal, despite all the general declarations to the contrary, although not explicitly referring to this phenomenon.[10] It is the constitutional duty of all ordinary courts to ensure that judicial proceedings, and thus decisions, are in accordance with the Constitution.[11] The Constitutional Court is therefore, in the context of the procedure under Article 27 of the Act on the Constitutional Court, investigating something that we should expect of an ordinary court in a constitutional democracy. As an appellate forum, it examines whether the judge who heard the case decided in accordance with the Constitution. From a perspective that goes beyond the specific case and shapes judicial practice

9 The individual findings are largely based on previous research, in many places textually identical, see Bitskey, Botond – Fröhlich, Johanna – Gárdos-Orosz, Fruzsina – Rajos, Krisztina: "Az alkotmányjogi panasz eljárások tapasztalatai az indítvány beérkezésétől az érdemi elbírálásig", in Bitskey, Botond – Török, Bernát (eds.): *Az alkotmányjogi panasz kézikönyve,* Budapest, HVG-ORAC, 2015, 102–225, for an extended, revised version, see Gárdos-Orosz Fruzsina: "A bírói döntések ellen benyújtott alkotmányjogi panaszok befogadhatósága I. Az Abtv. 26. § (1) bekezdése", *Alkotmánybírósági Szemle,* 2013/4, 74–81; Gárdos-Orosz, Fruzsina: "A bírói döntések ellen benyújtott alkotmányjogi panaszok befogadhatósága II. Az Abtv. 27. §-a", *Alkotmánybírósági Szemle,* 2014/1, 82–89.

10 E.g. Decision 3037/2014. (III. 13.) AB.

11 Vissy, Beatrix: "A bírói döntések alkotmánybírósági felülvizsgálata mint a politikai hatalom korlátozásának eszköze?", in Gárdos-Orosz, Fruzsina – Szente, Zoltán (eds.): *Jog és politika határán. Alkotmánybíráskodás Magyarországon 2010 után,* Budapest, HVG-ORAC, 2015, 349–374.

and, ultimately, legislation and the application of the law in general (objective legal protection), the Constitutional Court's decision is of course of great importance. On the one hand, the decisions of the Constitutional Court, by virtue of their position as a source of law, shape the legal order by their *erga omnes* effect, even through the individual case. The specific procedural act of the Constitutional Court also confirms that its law-making function is situated between the legislative and the judicial. It has already been widely recognised that the Constitutional Court is a "negative legislator" and, in view of its new powers, it must also be recognised that it is ultimately the "law judge" of the parties in a given case.[12] In constitutional complaint proceedings, the Constitutional Court acts as an appellate court in relation to the constitutional aspect of the specific litigation. However, the scope of constitutional review in individual cases is narrow.[13]

We sought to answer what traditional conceptual-logical methods of analysis can tell us about the relevance and effectiveness of the new constitutional complaint, and complemented this with an outline of the possibilities of quantitative analysis.

The introduction of the new powers, as I wrote above, was probably a "consolation prize" for the abolition of the *actio popularis;* at the time of the codification of the complaint under Article 27 of the Act on the Constitutional Court, its consequences for the interpretation and application of the law were not yet foreseeable. Although there was undoubtedly a limited literature on the German type of constitutional complaint in Hungary, there was no in-depth analysis of the debates on this complaint. The analysis of five years of practice has shown that the complaint can not only be a source of institutional conflicts, but also has the potential to shape the interpretation of the law by the courts on fundamental issues according to the new constitutional content. This is something that the Constitutional Court's powers have been able to do in the past, and indeed have served this purpose, but the fundamental difference is that since 2012, constitutional rules on the interpretation and application of the law will become normative, and failure to comply with them will lead to their invalidity, as the Constitutional Court will annul the court decisions taken in this way.

[12] This argument is not invalidated by the fact that the Constitutional Court does not decide the case.

[13] For example, a constitutional complaint may only refer to a violation of a right guaranteed by the Fundamental Law [Order 3252/2012. (IX. 28.) AB]; a question of application of law "of a purely private nature" cannot be of fundamental constitutional significance {Order 3072/2012. (VII. 26.) AB, Reasoning [9]}; the Constitutional Court cannot review an ordinary court decision based on a case-by-case assessment: it cannot review the "judicial assessment made in determining the outcome of the evidence" {Order 3237/2012. (IX. 28.) AB, Reasoning [12]}; the Constitutional Court does not have the power to review "[the] direction of the judicial decision, the judicial weighing of the evidence", nor to assess "how the ordinary courts have assessed a particular fact", in other words, it cannot review the entire judicial procedure {Order 3359/2012 (XII. 5.) AB, Reasoning [8]}.

4.2.3. Figures on inclusiveness and success rates

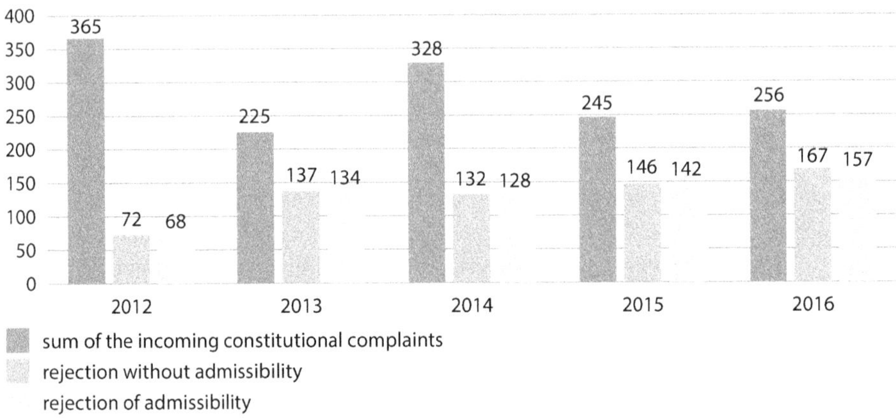

Figure 1: Total complaints received, rejected outright and rejected by admissibility

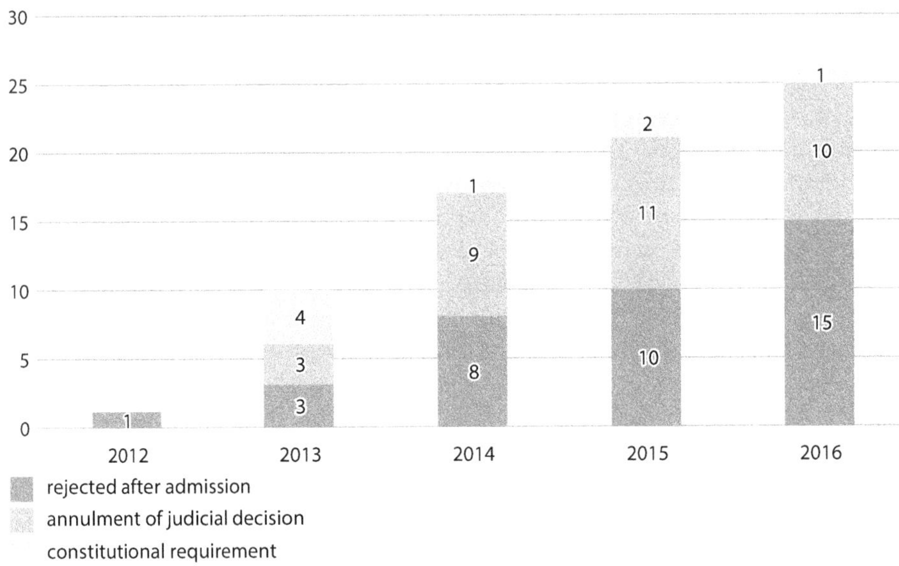

Figure 2: Complaints rejected on the merits, annulments of judicial decision, constitutional requirements
Figures by Zsolt Ződi

4.2.4. The traditional approach – the importance of the admissibility procedure in the relationship between the ordinary court and the Constitutional Court

The experience with the admission of constitutional complaints under Article 27 of the Act on the Constitutional Court shows that the Constitutional Court has a very strict practice when examining the admission criteria of the Act. The year 2012 was particularly characterised by a sense of transience, which was indicated not only by the relatively small number of motions based on Article 27 of the Act on the Constitutional Court compared to other constitutional complaints, but also by the low number of constitutional complaints[14] deemed admissible.

In a specific case, the Constitutional Court interpreted the concept of a decision on the merits in this context as follows: "The Constitutional Court first of all states that there is no obstacle to the admission of a constitutional complaint against a decision of the Curia in a review procedure (provided that the petitioner has not challenged the final decision before the Constitutional Court) if it concerns another decision on the merits or other decision that terminates the proceedings. Such a decision is deemed to be such if the Curia (a) upholds the contested decision in force, or (b) annuls the final decision in whole or in part and issues a new decision in its place or in place of the first instance decision in accordance with the law, or (c) reverses the final decision and issues a new decision in accordance with the law, or (d) annuls the contested decision and terminates the proceedings. {Order 3021/2013. (I. 28.) AB, Reasoning [6]}".[15]

4.2.4.1. Admissibility: what is "prejudice to a right guaranteed by the Fundamental Law?"

According to the wording of the Act on the Constitutional Court, it is possible to initiate a constitutional complaint against a judicial decision that violates a right guaranteed by the Fundamental Law. It is also typical of petitions under Article 27 of the Act on the Constitutional Court that in many cases the petitioners base their objection to the constitution on the rule of law or on one of the requirements of the rule of law derived from it. As with the other types of complaints, the question of infringement of rights raised questions in relation to the practice developed in this procedure as to which articles of the Fundamental Law can be used as a basis for an infringement of it, and within this, complaints based on the rule of law and legal certainty formed a distinct category of cases. The practice in relation to petitions

14 According to the statistics available on the website of the Constitutional Court, by 31 December 2012, a total of 72 constitutional complaint procedures initiated under Article 27 of the Act on the Constitutional Court were pending, of which only six had been received by the end of the year. The situation has not changed significantly since then.

15 A similar case is for example Order 3039/2013. (II. 12.) AB.

based on the rule of law and legal certainty can basically be divided into four directions in the complaint procedure under Article 27 of the Act on the Constitutional Court.

The first, though far from settled practice, is where the rule of law can be invoked, but only if it has been accompanied by other violations of rights. This is what the Constitutional Court said in a case concerning the dismissal of university teachers.[16]

According to the interpretation most consistently held by the Constitutional Court, the Court "examined the allegation of breach of the requirement of legal certainty in two main cases, the petitions based on retroactive legislation and the petitions based on lack of preparation time, vacation legis. {Order 3268/2012. (X. 4.) AB, Reasoning's [14]–[17]}".[17]

In a few decisions, the Constitutional Court has not allowed the rule of law to be invoked even in the case of the two exceptions – either explicitly or simply by silence on the above practice – but such decisions have been rare.[18]

Finally, only in the context of Article 27 of the Act on the Constitutional Court, the tendency appeared according to which the two exceptional cases cannot even arise, since both the sufficient preparation time and the prohibition of retroactivity exclusively formulate requirements towards the legislator, which, however, are excluded from being violated against judicial decisions.[19]

Due to the nature of the appeal against judicial decisions, there were several petitions alleging a lack of uniform application of the law by the courts or, in this context, a breach of legal certainty. In this context, the Constitutional Court has emphasised in several cases that it cannot review a decision of an ordinary court based on a case-by-case assessment, as regards the weighing of evidence and the interpretation of the law in relation to the facts. In these decisions, the Constitutional Court has stated that it is for the ordinary courts, in particular the Curia, to ensure

16 However, since in the case in question the petitioning university professors did not consider their dismissal to be unlawful in material terms, even by their own admission, they could not rely on an abstract violation of legal certainty. See Order 3018/2013. (I. 28.) AB, Reasoning's [12]–[13]. A similar case is the Decision 6/2013. (III. 1.) AB, which conducted a constitutional review of *Act CCVI of 2011 on the Right to Freedom of Conscience and Religion and on the Legal Status of Churches, Religious Associations and Religious Communities* in the procedure under Article 26 (2) of the Act on the Constitutional Court.

17 This direction was also confirmed in the following decisions: Order 3327/2012. (XI. 12.) AB; Order 3346/2012. (XI. 19.) AB; Order 3387/2012. (XII. 30.) AB; Order 3377/2012. (XII. 15.) AB; Order 3033/2013. (II. 12.) AB; Order 3065/2013. (II. 28.) AB; Order 3125/2013. (VI. 24.) AB, Reasoning [6]; Order 3157/2013. (VII. 24.), Reasoning [25].

18 Order 3236/2013. (XII. 21.) AB, Reasoning [36]; Order 3237/2013. (XII. 21.) AB, Reasoning [19].

19 For the time being, this direction cannot be regarded as established, as the Constitutional Court has examined the existence of the two exceptions in several cases in complaints under Article 27, e.g. Order 3160/2013. (VII. 24.) AB, Reasoning [27]; Order 3176/2013. (X. 9.) AB, Reasoning [27]; Order 3223/2013. (XII. 12.) AB, Reasoning [8].

uniform case-law.[20] A similarly rooted problem can be seen when the Constitutional Court ruled that the violation of the right to a trial within a reasonable time does not affect the merits of a judicial decision,[21] and therefore a constitutional complaint that does not provide any other justification for the violation of a right under the Fundamental Law cannot be admitted.

4.2.4.2. Admissibility: what is the fundamental constitutional issue?

As I have already pointed out, the Constitutional Court has rejected the admission of a constitutional complaint initiated under Article 27 on the grounds set out in Article 29 of the Act on the Constitutional Court in a remarkably large number of cases. In this context, it has interpreted the statutory requirement to raise a question of fundamental constitutional importance in a very restrictive manner and has strictly enforced it. This has resulted in many rejection orders based on the absence of a question of fundamental constitutional importance, yet no consistent jurisprudence has been developed in relation to this criterion. It is not clear what criteria, if any, the Constitutional Court uses to separate the examination of the fundamental constitutional question from the examination of the unconstitutionality of the substantive decision of the court and how these criteria relate to each other.

In the first period of its practice, the Constitutional Court often simply stated in its rulings that the petition did not raise any fundamental constitutional law violation or any question of fundamental constitutional significance that would have a substantial impact on the judicial decision. Since then, the reasoning has become both longer and, in some cases with reference to earlier rulings, has been able to capture certain recurrent interpretative trends.

The most frequently invoked grounds for refusal include the ordinary interpretation of the law by the judiciary and the refusal to review discretionary decisions, the denial of the admissibility of an argument based on a mere criticism of the judgment (and thus the concept of the court of fourth instance), as follows: the Constitutional Court has ruled in several decisions that a constitutional complaint against a judicial decision "cannot be considered as a means of remedying all the harm caused by judicial decisions that are (no longer) subject to appeal within the judicial system. [...] Alleged or actual breaches of the law committed by ordinary courts cannot in themselves constitute grounds for a constitutional complaint. [...] This power cannot, however, provide a basis for [the Constitutional Court] to intervene in the activity of the courts in all cases where an (alleged) infringement of

[20] Order 3325/2012. (XI. 12.) AB, Reasoning [14]; Order 3146/2013. (VII. 16.) AB, Reasoning's [32]–[33]; Order 3176/2013. (X. 9.) AB, Reasoning [27]. It should be noted that this admissibility criterion is often intertwined with the criteria to be examined under Article 29 of the Act on the Constitutional Court, e.g. Order 3297/2012. (X. 19.) AB, Reasoning [8].

[21] "The prejudice caused by the delay in the procedure cannot therefore be remedied in the Constitutional Court procedure." Order 3237/2012. (IX. 28.) AB, Reasoning [8].

the law has been committed which cannot be challenged by other means of legal remedy [...] {Order 3268/2012. (X. 4.) AB, Reasoning [28]}".[22]

In one case, the Constitutional Court pointed out that errors and mistakes in the application and interpretation of the law are not constitutional issues. Therefore, the mere fact that judicial decisions are subsequently found to be wrong – without being manifestly wrong – cannot in itself lead to either the imposition of liability for damages or the unfairness of the proceedings.[23]

When assessing the admissibility of a constitutional complaint – following the German practice[24] – the assessment will include whether the significance of the decision examined in the context of the constitutional complaint goes beyond the given case, whether the given petition can be used as a basis for examining a new segment of the content of a fundamental right, or whether the case gives the Constitutional Court the opportunity to formulate guidelines for the constitutional institutions on the content and enforcement of the given fundamental right. In the practice of the German Constitutional Court in relation to constitutional complaints, a constitutional complaint may also be admissible if it concerns a matter of social importance. This does not mean, however, that the number of people affected or the social importance of the issue in question is a factor in determining admissibility where a significant constitutional issue is raised. Similarly, in Hungarian constitutional court practice, the admissibility argument of social significance extending beyond the individual case can be found as an independently invocable admissibility criterion for a question of fundamental constitutional significance in Article 29 of the Fundamental Law.[25]

The content of the admissibility criterion of a question of fundamental constitutional importance thus seems to be outlined in the practice of the Constitutional Court, but this is rather reflected in the definition of the negative side of this concept, i.e. what does not constitute a question of fundamental constitutional importance.

4.2.5. Conclusions

Together with my colleagues Zsolt Ződi and Viktor Olivér Lőrincz, we set out to examine how the significance of constitutional complaints could be measured in our legal system. Among the constitutional complaints, we examined in particular the complaint under Article 27 of the Act on the Constitutional Court, because in our opinion this complaint has brought the greatest change in the relationship between the ordinary courts and the Constitutional Court. In addition, we have

22 See also Order 3325/2012. (XI. 12.) AB, Reasoning [15]; Order 3018/2013. (I. 28.) AB, Reasoning [9].

23 Order 3003/2013. (I. 15.) AB, Reasoning [13].

24 For a summary, see, e.g., Kadlót, Erzsébet: "Az indítványok szűréséről", *Alkotmánybírósági Szemle*, 2012/1, 96–105.

25 Decision 3/2013. (II. 14.) AB, Reasoning [33]; Decision 7/2013. (III. 1.) AB, Reasoning [20].

also analysed the recent experience of the complaint procedure under Article 26 (1) of the Act on the Constitutional Court in the light of the data, since the two complaints are fundamentally interrelated and the legislator has therefore ensured interoperability between them. The number of cases in which legal protection is provided through the constitutional complaint procedure is relatively small. This does not mean, of course, that legal protection is not provided, but the figures show that it is not the constitutional complaint that plays an important role in terms of volume in individual legal protection. The conclusion that can be drawn from the data is rather that constitutional complaints may be of greater importance in the protection of the objective legal order, but that the day-to-day work is done by the ordinary courts and the administration in the protection of constitutional rights and interests.

The aim of this article was to review the filtering mechanisms in the constitutional complaint procedure, i.e. how the Constitutional Court decides which cases to deal with on the merits. In conclusion, it can be concluded that the Constitutional Court can, by the very nature of constitutional adjudication, enforce objective constitutional protection aspects rather than remedying individual rights. Our research on the first five years of the Constitutional Court's practice is confirmed by the most recent study on the subject by Kinga Zakariás, which not only provides a systematic summary of the relevant practice, but also offers a theoretical framework for a precise understanding of it.[26]

4.3. The enforcement of fundamental rights in the practice of ordinary courts and the role of the Constitutional Court[27]

4.3.1. Introduction

In examining the horizontal effect of fundamental rights, we sought to answer the question of what role the Constitutional Court has played and what role it has assumed since the entry into force of the Fundamental Law in the private (horizontal) enforcement of fundamental rights. Our research question was what principles have been developed by the Constitutional Court to determine what it examines from the point of view of admissibility, and during the substantive examination in

26 Zakariás, Kinga: "A bírói döntések alkotmánybírósági felülvizsgálata terjedelmének dogmatikai keretei – a jogalkalmazás közvetlen és közvetett alapjogsértésének kontrollja a német és magyar gyakorlat tükrében", *Állam- és Jogtudomány,* 2021/4, 101–127.

27 The chapter is partly based on the study by Gárdos-Orosz, Fruzsina – Bedő, Renáta: "Az alapvető jogok érvényesítése a magánjogi jogviták során", *Alkotmánybírósági Szemle,* 2018/1, 3–15.

the context of certain procedures, in particular the constitutional complaint[28] under Article 27 of the Act on the Constitutional Court, and what principles are used to decide whether it should intervene in the adjudication of private law disputes by annulling the judicial decision or declaring a constitutional requirement in order to enforce constitutional rights.

The horizontal effect of fundamental rights in Hungary was declared by Decision 8/2014. (III. 20.) AB. The horizontal scope of a right enshrined in the Fundamental Law means that it can also be invoked in private law relationships. The horizontal scope/effect is indirect if the parties cannot directly rely on provisions of the Fundamental Law, they must be taken into account only when interpreting the applicable law. In the case of the direct horizontal effect, on the other hand, the provisions of fundamental law may be invoked directly before the court, without the intervention of a statute, so that the court may base its judgment on the provisions of the constitution.

In recent times, both private law and fundamental human rights have evolved considerably.[29] As a result of historical developments, it can be seen that the fundamental human rights enshrined or understood in the constitution are becoming increasingly important in horizontal, private legal relationships.

Since the entry into force of the Fundamental Law, i.e. since January 1, 2012, numerous studies have dealt with the question of how the constitutional complaint introduced by Article 27 of the Act on the Constitutional Court, Article 28 of the Fundamental Law and the new powers and new positioning of the Constitutional Court in general have changed the private enforcement of fundamental rights in judicial practice.[30] In general, these studies have looked at how the Constitutional

28 Article 27 of the Act on the Constitutional Court: "In accordance with Article 24 (2) *d)* of the Fundamental Law, persons or organisations affected by judicial decisions contrary to the Fundamental law may submit a constitutional complaint to the Constitutional Court if the decision made regarding the merits of the case or other decision terminating the judicial proceedings a) violates their rights laid down in the Fundamental Law, and b) the possibilities for legal remedy have already been exhausted by the petitioner or no possibility for legal remedy is available for him or her."

29 For a description, see Sólyom, László: *A személyiségi jogok elmélete,* Budapest, Közigazgatási és Jogi Könyvkiadó, 1983.

30 Orbán, Endre: "A bírói döntések ellen benyújtott alkotmányjogi panaszok tapasztalatai", *Magyar Jog,* 2016/10, 577–588; Vissy, Beatrix: "A bírói döntések alkotmánybírósági felülvizsgálata mint a politikai hatalom korlátozásának eszköze?", in Gárdos-Orosz, Fruzsina – Szente, Zoltán (eds.): *Jog és politika határán. Alkotmánybíráskodás Magyarországon 2010 után,* Budapest, HVG-ORAC, 2015, 349–374; Vissy, Beatrix: "A valódi alkotmányjogi panasz legitimitása Hans Kelsen szemszögéből", *Közjogi Szemle,* 2015/3, 35–41; Csehi, Zoltán: "A német alkotmányjogi panasz hatása – biztató kezdetek a magyar gyakorlatban", *Acta Universitatis Szegediensis – Acta Iuvenum,* 2016/2, 17–32; Gárdos-Orosz, Fruzsina – Lőrincz, Viktor Olivér – Ződi, Zsolt: "Egy új alkotmányjogi panaszeljárás (Abtv. 27. §) jelentőségének mérhetősége a bírósági és az alkotmánybírósági alapjogvédelem rendszerében", *MTA LAW Working Papers,* 2017/23, 1–24, https://jog.tk.mta.hu/uploads/files/2017_23_GardosOrosz_Lorincz_Zodi.pdf; Bitskey, Botond – Fröhlich, Johanna – Gárdos-Orosz, Fruzsina – Rajos, Krisztina: "Az egyes alkotmányjogi panasz eljárások különös szabályai. Az Abtv. 27. §-a szerinti panasz", in Bitskey, Botond – Török,

Court enforces the law in its decisions in relation to certain fundamental rights, and whether the number of references to the Fundamental Law has increased or decreased in ordinary court practice since the entry into force of the Fundamental Law, i.e. whether the new positive legal environment has changed the sensitivity of the courts towards the enforcement of the norms of the Constitution.[31]

In 2011[32] I argued that the introduction of a German-style constitutional complaint in Hungary is necessary to ensure that fundamental rights are satisfactorily enforced in private law litigation in judicial practice. Numerous writings and research works have shown that the provisions of *Act XX of 1949 on the Constitution* (the Constitution) are not sufficiently enforced in the interpretation of the courts, and that the ordinary judicial practice often ignores fundamental rights norms.[33]

Bernát (eds.): *Az alkotmányjogi panasz kézikönyve*, Budapest, HVG-ORAC, 2015, 186–201; Chronowski, Nóra: "Alkotmányjogi panasz és alkotmányvédelem", *Fundamentum*, 2014/1-2, 91–95; Naszladi, Georgina: "A német alkotmányjogi panasz hatása a hazai szabályozásra és az alkotmánybírósági joggyakorlatra", *Jura*, 2014/1, 235–240; Tóth J., Zoltán: "A »valódi« alkotmányjogi panasz használatba vétele: az Abtv. 27. §-a szerinti panasz első két éve az Alkotmánybíróság gyakorlatában", *Jogtudományi Közlöny*, 2014/5, 224–238; Vissy, Beatrix: "Támpontok a valódi alkotmányjogi panasz hatókörének megállapításához", *Közjogi Szemle*, 2014/2, 40–46; Csehi, Zoltán: "A valódi alkotmányjogi panasz és a magánjog lehetséges jövőjéről", *Alkotmánybírósági Szemle*, 2012/2, 126–130; Gárdos-Orosz, Fruzsina: "Az actio popularistól az alkotmányjogi panaszig: a magyar Alkotmánybíróság új hatáskörei", in Boóc, Ádám – Fekete, Balázs (eds.): *Il me semblait que j'étais moi-même ce dont parlait l'ouvrage. Liber amicorum Endre Ferenczy*, Budapest, Patrocinium, 2012, 118–133; Vissy, Beatrix: "Az individuális alapjogvédelem kilátásai az alkotmánybíráskodásban. Merre mutat az alkotmányjogi panasz iránytűje?", *Magyar Közigazgatás*, 2012/2, 199–211; Tóth J., Zoltán – Térey, Vilmos: "A bírói döntésekre is kiható alkotmánybírósági jogvédelem tapasztalatai (2012–2017)", *Alkotmánybírósági Szemle*, 2017/2, 102–107; Chronowski, Nóra: "Az alkotmánykonform értelmezés és az Alaptörvény", *Közjogi Szemle*, 2017/4, 7–15; Szilágyi, Emese: "Az Alkotmánybíróság az alkotmánykonform bírói jogértelmezésről – terítéken az Alaptörvény 28. cikke", *Közjogi Szemle*, 2015/1, 66–68; Téglási, András: "Az alapjogok hatása a magánjogi viszonyokban az Alkotmánybíróság gyakorlatában az Alaptörvény hatálybalépését követő első három évben, különös tekintettel a tulajdonhoz való jog alkotmányos védelmére", *Jogtudományi Közlöny*, 2015/3, 148–157; Somody, Bernadette – Szabó, Máté – Szigeti, Tamás – Vissy, Beatrix: "Alapjogi igények, alapjogi szabályok: az alapjogi ítélkezés egy koncepciója", in Somody, Bernadette (eds.): *Alapjogi bíráskodás – alapjogok az ítélkezésben*, Budapest, L'Harmattan, 2013.

31 For a presentation of the research conducted in the framework of the CSS Institute of Legal Studies, see Gárdos-Orosz, Fruzsina: "A rendes bíróságok és az Alkotmánybíróság kapcsolata az alapjog-érvényesítésben", in *Az Alaptörvény érvényesülése a bírói gyakorlatban III. Alkotmányjogi panasz: az alapjog-érvényesítés gyakorlata*, Budapest, HVG-ORAC, 2019, 11–18.

32 Gárdos-Orosz, Fruzsina: *Alkotmányos polgári jog? Az alapvető jogok alkalmazása a magánjogi jogvitákban*, Budapest–Pécs, Dialóg Campus, 2011.

33 See, e.g., Halmai, Gábor: "Az alkotmányjogi panasz – jelen és jövendő?", *Bírák Lapja*, 1994/3–4, 63–74; Uitz, Renáta: "Egyéni jogsérelmek és az Alkotmánybíróság", *Fundamentum*, 1999/2, 39–52; D. Tóth, Balázs – Enyedi, Krisztián – Halmai, Gábor – Németh, Attila – Polgári, Eszter – Sólyom, Péter: "Alkotmányos és nemzetközi emberi jogi követelmények a rendes bíróságok gyakorlatában", in Fleck, Zoltán (ed.): *Bíróságok a mérlegen II.*, Budapest, Pallas, 2008, 75–88; Bencze, Mátyás: "Az Alapjogok bíróság előtti érvényesülésének szociológiai háttere", in Somody, Bernadette (ed.): *Alapjogi bíráskodás – alapjogok az ítélkezésben*, Budapest, L'Harmattan, 2013, 95–117.

Of course, the proposal was not intended to replace other constitutional powers with the German-style constitutional complaint, and I followed with concern that the constitutional complaint was conceived by the legislator as a substitute for effective control of the legislative and executive branches.[34] A new problem has come to the fore in Hungarian constitutional adjudication: the conflict between the ordinary judiciary and constitutional adjudication.

Although the question of horizontal effect is still very exciting from a doctrinal point of view, the public law context of the interpretation of constitutional complaints has changed completely since 2011. The ability of independent and impartial courts to carry out their advocacy activities unhindered by a stable legal doctrinal framework developed over centuries has become a much-appreciated asset. The problem of the private enforcement of fundamental rights cannot be assessed in domestic practice without taking into account the public law context, since we are talking about the enforcement of a Fundamental Law freely created by a specific government majority and which can be amended almost without constraints.

Taking all this into account, we considered it important to reiterate the reasons for the private enforceability of fundamental rights. Horizontal effect as a doctrine – a legal construction – was conceived as an institution of constitutional democracy and can only be understood in accordance with its original purpose. The horizontal scope of fundamental rights is always linked to a specific, universal conception of fundamental rights. In addition to the Hungarian literature analysing post-2012 case law, we reviewed all decisions in which the subject word horizontal effect identifiable by the citation index cited one of the three most important fundamental decisions dealing with the topic, Decisions 8/2014. (III. 20.) AB, 34/2014. (XI. 14.) AB or 3/2015. (II. 2.) AB, or where the reference to Article 28 of the Fundamental Law was included in this context, related to the horizontal scope of fundamental rights. Enforcement of fundamental rights in private law may generally arise in constitutional complaint proceedings, but we cannot exclude that the Constitutional Court may also address the issue in its decisions in other proceedings, and therefore we have not limited our analysis to the constitutional complaint. Two final questions are addressed by this review: first, whether the level of legal protection has changed since the Constitutional Court ruled in 2014 that the Fundamental Law has indirect horizontal effect and, if so, whether this change is due to the introduction of the constitutional complaint under Article 27 of the Act on the Constitutional Court.

34 For a detailed analysis of the changes in the powers of the Constitutional Court, see GÁRDOS-OROSZ, Fruzsina: "Alkotmánybíróság 2010–2015", in JAKAB, András – GAJDUSCHEK, György (eds.): *A magyar jogrendszer állapota 2010–2015*, Budapest, MTA TK Jogtudományi Intézet, 2016, 442–479.

4.3.2. The starting point – the purpose of the legal construct

In constitutional law, following the development of law since the French Revolution, the protection of fundamental human rights has been recognised as the primary objective of the state, both at national and international level.[35] At first, the protection of fundamental rights was only a declaration, but later the subjective rights, the rights derivable from the constitution and the more detailed rights formulated in the specific law, appeared. The subject of these rights can prevent the state from interfering in private legal relations through the state's enforcement mechanisms. This is called the negative, abstentionist obligation of the State, the protection of liberties.

The later development was marked by the fact that at the end of the 19th century, in addition to these rights, there was a demand for the state to be actively involved in the protection of fundamental rights. More and more rights were recognised in constitutions, most of which now included a catalogue of fundamental rights. For the vast majority of rights, the state is not only obliged to refrain from infringing them, but must also take action to ensure that they are respected. This includes not only the organisation and conduct of elections by the state, or the punishment of behaviour that may cause injury to life or limb, but also the state's support for a free and balanced press or the creation of an education system.

In the 20th century, the social and economic changes brought about by wars and economic crises have greatly shaped expectations of the law. Constitutional law, at both theoretical and practical levels, has increasingly sought to ensure that fundamental human rights are respected: the doctrine of the state's obligation to provide what might be called institutional protection in the *technicus* of constitutional law has been emphasised, and the state has been given more and more responsibility for recognising and enforcing the rights of subjects.

This development of law has led to the need for the state to strengthen the protection of fundamental rights between individuals through the instruments of constitutional law, by ensuring that the fundamental human rights enshrined in the constitutions are not only applied in the relationship between the state and the individual, but also between individuals. This is the problem of the so-called horizontal effect/scope.

It was already established in Roman law and jurisprudence that the scientific study of public law and private law can be separated.[36] However, this separation has now led to a situation in which the two disciplines are sometimes difficult to link

[35] Nor can we ignore the fact that the rationality of the emerging capitalist economic order also required in many cases the protection of fundamental human rights, in particular the rights of the individual. László Sólyom, in his monograph on the rights of the individual, sees the interconnection between the rights of the individual and property rights as the main driving force of development, see Sólyom, László: *A személyiségi jogok elmélete,* Budapest, Közigazgatási és Jogi Könyvkiadó, 1983.

[36] See Ulpianus: "*publicum ius est quod ad statum rei Romanae spectat, privatum quod ad singulorum utilitatem.*" D.1.1.1.2.

for dogmatic reasons; despite this, there is no doubt that private law has undergone changes in the last century along similar lines and with similar aims to public law. Private law has sought to respond to social and economic problems along the same lines as constitutional law. The classical liberal approach, which centred on property law, has been complemented in private law by an egalitarian approach to the protection of individual rights.

The research question concerned how the horizontal scope established in constitutional law operates in the jurisprudence, in the interpretation of certain fundamental rights in the current practice of the Constitutional Court – to what extent the Hungarian Constitutional Court intends to regulate the development of private law in the area of the task of enforcing the Fundamental Law.

This inevitably implies that the court must take into account constitutional interests in addition to the classical private law interest assessment, which requires the court to be open-minded and to be well-prepared in constitutional law beyond private law.

In Germany, the Federal Constitutional Court has ruled that the *Basic Law (Grundgesetz)* is based on an objective set of values that must be applied in all legal relationships and that the state must ensure is enforced. This is possible if the judge interprets the law, in particular by means of the general rules, in such a way that the German Basic Law is taken into account above all.[37]

In Hungary, a similar concept to the German one emerged after the entry into force of the Fundamental Law. The Hungarian constitutional and legislative power has achieved remarkable results in making certain constitutional provisions applicable by the operation of law in certain private legal relationships.[38]

Before we turn to the practice of the Constitutional Court after 2012, it is worth recalling what our expectations were in 2011 regarding the introduction of the constitutional complaint and the declaration of horizontal scope: "The amendment of the law can be an incentive for the development of judicial practice in line with the achievements of the last twenty years in the protection of fundamental rights. The introduction of a German-style 'genuine constitutional complaint' to review the case-by-case interpretation of the constitution by the courts could also facilitate this process. There is scope for amending the rules of both the Civil Code and the Constitution.

Before drawing a legal-dogmatic conclusion, it is worth emphasising that, as the study shows, it is primarily up to the discretion of the courts to develop a jurisprudence that respects the fundamental and sound doctrinal concepts of private law and also meets the requirements dictated by the Fundamental Law."[39]

---

[37] Szalbot, Balázs Mihály: "A közvetlen alkotmányjogi panasszal támadható normák körének meghatározása", *Magyar Jog*, 2017/6, 347–361.

[38] Article 1:2 (1) of the *Act V of 2013 on the Civil Code*: "The provisions of this Act shall be interpreted in accordance with the constitutional order of Hungary."

[39] Gárdos-Orosz, Fruzsina: *Alkotmányos polgári jog? Az alapvető jogok alkalmazása a magánjogi jogvitákban*, Budapest – Pécs, Dialóg Campus, 2011.

4.3.3. The doctrine of horizontal effect and the new constitutional bases – lessons from the judicial practice

The entry into force of the Fundamental Law has brought about a number of changes in the protection of fundamental rights by the judiciary, which also affect the question of horizontal effect of the Fundamental Law. Although Article 70/K of the former Constitution provided for the enforceability of claims of the violation of fundamental rights before the courts, the Fundamental Law no longer contains an explicit provision on the enforcement of fundamental rights by the courts.[40]

Article 28 of the Fundamental Law, which stipulates that in the application of the law, the courts shall interpret the text of legislation primarily in accordance with its purpose and the Fundamental Law, lays down the constitutional interpretation in the protection of fundamental rights.[41] Constitutional interpretation[42] means that if the legislation in question allows for different interpretations, one of the interpretations in conformity with the Constitution must be adopted over the unconstitutional one.[43] The requirement of constitutional interpretation is complementary to traditional methods of interpretation, i.e. the result obtained by the methods of interpretation must also be examined to see whether the resulting normative content is in conformity with the constitution. The Fundamental Law has also institutionalised the legal institution of a constitutional complaint for the review of judicial decisions, which in fact makes explicit that the legality of judicial decisions is subject to compliance with the Fundamental Law.[44]

Since the Constitutional Court interprets the exercise of certain fundamental rights in private relations mainly through the role of the constitutional complaint for the review of judicial decisions in the protection of fundamental rights and through the interpretation of the constitutional conformity of the constitution, the outlines of the doctrine of horizontal scope emerge from the practice of the Constitutional Court in a mosaic. Examining this practice, it can be concluded that three basic decisions of the Constitutional Court can be identified in the issue of horizontal scope and constitutional interpretation: Decisions 8/2014. (III. 20.) AB, 34/2014. (XI. 14.) AB and 3/2015. (II. 2.) AB, which the Constitutional Court refers to as basic decisions in its subsequent cases.

---

40 Article XXVIII of the Fundamental Law.

41 Jakab, András: "A bírói jogértelmezés az Alaptörvény tükrében", *Jogesetek Magyarázata*, 2011/4, 86.

42 Petrétei, József: *Az alkotmányos demokrácia alapintézményei*, Budapest – Pécs, Dialóg Campus, 2009, 137–138; Chronowski, Nóra: "Alkotmányjogi panasz és alkotmányvédelem", *Fundamentum*, 2014/1-2, 91–95; Chronowski, Nóra – Drinóczi, Tímea – Kocsis, Miklós: "Mozaikok, azaz milyen értelmezési kérdéseket vethet fel az alaptörvény?", in Drinóczi, Tímea (ed.): *Magyarország új alkotmányossága*, Pécs, PTE ÁJK, 2011, 49–50.

43 Petrétei, József: *Az alkotmányos demokrácia alapintézményei*, Budapest – Pécs, Dialóg Campus, 2009, 137–138.

44 Somody, Bernadette – Szabó, Máté Dániel – Vissy, Beatrix: *Az alapjogi bíráskodás kézikönyve*, Budapest, HVG-ORAC, 2013, 31.

For the first time, in Decision 8/2014. (III. 20.) AB, the panel acknowledged that the rights contained in the Fundamental Law are infiltrated into private law through the general rules of the specific law, as the Fundamental Law and the legislation are binding on everyone, and the norms of the Fundamental Law must be applied throughout the legal system. However, the extent to which the rights contained in the Fundamental Law affect private law relations and litigation has not been further developed in the process of abstract constitutional interpretation initiated by the Government. However, the Constitutional Court has pointed out that the enforcement of fundamental rights differs between public and private law, since while in public law the Fundamental Law is enforced directly by means of legislation and directly on the state, in private law it is enforced indirectly, through the interpretation of private law norms, by the transmission of fundamental rights and constitutional values contained in the Fundamental Law. The Constitutional Court has ruled that fundamental rights can only be infiltrated into the private legal system through the general rules of private law and in cases where general rules cannot be applied, fundamental rights cannot have a direct effect in private law. The Constitutional Court has also pointed out that the question of horizontal effect is not a question of whether certain treaties can be directly contrary to the Fundamental Law on the basis of this, but of the requirement that the court must take account of the provisions of the Fundamental Law in its application and interpretation of the law. On the basis of Article 28 of the Fundamental Law, the Constitutional Court has concluded that courts must take due and differentiated account of all legal provisions in their judgments.[45]

In its Decision 34/2014. (XI. 14.) AB, the Constitutional Court explains that under Article 28 of the Fundamental Law, when interpreting legislation, courts must take into account the duty to help the poor and the needy as set out in the National Avowal, and must also bear in mind Article M) (2) of the Fundamental Law, i.e. the protection of the fundamental rights of the weaker parties. In this decision, the Court confirms the infiltration of the rights enshrined in the Fundamental Law through the general rules of private law by illustrating them by the example of the requirement of good faith and fair conduct, and explains that the requirement of good faith and fair conduct is a legal principle codified at the level of the Civil Code and is a constitutional value under Article M) (2) of the Fundamental Law, in particular with regard to the system of private law and its legal relations.[46]

The Constitutional Court has set out further criteria for the interpretation of Article 28 of the Fundamental Law in its Decision 3/2015. (II. 2.) AB. Article 28 of the Fundamental Law does not provide for the courts as an option, but as a constitutional obligation to interpret the law in accordance with the Fundamental Law

45 Decision 8/2014. (III. 20.) AB, Reasoning's [54]–[56].
46 Decision 34/2014. (XI. 14.) AB, Reasoning's [51], [94].

in their adjudicative activity. This is also ensured by the constitutional complaint which allows for a constitutional review of judicial decisions. The Constitutional Court has interpreted that, within the margin of interpretation provided by the law, the courts must identify the fundamental rights aspects of the case before them and interpret the law applied in the judicial decision in the light of the constitutional content of the fundamental right concerned. This does not mean that the courts should base their decisions directly on the provisions of the Fundamental Law, but that they should take into account the relevant constitutional aspects when interpreting the law and apply it to the specific facts of the case. Furthermore, the Constitutional Court has ruled that it will find a judicial decision unconstitutional when, in a case relevant to fundamental rights, the judge has failed to have regard to fundamental rights or his or her interpretation of the law is not in accordance with the content of the fundamental right. In relation to the application of the necessity-proportionality test, the Constitutional Court stated that Article 28 of the Fundamental Law imposes a constitutional requirement on the courts that, when interpreting a rule of law which restricts the exercise of a fundamental right, they must, within the margin of interpretation allowed by the law, limit the restriction of the fundamental right concerned to the level of necessary and proportionate intervention.[47]

In these decisions, the Constitutional Court laid the foundations for an interpretation of the law and horizontal effect in line with the Fundamental Law. It can be seen that, by interpreting Article 28 of the Fundamental Law and pushing its limits, it has taken a position on the question of horizontal scope by recognising the indirect application of fundamental rights in private law relations. It defined the criteria for the conformity of judicial decisions with the Fundamental Law, first by interpreting the general rules, then by interpreting legislation, and finally by applying the necessity-proportionality test to certain fundamental rights.

In the following article, we will show, through different groups of cases, how the doctrine of horizontal effect has been applied in the practice of the Constitutional Court since 2014, and to what extent the practical implementation of the doctrine of horizontal effect leads to the enforcement of increasing or decreasing judicial protection, depending on the wording of the right contained in the Fundamental Law and the interpretation of the Constitutional Court.

47 Decision 3/2015. (II. 2.) AB, Reasoning's [17]–[18], [20]–[21]. In this decision, Béla Pokol rejected the recognition of horizontal scope and in his dissenting opinion he explained that the enforcement of fundamental rights in private relations entails the risk that any area of law which does not regulate the relationship between the state and the individual is forced to abandon its original conceptual framework and legal doctrine. Reasoning's [77]–[81].

4.3.3.1. Right to property[48]

As a consequence of the foreign currency loan cases, the Constitutional Court has invoked the doctrine of horizontal scope in several subsequent decisions. In relation to the constitutional assessment of the underlying liability construct in the legal relationship between private parties in the context of the right to property, the Court has also held that, while respecting freedom of contract, constitutional requirements can ultimately serve as a constitutional yardstick for assessing the relationship between private parties through the general rules of private law. However, citing an earlier decision,[49] it also stated that the protection of the weaker party in contractual relations must be ensured primarily by private law. According to the Constitutional Court's interpretation, the right to property, as a fundamental right in the first place, requires the State not to interfere in the ownership position of the subject of the fundamental right, and the State is therefore obliged to lay down the appropriate rules in accordance with its duty to protect institutions.[50]

The right to inheritance was the subject of the Decision 5/2016. (III. 1.) AB, which was based on a case in which the petitioner could not receive a beneficial interest in the event of death as testamentary heir. The Constitutional Court confirmed, on the basis of Article 28 of the Fundamental Law, that it is the task of the Constitutional Court to establish a judicial interpretation of the law in conformity with the Fundamental Law, one of the means of which is the new type of constitutional complaint. In this case, the Constitutional Court found that the right of succession is to be considered in the same context as the right to make a will and therefore examined the case from the point of view of the right of disposal, which is part of the right to property. It ruled that in this case the courts had restricted the testator's right to dispose of the property belonging to him without any constitutional justification,

---

48 From the literature, see in particular Karsai, Dániel – Mihály, Eszter: "Elefántsirató – a sikeres alkotmányjogi panaszok utóélete", *MTA Law Working Papers,* 2017/21, 1–31, https://jog.tk.mta.hu/uploads/files/2017_21_Karsai_Mihalyi.pdf; Drinóczi, Tímea: "A tulajdonhoz való alapjog értelmezésének eltérései a rendes bírósági és az alkotmánybírósági gyakorlatban: a bírói kezdeményezések és az alkotmányjogi panaszok tapasztalatai", *MTA Law Working Papers,* 2017/24, 1–37, https://jog.tk.mta.hu/uploads/files/2017_24_Drinoczi.pdf; Téglási, András: "Az alapjogok hatása a magánjogi viszonyokban az Alkotmánybíróság gyakorlatában az Alaptörvény hatálybalépését követő első három évben, különös tekintettel a tulajdonhoz való jog alkotmányos védelmére", *Jogtudományi Közlöny,* 2015/3, 148–157; Téglási, András: "A tulajdonhoz való jog védelme az Alkotmánybíróság gyakorlatában az Alaptörvény hatálybalépését követően", in Cservák, Csaba – Horváth, Attila (eds.): *Az adekvát alapjogvédelem,* Budapest, Porta Historica, 2017; Pongrácz, Alex: "Gondolatok a tulajdon(jog)ról, figyelemmel az Alaptörvény szabályozására", in Deli, Gergely – Szoboszlay-Kiss, Katalin (eds.): *Tanulmányok a 70 éves Bihari Mihály tiszteletére,* Győr, Universitas, 2013, 505; Holló, András: *Az alkotmányjognak asztalánál,* Budapest, HVG-ORAC, 2015, 407–418; Stumpf, István: *A tulajdonhoz való jog* (lecture, Győr, 3 March 2016).

49 Decision 3009/2012. (VI. 21.) AB, Reasoning [51].

50 Decision 3052/2016. (III. 22.) AB, Reasoning [53].

but stressed that the ruling did not mean that the owners had a substantive right to dispose of the property without restriction in the event of their death.[51]

In another case, the Constitutional Court examined the extent to which the courts had taken into account the petitioner's right to physical and mental health when ruling on an action alleging trespass and infringement of neighbouring rights, in relation to noise caused by a civil shooting range next to a property. In that decision, the Constitutional Court pointed out that, although protection against environmental nuisance applies in both public authority proceedings and civil law proceedings, the courts and the public authorities do not act according to the same rules. Courts rule on a case primarily on the basis of civil law rules and do not follow administrative rules in their decision-making. The Constitutional Court found that the courts had taken due account of the petitioner's right to health when making their decision, and therefore, when applying the civil law provisions, they had taken the relevant fundamental right into account, even if the judgment was not based on it.[52]

4.3.3.2. Freedom of the press and freedom of expression[53]

The Constitutional Court dealt with the interpretation of the prohibition of market manipulation in accordance with the Fundamental Law in the aforementioned Decision 3/2015. (II. 2.) AB in relation to an article published by the press on a public matter closely related to the economic and financial life of Hungary. The Constitutional Court held that the freedom of the press occupies a prominent place among fundamental rights, as the press is an indispensable means of forming and expressing opinions. As a consequence, freedom of the press is a fundamental right of paramount importance, and the constitutional aspects of its restriction must be taken into account. In the present case, the Constitutional Court ruled that the prohibition of unlawful interference in the market is a constitutional value under Article M) (2) of the Fundamental Law, for the protection of which restrictions on press freedom may be necessary, but that constitutional considerations must also be taken into account when assessing the proportionality of the restriction. It stated that, since the primary constitutional task of the press is to uncover and publish facts and contexts, the prohibition of market interference should not be interpreted in an expansive manner in order to achieve this.[54]

---

51 Decision 5/2016. (III. 1.) AB, Reasoning [43]–[44].

52 Decision 3075/2016. (IV. 18.) AB, Reasoning's [26]–[28].

53 From the literature, see in particular Török, Bernát: "A közügyek vitájának körvonalai a véleményszabadság magyar doktrínájában", in Koltay, András – Török, Bernát (eds.): *Sajtószabadság és médiajog a 21. század elején 4.*, Budapest, Wolters Kluwer, 2017, 425–460; Török, Bernát: "A szólásszabadság védelmének dinamikája", *Magyar Jog*, 2017/12, 721–733.

54 Decision 3/2015. (II. 2.) AB, Reasoning's [24]–[26], [28]. Pozsár-Szentmiklósy, Zoltán: "Az arányossági teszt a jogalkalmazásban", *Alkotmánybírósági Szemle*, 2016/2, 97–107; Török, Bernát: "Alkotmányjogi tesztek hálójában: a sajtószabadság esete a tőkepiaccal", in Fejes, Zsuzsanna – Török, Bernát (eds.): *Suum cuique. Ünnepi tanulmányok Paczolay Péter 60. születésnapja tiszteletére*, Szeged, Pólay Elemér Alapítvány, 2016, 671–684.

The Constitutional Court also dealt with the freedom of expression, the constitutional purpose of the press and the requirement of credible and unbiased information in relation to the case of a programme in which the presenter described the Jobbik Movement for Hungary with the term "extreme right-wing". According to the Constitutional Court's case-law, the right to freedom of expression is not only a fundamental subjective right, but also includes its objective, institutional aspect, which also implies the guarantee of public opinion as a fundamental political institution. The Constitutional Court has pointed out that, since the legal provisions restricting freedom of expression are also shaped by the interpretations of those applying the law, the constitutional function of freedom of the press must also be taken into account when interpreting the law.[55]

Pursuant to Decision 34/2017. (XII. 11.) AB on the legal requirements of reporting on press conferences of public figures and the related liability issues, the Constitutional Court's task is to act as the supreme body for the protection of the Fundamental Law, to guard the constitutionality of professional interpretations and, if necessary, to set the direction and constitutional limits of the interpretation to be followed. In this case, the Constitutional Court held that the usual interpretation of the civil law concept of 'rumour' does not take sufficient account of the specific constitutional value of the activities of the press. As a consequence, it has consistently defined the constitutional aspects to be considered by the court in this particular case, building on its previous decisions. On the basis of the case-law of the Constitutional Court in the field of freedom of the press, it can be stated that if the court judgment finding a violation of the right of personality did not sufficiently respect the constitutional content of the freedom of the press, this is grounds for annulment of the court decision by the Constitutional Court.[56]

4.3.3.3. "Police officer's portrait"[57]

The most controversial case was the so-called police officer's portrait case, because in this case the Constitutional Court's interpretation of the law was largely contrary to the previously established civil law doctrine, and in its Decision 28/2014. (IX. 29.) AB the Constitutional Court overruled the consistent practice of the ordinary court

---

55 Decision 3264/2016. (XII. 14.) AB, Reasoning's [23]–[27], [41].

56 Decision 34/2017. (XII. 11.) AB, Reasoning's [19]–[20].

57 From the literature, see Szilágyi, Emese: "Homályos kép. Alkotmánybírósági határozat a rendőrök arcának kötelező kitakarásáról", *Közjogi Szemle,* 2014/4, 59–60; Szeghalmi, Veronika – Papp, János Tamás: "A rendőr képmásának védelme – a vita jelenlegi állása", *Iustum Aequum Salutare,* 2015/4, 109; Zakariás, Kinga: "A képmáshoz való alapjog. A bírói döntések alkotmánybírósági felülvizsgálatának terjedelme a rendőr képmás ügyekben", *Alkotmánybírósági Szemle,* 2017/2, 108–114; Somody, Bernadette: "A rendőrarcképmás-ügy mint az alapjogi ítélkezés próbája", *Fundamentum,* 2016/1, 103–112; Kiss, Tibor: "Pillanatfelvétel a képmás védelméhez fűződő jog bírói gyakorlatáról 2. rész", *Debreceni Jogi Műhely,* 2017/3–4, http://www.debrecenijogimuhely.hu/archivum/3_4_2017/pillanatfelvetel_a_kepmas_vedelmehez_fuzodo_jog_biroi_gyakorlatarol; Török, Bernát: "A szólásszabadság hatóköre és az általa nyújtott védelem", *Magyar Jog,* 2015/7–8, 385–393.

on the basis of constitutionality criteria. Moreover, the Constitutional Court, while maintaining its previous practice on the general right of personality, defined the limitation on the unauthorised disclosure of pictures of police officers not on the basis of its previous practice, but as an unlimited aspect of human dignity.[58] The question is whether such an interpretation of the power was in line with the provisions of Decision 8/2014. (III. 20.) AB and did not go beyond the horizontal scope of the decision. In this 2014 decision, Article 28 of the Fundamental Law was already more prominently expressed, and on the basis of this, the Constitutional Court decided that it could also review the aspects of the balancing between fundamental rights.[59] The literature is not unanimous on whether this type of intervention is acceptable; many welcomed the Constitutional Court's decision and did not see its interpretation of competence as a cause for concern, while others would have preferred a different interpretation.[60]

We can consider Decision 13/2014. (IV. 18.) AB on defamation proceedings as well,[61] in which the Constitutional Court set out the criteria, based on a balancing of fundamental rights, necessary to ensure that the criminal assessment of a public communication concerning the discussion of public affairs is in line with the requirements of the Fundamental Law. It should be stressed that, in this decision, the Constitutional Court has underlined the competence of the courts in the field of specialised law and, while respecting this competence, has defined the role of the constitutional complaint as a legal protection, according to which the Constitutional Court is responsible for enforcing fundamental rights in individual cases, thereby defining a framework for the application of the law in accordance with the requirements of the rights recognised by the Fundamental Law. It stated that its competence did not extend to interpreting legislation in accordance with the rules of specialised law and to assessing the validity of positions in the area of legal doctrine, and therefore did not take a position on the legal issues involved. Nevertheless, in this case, unlike in the past, it has already stressed the need to argue from a constitutional point of view, referring also to its specific system of criteria.[62]

The Constitutional Court has consistently applied the criteria it followed in its decision in the context of defamation proceedings in relation to the publication of police officers' photographs. In this case, too, the Constitutional Court applied the

---

58 Zakariás, Kinga: "A képmáshoz való alapjog. A bírói döntések alkotmánybírósági felülvizsgálatának terjedelme a rendőr képmás ügyekben", *Alkotmánybírósági Szemle*, 2017/2, 108–114.

59 Téglási, András: "Az alapjogok hatása a magánjogi viszonyokban az Alkotmánybíróság gyakorlatában az Alaptörvény hatálybalépését követő első három évben, különös tekintettel a tulajdonhoz való jog alkotmányos védelmére", *Jogtudományi Közlöny*, 2015/3, 151.

60 Somody, Bernadette: "A rendőrarcképmás-ügy mint az alapjogi ítélkezés próbája", *Fundamentum*, 2016/1, 103–112.

61 Tóth J., Zoltán: *A büntetőjogi rágalmazás és becsületsértés. A defamatorikus bűncselekmények elméleti és gyakorlati megítélése a véleménynyilvánítási szabadság és az emberi méltósághoz való jog kontextusában*, Budapest, Médiatudományi Intézet, 2017; Szomora, Zsolt: "Az alkotmányos követelmények hivatkozási tipológiája becsületsértési és rágalmazási ügyekben hozott büntetőítéletekben", *Jogtudományi Közlöny*, 2014/10, 469–476.

62 Decision 13/2014. (IV. 18.) AB, Reasoning's [38]–[42], [51].

same balancing test between fundamental rights as the court should have applied when considering the aspects of freedom of information and protection of the right to privacy. The Constitutional Court held that the provisions of civil law are given substance by ordinary judicial practice, but also considered that, on the basis of Article 28 of the Fundamental Law, it was necessary to take into account the constitutional aspect of freedom of the press in this case.[63]

The constitutionality criteria set by the Constitutional Court were not applied by the courts, and the police mug shot case continued. The courts first applied the Constitutional Court's interpretation restrictively.[64] The next time, the courts did not even follow the criteria based on the balancing of fundamental rights as defined by the Constitutional Court.[65] The next stage in the police mug shot cases was when the Constitutional Court annulled the decision of the Metropolitan Court of Appeal. The Constitutional Court reaffirmed its previous decisions and stressed that the image of a police action may be made public. It ruled that ordinary courts cannot ignore, selectively or restrictively apply the Constitutional Court's interpretation of certain provisions of the Fundamental Law.[66]

The constitutional issues raised by the police photograph case were examined from a different angle by the Constitutional Court when a court hearing was held and the legal advisers representing the police were filmed. The Constitutional Court pointed out that the standards for the exercise of freedom of expression and freedom of the press in the courtroom and in public places differ when taking photographs and videos. The panel drew attention to the purpose and guarantees of the court hearing when considering its constitutionality.[67]

4.3.3.4. Violation of the right to privacy[68]

In the case before the Constitutional Court, the petitioner was listed by a private individual as one of his pets on the iWiW community page, and published posts that were damaging to his reputation, including his status as a lawyer. The Constitutional Court examined the relationship between the right to reputation and

[63] Decision 28/2014. (IX. 29.) AB.

[64] Decision 16/2016. (X. 20.) AB.

[65] Decision 17/2016. (X. 20.) AB.

[66] Decision 3/2017. (II. 21.) AB.

[67] Decision 3021/2018. (I. 26.) AB, Reasoning's [24]–[28].

[68] From the literature, see Koltay, András: "Az »általános személyiségi jog« azonosítása felé. Alkotmányjogi, magánjogi és büntetőjogi vizsgálódás", in Koltay, András – Török, Bernát (eds.): *Sajtószabadság és médiajog a 21. század elején 4.*, Budapest, Wolters Kluwer, 2017, 267–296; Koltay, András: "A becsület, a jóhírnév és az emberi méltóság fogalmi elhatárolása a magyar magánjogban", in Koltay, András – Darák, Péter (eds.): *Ad astra per aspera. Ünnepi kötet Solt Pál 80. születésnapja alkalmából*, Budapest, Pázmány Press, 2017, 435–458; Koltay, András: "A jó hírnév és a becsület védelme, különös tekintettel a közéleti szereplőkre és a közügyek vitáira", in Koltay, András – Nyakas, Levente (eds.): *Magyar és európai médiajog*, Budapest, Wolters Kluwer, 2015, 309–347; Deli, Gergely: "Az emberi méltóság alapjoga Magyarországon", in Kukorelli, István (ed.): *Hány éves az Alaptörvény? A régi-új kérdése az Alaptörvényben*, Budapest, Gondolat, 2017, 121–152.

freedom of expression in the case. Referring to its previous case-law, it explained that the scope of constitutionally protected freedom of expression is broader in relation to persons exercising public authority and politicians in public office than in relation to other persons, but that the exercise of freedom of expression cannot, in principle, be directed at violating the human dignity of others, even if it is aimed solely and exclusively at discrediting the person concerned. A person acting as a lawyer cannot, however, be regarded as a person exercising public authority or as a politician acting in a public capacity by virtue of his or her status as a lawyer, and there is therefore no constitutional reason why an act which would otherwise be punishable should not be punishable on the ground of the victim's status as a lawyer. The Constitutional Court ruled that the judicial position that the impugned expressions are not unlawful is not in accordance with the Constitution, when the above constitutional aspects are properly weighed.[69]

The Constitutional Court has, however, set out an exception to the prohibition of discrimination in private law relations in the context of the enforcement of the constitutional aspects of a given case. Inferring from the human dignity enshrined in the Fundamental Law, it found that the prohibition of discrimination is more strongly and directly enforced in private legal relations than other constitutional freedoms, since if the provision of services takes place in a public place, the direct enforcement of the prohibition is also required. This enforcement is also contained in the Civil Code, which also prohibits discrimination against persons in the area of the named personal rights.[70]

In the context of the interpretation of the right to private property, the Constitutional Court pointed out that Article 28 of the Fundamental Law made it an obligation of the state to enforce fundamental rights in relations between private law subjects. This is reinforced by the introduction of a constitutional complaint for review of judicial decisions. As a consequence, the judicial activity of ordinary courts is effectively subject to constitutional control. Furthermore, Article 28 of the Fundamental Law imposes an obligation on the courts to recognise the fundamental rights relevance of the cases to be decided, to identify the content of the fundamental rights involved and to interpret and apply the law in the light of this in the specific legal disputes.[71]

---

[69] Decision 1/2015. (I. 16.) AB, Reasoning's [35]–[36], [39].

[70] Decision 3001/2016. (I. 15.) AB, Reasoning's [56]–[57]. On the issue, see also Lápossy, Attila – Szajbély, Katalin: "Egy nem lovagias ügy", *Szuverén*, 4 December 2013, http://szuveren.hu/jog/egy-nem-lovagias-ugy; Reiner, Roland: "Védett nők?", *Republikon blog*, 28 November 2013, http://republikon.blog.hu/2013/11/28/vedett_nok_589; Orbán, Endre: "Teczár-ügy reloaded", *Arsboni*, 12 October 2016, https://arsboni.hu/teczar-ugy-reloaded

[71] Decision 3312/2017. (XI. 30.) AB, Reasoning [31]. In his dissenting opinion, Péter Szalay, Judge of the Constitutional Court, pointed out that not only and exclusively the general clauses of the Civil Code can help the enforcement of fundamental rights, but any private law norm that needs interpretation or raises discretionary aspects in its application can be suitable for the mediation of the constitutional rights and values enshrined in the Fundamental Law through the judicial activity of ordinary courts. In particular, the *clausula rebus sic stantibus*, which applies to private law, consumer protection rules, social responsibility in relation to property or the system of per-

The Constitutional Court considered in Decision 3313/2017. (XI. 30.) AB whether the prejudice alleged by the petitioner, which arises from the fact that he is shown in a press release reporting on the criminal proceedings against him with a prison guard, a belt and handcuffs, is related to the presumption of innocence. The applicant's claim for the protection of his personality is essentially based on the fact that a photograph of him was taken and used as an illustration in the report on the criminal proceedings against him. The Constitutional Court has confirmed that, under Article 28 of the Fundamental Law, the courts must identify the fundamental rights aspects of the case before them within the margin of interpretation provided by the law and interpret the law applied in a judicial decision in the light of the constitutional content of the fundamental right concerned.[72]

In connection with the violation of the reputation of a historian, the Constitutional Court examined whether the interpretation of the law by the courts and the legal assessment of the historical facts were in line with the right to freedom of expression guaranteed by Article IX (1) of the Fundamental Law and the right to reputation deriving from the right to human dignity enshrined in Article VI (1) of the Fundamental Law. The Constitutional Court has examined the decisions of the courts on the basis of the criteria of constitutionality established in previous decisions, in particular, with regard to the relevant fundamental rights aspects, whether the contested decision suffers from a lack of discretion which raises a problem of fundamental constitutional importance or an infringement of the fundamental rights which would substantially affect the judicial decision.[73]

In its Decision 3002/2018. (I. 10.) AB on the objective responsibility of the press, the Constitutional Court also explained, in addition to the context, that the Constitutional Court may review the interpretation of judicial law under Article 27 of the Act on the Constitutional Court only if the case has fundamental rights relevance. Thus, the mere fact that a case has a fundamental rights relevance does not in itself lead to a disregarding of the assessment of the case-law, but it does impose an additional requirement. It stated that the courts must endeavour to have regard to the fundamental rights implications of the case within the margin of interpretation provided by the substantive and procedural rules applicable to the case before them and to give effect in their decision to the constitutional content of the fundamental right concerned. If the applicable rule is not so interpreted, the Constitutional Court considers that the rule itself is unconstitutional.[74] Therefore, it is also possible for the Constitutional Court to switch from the procedure under Article 27 of the Act on the Constitutional Court to the procedure under Article 26 of the Act on the Constitutional Court.

sonal rights, are also the means by which constitutional law norms can be transmitted in relations between private law subjects. Reasoning [88].

72 Decision 3312/2017. (XI. 30.) AB, Reasoning [48].

73 Decision 3001/2018. (I. 10.) AB, Reasoning's [29]–[40].

74 Decision 3002/2018. (I. 10.) AB, Reasoning [60].

The Constitutional Court also ruled that the courts must play a mediating role in cases where the exercise of a fundamental right of one individual is threatened by the exercise of a fundamental right of another individual. This mediation role means that the courts must take into account the inalienability of the essential content of fundamental rights and the principle of proportionality, which the Constitutional Court can verify. Accordingly, courts must decide by identifying the scope of protection of the fundamental rights concerned and by weighing up the relevant fundamental rights. According to the interpretation of the Constitutional Court, the essential aspect is that the courts, in making their decision, do not empty the relevant fundamental rights of their essential content, and ensure the obligation to protect fundamental rights under Article I (1) of the Fundamental Law.[75]

4.3.4. Sub-summary: the horizontal effect and its practice under the Fundamental Law

In my 2011 monograph entitled *Alkotmányos polgári jog? (Constitutional Civil Law?)*, I argued that the horizontal scope of the Constitution is a concept that needs to be implemented in Hungarian law, partly by providing for it in the new Civil Code and partly by introducing the German-style constitutional complaint. However, the above examples show that the enforcement of constitutional content can have very different results depending on what the positive constitutional legal content is. It can be concluded that the procedure alone is not a guarantee of the exercise of a fundamental right if we cannot assume that the content of the constitution is in line with the legal development of constitutional democracies. The horizontal effect as a procedure is therefore only accompanied by stronger legal protection if the constitution provides stronger legal protection than that offered by civil law.

The issue of horizontal effect is a sensitive topic in Hungarian law because it has partly been transformed into a debate on the relationship between the ordinary courts and the Constitutional Court, of which the police officer's face photo cases are a striking example. Accordingly, the Hungarian legal literature also deals extensively with the question of how to delimit the competence of the Constitutional Court and the ordinary courts in relation to the tasks related to the enforcement of the Fundamental Law.

The indirect horizontal effect introduced in Hungary is based on the fact that it is difficult to imagine a legal vacuum in civil law, i.e. a case that cannot be decided on the basis of the Civil Code. It is difficult to imagine cases that cannot be decided on the basis of the fundamental principles of contract law, such as freedom of contract, the principle of performance of contracts *(pacta sunt servanda)* and the general principles of civil law (good morals, good faith and fairness, etc.). In the case of rights relating to persons, it is also difficult to imagine a legal vacuum, since the article providing general protection for named and unnamed rights provides suffi-

[75] Decision 3145/2018. (V. 7.) AB, Reasoning's [69]–[70].

cient guidance for all cases of rights relating to persons. Private law disputes should therefore be dealt with primarily on the basis of private law, with the question of the enforcement of fundamental rights being raised as an additional issue. In the present public law situation, that we called populism above, a contrary approach to the enforcement of fundamental rights may be abusive if the constitutional amending power seeks to impose the new fundamental rights standards and the desired interpretation of fundamental rights in the ordinary judicial practice by means of a constitutional complaint. The review has shown that the enforcement of the horizontal effect of fundamental rights is nowadays more a case-by-case process, that the Constitutional Court is generous in its formulation of principles, and that it is thus ultimately up to the decision and interpretation of the Constitutional Court how the ordinary court enforces the constitutional content it has defined in individual cases and on individual constitutional issues.

4.3.5. Conclusions

After reviewing the jurisprudence in Hungary since 2014 related to the sometimes conflictual cooperation of the ordinary judiciary and the Constitutional Court, the following observations can be made regarding the enforcement of the Fundamental Law in ordinary court jurisprudence.

The introduction of the constitutional complaint is significant, and the fact that it is through this procedure that the issue of ensuring the enforcement of the rights enshrined in the Fundamental Law is most often raised. The practice of the Constitutional Court is case-by-case, particularly because of the nature of the constitutional complaint. The degree of activity of the Constitutional Court varies from one fundamental right to another and from one subject to another.

As the Fundamental Law does not specifically provide for the question of horizontal effect, the Constitutional Court determines the relevant constitutional aspects to be applied in the case practice of the courts, which the courts must consider in order to interpret the case in accordance with the Fundamental Law. All these factors mean that it takes a very long time for the constitutional requirements to be established in a given area.

In the practice of the Constitutional Court, therefore, the individual groups of cases must be distinguished, and within them the horizontal effect can be examined, because within the group of cases the Constitutional Court consistently refers to its previous findings. However, the fact that it defines the not always concrete – and often very abstract – aspects of constitutional law on a case-by-case basis makes the development of the case-law of the Court difficult and slow.

Furthermore, there are cases where the Constitutional Court only requires the ordinary court to have some form of fundamental right assessment taken into consideration, while there are also cases where it clearly requires a necessity-proportionality test to be constitutional. In some cases, it also reviews the criteria and the result of the balancing exercise, i.e. it leads to unconstitutionality if it was not carried out by the ordinary court in the way and with the result that would have been the case if the Constitutional Court had been involved. The problem with this third solution is that, in the event that the Constitutional Court reviews the fundamental rights assessment, its criteria and its outcome, it cannot in fact avoid becoming a super-court, since it may change one aspect of the ordinary court's interpretation of the law and thus impose a different result from the one that the ordinary court has arrived at, taking into account the constitutional aspects.

In sum, it can be concluded that the horizontal effect of the Fundamental Law is not a constitutional concept that can be evaluated on its own, since whether it generates forward-looking results in the field of legal protection depends fundamentally on the positive legal content that the Constitutional Court enforces when implementing the Fundamental Law and the method of interpretation that the Constitutional Court expects to be applied. A key question may be whether the Constitutional Court can consistently leave the application of the necessity-proportionality test to the ordinary courts or whether it also holds the courts to account for the outcome of the constitutional balancing exercise. In the latter case, which appears only sporadically in the case law of the Constitutional Court, the Constitutional Court would inevitably become a super-court, which it does not consider desirable. The introduction of the constitutional complaint could therefore be a step forward in the development of legal protection (we can see that constitutional concerns are mostly, but not exclusively, addressed in private litigation through the constitutional complaint procedure), but it requires the development of a very careful and considered constitutional court practice to ensure that the doctrine of horizontal effect, as a constitutional concept in a constitutional democracy, does not become a unilateral control of the interpretation of the law by ordinary courts dictated by the constitutional majority. This is particularly important in Hungary because, as I have shown, the case law is very uncertain and varies from case to case, and in its present form it does not represent a point of reference for the courts, so the increased exposure of ordinary law to constitutional court decisions has a rather negative effect on the legal certainty derived from the rule of law. For all these reasons, I would be cautious today with the *de lege ferenda* proposal formulated in my monograph published in 2011, because although the theoretical and normative considerations are still valid today, the practical advantages of horizontal effect and the use of constitutional complaints for the purpose of legal development are hardly visible in the current constitutional environment.

5. FROM CRISIS TO CRISIS. HUNGARIAN CONSTITUTIONAL REVIEW IN THE EUROPEAN SPACE[1]

There is good reason to believe that regional or global problems of recent years, such as the pandemic, the migration crisis, the financial crisis, Brexit, the climate crisis, the surrounding war, etc., have had an impact on the practice of constitutional courts. It is clear that in their judgments, constitutional courts have also had to take increasing account of the social and economic context, which is full of obstacles. The legal model of constitutional adjudication, as I explained in the introduction to this volume, is based on a basic state of constitutional democracy, i.e. the experience of the past decades does not necessarily offer well-tested solutions to crises, emergencies, and political and economic constraints, or to the limits within which constitutional principles, rights and values can be enforced in these situations. The question is how constitutional courts can maintain both their identity and their adaptability in this situation, how their function, their tasks, powers and their practice will change, whether they will remain constitutional courts in the classic sense of the word, according to the legal model, or whether crises will also cause fundamental changes in the institutional system. In the following chapter, I will also analyse the functioning of the Hungarian Constitutional Court using a comparative method in order to see whether we are talking about particular problems. What are the European trends in the changes in the practice of the Constitutional Court? What are the benchmarks for Hungary?

In Hungary, the practice of the Constitutional Court in the 1990s, following the democratic change of regime, was markedly activist, i.e. the Court interpreted its powers very broadly and was also characterised by interpretative activism. In general, this is true even if many analyses suggest that this activism was more prevalent in fundamental rights cases, while the body was more restrained in matters of state

[1] The chapter draws in large part on Szente, Zoltán – Gárdos-Orosz, Fruzsina: "Constitutional courts under pressure – An assessment", in Szente, Zoltán – Gárdos-Orosz, Fruzsina (eds.): *New Challenges to Constitutional Adjudication in Europe,* London, Routledge, 2018, 291–312; Szente, Zoltán – Gárdos-Orosz, Fruzsina: "Judicial deference or political loyalty?", in Szente, Zoltán – Gárdos-Orosz, Fruzsina (eds.): *New Challenges to Constitutional Adjudication in Europe,* London, Routledge, 2018, 89–110.

organisation.[2] The Constitutional Court has also defined new methods of interpretation, for example the general construction of fundamental rights protection, the necessity-proportionality test, which is still in force today, and the yardsticks relating to other fundamental rights or constitutional principles.[3]

In each case, the Constitutional Court has always borne in mind the need to decide the question raised by the petition, and if the Constitution did not give precise guidance, it has decided in the spirit of the Constitution. It did not invoke lack of jurisdiction even when (as in the case of the death penalty) there was a strong dispute under the Constitution as to whether the constitutional dispute could be decided by constitutional interpretation. Thus, in the 1990s, the Constitutional Court interpreted its jurisdiction broadly, including the politically sensitive social and economic issues of constitutionality.

However, the new parliamentary majority, the constituent power in 2011, envisaged a different kind of constitutional court. Although such ideas were echoed during the constitution-making process, the Fundamental Law did not abolish the Constitutional Court, nor did it transfer the constitutional function and the tasks that go with it to the Curia and the ordinary courts.

In 2010, the Constitutional Court's powers were severely limited by the constitutional majority, which essentially eliminated the possibility of constitutional review of central budget laws. The number of members of the Constitutional Court increased from 11 to 15, but the status of the constitutional court judges remained essentially the same. Some of the standards set by the Fundamental Law for the Constitutional Court, such as the general test of limitation of fundamental rights, have been codified in the Fundamental Law [in Article I (3)], while in 2013, with the Fourth Amendment to the Fundamental Law, the previous Constitutional Court decisions were repealed. Although the restructuring of the Constitutional Court's powers by the Fundamental Law and the Act on the Constitutional Court, the new rules on the election of constitutional judges or the repeal of previous decisions have been done in a very controversial way, there

[2] Halmai, Gábor: "The Hungarian Approach to Constitutional Review: The End of Activism? The First Decade of the Hungarian Constitutional Court", in Sadurski, Wojciech (ed.): *Constitutional Justice, East and West. Democratic Legitimacy and Constitutional Courts in Post-Communist Europe in a Comparative Perspective,* Hague – London, Kluwer Law International, 2002, 189–211; Schwartz, Herman: *The Struggle for Constitutional Justice in Post-Communist Europe,* Chicago, University of Chicago Press, 2000.

[3] In the Hungarian literature, the term "judicial activism" refers to the court's efforts to extend its own jurisdiction, while "interpretive activism" refers to the practice of the court's inclusion of extra-constitutional sources in its reasoning. On the interpretative practice of the Constitutional Court, see Szente, Zoltán: "Breaking and Making Constitutional Rules – The Constitutional Effects of Financial Crisis in Hungary", in Contiades, Xenophon (ed.): *Constitutions in the Global Financial Crisis. A Comparative Analysis,* Farnham, Ashgate, 2013; Jakab, András – Fröhlich, Johanna: "The Constitutional Court of Hungary", in Jakab, András – Dyevrea, Arthur – Itzcovich, Giulio (eds.): *Comparative Constitutional Reasoning,* Cambridge, Cambridge University Press, 2017.

is no doubt that the Constitutional Court has, by and large, retained its constitutional position, as described in detail in the introductory chapter of this volume: by the letters of the Fundamental Law.

The Fundamental Law contained a number of provisions, which were intended to influence practice as a principle of interpretation. As I have explained in the third part of this book, Articles N) and R) of the Fundamental Law, or even Article I (3), were all intended to limit the interpretative practice of the Constitutional Court. The abolition of the *actio popularis* and the reorganisation of jurisdiction have also been discussed above, and I have also shown how this has affected the number of cases coming within each jurisdiction, i.e. how the Constitutional Court has turned towards ordinary court review, in parallel with the reduction in the intensity of review against legislative acts of the legislative and executive branches.[4]

However, in addition to institutional and political changes, I was also curious about the external influences, the "social problems" that shaped the constitution-making process. My assumption was that political changes and the resulting institutional, jurisdictional and procedural changes are often formulated as a response to changes in the social, economic or even natural environment. In order to understand the complexities of the functioning of the constitutional order, it is also worth examining whether the institutional and legal changes that we see are not due to legal responses to specific societal challenges. Could the end of the earlier activism on fundamental rights and the narrowing of jurisprudence on the limitation of public power and judicial constitutional protection in general be due to a changed social, economic, technological or natural environment?

5.1. Changes in the practice of the Constitutional Court in the context of the economic crisis, the migration crisis, the fight against terrorism, national security and the pandemic

In the past ten to fifteen years, before the 2020 COVID-19 crisis, constitutional debates in Hungary that usually accompany the extraordinary situation were quite rare. The crises may have affected the country sometimes less severely as other countries, as has been the case e.g. with the migration crisis, or terrorist threats, but sometimes the discussions on the special authorisations were simply not very

4 For a further detailed analysis of recent cases, see Gárdos-Orosz, Fruzsina: "Alkotmánybíróság 2010–2015", in Jakab, András – Gajduschek, György (eds.): *A magyar jogrendszer állapota 2010–2015,* Budapest, MTA TK Jogtudományi Intézet, 2016, 442–479. For an overview of the transition, see Gárdos-Orosz, Fruzsina: "The Hungarian constitutional court in transition: from actio popularis to constitutional complaint", *Acta Juridica Hungarica,* 2012/4, 302–315.

intensive. However, the effects have undoubtedly been the formal justification for the introduction of certain legal changes to the constitutional order and especially to the constitutional court's functions, powers or jurisprudence in general, in the form of constitution-making, legislation or constitutional court decisions, which, building on and by smaller elements, have fundamentally reshaped the constitutional order.

5.1.1. The standards of fundamental rights protection in normalcy and in emergency in Hungary

In Hungary, the main lines of human rights protection were introduced in the democratic transition of 1989-1990.[5] The Constitutional Court of Hungary, operating from 1 January 1990, had a major role in elaborating on the rules that were agreed by the parties and adopted in the constitutional text and in further legislation consented to by the first democratically elected Parliament. The Fundamental Law, adopted in 2011 by the two-thirds majority in the National Assembly of the Fidesz–KDNP (Orbán) Government, preserved the conceptual considerations of the former Constitution and, as to the rules on the scope, objectives and limitations of human rights protection, it adopted very similar if not identical wordings. Although in 2013 the Fourth Amendment to the Fundamental Law declared all Constitutional Court decisions that were issued before 2012 ineffective, and in spite of the constantly changing practice of fundamental rights protection, especially with regard to certain rights, interestingly enough, the doctrine itself or at least the main lines of the doctrine did not change, but were rather colored by for example compulsory elements of constitutional interpretation or the change in fundamental rights enforcement measures.[6] In this subchapter, I will describe the main elements of the standards of fundamental rights protection in normalcy and in emergency in Hungary in order to give basis for further discussion on the jurisprudence in crisis situation. My main argument is that the emergency standards of human rights protection are not only underdeveloped in the Hungarian legal system, even though the development has been in progress since 2015, but are also in contradiction with the main undertakings of the constitutional state in relation to the greatest possible, guaranteed protection of human rights.

[5] This chapter uses an English translation of Gárdos-Orosz, Fruzsina: "Az alapvető jogok korlátozása", in Jakab, András (ed.): *Az Alkotmány kommentárja,* Budapest, Századvég 2009, and is a revised short version of the chapter: Gárdos-Orosz, Fruzsina: "The normative standards of human rights protection in normalcy and in emergency in Hungary", in Florczak, Monika – Gárdos-Orosz, Fruzsina – Wator, Jan Malir – Steuer, Max (eds.): *Emergencies and human rights protection in the Visegrad countries,* Routledge, 2024 (forthcoming).

[6] I wrote extensively about this in Gárdos-Orosz, Fruzsina: "Constitutional interpretation in Hungary", in Gárdos-Orosz, Fruzsina – Szente, Zoltán (eds.): *Constitutional interpretation in the Populist Regimes in Europe and Beyond,* Routledge, 2021.

5.1.1.1. The history of fundamental rights protection in Hungary

A human rights standard similar to the one contained in the Constitution after the 1989 democratic transition of the country from socialism to constitutional democracy first appeared in Hungary in the preamble of *Act I of 1946 on the Form of the Hungarian State* (Small Constitution).[7] The text of this norm of the first democratic constitution after the Second World War, which never became fully effective and which was fast overruled by the 1949 Stalinist constitution, stipulated that the state shall guarantee the natural and inalienable rights of man to the citizens of the Republic of Hungary. An exemplary list of rights was drawn up and a general equality clause was introduced, ensuring that rights are exercised equally and without discrimination. In addition, there was a guarantee that a citizen could only be deprived of his rights through legal proceedings. The period from 1946 to 1949 (the liquidation of democratic parties, electoral fraud, elections brought forward by force, etc.) destroyed democratic aspirations. In 1949, *Act XX of 1949 on the Constitution of the Hungarian People's Republic* was adopted, which formally remained the constitution (but with significant amendments after 1989) until 31 December 2011. At the time of its creation, this act did not provide for the protection of fundamental rights.[8] The constitutional rules on rights were introduced into the Constitution at the level of declaration with the 1972 constitutional amendment,[9] but this did not represent a significant change in the content of the protection of fundamental rights compared to the previous period, as the party-state's attention was not focused on the protection of rights. That turn had to wait until the 1989 democratic revolution under the rule of law. It was then that the current system of

---

7 "The Republic shall guarantee to the citizens of the Republic the natural and inalienable rights of man, and to the Hungarian people the right to orderly coexistence and peaceful cooperation with other peoples. In particular, the natural and inalienable rights of citizens are: personal liberty, the right to a human life free from oppression, fear and want, freedom of thought and expression, freedom of religion, freedom of association and assembly, the right to property, security of person, work and a decent livelihood, freedom of education and the right to participate in the life of the State and of local government. No citizen shall be deprived of these rights without due process of law, and the Hungarian State shall guarantee these rights to all its citizens equally and without discrimination in any direction, within the framework of the democratic system of the State." For more on this and on the history of the first text, see Sólyom, László: "Az Alkotmány emberi jogi generálklauzulájához vezető út", *Iustum Aequum Salutare*, 2005, 28.

8 The notion of human rights was considered an unscientific vestige of *natural law* by the doctrine of the time, and was replaced by the term "civil rights". This socialist conception (which confused two problems, i.e. 1. natural rights vs. positivist fundamental rights, and 2. fundamental rights for all people vs. fundamental rights for citizens only) continued to exist for some time after the 1989–90 regime change. For a critical discussion of the socialist doctrine in question and its survival, see Jakab, András: "A szocializmus jogdogmatikai hagyatékának néhány eleméről", *Iustum Aequum Salutare*, 2007, 189, 202–203.

9 *Act I of 1972 amending Act XX of 1949 and on the unified text of the Constitution of the Hungarian People's Republic.*

fundamental rights protection was established, which is not just a declaration, but a real state guarantee, backed by guarantees and an institutional basis, to ensure that people can exercise their fundamental rights in the way in which they are entitled to under the constitution.[10]

It was during the regime change, when the requirement of respect and protection of human rights was formulated, that the legislator created the legal basis, the consistent enforcement of which established the protection of human rights in Hungary. *Act XXXI of 1989 amending the Constitution,* which provided for a complete revision of the former Socialist constitution stated in Article 8: "(1) The Republic of Hungary recognises the inviolable and inalienable fundamental rights of man, and the respect and protection of these rights shall be the primary duty of the State. (2) Rules concerning fundamental rights and duties may be established only by an Act of the Constitution. (3) The exercise of a fundamental right may be subject only to restrictions laid down by a constitutional law which are necessary for the protection of the security of the State, internal order, public safety, public health, public morals or the fundamental rights and freedoms of others. (4) The fundamental rights laid down in Articles 54–56, 57(2)–(4), 60, 66–69 and 70/E may not be restricted or suspended even in times of emergency, state of emergency or danger."

It became an important constitutional guarantee of fundamental rights and duties that the rules governing them could only be enacted by a qualified two-thirds majority, i.e. by a unanimous vote of a two-thirds majority of all the deputies,[11] in so-called constitutional acts. The aim was to ensure that restrictions on fundamental rights could be imposed under the strictest conditions, in accordance with international conventions. In addition, the constitutional amendment specified in detail those fundamental rights that could not be restricted, even in exceptional situations.

However, the rule that only a constitutional act could regulate fundamental rights made governance very difficult, as the Antall Government did not have a two-thirds majority in parliament. This situation led to Decision 4/1990. (III. 4.) AB, which made it a constitutional requirement that rules on fundamental rights and duties must always be regulated in a constitutional act regardless of their content. In the end, however, as part of the MDF–SZDSZ (Hungarian Democratic Forum and Alliance of Free Democrats – Hungarian Liberal Party) pact between the two then most significant democratic parties, the category of constitutional act was abolished by constitutional amendment. After this amendment, the Constitution required the unanimous vote of a two-thirds majority of the members present (i.e. not all of them) only for legislation affecting a fundamental right in certain most

[10] For a summary of the history of human and civil rights in Hungary before 1949, see Sári, János: *Alkotmányjog II. Alapjogok,* Budapest, Osiris, 2004, 25–27.

[11] Article 10 (3) of the *Act XXXI of 1989 amending the Constitution.* This majority is called a qualified two-thirds majority; see the terminology developed in the commentary to Article 34 (2).

important cases, such as politically sensitive issues, where the high level consensus is important.[12]

Following the first free elections, the so-called general restriction clause of the Constitution was also affected[13] by the introduction of the concept of 'the essential content of fundamental rights' *(Wesensgehalt),* following the German model, in addition to the emphasis on the importance of procedural guarantees of constitutionality[14] and the abolition of the list of specific grounds of public goods/interests for the limitation of fundamental rights.

The Fundamental Law that entered into force on 1 January 2012 stipulates in part Freedom and responsibility, in Article I: "(1) The inviolable and inalienable fundamental rights of MAN must be respected. It shall be the primary obligation of the State to protect these rights. (2) Hungary shall recognise the fundamental individual and collective rights of man. (3) The rules for fundamental rights and obligations shall be laid down in an Act of Parliament. A fundamental right may only be restricted to allow the effective use of another fundamental right or to protect a constitutional value, to the extent absolutely necessary, proportionate to the objective pursued and with full respect for the essential content of that fundamental right. (4) Fundamental rights and obligations which, by their nature, do not only apply to man shall be guaranteed also for legal entities established by an Act."

The text of the Fundamental Law does not contain the rules that apply to the special legal order human rights protection. It is placed in a separate part of the Fundamental Law, which regulates the special legal order.

Article 52: "(1) During the period of special legal order, the application of the Fundamental Law shall not be suspended. (2) During the period of special legal order, the exercise of fundamental rights, except for the fundamental rights provided for in Articles II and III, and Article XXVIII (2) to (6), may be suspended, or may be restricted beyond the extent specified in Article I (3). (3) During the period of special legal order, the Government shall be obliged to take every measure to guarantee the continuous operation of the National Assembly. (4) During the period of special legal order, the operation of the Constitutional Court shall not be restricted. During the period of special legal order, the Government shall be obliged to take every measure to guarantee the continuous operation of the Constitutional Court. (5) The detailed rules to be applied during the period of special legal order shall be laid down in a cardinal Act."

---

12 On this, see in detail Sólyom, László: "Az Alkotmány emberi jogi generálklauzulájához vezető út", *Iustum, Aequum, Salutare,* 2005, 48.

13 For a summary of constitutional amendments and new constitutional concepts, see Kukorelli, István (ed.): *Alkotmányjog I.,* Budapest, Osiris, 2007, 70–73.

14 Tóth, Attila Gábor: "Az eljárási alkotmányosság tartalma", *Fundamentum,* 2004/3, 5–33.

5.1.1.2. What is a fundamental right in normalcy and in emergency in Hungary?

According to the ruling constitutional doctrine in Hungary, the constitution is the foundation of the protection of fundamental rights. Hungary recognises the fundamental rights of man: the constitution thus declares that these rights exist independently of the state. The state does not only recognise these rights, but also respects and actively protects them. This conception of rights follows international and European human rights standards:[15] the meaning of entitlement is that the state has a special obligation to justify any derogation from the guarantee of these rights.[16]

A fundamental right is, therefore, a group of human rights that are recognised as fundamental rights in national constitutions and international conventions, and thus become parts of the substantive law.[17] The guarantee of fundamental rights in written constitutions consists of two phases: on the one hand, fundamental rights must be enshrined in a constitutional act and, on the other, the effective institutional guarantee of these rights must be ensured. Therefore, modern constitutions no longer only solemnly declare fundamental rights, but also provide for the means and methods of protecting them.[18] The Hungarian Fundamental Law contains fundamental rights, including fundamental rights and constitutional rights, duties, constitutional values and objectives.

Fundamental rights are enforceable, and although originally the right holder could only claim their enforcement against the state, today constitutional law thinking increasingly calls for fundamental rights to be enforceable in certain private, horizontal legal relationships as well.[19] However, fundamental rights do not generally imply unlimited rights and freedoms. Most rights can be limited; the criteria for limitation are either contained in the text of constitutions and/or in the principles formulated by constitutional court practice. The content of human rights as protected by the state can be understood by considering the fundamental rights in the constitution together with the possibilities for limiting them.

The declaration of the inviolability and inalienability of fundamental rights is a legacy of *Act I of 1946* and was inspired by international treaties. The Round Table negotiators at the time of the change of regime went back to this document to settle debts relating to respect for human rights.[20]

---

15 Klein, Eckhart: "Az alapjogok meghatározása az alkotmányban" in Ádám, Antal (ed.): *Alkotmányfejlődés és jogállami gyakorlat,* Budapest, Hanns Seidel Alapítvány, 1994, 67.

16 Dworkin, Ronald: *Taking Rights Seriously: With a New Appendix, a Response to Critics,* Duckworth, 1977, 191.

17 Halmai, Gábor – Tóth, Gábor Attila (eds.): *Emberi jogok,* Budapest, Osiris, 2003, 28–29.

18 Pikler, Kornél: *A bourzsoá alkotmánybíráskodás,* Budapest, Közgazdasági és Jogi Könyvkiadó, 1965, 212–213.

19 See Sajó, András – Uitz, Renáta: *The Constitution in Private Relations,* Eleventh Publishing, 2006; Sajó, András (ed.): *Alkotmányosság a magánjogban,* Complex, 2006.

20 Sólyom, László: "Az Alkotmány emberi jogi generálklauzulájához vezető út", *Iustum Aequum*

In the French Revolutionary Declaration *(Déclaration des droits de l'homme et du citoyen)*, the inalienability of rights originally meant only that a person could not renounce his/her rights. The concept is historically and politically mainly declarative, yet it also carries fundamental positive legal content. The terms inviolability and inalienability derive from the philosophy of human rights and have a positive constitutional meaning, referring to the validity of human rights. The conceptual pair can be understood as meaning that fundamental rights are not at the disposal of either the constitution-making authority or the legislator.

In emergency situations, the concept of fundamental rights remains the same as it is not repeated in part V on the special legal order in the Fundamental Law. Certainly, it would be strange to question the inalienable nature of these rights. The Fundamental Law allows alteration from the general close of restriction, but not from the general provision that defines the task of the state in fundamental rights protection. This means that, if we examine the legal text that although a full suspension of certain rights (almost all of them) becomes possible in times of a special legal order, the task of the state to handle fundamental rights protection as a primary task does not change. Furthermore, the notion of fundamental rights with the above attributes should also be observed. It appears to be a full contradiction to the first, but the temporal nature of emergency situations might ease this contraction, if we claim that the full restriction, the suspension of the state protection of a specific right serves its greater protection in the long run.

5.1.1.3. Content of the state obligation to protect rights

The strictest liberal conception of the state holds that the state only has a duty of restraint in relation to fundamental rights; the point is that the organs of the state should not violate fundamental rights by their conduct. The more modern constitutional conception holds that the state must also actively ensure the protection of fundamental rights. The institutional conception of fundamental rights assumes that the protection of fundamental rights must permeate the entire legal system. This theory sees the creation of a comprehensive institutional system as a guarantee of individual fundamental rights protection. In Hungary, the Fundamental Law establishes the obligation to respect and protect the rights of individuals, but in addition, according to the practice of the Constitutional Court, the state has an objective obligation to protect institutions, which is not a subjective legal protection of rights, but an institutional protection.

According to the Fundamental Law, the State respects the fundamental rights of the people. This means that state organs exercising public authority, that is to say, the duty bearers of fundamental rights, may not, by active or passive conduct, un-

Salutare, 2005, 43. According to Sólyom, this formulation also quotes the Convention *(inherent righs)* and definitely refers to the roots of natural law. The wording of Article 8 of the Constitution also corresponds to the Grundgezets declaration, but there is no evidence that this was used as a model.

constitutionally restrict the fundamental rights of those entitled to them. There has been a discrepancy in this doctrine since 2019 when state organs became entitled to launching a constitutional complaint according to Article 27 of the Act CLI on the Constitutional Court, by an amendment, as holders of certain fundamental rights before the courts as legal persons.

Respect guaranteed by the state also means non-interference. In this case, it means that the State, acting on its own interests, does not interfere with the system of relations between persons and does not regulate their behaviour. This does not mean that the State does not protect the individual from having her fundamental rights restricted by another person, but merely that the State does not interfere in the life and relations between private and legal persons in a way that restricts the fundamental rights of one or both parties.

The Constitutional Court has deduced from the duty to protect that, in addition to the classical constitutional content, the duty to abstain, the state also has an active duty to protect in the area of guaranteeing fundamental rights.[21]

The exercise of fundamental rights requires, to some extent, the active behaviour of the state. This means that the realisation of citizens' substantive rights requires the State to establish and maintain a system of institutions,[22] which includes, firstly, the creation of normative provisions applicable to the same life situation, and, secondly, the organisational system that these provisions create.

In short, we can say that the objective institutional protection aspect of certain fundamental rights is also a constitutional value, which cannot be enforced as a subjective right, but which the state is obliged to ensure. There are, therefore, no constitutional values behind the Constitution that are separate from it; the objective and subjective aspects of fundamental rights can be called constitutional values, or dynamic values, for each fundamental right and the system together [Decision 47/2007. (VII. 3.) AB].

Article I of the Fundamental Law defines the protection of fundamental rights as a primary duty. This is not a declaration but a guiding principle of constitutional democracy that should apply in emergency situations in the special legal orders as well. For example, it follows from this primary duty that, even when the Constitutional Court – creating a coherent system of protection of fundamental rights – expands the detailed rules for the restriction of fundamental rights, or when the Constitution regulates the standards for states of emergency, it recognises that the most important duty of the state is to respect and protect fundamental rights. Primacy in this case, therefore, means that all other considerations – the public interests and organisation of the State – can only prevail if they do not prevent the State from fulfilling its primary duty. The fact that the protection of fundamental

---

21 Sajó, András: *Az önkorlátozó hatalom,* Budapest, Közgazdasági és Jogi Könyvkiadó – MTA Állam- és Jogtudományi Intézet, 1995, 349–350.

22 Farkas, Zoltán: "Az intézmény fogalma, fedezete és funkcionalitása", *Miskolci Jogi Szemle,* 2007/2, 33–55.

rights is the primary duty of the State therefore means that fundamental rights are formulated as core values of the legal system[23] and that constitutional considerations concerning the effectiveness of the organisation of the State are secondary to the protection of fundamental rights.

The Constitutional Court has deduced from the same provision on the rule of law that the state must enable the most favourable exercise of fundamental rights [Decision 34/1992. (VI. 1.) AB, ABH 1992, 192, 201]. If the most favourable exercise of fundamental rights is to be made possible, and this is the primary duty of the State, then the system of criteria for limiting fundamental rights developed by the Constitutional Court must comply with this constitutional norm in all situations.

5.1.1.4. The test of fundamental rights restrictions

In the Fundamental Law we find the formal and substantive criteria for the restriction of fundamental rights. By formal criteria, we mean the procedural rules, namely that the rules on fundamental rights and obligations are laid down by law. Parliament shall enact a law. A law is a statute which is subordinate to the Fundamental Law in the legislative hierarchy and which is adopted by Parliament with a majority support, varying according to the content of the legislation, in accordance with a specific procedural order. The Fundamental Law requires a two-thirds majority to regulate certain fundamental rights.

The substantive requirement is that a law may not restrict the essential content of a fundamental right. The meaning of essential content, which is the inviolable core of the regulation of fundamental rights, has been defined in a less general way in relation to the individual fundamental rights. However, the notion of essential content does not play a decisive role in the control of norms; like the German Constitutional Court, the Hungarian Constitutional Court has rather considered other, necessity-proportionality criteria of restriction as the guiding principle for its analysis.[24]

The test for the protection of fundamental rights, which can be called general, has developed without major controversy. The Constitutional Court has developed the content of fundamental rights and the yardstick for their limitation following a functional and formalised constitutional interpretation.[25] The most complex and stringent version of the standard (also known as the test or method) is the following: the state may resort to the means of restricting a fundamental right if the protection or exercise of another fundamental right and freedom or the protection of other constitutional values cannot be achieved in any other way. Thus, for a restriction of a fundamental right to be constitutional, it is not in itself sufficient that it is imposed in order to protect another fundamental right or freedom or in order to

[23] Pokol, Béla: "Az alapjogok és az »alapjogi« bíráskodás", *Társadalmi Szemle*, 1991/5, 56.

[24] For a summary of the development and differentiation of the criteria, see Sólyom, László: *Az alkotmánybíráskodás kezdetei Magyarországon*, Budapest, Osiris, 2001, 395–441.

[25] See Holló, András: *Az alkotmányvédelem kialakulása Magyarországon*, Miskolc, Bíbor, 1997, 172.

achieve another constitutional objective, but it must also meet the requirement of proportionality: the importance of the objective pursued and the seriousness of the harm caused to the fundamental right must be in proportion to each other. The legislator must choose the least restrictive means of achieving the objective in question. A restriction of the content of a right is unconstitutional if it is arbitrary and without compelling reason, or if the severity of the restriction is disproportionate to the objective pursued [Decision 30/1992. (V. 26.) AB, ABH 1992, 169, 171].[26] Although the main lines of the standard of review were soon established, there is still no consistently validated Constitutional Court practice as regards the details, and applies the tests with minor modifications. The variations are partly due to the fact that the Constitutional Court applies the general test with conceptually different degrees of rigour to different fundamental rights.[27]

The rule of the Fundamental Law on the essential content is fundamental because it is capable of giving effect to human dignity in the spirit of the general rule of equality.[28] The criterion of the inalienability of the essential content of the former Hungarian Constitution was transposed by the codifiers of the Hungarian Constitution based on a German model. Article 19 (2) of the German Basic Law contains the same rule.[29] However, German case law has not developed this provision in such a way that it forms the basis for the protection of fundamental rights.[30] The Hungarian Constitutional Court took a similar position on this issue. The substantial content, the substantive analysis of fundamental rights as a group, is almost not dealt with by the Constitutional Court at all, but the meaning of the substantial content is examined for each fundamental right.

The reason for the different positions may also be that the Constitutional Court did not clearly distinguish between the case of a simple conflict of fundamental rights and the case of a conflict of fundamental rights that cannot be resolved by the necessity-proportionality test.[31] The essential content is not compromised up to a certain point in a necessary and proportionate restriction of fundamental rights. A genuine conflict between fundamental rights arises when the conflict cannot be resolved without affecting the essential content of one of the fundamental rights.[32]

---

[26] Decision 2/1990. (II. 18.) AB, Decision 20/1990. (X. 4.) AB, Decision 7/1991. (II. 28.) AB, etc. [Decision 22/1992. (IV. 10.) AB, ABH 1992, 122, 123].

[27] For more on the differentiation of the general measure, see Sólyom, László: *Az alkotmánybíráskodás kezdetei Magyarországon*, Budapest, Osiris, 2001, 401.

[28] Bragyova, András: *Az új alkotmány egy koncepciója*, Budapest, Közgazdasági és Jogi Könyvkiadó - MTA Állam- és Jogtudományi Intézet, 1995, 69.

[29] Which has also been adopted in Article 33 (1) (b) of the South African Subsection.

[30] 22 BVergE 180, 220. See Currie, David P.: *The Constitution of the Federal Republic of Germany*, University of Chicago Press, 1994, 306–307.

[31] According to Tamás Győrfi, this is partly why the passage on essential content in the Constitution is meaningless. Győrfi, Tamás: *Az Alkotmánybíráskodás politikai karaktere. Értekezés a magyar Alkotmánybíróság első tíz évéről*, Budapest, INDOK, 2001, 90.

[32] See Zucca, Lorenzo: *Constitutional Dilemmas*, OUP, 2007, 52–55.

The Constitutional Court applies the necessity-proportionality test to the constitutionality of the restriction of the rights that are fundamental rights. It can only alter from it if one of the special legal orders is declared according to the Fundamental Law. In this case, however, the test does not apply, or applies only in the case if human dignity or the other rights which are enshrined in the Fundamental Law special legal order are affected by the restriction. This is why it has a special importance that in the exceptional situation from financial crisis to migration to Covid-19 pandemic when the Fundamental Law allows to declare the special legal order and which state institution is responsible to decide about the declaration of it.

Contrary to its name, the necessity-proportionality test has three main elements. The first element, the legitimate legislative aim, the constitutionally acceptable justification for the restriction and the logical relationship between the aim and the means (legal provision), is generally examined by the Constitutional Court within the framework of the necessity element, with or without a specific designation. Under the second element, necessity, the Constitutional Court understands the inevitability of the restriction, the existence of a compelling reason. The third step of the test is proportionality, where the Constitutional Court checks whether the restriction was proportionate to the importance of the aim pursued by the restriction.[33] In theory, the steps are equivalent, meaning that unconstitutionality can be established at any stage of the analysis – if the legislation does not meet one of the criteria, it is unconstitutional. Legislation can only be constitutional if, in the course of the constitutionality review, the Constitutional Court is satisfied that the legislation was enacted in pursuit of a legitimate legislative objective, that the legislation was capable of serving that objective, that the rule was strictly necessary to achieve that objective and that it was proportionate to the objective pursued. The Constitutional Court generally examines these elements in turn. If the Constitutional Court finds that the legislation fails at either the first or the second step, the examination is usually discontinued and the unconstitutionality is established.

The constitution in force does not formulate the interests and objectives that may serve as a justification for the restriction of fundamental rights, nevertheless, as the first element of the necessity-proportionality test, the Constitutional Court examines whether there is a constitutionally acceptable justification for the restriction and whether the measure under examination is indeed capable of serving the legitimate legislative objective.

The absence of necessity should be generally justified in two ways in Constitutional Court decisions. If the restriction is inappropriate to achieve the objective, it may not be necessary, or if the legislator's objective can be achieved by other means, it may not be necessary.[34] Therefore, the legislator is obliged to use the least restrictive means suitable for achieving the given objective, because if the restric-

33 This triple-structured study is referred to in the international literature as a "proportionality".

34 Gadó, Gábor: "Alapjogok védelme és korlátozása az Alkotmánybíróság döntéseinek tükrében", *Gazdaság és Jog*, 1994/9, 7.

tion is not suitable for achieving the objective, the fundamental right can be found to be infringed (ABH 1991, 18, 23). According to the principles developed in the 1990s but reinforced after 2010 by the Fundamental Law and never denied by the Constitutional Court after 2012: the state may resort to the last resort of restricting a fundamental right if the protection or enforcement of another right or the protection of other constitutional objectives cannot be achieved in any other way, and the restriction may only be to the extent that is strictly necessary for these purposes (ABH 1991, 22, 25).

This interpretation of necessity is a constant in the Constitutional Court's present doctrinal approach, but in practice the necessity is handled quite loosely, and especially in the special legal order, as I will explain, there is a great deference towards Government action that means that the scope of necessity is quite vague in order to leave room for Government considerations.

The development of proportionality in the constitutional sense is a relatively late development. The term was first established in administrative law, more specifically in German rules on the maintenance of order. There, proportionality meant that police intervention should be limited to the extent necessary to achieve the objective pursued. In order to protect citizens' rights against administrative interference, the principle of the liberal state was introduced. This meant that the power of the state was essentially limited, while the power of the individual was essentially unlimited.[35]

The German constitutional court developed the constitutional standard from the concept of administrative law. As it was developed to assess police action, in my opinion points to the fact that the test is capable to handle extraordinary situations, furthermore, it was developed precisely for the assessment of an extraordinary action. Already in a decision of 11 June 1958,[36] the German Federal Constitutional Court stated that the legislator may only use means to restrict the economy which are proportionate to the objective pursued.[37]

Following the German model, the last step of the constitutional court's examination in Hungarian constitutional law is the proportionality test. Proportionality means that the regulation restricts a fundamental right less than the legislator increases the protection of another fundamental right or constitutional value, i.e. the harm is less than the benefit that can be assessed on the other side. In Decision 20/1990. (X. 4.) AB the Constitutional Court stated and on a doctrinal level this still applies that the constitutionality of norms restricting a fundamental right requires proportionality, i.e. that the importance of the objective to be achieved and the

---

35 Nishihara, Hiroshi: *Constitutional Meaning of the Proportionality Principle in the Face of "Surveillance State"*, www.enelsyn.gr/en/workshops/workshop15(en).htm

36 BVerfGE 7, 377 – "Apothekenurteil".

37 There was some debate about whether a court had the authority to develop such a set of fact-based criteria, but the argument that even at that cost it was worth the legislative scrutiny became persuasive. Nishihara, Hiroshi: *Constitutional Meaning of the Proportionality Principle in the Face of "Surveillance State"*, www.enelsyn.gr/en/workshops/workshop15(en).htm

seriousness of the damage to the fundamental right caused in order to achieve it must be in harmony (ABH 1990, 69, 71).[38] When carrying out the analysis, it is important to take into account that a restrictive provision to be considered against a fundamental right is more serious if it directly serves to enforce and protect another subject's fundamental right, less serious if it protects such rights only by means of an "institution", and less serious if it is only the object of an abstract value.

In the first years of its operation, the Constitutional Court always seemed to make the restriction of fundamental rights subject to increasingly lenient conditions. Later on, in the drafting of each decision, the Constitutional Court has always reverted to different early tests, which is why the general test for the protection of fundamental rights, although identical in content, is still used differently in its wording. The Fundamental Law finally adopted a standard formulation in Article I (3) of the Fundamental Law.

The balancing of fundamental rights, constitutional rights, state objectives and constitutional values is a constitutional power. The fundamental rights in the Fundamental Law are abstract in their wording.[39] This means that their content cannot be extracted, or is difficult to extract, by traditional methods of legal interpretation, hence the need to define criteria for constitutional interpretation is a new enabling tool.[40] However, the balancing exercise is a way for the interpreter of the text to strike a balance between the fundamental rights and to apply the rules to each constitutional question in such a way that the constitutional content is upheld. A clearly traceable method is essential because it provides, in an abstract way, a basis for keeping the reflection within an objective framework.[41] The main dilemma with regard to the emergencies and suboptimal situations in Hungary, including the populist Government, but apart from the problems of the state and law discussed above, the external challenges of the financial crisis, environmental and health crisis, migration etc. whether the so-called necessity and proportionality test can be upheld and will be upheld by the Hungarian Constitutional Court. The deference towards the two-thirds constituent majority does not provoke insistence towards the preservation of this test assessing the constitutionality of the limitation of rights, but on the other hand it gives empowerment to the Constitutional Court

[38] See Balogh, Zsolt – Holló, András (eds.): *Az értelmezett Alkotmány,* Budapest, Magyar Hivatalos Közlönykiadó, 2005, 205.

[39] For a critique of this, see Takács, Albert: "Magyarország alkotmánybírósága tegnap és holnap között", in Ádám, Antal (ed.): *Alkotmányfejlődés és jogállami gyakorlat,* Budapest, Hanns Seidel Alapítvány, 1994, 114. In the case of certain institutions, more detailed regulation would be necessary (criminal procedure, punishments, special restrictions on the right of assembly) rather than declarations of law. Sajó, András: *Az önkorlátozó hatalom,* Budapest, Közgazdasági és Jogi Könyvkiadó – MTA Állam- és Jogtudományi Intézet, 1995, 364.

[40] See, e.g,. Bragyova, András: *Az alkotmánybíráskodás elmélete,* Budapest, Közgazdasági és Jogi Könyvkiadó – MTA Állam- és Jogtudományi Intézet, 1994; Paczolay, Péter (ed.): *Alkotmánybíráskodás és alkotmányértelmezés,* Budapest, ELTE ÁJK, 1995.

[41] Kiss, Barnabás: "Az alapjogok alkotmányi szabályozásának általános kérdései", in Ádám, Antal (ed.): *Alkotmányfejlődés és jogállami gyakorlat,* Budapest, Hanns Seidel Alapítvány, 1994, 140.

to carry out interpretation by balancing according to its proper imaginary of the value of the constitutional provision. Furthermore, these standards apply in international and EU law in different forms and I believe that an open rejection might have serious political connotations as well.

5.1.1.5. Standards of human rights protection in the special legal order

In the former Constitution, Article 8 (4) listed the rights that may not be suspended or restricted even in a state of emergency or a state of danger. These rights include the right to life and human dignity, legal capacity and the rights to liberty, security of person, presumption of innocence and the right to defence, freedom of conscience and religion, the provisions of the Constitution relating to equality, non-discrimination, the rights of the child, minority rights, rights relating to citizenship, and the right to social security and benefits. The formal end of a state of emergency automatically ends all restrictions on fundamental rights.[42] In Article 8 (4), the former Constitution defined the scope of the rights which cannot be restricted or suspended even in special situations. The new Fundamental Law, which entered into force in 2012, continued this tradition of rights restriction in the special legal orders. Article 52 of the Fundamental Law states that during the period of special legal order, the application of the Fundamental Law may not be suspended. During the period of special legal order, the exercise of fundamental rights, except for the fundamental rights provided for in Articles II (human dignity) and III (prohibition of torture), and Article XXVIII (2) to (6) (fundamental procedural rights), may be suspended, or may be restricted beyond the extent specified in Article I (3). The structure and the fundamental considerations in the human rights protection in emergencies has, therefore, been the same since the 1989 democratic transition at the constitutional level.

The Hungarian constitution, the Fundamental Law of 2011, is probably unique in the sense that until November 2022 it recognised six different forms of special legal order, and there are two other kinds of emergencies in effect, the so-called "crisis situation caused by mass immigration"[43] and the "health crisis situation"[44] which are regulated at sub-constitutional level. In fact, there are some other types of possible crisis situations such as energy supply or nuclear crises, but in those cases the crisis management systems are narrowly tailored and the range of tools available are very limited.[45] One of these emergency situations, the so-called state of danger has been declared and extended several times to manage the health crisis caused by the corona virus pandemic. According to the Fundamental Law, this

[42] *States of Emergency: Their Impact on Human Rights,* International Commission of Jurists, 1983, 460.

[43] See Articles 80/A–80/K of the Act LXXX of 2007 (on the Asylum).

[44] See Articles 228–254/E of the Act CLIV of 1997 (on the Public Health).

[45] Kádár, Pál – Hoffman, István: "A különleges jogrend és a válságkezelés közigazgatási jogi kihívásai: a »kvázi különleges jogrendek« helye és szerepe a magyar közigazgatásban", *Közjogi Szemle,* 2021/3, 1.

kind of special legal order may be declared by the Government "in the event of a natural disaster or industrial accident endangering life and property, or in order to mitigate its consequences". In case of a state of danger, the Government is endowed with special powers, like introducing emergency measures defined by a so-called cardinal law (a form of parliamentary legislation requiring a two-thirds majority vote of all MPs present), adopting decrees by means of which it may suspend the application of certain legislative acts, derogate from the provisions of acts, and taking other extraordinary measures. That constitutional empowerment is, however, not unlimited. The exceptional powers can be exercised only within the framework specified in a cardinal law and, on the other hand, only such extraordinary measures can be taken as are necessary to eliminate the consequences of an emergency. Moreover, the emergency decrees of the Government can remain in force beyond 15 days only with the consent of the National Assembly. The state of danger can be terminated only by the Government, which is, in fact, a constitutional obligation since it is the duty of the Government to cease the special legal order "if the conditions for its promulgation no longer exist". Emergency decrees[46] issued by the Government at the time of a state of danger automatically cease on the same day when the special legal order is terminated, even if the Parliament has previously agreed to extend their temporal effect. Nevertheless, the National Assembly may adopt a law with the same content as the repealed Government decree(s). According to the Ninth Amendment to the Fundamental Law from 2022, Article 48 of the FL in part Special legal orders states that "Special legal order shall be a state of war, a state of emergency and a state of danger".

The most serious restriction of a fundamental right is the suspension of the fundamental right by the state power. Thus, the possibility of restriction and suspension mean a difference in degree. However, the former Constitution after the democratic transition did not specify which rights may be restricted but not suspended, even in times of emergencies. It was, therefore, up to the legislator and the Government, in addition to the constitutional review by the Constitutional Court, to determine which rights can be completely withdrawn in a given situation within the framework of the Constitution.[47] With regard to the question of the sustention and the restriction, the case remained the same with the text of the Fundamental Law which means the extraordinary power given to the Constitutional Court in this situation.

In the Ninth Amendment of the Fundamental Law we find rules in Article 52 (Common rules which apply to all special legal orders) that "(1) During the period of special legal order, the application of the Fundamental Law may not be suspend-

46 It can be observed that the Fundamental Law does not use the term "emergency decrees" but refers simply to (Government) decrees.

47 Article 15 of the Convention provides for restrictions on fundamental rights in times of qualified situations ("state of emergency"). The text expressly states that derogations from the obligation to protect fundamental rights may be made only "to the extent strictly required by the exigencies of the situation".

ed. (2) During the period of special legal order, the exercise of fundamental rights, except for the fundamental rights provided for in Articles II and III, and Article XXVIII (2) to (6), may be suspended, or may be restricted beyond the extent specified in Article I (3)."

The struggles around the suspendability and the limitation problem remained lively in the Covid-19 jurisprudence of the Hungarian Constitutional Court. The new text of the Fundamental Law did not make it clear if either the full restriction or suspension should have special reasons, when the essential content of the right is limited, or the Government can freely decide between the special restriction and the suspension according to the situation of emergency. In this latter case, do Government rules other than the necessity and proportionality standards decide between the two options in the end? Could we identify any other standards according to the text of the Fundamental Law to measure the Government decision on the special restriction or the suspension?

We must mention Decision 23/2021. (VII. 13.) AB about the general ban on demonstrations. This was the most contested case with five separate opinions. The petitioners were participants or organisers of a pre-announced motoring protest in April and May 2020, during the general ban on gatherings due to the state of danger, and they also raised awareness of the protest on social media. They stayed in their cars with a banner expressing their demands and drove around a roundabout where the rally was to take place, in accordance with the epidemiological regulations, while honking their horns in protest at the crisis management measures. The participants were taken into custody and fined by the police. The constitutional complaint procedures were based on the decisions of the Pest Central District Court in these cases.

The ordinary court in these contested decisions partially reversed the authorities' decisions and reduced the fine. The petitioners complained, however, that the court had classified their action under the restrictive measures adopted in the extraordinary legal regime, although the freedom of expression was lawfully exercised from cars not violating the rules of social distancing and violating traffic rules in a proportionate manner only for the sake of exercising the freedom of expression.

The Constitutional Court explained that the district court had taken into account the fact that the petitioner had announced the event as a public event for the purpose of expressing opinions on public matters. This amounted to a non-lawful assembly under the general assembly ban; therefore, honking and other violations of the traffic rules counted as actions outside the scope of the fundamental rights protection. The Constitutional Court majority opinion emphasised that it is not in a position to evaluate in a state of danger if such a general ban on assemblies is necessary to hinder the spread of the virus. The Constitutional Court, therefore, dismissed the constitutional complaints against the ordinary court's decision.

As to the competence of the Constitutional Court in evaluating Covid-19-related rights restrictions, the Court explicitly further reinforced this approach in a politically sensitive case on mining rights, that its jurisdiction is limited to the examination of whether the emergency legislator had the power to enact the contested provision of the decree. The examination of whether the enactment of a new rule on the exploitation of mining rights, different from the previous one, was expedient, was no longer within the jurisdiction of the Constitutional Court. However, the Constitutional Court examined, on the basis of legislation adopted on appropriate authorisation during a period of emergency, whether the content of the legislation was in conformity with the Fundamental Law and it found it constitutional.[48]

This deferential approach to the review tests was debated in parallel and separate opinions within the court, but even when the Court used stricter tests, the Government decrees and other pandemic related legislation were found equally constitutional.

We can see that although it is a narrower list of rights that are not restrictable under the special legal order, still there is a certain scope where the possibilities of the special limitations are excluded. An example in the Covid-19 case law of the Hungarian Constitutional Court for this rule of exclusion is the case of mandatory vaccination as I will explain later.

The reasoning why certain rights were selected for special protection in emergency situations was not clear in a doctrinal sense either before or after the 2012 adoption of the Fundamental Law. In the explanatory memorandum of the Fundamental Law and that of the Ninth Amendment to the Fundamental Law that reinforced the rules of exception we do not receive any explanation for the narrowing of the list of rights where the special restrictions could be applied or the differences from the limitation closes of the most important international documents such as Article 15 of the ECHR or Article 4 of the Universal Declaration. On the other hand, the exception was clearly applied in the Covid-19 jurisprudence of the Constitutional Court with regard to the protection of human dignity in such a classic case of rights restriction as mandatory vaccination in times of pandemic.

5.1.1.6. Conclusions

In this subchapter, I have described what the main rules of the protection of fundamental rights are in normalcy and in the special legal order in Hungary. I have explained that the major standards did not change with the entering into force of the Fundamental Law. This does not mean that there is no change in the related constitutional text of certain rights but that the standard of the protection, the so-called test preserved its main attributes, in essence remained the same so-called necessity proportionality test in doctrine. I called attention to the fact that another paragraph of the Fundamental Law declares that the protection of the inalienable rights is the primary duty of the state. I argued that although it is possible in the special legal order to suspend or limit rights and although it is not clear if the re-

48 Decision 3152/2022. (IV. 12.) AB.

striction or the suspension prevails in certain cases, finally it will be the principal rules that the state should protect as much rights as possible also in a special legal order. I illustrated, however, with some cases that it is not a well-established doctrine of the Constitutional Court based on the text of the Fundamental Law.

5.1.2. The impact of the economic crisis on constitutional jurisprudence[49]

The practice of the Constitutional Court in the context of the economic crisis has already been briefly discussed above, when I described the functioning and the exercise of jurisdiction of the Constitutional Court. Therefore, I will now only briefly discuss the case-law and then deal specifically with the way in which the reference to the social problem has appeared in the practice of the Constitutional Court.

5.1.2.1. Background

Hungary is an open economy, highly dependent on European and world trends. Hungary has been a member of the European Union since 2004, with GDP growth of around 60-70% of the European average, according to Eurostat. The issue of economic catching-up has always posed problems. Even in 2004, before the economic crisis, the European Commission launched a deficit procedure against Hungary for its long-term unbalanced budget. The onset of the economic crisis in this situation in autumn 2008 had serious consequences: by 2009, GDP had fallen by almost 7%. In response to this, the government adopted an unorthodox economic policy, which tackled the crisis with innovative solutions rather than traditional economic policy instruments.[50] Some of these were at the level of constitutional arrangements, building a state in which state interference in economic competition, centralised economic governance and centralisation of resources played a major role. It was also essential to keep the state in control of sectors of high importance, including by influencing the ownership structure. The system of state aid also changed, and the Hungarian state, seeking to limit EU rules, sought to give preferential treatment to domestic companies, even by introducing special taxes on foreign-owned companies in the banking or telecommunications sectors. Trade turned from the West

[49] For more on this, see the full papers underlying this chapter, Gárdos-Orosz, Fruzsina – Gárdos, Péter: "Az Alkotmánybíróság első határozata a pénzügyi intézmények fogyasztói kölcsönszerződéseiben alkalmazott egyoldalú szerződésmódosítási jogra vonatkozó törvényi szabályozásról", *Jogesetek Magyarázata*, 2015/2, 3–15; Gárdos-Orosz, Fruzsina – Gárdos, Péter: "Az Alkotmánybíróság második határozata a pénzügyi intézmények fogyasztói kölcsönszerződéseiben alkalmazott egyoldalú szerződésmódosítási jogra vonatkozó törvényi szabályozásról", *Jogesetek Magyarázata*, 2016/3, 21–32; Gárdos-Orosz, Fruzsina: "Rendhagyó alkotmányossági mércék az Alkotmánybíróság »devizahiteles« határozataiban", in Gárdos-Orosz, Fruzsina – Szente, Zoltán (eds.): *Jog és politika határán. Alkotmánybíráskodás Magyarországon 2010 után*, Budapest, HVG-ORAC, 2015, 373–409.

[50] On the effectiveness of such arguments for constitutional change, see Pap, András László: *Democratic Decline in Hungary. Law and Society in an Illiberal Democracy*, London, Routledge, 2018.

to the East in the hope of expanding economic links and economic growth, and the public works programme was launched, which the state hoped would lead to higher employment rates.

Almost all similar measures have had a constitutional impact. Among the provisions of the 2011 Fundamental Law, the most interesting from the point of view of economic governance is perhaps Article N) of the Fundamental Law, which states that Hungary shall apply the principle of balanced, transparent and sustainable fiscal management. The Constitutional Court, the courts, local governments and other state bodies are obliged to respect these principles in the performance of their duties. Although there has not yet been a Constitutional Court decision explaining the content of this provision, and the Constitutional Court has not yet referred to it in its reasoning on its own activities and their limits, this provision is perhaps the most striking illustration of the constitutional change in the nature of economic governance. The role of social rights has also changed in relation to Hungary's economy: the Fundamental Law makes it clear that they are not given the status of fundamental rights, and therefore the extent of their protection depends on the performance of the economy.

Although this provision is not identical to the previous protection of fundamental rights, it is similar in that the previous Constitutional Court practice also emphasised – in addition to formulating the scope of protection and the essential content of the rights – which the provision of rights outside the scope of fundamental rights depends on the economic performance of the state. In any case, from a legal policy point of view, it is clearly significant that the Fundamental Law uses a different wording from the text of the former Constitution, by stating that property entails social responsibility, and also limits the budgetary competence of the Parliament by stating that a budget cannot be drawn up which increases the public debt if it already exceeds 50% of GDP.[51] The policy, also reflected in the Fundamental Law, of prioritising centralised regulation of the economy and limiting the powers of individual state institutions was probably not followed by a major professional, social or political debate because in 2011 the shock of the economic crisis seemed to call for new regulation in this area. Some authors have even suggested that the reason for the new approach of the Fundamental Law may be that it was drafted in a period following the economic crisis.[52]

5.1.2.2. Changes in the practice of the Constitutional Court

After the economic crisis, the framework for constitutional review was fundamentally determined by the restriction that the Constitutional Court has essentially no power to conduct constitutional review on issues concerning the central budget. This has led to certain issues not being brought before the Constitutional Court,

[51] Article 36 (4)–(5) of the Fundamental Law.

[52] Chronowski, Nóra – Vincze, Attila: "Two Eras of Hungarian Constitutionalism: From the Rule of Law to Rule by Law", *Hague Journal on the Rule of Law*, 2016/2, 271–289.

because the lack of competence has led to the absence of a corresponding motion. Shortly after this limitation of jurisdiction, although there were still attempts by petitioners to influence the constitutionality of the body's position in borderline situations, and in some cases the Constitutional Court's dogmatic reasoning allowed it to establish jurisdiction even in matters with budgetary implications, the picture has now become clearer and the Constitutional Court does not deal with financially and economically sensitive matters. This is also due to the fact that in cases such as the 98% special tax[53] the Constitutional Court found it unconstitutional,[54] and a two-thirds majority in Parliament made the possibility of imposing such special taxes part of the Fundamental Law by constitutional amendment.[55] The Constitutional Court was then again called upon to take a position on the issue against the will of the government, but this time it took a more restrained position, according to which a rule could be made retroactively for a given tax year, if the tax year had not yet ended.[56] The Constitutional Court thus sought to limit the legislator's room for manoeuvre in even more cases after 2010, when the rule violated fundamental guarantees of the rule of law. This may have been partly due to the fact that the majority of the judges on the panel were long-standing members of the Constitutional Court who did not wish to change their professional position on certain constitutional issues.[57]

One of the most controversial issues in the post-2010 constitutional changes and changes in constitutional court practice has been the reinterpretation of the right to property. Interestingly, the wording on the right to property has not changed much compared to the past.[58] However, the overall impact of the whole regulatory regime of the Fundamental Law has led to markedly different interpretations, both in legislation and in the practice of the Constitutional Court, which examines the constitutionality of legislation. In 2012, the forced integration of cooperative credit institutions caused a stir, and a number of constitutional concerns were raised, but the Constitutional Court found the provision to be appropriate and did not find any violation of the right to property. The government sought to integrate credit

53 In this case, a legal provision was reviewed to allocate resources because the government considered it contrary to good morals to impose a special tax of 98% on the high severance payments that had been agreed and in many cases already paid. In its reasoning, the Constitutional Court invoked the rule of law and, in a bold argument, reverted its jurisdiction to the right to human dignity in the review.

54 Decision 184/2010. (X. 28.) AB.

55 See also Kovács, Kriszta – Tóth, Gábor Attila: "Hungary's Constitutional Transformation", *European Constitutional Law Review,* 2011/2, 183–203.

56 Decision 37/2011. (V. 10.) AB.

57 Szente, Zoltán: "The Interpretive Practice of the Hungarian Constitutional Court: A Critical View", *German Law Journal,* 2013, 1591–1614.

58 Article XIII of the Fundamental Law: "(1) Everyone shall have the right to property and inheritance. Property shall entail social responsibility. (2) Property may only be expropriated exceptionally, in the public interest and in those cases and ways provided for by an Act, subject to full, unconditional and immediate compensation."

institutions in the form of cooperatives because it could control the activities of this sector by acquiring majority ownership. The shareholders saw this provision as a restriction of their right to property, and specifically of certain of their partial rights, and therefore lodged a constitutional complaint.[59] The Constitutional Court's reasoning, on the other hand, was that, although the scope for manoeuvre of the individual credit institutions had obviously been reduced as a result of the integration, their position had been strengthened and the capital behind them had increased, and therefore no infringement of the right to property could be established.

This is the background to the start of the crisis for foreign currency borrowers. The question was how much leeway the Government would give to the banks to improve the position of foreign currency borrowers who were in a very difficult situation. It was obvious that a large number of people and legal entities were in an unfavourable or downright crisis situation because the economic crisis had caused the risky contractual arrangements under which they had taken out loans to become suddenly and heavily burdened in an unpredictable way. The role of the State in such a situation is undoubtedly to mitigate the damage caused by the crisis. The question is who should bear the burden and by what legal means. There was also a consensus among the experts who took different positions on the case that, in this case, legislation, as opposed to the application of the law, was the instrument that could have been used to remedy the problem, which was on a large scale. The question addressed to the Constitutional Court was therefore whether the laws adopted in the case were suitable to achieve the legislative objective pursued and whether the legal restrictions imposed on the credit institutions in order to achieve that objective were necessary and proportionate. In addition, there was of course the question of whether the legal certainty resulting from the rule of law permitted such a regulation, and how and by what constitutional means the State could intervene in contractual relations already concluded.

The Constitutional Court has examined the different stages of the legislation in several cases and even recorded its position in an abstract constitutional interpretation procedure [Decision 8/2014. (III. 20.) AB]. The message of the decision was that the crisis opens up new legal possibilities and requires more lenient constitutional legislation, even if it is not a case of an extraordinary legal order provided for by the Fundamental Law, but simply a case of a social problem requiring specific legislation to solve it. The Constitutional Court's approach to new social problems is clearly illustrated by Decision 34/2014. (IX. 14.) AB, in which it stated that different standards apply when the financial crisis has had a major impact on the country's economy and that, in this situation, it is inevitable that the Government should set long-term objectives to stabilise the economy and use instruments that are capable of achieving this objective.

Even before, in the 1990s, the question was raised whether in a crisis situation, when a social problem becomes acute, it is possible to apply new standards in prac-

[59] Decision 20/2014. (VII. 3.) AB.

tice, and in the case of foreign currency credit loans, the Constitutional Court was not encountering this problem for the first time. For example, in the early 1990s, in Decision 26/1992. (IV. 30.) AB, the Constitutional Court stated in a case concerning trade union property that, as a general principle, it cannot be accepted that in a conflict situation the Constitutional Court may depart from its consistent interpretative practice, but that it may be possible – and the Constitutional Court sought to justify the exception in this situation – to depart from the scope of protection of the right to property on an individual basis in the interests of a legitimate legislative objective, if the legitimate legislative objective justifies this. When the constitutionality of the abolition of early retirement pensions for members of the armed forces[60] was under consideration in the Decision 23/2013. (IX. 25.) AB, the Constitutional Court also acknowledged that the economic crisis and the financial situation of the country may justify such interventions, even if it is a question of fact that those who chose the armed forces as their profession, having been aware of the early retirement rules that had existed for decades, decided to enter the profession and were entitled to an early retirement pension during the period of service.

In another decision, the Constitutional Court had to examine the constitutionality of a piece of legislation containing market management instruments relating to trade in tobacco products.[61] Here, too, the right to property was infringed, and the Constitutional Court held that the right to property did not include the expectation of a tobacconist that he could continue to operate a business, which he had been running for a considerable period under various licences in a legal environment, which made this foreseeable.

The question formulated in the famous decision in Hungarian constitutional law is therefore still valid, i.e. whether it is possible to build the rule of law against the rule of law,[62] i.e. what concessions can be made while preserving constitutionality in the context of the government's crisis management measures.

At the beginning of the 1990s, when the Constitutional Court formulated the concept of the right to property, it was formulated as a material basis for individual autonomy, and thus the scope of protection was much wider than in the case of civil law property. If this interpretation is taken as a starting point, it also means that, in some cases, the legislative environment related to the permanent pursuit of an occupation can be considered as having a direct impact on access to the material basis of individual autonomy. The original interpretation of the right to property[63] has therefore changed fundamentally in that it is now protected in a much narrower sense, namely that of acquired rights or legitimate *expectations*, the latter being explicitly understood in conjunction with the rule of law and legal certainty.

60 Article 14 (1)–(2) of the *Act CLXVII of 2011 on the termination of old-age pensions before the age of retirement, on provision before the age of retirement and on service contributions.*

61 Decision 3194/2014. (VII. 14.) AB.

62 Decision 11/1995. (III. 5.) AB.

63 See, e.g., Decision 17/1992. (III. 30.) AB; Decision 64/1993. (VI. 3.) AB; Decision 1138/B/1995. AB; Decision 51/2001. (IX. 15.) AB; Decision 109/2008. (IX. 26.) AB; Decision 867/B/1997. AB.

In the tobacconist's shop case, therefore, the ECtHR did not agree with the Constitutional Court on the interpretation of Article 1 of the First Additional Protocol to the European Convention on Human Rights, in the context of the revocation of licences, which allow a business to be run as a lifelong career. According to the ECtHR, the complainant had to bear an excessive individual burden as a result of the change in the legislation and his right to property was therefore infringed.[64]

The Constitutional Court's decision on the nationalisation of private pension funds was perhaps the first case in which the right to property was challenged in the literature: the Constitutional Court upheld the government's decision, holding that the reorganisation did not violate the right to property.[65] Since this decision, all Constitutional Court rulings in the context of the right to property have narrowed the scope of property protection, moving away from the Constitutional Court's previous understanding and emphasising that property is socially bound. The change of concept was also motivated by the fact that in 2008 the country was undoubtedly facing a crisis situation that was also felt at a global level. The question is, as I will point out later, to what extent this shaken global economy provided a constitutional justification in Hungary for narrowing the scope of protection of a fundamental right.[66]

5.1.2.3. Foreign currency credit loan cases

The Decision 34/2014. (III. 20.) AB introduced new benchmarks, which are worth briefly reviewing, because they illustrate the magnitude and nature of the doctrinal shift. Apparently, all that has happened is that the Curia has determined when a clause on the unilateral modification of interest, costs and fees in consumer loan agreements meets the requirements of the Civil Code. This was the basis on which the legislator drafted the Foreign Currency Credit's Loans Act, partly on the mandatory interpretation of the law itself and partly on the procedural consequences. The Constitutional Court has held that this interpretation is the constitutional content of the norm and that any contrary interpretation is contrary to the Fundamental Law.

64 Vékony v. Hungary, Judgement of 13 January 2015, no. 65681/13.

65 Decision 184/2010. (X. 28.) AB.

66 Szilágyi, Emese: "A kommunikációs alapjogok általános értelmezése és alkalmazása a rendes bírósági és az alkotmánybírósági gyakorlatban – a bírói kezdeményezések és az alkotmányjogi panaszos ügyek tapasztalatai", in *Az Alaptörvény érvényesülése a bírói gyakorlatban III. Alkotmányjogi panasz: az alapjog-érvényesítés gyakorlata,* Budapest, HVG-ORAC, 2019, 98–121; Hollán, Miklós: "Büntetőbírói döntések az Alkotmánybíróság ítélőszéke előtt a *nullum crimen et nulla poena sine lege* elv tükrében", in *ibid.* 64–97; Tordai, Csaba: "Az alkotmánybírósági esetjog hatása a rendes bírói ítéletekre az információszabadság és a képmáshoz való jog területén", in *ibid.* 245–259; Sepsi, Tibor: "Az Alaptörvény személyes adatok védelméhez való joggal összefüggő rendelkezéseinek érvényesülése – az alkotmánybírósági gyakorlat a rendes bíróságok eljárásában az Alaptörvény hatálybalépése óta", in *ibid.* 260–276; Drinóczi, Tímea: "A tulajdonhoz való alapjog értelmezésének eltérései a rendes bírósági és az alkotmánybírósági gyakorlatban: a bírói kezdeményezések és az alkotmányjogi panaszok tapasztalatai", in *ibid.* 277–312.

As a starting point, the decision stated that as a result of the economic crisis of 2008, "[a] large number of households found themselves in a difficult living situation, tens of thousands of families were threatened with eviction, etc. The negative consequences of the problem are borne by society and the national economy as a whole, and it was not possible to address and remedy them through judicial means (in the framework of individual legal protection)."

The decision – referring to Decision 13/2013. (VI. 17.) AB – stated as a starting point that there is no obstacle to the application of the previous findings on the requirement of legal certainty. However, it pointed out that, in the light of Article R) (3) of the Fundamental Law, Article M) (2) provides that, in the event of a serious crisis situation affecting the fundamental rights of the masses of the weaker parties, the protection of consumers' rights and the duty to assist the victims of such a crisis are the primary duty of all branches of government. "In the absence of such 'intervention' by the State, the fundamental rights of vulnerable debtors, and ultimately their right to human dignity, would be irreversibly affected. The courts would have had to interpret the legislation in this way under Article 28 of the Fundamental Law even in the absence of the law in question."

The decision is one of a series of decisions in which the Constitutional Court has not clearly interpreted the rule of consumer protection laid down in the Fundamental Law as a state objective.[67] The summary statement of the decision, according to which the courts should have acted in the same way as the law in the absence of the law with regard to Article R) (3) and Article M) (2) of the Fundamental Law, is not clear in its content. Indeed, it is not clear whether this finding follows from the provisions of the Civil Code subsequently examined by the decision, with the argument that the provision had previously carried the content corresponding to the constitutional interpretation and that the courts should therefore have applied that interpretation, or whether, on the contrary, the Constitutional Court's assertion is that the courts should have applied that system of requirements even in the absence of an express statutory provision.[68] Both lines of reasoning can be deduced from the text of the decision. This is a matter of concern because, according to both interpretations, the Constitutional Court has consistently held that previous judgments which did not examine the unfairness of the clauses in the proceedings in accordance with the principles laid down in the law in a novel way are contrary to the Fundamental Law.

67 See, first of all, the special opinion of Barnabás Lenkovics, Decision 8/2014. (III. 20.) AB, ABH 2014, 300, 312–313, and following the present decision, Decision 2/2015. (II. 2.) AB, ABH 2015, 132, 138–139. For a brief summary of the relevant decisions, see Téglási, András: "A devizahitelezés problémája és kezelésének alkotmányos kérdései az Alkotmánybíróság gyakorlatának fényében", in Lenter, Csaba (ed.): *A devizahitelezés nagy kézikönyve,* Budapest, Nemzeti Közszolgálati és Tankönyvkiadó, 2015, 315–334; Drinóczi, Tímea: "Az Alkotmánybíróság határozata a devizahitelekről. A szerződési szabadság régi-új korlátai", *Jogesetek Magyarázata,* 2014/2, 3–12.

68 On the difference between the two interpretations, the indirect and the direct horizontal scope, see Gárdos-Orosz, Fruzsina: *Alkotmányos polgári jog? Az alapvető jogok alkalmazása a magánjogi jogvitákban,* Budapest – Pécs, Dialóg Campus, 2011.

However, since, taking into account the decision as a whole, it can be concluded that the Constitutional Court undoubtedly did not intend this legal effect in this form, the above statement can only be interpreted as *obiter dictum*, which means that it cannot be included in the scope of the reasoning underlying the operative part, i.e. it has no precedential value and the *erga omnes* effect does not extend to this statement. Of course, in accordance with the specific nature of *obiter dictum*, one could certainly attribute to that statement an explanatory force for the future if its content could be clearly established. Based on the above, we can continue to align ourselves with the above-mentioned findings of Decision 8/2014. (III. 20.) AB on the question of horizontal effect, which recognises the role of indirect horizontal effect in Hungarian law and does not accept that the Fundamental Law can be directly invoked if the judge cannot find any other applicable norm in the legal system.

The Constitutional Court first examined the issue of the preparation period in relation to the breach of legal certainty.

As regards the preparation period, the Constitutional Court's reasoning was based on the fact that the principles on the basis of which the courts will examine the unfairness of clauses after the entry into force of the legislation were known from December 2012, when the opinion of the Civil Department of the Curia was adopted. This statement is undoubtedly correct. However, the problem of the preparation time was not primarily raised by the petitions in relation to the emergence of criteria for fair contract terms, but rather to the fact that, after the entry into force of the law, financial institutions had only a very short period of time to review dozens of contracts over a ten-year period in view of the changed litigation position, to determine which clauses were covered by the law and to decide whether to bring an action in the absence of knowledge of the legal consequences. However, in response to this argument, the decision merely stated, in a very vague manner, that "[t]he identification of those elements, even over a contractual period of approximately 10 years, should not give rise to a problem which would make it impossible to meet the time limit for bringing an action". A novel constitutional argument in favour of a change in the previous practice regarding the preparation period is that the relevant date for the starting date of the preparation period would not be the date of publication of the legislation, but an earlier date. The Constitutional Court has stressed in several decisions the fundamental importance of a sufficient preparation period, but has always calculated it from the date of publication of the legislation and not from an earlier date, in accordance with the guarantees of the rule of law (publication in the Official Journal is a condition for the validity of the main rule).[69]

[69] See, e.g., Decision 28/1992 (IV. 30.) AB, ABH 1992, 155, 156–157. On recent practice and the interpretation of the sufficient preparation time by the Constitutional Court – which also confirms that reference to well-known facts in this context has never appeared in either domestic, foreign or international practice – see Papp, Imre: "A jogbiztonság formai eleme: a kellő felkészülési idő követelménye", *Kodifikáció*, 2013/1, 5–60.

In the context of legal certainty, the Constitutional Court also examined in detail whether the *Act XXXVIII of 2014 on the Resolution of Questions Relating to the Uniformity Decision of the Curia Regarding Consumer Loan Agreements of Financial Institutions* (Foreign Currency Credit's Loans Act) violates the prohibition of retroactive legislation. To this end, the decision considered it necessary to examine whether the substantive provisions of the law created a new regulatory environment in terms of content. In its examination, the panel starts from the fact that Article 4 (1) of the Civil Code, which lays down the principles of good faith and fair dealing, Article 5 (1), which prohibits abuse of rights, and Article 200 (2), which penalises infringements of good morals by nullity, have remained unchanged since 2004. These rules are now enshrined as constitutional values in Article M) (2) of the Fundamental Law. The provisions appearing in the sectoral laws did not override the provisions of the Civil Code, which have always been in force as underlying law, and therefore the Foreign Currency Credit's Loans Act did not create a new legal environment. According to the Constitutional Court, therefore, in the present case, the law has created a presumption of unfairness in contractual terms, which did not previously comply, with the general prohibition of general clauses. "The content of the law is thus nothing more than an authentic interpretation of the law by the legislature (in this case, the legislator), as deduced from the practice of the legislature." In view of this, the decision also considered the petition to be unfounded in this respect.

The decision is very vague on the issue of retroactivity. According to the decision, the Articles 4–5 and 200 (2) of the Civil Code have always imposed the same requirement as Article 4 (1) of the Foreign Currency Credit's Loans Act with regard to Article M (2) of the Fundamental Law. Although the decision quotes the commentary to the Civil Code for almost a page, it is not suitable to support the decision's assertion, as no concrete conclusions can be drawn from it in this case. In this respect, the majority reasoning does not address the question of how the general rules relied on have actually been applied (as a matter of settled law) in the settled practice of the ordinary court or how they have shaped the outcome of the specific litigation. The Constitutional Court therefore submits that the requirements laid down in Article 4 of the Foreign Currency Credit's Loans Act have not brought about any change in relation to the Civil Code, since the rules of the Civil Code have always had to be interpreted in this way.

While the majority opinion does not refer to any judgments, László Kiss' dissenting opinion refers to several court decisions that represent the opposite interpretation of the Constitutional Court. In László Kiss's dissenting opinion, the law clearly infringes the prohibition of retroactive legislation by excluding, in the case of loan agreements falling within its scope, the provisions of the law in force at the time of the conclusion of the contract, or by providing for derogations from them. In support of that argument, the dissenting opinion submits, inter alia, that the law also interferes with legal relationships which are time-barred and have already come to an end by reason of the rule in Article 1 (6) and precludes the court from examining all the circumstances of the transaction when giving judgment. The dissenting opinion demonstrates with a long series of Hungarian and foreign studies that the principles set out in Article 4 (1) of the Foreign Currency Credit's Loans Act did not exist in such a form or with such content in Hungarian law or in EU law. Although the reports of the Hungarian Competition Authority, the Hungarian Financial Supervisory Authority and the National Office for the Judiciary (OBH) have pointed to the worrying nature of the regulation since 2005, this does not change the fact that the principles laid down in the Foreign Currency Credit's Loans Act did not exist at the time the contracts were concluded. "By laying down new statutory nullity criteria for contractual provisions that had been in force for a long time, Article 4 (1) of the Act in fact changed the parties' contractual relations in a formative way, with retroactive effect to the date of conclusion of the contract, by Parliament's legislative power."

The parallel reasoning of Tamás Sulyok was based on the argument, without precedent, that a statute can modify the content of a contract in two ways. A constitutional amendment is deemed to have constitutional effect "if the law contains provisions relating to contracts which were not in force at the time the contract was concluded". By contrast, a declaratory amendment is made "where the content of the law which determines the content of the contract is subsequently reproduced in another law, with substantially the same content but with a more elaborate system of doctrine [...]. In the case of a declaratory amendment, the legislation has no law-making effect on the contract, but a declaratory provision may facilitate more effective application of the law." The parallel explanatory memorandum considered the legislation at issue to have declaratory effect because "the positive law rules in force on 1 May 2004 already contained the (compiled) legal principles summarised in Article 4 (1) of the Act on the case of unilateral amendments to contracts by financial institutions".

According to the parallel reasoning, the principles of clarity, objectivity, factuality, proportionality and terminability were already valid in civil law on the basis of the general clauses of the old Civil Code, in the absence of an explicit provision in the Foreign Currency Credit's Loans Act or even in the opinion of the Civil Law Department (Collegium) of the Curia. This reasoning is, in my view, without any legal basis. In accordance with Articles 4–5 of the Civil Code, the courts have never previously deduced the reasoning set out in the parallel reasoning. The parallel reasoning also asserts, without any support, that certain principles can be derived from Article 209 of the Civil Code or Article 210 of the *Act CCXXXVII of 2013 on Credit Institutions and Financial Enterprise* (Hpt.), whereas this has not previously appeared in judicial interpretative practice either. This reasoning does not take account of the interpretation of the legislation referred to in practice, i.e. – as the illustrative examples in László Kiss's dissenting opinion also show – it arbitrarily derives certain principles from the provisions of the Civil Code and therefore wrongly concludes that Article 4 (1) of the Foreign Currency Credit's Loans Act has declaratory effect.

The decision also found that the application based on the infringement of judicial independence was unfounded and rejected. In this context, the decision, citing in detail Decision 19/1999. (VI. 25.) AB, pointed out that the essence of judicial independence is that the judge is subject only to the law, i.e. cannot be instructed. However, the fact that a judge is not subject to instructions cannot, of course, mean that he is not subject to the law. It is precisely the judge's task to form, based on the established facts, "his own internal convictions on the case before him, which enable him subsequently to take his decision on the basis of the relevant legislation". Invalidity must therefore be decided in accordance with the provisions of the law.

In a detailed dissenting opinion, Miklós Lévay stated his position that the Foreign Currency Credit's Loans Act violates the principle of judicial independence, and that the new majority interpretation is flawed. The reason for this is that the judge has to prepare and decide within extremely tight time frames, having to familiarise himself with a large volume of documents, while his discretionary tools have been greatly reduced by the Foreign Currency Credit's Loans Act which has made court proceedings and decision-making a mere formality. Miklós Lévay's dissenting opinion shows very clearly how the law violates the principle of separation of powers by infringing the independence of the judiciary. If the law does not allow the judge to exercise discretion in the proceedings because the procedural framework does not actually allow this, not only is the independence of the judiciary infringed, but ultimately also the principle of the division of powers enshrined in Article C) of the Fundamental Law. In such cases, the legislator, by excluding judicial discretion in the specific case, decides for the judge, depriving him of his constitutional duty. According to the dissenting opinion, the majority position suggests that the judge must blindly follow the will of the legislator, his freedom of interpretation resulting from judicial independence extending only to acting in accordance with the law.

The decision then examined whether the challenged legal provisions, taken as a whole, rendered the Foreign Currency Credit's Loans Act unconstitutional. In this respect, the decision pointed out that "[the] set of special procedural rules [...] gives rise to a special procedural order which, by virtue of the cumulative effect of the legal restrictions, raises constitutional doubts as to the fairness of the procedure as a whole". The decision concludes, however, "the constitutional concerns about the procedural order as a whole do not rise to the level of an infringement of the fundamental law in the present case". The decision does not contain any reasoning on this point.

From the reference to the cumulative effect of the restrictions, it seems that the Constitutional Court found that the Foreign Currency Credit's Loans Act as a whole restricts the right to a fair trial, but the Constitutional Court considers the restriction of the fundamental right to be constitutional under Article I (3) of the Fundamental Law. However, the majority decision does not contain any information on the assessment carried out. Past Constitutional Court practice shows that the test of limitation of fundamental rights must be applied separately to each challenged provision and each of its elements, as it is possible that only some elements are found to be unconstitutional, while other challenged elements pass the test of necessity-proportionality. A novel approach is to examine the legislation as a whole. The majority decision, the parallel reasoning and the dissenting opinions all reflect the fact that, although the petition identified a number of fundamental unconstitutionalities, the fundamental question of the Foreign Currency Credit's Loans Act was at the heart of the assessment, namely whether the requirement of seven principles for identifying unfair contract terms is contrary to the prohibition of retroactive legislation, which the Constitutional Court did not consider unconstitutional overall.

According to the Constitutional Court, the constitutional concerns related to the procedural rules do not reach the level of unconstitutionality either in detail or as a whole; they do restrict the fundamental rights in question to a large extent, but the restriction is not considered unconstitutional under Article I (3) of the Fundamental Law.

The decision of the Constitutional Court attempts to derive the seven principles of fairness set out in the Foreign Currency Credit's Loans Act from the general clauses and Article 209 (1) of the Civil Code. However, it is a fact that the seven principles were not part of the existing body of law before the opinion of the Civil Law Department was drafted. This is clearly demonstrated by the fact that the seven principles have never appeared either in legal literature or in case law.

The concept of unfairness set out in Article 209 (1) of the Civil Code is a general term, the content of which is necessarily shaped by judicial practice. In the case of general clauses, the framework within which the court makes a law-forming decision is even wider than the average. The special feature of the case under examination is precisely that the requirements set out in the opinion of the Civil Department had not previously appeared in law, and the Curia, and subsequently the legislature, enacted an interpretation of the law which was contrary to and disregarded the existing law, and which, for a decade, had been applied uniformly and had never been questioned by the legal literature or the courts, despite the requirement that unfairness be detected by the courts.

By considering the way in which the new rules of conduct were introduced, i.e. the procedure, to be in compliance with the Fundamental Law, the Constitutional Court decision in fact set a new constitutional standard for the concepts of the rule of law and legal certainty, as well as the right to due process, its partial rights and, above all, the prohibition of retroactive legislation, by means of a new, different interpretation of the Fundamental Law. As can be seen above, the new yardstick runs counter to the theoretical and doctrinal principles and settled practice of constitutional law on several points, and is simply blatantly contradictory on several points. The cavalcade of parallel and dissenting opinions illustrates this.

In the case of the Decision 2/2015. (II. 2.) AB, we also see that the decision has changed the previous interpretation of the crisis situation on several points. Perhaps the most important of these relates to the right to human dignity. The Constitutional Court also referred *obiter dictum* to the fact that in its Decision 8/1990. (IV. 23.) AB it stated that human dignity as a general right of personality includes the right to the free development of personality and the right to freedom of self-determination, and the autonomy of action (ABH 1990, 42). In Decision 64/1993. (XII. 22.) AB it was held that the right to property as the traditional material basis of individual autonomy of action is protected (ABH 1993, 373, 380).

According to the Constitutional Court, the global financial crisis of 2008–2009 and the social crisis situation have emptied the autonomy of action and the freedom of self-determination of the victims of the situation, "and this situation is also an affront to their human dignity". "And human dignity is inviolable (Article II of the Fundamental Law), and its protection is a primary duty of the state [Article I (1) of the Fundamental Law]."

This surprising interpretation of the material basis for general autonomy of action and the right to human dignity has been disputed by many within the body. For example, Ágnes Czine did not consider it acceptable that the majority opinion also invoked the right to human dignity when examining the violation of the principle of equality. In Czine's view, the violation of equality in the present case would not lead to the elimination of the general autonomy of action, and thus to a violation of the right to property and the right to human dignity.

The analysis of the decisions shows that the practice of the Constitutional Court is inconsistent. Some standards are changing,[70] new standards are emerging, but no coherent and justifiable new interpretative order is emerging.[71]

As the legitimacy of the Constitutional Court does not derive from its authority, but from the publicly justifiable interpretative framework to which its decisions are aligned, without a definable and thus contestable framework,[72] the legitimacy of constitutional adjudication is easily lost. Meaningful legal professional criticism is not possible if the dogmatic basis disappears. In this case, only political action and political relations remain. Without a legal basis and consistent reasoning closely aligned with it (constant practice), Constitutional Court decisions are also political decisions.

The experience of the foreign currency credit loan decisions is that the "crisis situation" and the approach of the majority of the Constitutional Court were capable of obliterating many standards that were considered normative even under the text of the Fundamental Law. These included the principle of separation of powers, judicial independence, the prohibition of retroactive legislation and the right to a fair trial. The level of protection of these constitutional principles and

[70] Chronowski, Nóra – Vincze, Attila: "Alkotmánybíráskodás (gazdasági) válságban", *Alkotmánybírósági Szemle*, 2014/2, 104–112.

[71] Téglási, András: "A szociális jogok (alap)jogvédelmi szintjének csökkenése a gazdasági válság hatására. Avagy a jogrendszerek versenye „rückwärts"-ben (?)", *Justum Aequum Salutare*, 2016/2, 141–170.

[72] Dworkin, Ronald: "Objectivity and truth: You'd better believe it", *Philosophy and Public Affairs*, 1996/2, 87–139.

rights has changed significantly as a result of the decisions under review here, and certain rights, such as the right to human dignity, and certain state objectives, such as consumer protection, have been given a new constitutional position and meaning.

In any case, the consequence of the decisions under review is legal uncertainty, which is not conducive to a stable constitutional order that seeks to interact with international law and EU law.

5.1.3. Migration

The volume has already pointed out that the migration crisis has brought fundamental changes in the practice of constitutional courts, despite the fact that Hungary was not seriously affected by the refugee flow, apart from a very short and limited period. There was a moment in 2015 when the migration crisis reached Hungary, with more than 400 000 people arriving in the country,[73] most of whom then went on to Austria and Germany. Hungary could not control its borders. Hungary was criticised by the European Union for creating chaos and for seeking to control the situation through austerity measures. The Government called for a referendum to give Hungary's voters the opportunity to express their views on the legal measures that the EU's pro-accession policy entails.[74] The EU rule was that Member States should allocate refugees arriving in Italy and Greece on the basis of a pre-quota for the purposes of the asylum procedure, in order to relieve the burden on countries in difficulty and to share fairly the burden of the migration crisis. Hungary would have received a first round of 1 294 out of 160 000 asylum seekers. The Hungarian Government did not find the regulation on the transfer of people to the EU acceptable and appealed to the CJEU to declare that the EU had no competence to regulate such a measure, and that the regulation was *ultra vires*. In addition, Hungary built a fence along the Serbian and Croatian borders to prevent illegal border crossings.

The Constitutional Court was not left out of this legal and political conflict. As a first step, it received a petition on the constitutionality of the so-called quota referendum.[75] The constitutionality of the referendum, i.e. whether the question can be put to a referendum or whether it falls within the prohibited subject matter of Article 8 of the Fundamental Law, has been questioned by several constitutional scholars in their writings.[76] However, the Constitutional Court interpreted its jur-

[73] Source: National Directorate for Aliens Policing and www.police.hu

[74] Council Decision (EU) 2015/1601 of 22 September 2015 establishing provisional measures in the area of international protection for the benefit of Italy and Greece.

[75] Decision 12/2016. (VI. 22.) AB.

[76] For details, see Szente, Zoltán: "The Controversial Anti-Migrant Referendum in Hungary is Invalid", 2016, http://constitutional-change.com/the-controversial-anti-migrant-referendum-in-hungary-is-invalid; Halmai, Gábor: "The Invalid Anti-Migrant Referendum in Hungary", *Verfassungsblog*, 4 October 2016, https://verfassungsblog.de/hungarys-anti-european-immigration-laws

isdiction in this respect as not extending to the examination of the substance of the referendum, since the question does not fall within any of the prohibited subjects of the referendum as defined in Article 8 of the Fundamental Law, and it can therefore only review the decision of the Curia on the validity of the referendum initiative from a procedural point of view.[77] While it is true that the Constitutional Court's powers are indeed limited in matters relating to the constitutionality of referendums, it is surprising that, compared to the activism that has been so characteristic of Hungarian constitutional jurisprudence in other referendum cases,[78] here we read a very reserved, textual interpretation. The Constitutional Court, examining only procedural issues, found that the decision of the Curia was lawful and therefore cannot raise any questions of constitutionality.[79] The Constitutional Court also ruled that the constitutional complaints lodged on the matter could not be upheld because the Constitutional Court had ruled that no one could be directly involved in the case of such a referendum. Direct involvement, as explained above, is a condition for admissibility, but the interpretation put forward here is interesting because in other cases the Constitutional Court has interpreted the condition of personal involvement more broadly.[80]

In another case, which has become the reference point of constitutional discourse and perhaps the most important fundamental decision of the Hungarian constitutional review of today, the Constitutional Court interpreted the prohibition of mass expulsion in the Fundamental Law, following the motion of the Commissioner for Fundamental Rights. According to the motion submitted by the Commissioner for Fundamental Rights in December 2015, the above-mentioned EU provision may violate the Fundamental Law if it is understood to deprive persons arriving on the territory of a Member State of their individual human dignity by

77 Article 33 (1)–(2) of the Act on the Constitutional Court: "(1) Parliamentary resolutions ordering a referendum or dismissing the ordering of a referendum to be obligatorily ordered shall be reviewed by the Constitutional Court with regard to conformity with the Fundamental Law and legality on the petition of anyone within thirty days. The petition shall arrive within fifteen days of the publication of Parliament's resolution. (2) In the procedure described in paragraph (1), the Constitutional Court shall only carry out an examination regarding the merits of the resolution if, between the authentication of the signature-collecting sheets and the ordering of the referendum, the circumstances changed to a significant degree in a manner that may significantly affect the decision, and if said changes could not be taken into account by the National Election Committee or the Curia when making a decision on the authentication of the question or the decision on the review thereof."

78 Halmai, Gábor: "The Hungarian Approach to Constitutional Review: The End of Activism? The First Decade of the Hungarian Constitutional Court", in Sadurski, Wojciech (ed.): *Constitutional Justice, East and West. Democratic Legitimacy and Constitutional Courts in Post-Communist Europe in a Comparative Perspective,* Hague – London, Kluwer Law International, 2002, 189–211; Schwartz, Herman: *The Struggle for Constitutional Justice in Post-Communist Europe,* Chicago, University of Chicago Press, 2000.

79 Decision 3130/2016. (VI. 29.) AB; Decision 3150/2016. (VII. 22.) AB; Decision 3151/2016. (VII. 22.) AB.

80 Decision 3127/2015. (VII. 9.) AB on the reduced retirement age for women and men.

not having their cases judged individually by the Member State, but by transferring them en masse from one country to another without their consent.

According to the Commissioner for Fundamental Rights, the decision to transfer people without an individual assessment constitutes collective expulsion.[81] Interestingly, the motion was tabled at a time when the Government saw the need to take action against the EU measure, and the Commissioner's initiative reinforced this position. The other provision which the Ombudsman asked to interpret was Article E) (2) of the Fundamental Law, which provides for the extent of the delegation of powers by the EU. For Hungarian constitutional law, this had been an unclear issue since accession.[82] It is a serious constitutional dilemma whether the Hungarian state is obliged to implement EU rules which the Hungarian state bodies, in particular, and ultimately the Constitutional Court, consider to be unconstitutional. Furthermore, if there is a constitutional possibility for a Hungarian constitutional institution to examine EU law in comparison with the Fundamental Law, the question is which one it will be. The motion of the Commissioner for Fundamental Rights suggested that if the EU exceeds its legislative powers and thereby violates the state constitution, it logically follows that the Constitutional Court has the power to review it.

The Constitutional Court responded to the petition in its Decision 22/2016. (XII. 5.) AB, which was issued a year later and was already described in the discussion of constitutional identity, without having ruled on the specific question of the constitutionality of mass-procedure. Referring to the National Avowal and Article E) of the Fundamental Law, it ruled that the joint exercise of competences with the European Union cannot lead to a violation of Hungary's sovereignty and identity.[83] The Constitutional Court, in line with the Government's position, deduced from the Fundamental Law that Hungary cannot enter into international obligations that infringe its sovereignty. It also stressed that sovereignty includes constitutional identity, the protection of which is the task of the Constitutional Court, the precise content of which it will determine on a case-by-case basis. While stressing that it does not judge the validity, invalidity or primary application of an EU law, the Constitutional Court considers it its duty to defend Hungary's sovereignty and constitutional identity in the face of EU law.

However, the decision detached the specific issue from the ombudsman's motion and did not examine whether the specific EU rule was contrary to the Fundamental Law, so we could not know what the legal consequence of such a future examination would be. The interesting aspect of the new decision, in terms of the interpretation of the Constitutional Court's role, lies mainly in its timing. Several previous Consti-

81 See the motion *http://public.mkab.hu/dev/dontesek.nsf/0/1361afa3cea26b84c1257f10005dd958/$-FILE/X_3327_0_2015_inditvany.002.pdf/X_3327_0_2015_inditvany.pdf*

82 Gárdos-Orosz, Fruzsina: "The Constitutional and statutory framework of the application of EU law in Hungary", *Acta Universitas Carolinae*, 2013, 315–337.

83 Decision 22/2016. (XII. 5.) AB.

tutional Court decisions dealing with the relationship between EU law and domestic law[84] have been criticised for failing to explain the relationship between EU law and the constitution in the legal system. It is true that earlier expectations in the literature had not yet anticipated a similar role for the concept of constitutional identity.[85] Even though the Constitutional Court in the new decision did not question the fact that the Constitutional Court does not have the competence to examine the legality of EU law – as it had already stated in several cases on the basis of almost identical wording of the Constitution in this respect –,[86] has now left room for some kind of internal constitutionality examination. However, the Constitutional Court also refused to examine the specific conflict of fundamental rights in this context.[87] The only decision that had previously discussed in more detail the possible limits to the application of EU law in Hungary was the so-called Lisbon decision,[88] on which I have published a detailed analysis.[89] The essence of the decision is that the delegation of powers in Article E) of the Fundamental Law is not unlimited, i.e. it indicates a fixed content, and if a claim for EU competence is notified beyond that content, it must be approved in advance by the Hungarian constitutional power at the level of the Fundamental Law. Some dissenting opinions have already called for the Constitutional Court to clarify the relationship between the Fundamental Law and EU law.

The Decision 22/2016. (XII. 5.) AB, which was issued after the migration crisis, thus provided a number of novelties for the Hungarian constitutional order. In addition to constitutional identity, the relationship between EU law and domestic law is a key issue in dealing with regional and global crises, and this has also been put in a new light here. This decision emphasised the international legal nature of the founding treaties, thus underlining that the EU is a cooperation based on the consensus of the Member States, which is therefore fundamentally dependent on the sovereign will of the Member States, and placed little emphasis on the *sui generis* nature of the EU legal order, which was formulated by the case law of the CJEU and became the basis of the EU legal order. As for the circumstances in which the decision was taken, it is worth highlighting that it followed an invalid referendum and an unsuccessful amendment to the Fundamental Law, which formulated the constitutional identity as a legal concept at the core of the Fundamental Law as opposed to EU law.[90]

---

84 Decision 1053/E/2004. AB; Decision 72/2006. (XII. 15.) AB; Decision 9/2007. (III. 7.) AB; Decision 143/2010. (VII. 14.) AB; Decision 32/2008. (III. 12.) AB.

85 Gárdos-Orosz, Fruzsina: "The Constitutional and statutory framework of the application of EU law in Hungary", *Acta Universitas Carolinae*, 2013, 315–337.

86 See, e.g., Decision 61/B/2005. AB; Decision 66/2006. (XI. 29.) AB; Decision 87/2008. (VI. 18.) AB.

87 Fazekas, Flóra: "EU law and Hungarian Constitutional Court", in Varju, Márton – Várnay, Ernő (eds.): *European Union Law in Hungary: Institutions, Processes and the Law,* Budapest, HVG-ORAC, 2014, 59.

88 Decision 143/2010. (VII. 14.) AB.

89 Gárdos-Orosz, Fruzsina: "The Constitutional and statutory framework of the application of EU law in Hungary", *Acta Universitas Carolinae,* 2013, 315–337.

90 The Decisions 2/2019. (III. 5.) AB and 32/2021. (XII. 20.) AB raise similar problems in recent practice.

5.1.4. Terrorism threat and security challenges

Unlike France, Britain or Germany, Hungary has not been hit by terrorist attacks in the past decade or more. As a result, perhaps, there are only two ordinary court decisions that have explicitly dealt with this issue and have influenced the development of the constitutional system and constitutional protection. The first case has its roots in 2007–2009, when the far-right group Hungarians' Arrows National Liberation Army committed a series of violent acts against politicians and other public figures, as well as Roma and Jewish communities. The trial in the ordinary court has been dragging on since 2011, but the detection of the case has made it clear that the group has no links to international terrorist organisations. The other case was the trial of Ahmed H., who was tried on terrorism charges. This happened at the height of the migration crisis, which led to strong criticism in the domestic and international press, as the accusation was simply that the Syrian-born perpetrator had called for violence while waiting to cross the border at the Hungarian-Serbian border in September 2015 and then joined the rioters.

The two cases could be considered insignificant, but they contributed to the justification of the sixth constitutional amendment of 14 June 2016 on the terrorist threat emergency, which introduced a new case of special legal order into chapter V of the Fundamental Law on special legal orders.

In this case, the constitutional authority did not respond to a current and present social problem, but to a politically relevant problem affecting other countries in Europe, by amending the constitution and allowing a new special legal order, i.e. extraordinary legislation, to be put in place in the event of a terrorist threat. As I have described above the evolution of the practice of constitutional review of constitutional amendments, i.e. the jurisdictional practice that emerged from the Fourth Amendment to the Fundamental Law did not allow the Sixth Amendment to the Fundamental Law to be subject to constitutional review.

Despite the fact that there has been a lot of talk about the threat of terrorism in government communications, especially in the context of the fight against migration, there has been little actual legal conflict and few resulting Constitutional Court decisions.

A constitutional complaint was initiated against the provisions of an act which allowed secret surveillance on the basis of the decision of the Minister of Justice without proper procedural control guarantees.

According to the petitioners, the fact that the anti-terrorism body is entitled to carry out secret surveillance without judicial control, solely on the basis of a ministerial authorisation, is a violation of their right to respect for private and family life, home and relations, and the protection of personal data, as guaranteed by Article VI of the Fundamental Law. The petitioners noted that they also consider unconstitutional the mere fact that a new body (the counter-terrorism body within the police) has been given the power to carry out secret surveillance, but that the similar powers of the national security services are also unconstitutional.

The Constitutional Court ruled that the amendment was constitutional, holding that the approval of the Minister of Justice was sufficient to ensure that the restriction was not unnecessary and disproportionate in the context of the constitutional protection of privacy.[91] This interpretation is contrary to the previous Constitutional Court practice derived from the former Constitution,[92] which is particularly interesting because, as we have seen, in the Constitutional Court decision on the right of assembly, the right to privacy in the context of other fundamental rights was given greater protection than before. Although the Constitutional Court reviewed its previous practice in this case in detail, this time it underlined that the protection of national security can be a justification for restricting fundamental rights. This decision was taken despite the fact that the ECtHR has also ruled that the secret collection of information can only be allowed if its control does not remain within the executive.[93] This case was also referred to the Strasbourg Court, which ruled that the Hungarian legislation was contrary to Article 9 of the European Convention on Human Rights and that the Constitutional Court had not provided effective legal protection against privacy-invading legislation in this case.[94]

However, shortly afterwards the Constitutional Court declared unconstitutional another provision that would have allowed greater control over certain segments of the public sector, transforming one-off controls into permanent controls. In this case, the Constitutional Court did not find adequate safeguards for measures limiting the protection of privacy.[95] In the context of domestic security challenges, it is also worth mentioning that the new law on assembly,[96] which was adopted on the basis of the Constitutional Court's decision finding an unconstitutional omission,[97] allows for an interpretation that in certain cases even a two person public assembly is subject to a notification requirement and thus to an administrative assessment. The need to address security challenges and to protect privacy justified the reconsideration of the 1989 law on public assemblies, and without further analysis it can perhaps be argued that the new legislation creates greater scope for public control than before, and that other fundamental rights (such as the right to privacy, including private housing) are more closely protected in the assessment of the lawfulness of assemblies. The fact remains that the previous 1989 legislation was generous and left many questions open for the legislator. However, it was in the spirit of the new legislation that the Constitutional Court's decision, which I will describe in detail in the next section, was taken at the time of the pandemic.

---

91 Decision 36/2005. (X. 5.) AB; Decision 2/2007. (I. 24.) AB.

92 Decision 2/2007. (I. 24.) AB.

93 Klass and Others, no. 5029/71, Report of the Commission, Series B no. 26; Malone v. United Kingdom, no. 8691/79, 2 August 1984; Leander v. Sweden, no. 9248/81, 26 March 1987.

94 Szabó and Vissy v. Hungary, no. 37138/14, 12 January 2016.

95 Decision 9/2014. (III. 21.) AB.

96 Decision 13/2016. (VII. 18.) AB.

97 Act LV of 2018 on the Right of Assembly.

5.1.5. Covid-19 and Constitutional Court in Hungary[98]

5.1.5.1. The special legal order

The Hungarian constitution, the 2011 Fundamental Law, is perhaps unique in the sense that it recognises six different forms of special legal order,[99] one of which – the state of danger – still exists at the end of 2022, when this research has been completed, and two other quasi-special legal orders below the constitutional level – the so-called mass immigration crisis[100] and the "health crisis" – are also in force.[101] Beyond these, there are some other types of crisis situations in the legal order, such as energy supply or nuclear crisis, but in these cases the crisis management systems are narrowly tailored and the range of instruments available is very limited.[102]

One of the six types of special legal order provided for in the Fundamental Law, the so-called state of danger, was proclaimed and extended several times to deal with the health crisis caused by the coronavirus pandemic, and later the Russian-Ukrainian war in Ukraine gave rise to its proclamation by means of the Tenth Amendment to the Fundamental Law.

In the case of the pandemic, the emergency rule of the Fundamental Law was applied, according to which the Government may declare a state of danger "in the event of a natural disaster or industrial accident threatening the safety of life and property, or in order to mitigate its consequences". In the event of this emergency, the Government has special powers, such as the power to introduce emergency measures provided for in a cardinal act, to adopt decrees having the force of legislative act to suspend the application of certain laws, to derogate from the provisions of laws and to take other emergency measures. However, the Government power is not unlimited. Exceptional powers may be exercised only within the limits set by a cardinal act, and only exceptional measures necessary to remedy or mitigate the consequences of the danger situation may be taken. Emergency decrees of the Government may remain in force beyond 15 days only with the authorisation of Parliament. Only the Government may terminate the state of danger, which is in fact a constitutional obligation, since the Government is obliged to terminate the special legal order "when the conditions for its promulgation no longer exist". Decrees is-

98 This chapter was supported by the Hungarian Academy of Sciences under Grant No. 05016764 (Resilience of the legal system in post Covid society: opportunities and risks).

99 The Ninth and Tenth Amendments to the Fundamental Law restructured and restructured the special legal order by extending the scope of the emergency situation and by introducing a new special legal order structure.

100 Article 80/A–K of the Act LXXX of 2007 on the Right of Asylum.

101 Article 228–254/E of the Act CLIV of 1997 on Health Care.

102 Kádár, Pál – Hoffmann, István: "A különleges jogrend és a válságkezelés közigazgatási jogi kihívásai: a kvázi különleges jogrendek helye és szerepe a magyar közigazgatásban", *Közjogi Szemle*, 2021/3, 1–11.

sued by the Government during a state of danger automatically expire on the date of termination of the special legal order, even if Parliament has previously agreed to extend their validity. However, Parliament may adopt law(s) with the same content as the repealed Government decree.

On 11 March 2020, the Government declared a state of danger "in order to protect the health and life of Hungarian citizens" due to the outbreak of the Covid-19 (SARS-CoV-2) coronavirus, which threatened the safety of life and property in the whole territory of Hungary.[103] The special legal order was in force until mid-June 2020, when the Government lifted it by decree.[104] At the same time, the Government introduced a so-called health emergency for six months on its own authority, which – although not formally a special legal order recognised by the Fundamental Law (see above) – gave the Government a very broad mandate to protect the population against the negative consequences of the pandemic.[105]

However, due to the worsening epidemic situation, the Government declared a state of danger again in November 2020.[106] This special legal order lasted until 8 February 2021, but was only lifted for technical reasons; on the same day that it was repealed by a decree, the Government declared a third state of danger.[107] Then, immediately after the adoption of the Tenth Amendment to the Fundamental Law, the Government declared a state of danger for the fourth time, but this time invoking the amended constitutional provision "in view of the armed conflict and humanitarian disaster in Ukraine and in order to avert the consequences of this situation in Hungary". This state of danger was introduced without any time limit.[108]

It is also worth noting that, although not related to the protection against the coronavirus pandemic, the above-mentioned "mass immigration crisis" has been in force since 2015 and is regularly extended by the Government.

It can be seen, therefore, that in Hungary, for many years, different types of emergency situations – regulated at constitutional or sub-constitutional level – have been in force, often in parallel.[109] Under these circumstances, it is reasonable to assume that the role of the institutions that control the activities of the Government, which is endowed with exceptional powers, and in particular that of the Constitutional Court, will increase in the future.

---

[103] Government Decree 40/2020. (III. 11.).

[104] Government Decree 282/2020. (VI. 17.).

[105] Government Decree 283/2020. (VI. 17.).

[106] Government Decree 478/2020. (XI. 3.).

[107] Government Decree 27/2021. (I. 29.).

[108] Government Decree 180/2022. (V. 24.).

[109] On the constitutionality problems related to the declaration of the state of emergency, see Szente, Zoltán: "A 2020. március 11-én kihirdetett veszélyhelyzet alkotmányossági problémái", *Állam- és Jogtudomány,* 2020/3, 115–139; Vörös, Imre: "A felhatalmazási törvénytől az egészségügyi válsághelyzetig és tovább", in Gárdos-Orosz, Fruzsina – Lőrincz ,Viktor Olivér (eds.): *Jogi diagnózisok. A COVID-19-világjárvány hatásai a jogrendszerre,* Budapest, L'Harmattan – Társadalomtudományi Kutatóközpont Jogtudományi Intézet, 2020, 1–28.

5.1.5.2. The complicated practice of the Constitutional Court[110]

Even if the two-thirds majority of the governing parties in Parliament meant that the Constitutional Court, rather than Parliament, could have examined the constitutionality of the circumstances surrounding the promulgation of the special legal order (if a constitutional institution with the power to do so had so requested), it could have counterbalanced the exceptional power of the Government, since the Constitutional Court's operation is not suspended in a state of danger. This idea has been confirmed by the Constitutional Court itself, as reflected in its first declaration, issued in March 2020, immediately after the declaration of the state of danger, according to which "as long as the declared state of danger persists, the members of the Constitutional Court are subject to increased responsibility". It is important to note that the availability of the Constitutional Court remained unchanged during this period, and its operation was uninterrupted even during periods when it was online and working from home. The case load and the number of completed cases show no difference between 2020 and the years before, meaning that day-to-day operations were stable.

The Constitutional Court started investigating Covid-19 cases in March 2020. Most of the cases were submitted as constitutional complaints, but the court also received some abstract norm control petitions (initiated by MPs) concerning Government decrees issued during the special legal order. In addition, some judicial initiatives have been filed to review the applicable norm in a specific case. On the basis of Articles 54 (1) and 53 (2) of the Fundamental Law,[111] the Constitutional Court has made a serious attempt to define its role in this period and the yardstick by which it can review restrictions of rights under the Fundamental Law, if the Fundamental Law allows restrictions of most rights to depart completely from Article I (3), the general test for the limitation of fundamental rights.[112]

Although the efforts of the Constitutional Court to establish the appropriate test or yardstick can be traced by reading the relevant decisions, the Constitutional Court ultimately recognised the constitutionality of all the regulations, so that during the more than two years of the state of danger, it did not find any constitutional defects that raised serious constitutional concerns that would have justified a declaration of unconstitutionality and annulment.

110 All the decisions of the Constitutional Court during and in the context of the pandemic can be found on the website of the Constitutional Court: https://alkotmanybirosag.hu/

111 Article 54 (1) of the Fundamental Law: "(1) Under a special legal order, the exercise of fundamental rights – with the exception of the fundamental rights provided for in Articles II and III, and Article XXVIII (2) to (6) – may be suspended or may be restricted beyond the extent specified in Article I (3)."

112 Erdős, Csaba: "Gondolatok a különleges jogrendi alapjogkorlátozás alkotmánybírósági gyakorlatáról", *Jog – Állam – Politika. Ünnepi különszám a 70 éves Kukorelli István tiszteletére*, 2022, 103–120.

During this jurisprudence, and especially at the beginning, the Constitutional Court rejected a number of applications on formal grounds. One of the reasons for this was the general limitation of the Constitutional Court's powers under Article 37 (4) of the Fundamental Law, according to which the Court may not in principle review the rules relating to the central budget of the State. In one of the very first cases, the Constitutional Court thus rejected the petition on the grounds of lack of competence. In Decision 3234/2020. (VII. 1.) AB, the challenged provision of the law provides that in 2020 local authorities are not entitled to the normal share of the motor vehicle tax collected by them, but that this amount becomes revenue of the central budget, specifically the Epidemic Protection Fund. The petitioner, a quarter of the MPs, argued that the revenue from the vehicle tax is a significant source of revenue for local self-government authorities in circumstances where they have been given a number of new tasks in the fight against the epidemic.

In the first period of the emergency, there was only one judicial referral, and that was rather on the grounds of a breach of the constitution concerning the autonomy of higher education in relation to the pandemic measures.[113] The case is relevant, however, because it highlights a significant and general constitutional problem that arose during the pandemic and is a good example of a debate that arose not because of the pandemic itself, but during and because of the pandemic, in which the pandemic was used not as a legitimate reason but rather as a pretext to change the rules in force.

In 2020, a number of Hungarian state universities, including the University of Theatre and Film Arts, were reorganised and privatised, and there were serious protests against this, the majority of which were organised by university students. The Board of Trustees of the University of Theatre and Film Arts declared the autumn semester invalid, claiming that the epidemic made it impossible to continue teaching. The students challenged the decision, saying that teaching could continue, but the new board of trustees, the new owner of the former state university, wanted to punish them for rebelling against the change.

The Constitutional Court rejected this petition, which asked to declare unconstitutional Government Decree 522/2020. (XI. 25.) on certain rules affecting higher education in times of emergency. In its decision, the Constitutional Court held that the application of the contested decree did not infringe the autonomy of higher education guaranteed by the Fundamental Law, provided that the Board of Trustees had taken the measure in cooperation with the higher education institution, in agreement with the depositary of the autonomy of higher education institutions when it took its decision. It is a normative requirement that the existence of the consent of the Senate must be examined by the ordinary court in the course of its proceedings.[114]

---

[113] Drinóczi, Tímea: "Loyalty, Opportunism and Fear. The forced privatisation of Hungarian universities", *Verfassungsblog,* 5 February 2021, https://verfassungsblog.de/loyalty-opportunism-and-fear

[114] Decision 28/2021. (XI. 5.) AB.

As regards constitutional complaints, very few cases were decided on the merits in 2020. Only nine cases were received in 2020, while many were received in 2021 and 2022, including hundreds of similar cases (mass petitions), on compulsory vaccinations or labour law issues. Most of these complaints were decided by the Constitutional Court panels in 2021 and 2022 in combined procedures. The Constitutional Court has six months to decide on admissibility and a further six months to decide on the merits of constitutional complaints. This means that, in the absence of an accelerated exceptional procedure, many of the constitutional complaints concerning restrictions of rights in the context of the case were not decided in due time.

A significant case of the Constitutional Court's pandemic-related jurisprudence was a constitutional complaint in which the Constitutional Court had previously rejected an abstract constitutional review motion on procedural grounds.

While the Constitutional Court rejected the MPs' initiative for an ex-post abstract review of the law, the constitutional complaint of the Göd municipality was deemed admissible. Under this Government Decree,[115] areas where industrial establishments of regional economic importance are located may be designated as special economic zones by government decision. The right to collect business tax paid by businesses operating in such areas was transferred from local to county level municipalities under the government decree affecting the area of the municipality of Göd. This resulted in a significant loss of revenue for the municipalities in which these economic zones were located, while the emergency decrees imposed a number of additional tasks on the same local authorities in order to protect against the Covid-19 epidemic.[116] The reorganisation of the ownership of the real estate used by these investments and the subsequent introduction of new tax rules were not, according to the proposal, necessary to achieve more effective protection against Covid-19. Unlike local governments, county-level governments do not have significant powers to organise an effective public response to a pandemic.[117]

The Constitutional Court rejected a constitutional complaint by the Göd municipality, which claimed that the municipality's right to property had been infringed and that without this revenue it would find it disproportionately difficult to carry out its tasks. In the operative part of the decision, however, it laid down a constitutional requirement with *erga omnes* effect, according to which Parliament

115 Government Decree 135/2020. (IV. 17.).

116 Balázs, István – Hoffman, István: "A közigazgatási jog rezilienciája - koronavírus idején", in Gárdos-Orosz, Fruzsina – Lőrincz, Viktor Olivér (eds.): *Jogi diagnózisok. A COVID-19-világjárvány hatásai a jogrendszerre,* Budapest, L'Harmattan – Társadalomtudományi Kutatóközpont Jogtudományi Intézet, 2020, 45–66.

117 IV/00839/2020. Constitutional complaint against the Government Decree No. 135/2020. (IV. 17.) on the measures necessary for the stability of national economy in the context of the state of danger and the Government Decree No. 136/2020. (IV. 17.) on the designation of a special economic zone within the administrative territory of the town of Göd (designation of a special economic zone).

is obliged to provide adequate financial compensation for the tasks entrusted to local authorities. The Constitutional Court stressed that in an emergency situation, the Government is entitled to take immediate and effective measures.

Another constitutional complaint sought to establish the contradiction between a new provision of the Criminal Code on fear mongering and the Fundamental Law, and asked to annul it.[118] At the beginning of the coronavirus epidemic, Parliament adopted an amendment to the Criminal Code, effective from 31 March 2020, which provides that the dissemination of scare stories in public is to be punished more severely in a special legal regime, such as a pandemic emergency. The petitioner argued that the new legislation unnecessarily and disproportionately restricts their right to freedom of expression and is completely unpredictable, leaving wide scope for arbitrary police and judicial enforcement. Furthermore, the rule is incomprehensible and leaves the addressees of the norm in limbo.

In its decision, the Constitutional Court stated that the dissemination of rumours under the contested provision of the law concerns a narrow range of communications: it prohibits the public communication of knowingly false or distorted facts, but only if it is done in a manner that is likely to hinder the defensive measures taken during a period of special legal order. The prohibition therefore only applies to the communication of knowingly false or distorted facts, not to critical opinions. Critics of the decision argue that, instead of annulling the amendment to the Criminal Code, the Court has in fact added an element of intentionality to the text of the provision in order to comply with the requirements of freedom of expression, which is more a guideline for the legislator in the context of the interpretation of the norm than a decision on the constitutionality of the norm within the competence of the Constitutional Court. The guidance is presumed to coincide luckily with the interpretation under the prevailing criminal law doctrine.[119]

There was also a highly publicised decision in April 2021. The Constitutional Court, in its Decision 3413/2020. (XI. 26.) AB, had previously rejected a constitutional complaint by an individual MP challenging a government regulation [Government Decree 179/2020. (V. 4.)], which extended the 15-day deadline for providing data of public interest to 45 days, and may extend it by a further 45 days if the public administration is prevented from providing the data due to the epidemic. However, according to the Decree regulation, this did not require further justification.[120]

In 2020, the petition was rejected by the Constitutional Court on the grounds of the expiry of the regulation due to the end of the emergency. In the new autumn state of danger, the MPs re-filed a motion on 21 January 2021 against the new reg-

118 Decision 15/2020. (VII. 8.) AB.

119 Ambrus, István – Gárdos-Orosz, Fruzsina: "Rémhírterjesztés", in Gárdos-Orosz, Fruzsina – Zakariás, Kinga (eds.): *Az alkotmánybírósági gyakorlat. Az Alkotmánybíróság 100 elvi jelentőségű határozata 1990–2020,* Budapest, Társadalomtudományi Kutatóközpont Jogtudományi Intézet – HVG-ORAC, 2021, 1013–1034.

120 Decision 15/2021. (V. 13.) AB.

ulation with the same content. The Constitutional Court decided the case on the merits and rejected the motion, restating a constitutional requirement, which stated that the Fundamental Law requires that, when applying the regulation, public authorities must justify the reasons for withholding the data of public interest in the context of the pandemic and must provide the data of public interest as soon as possible.[121]

In relation to the restriction of political rights, we should also mention Decision 23/2021. (VII. 13.) AB on the general prohibition of demonstrations. This was the most controversial case, with five dissenting opinions against the majority decision. In April and May 2020, during the general ban on gatherings due to the state of danger, the petitioners were participants or organisers of a pre-announced demonstration by car and raised awareness of the demonstration on social media. They stayed in their cars with banners expressing their demands and drove around the roundabout where the rally was to take place, honking their horns in protest against the crisis management measures. The participants were detained and fined by the police. The administrative decisions in these cases were subject to judicial review by the Pest Central District Court.

In these contested decisions, the ordinary courts partially annulled the authorities' decisions and reduced the fine. However, the petitioners complained that the court had classified their action as part of the general prohibition of assembly adopted under the extraordinary legal order, whereas they had lawfully exercised their freedom of expression in a manner that did not infringe the rules of social restraint and that imposed proportionate restrictions on traffic rules in order to exercise their freedom of expression.

The Constitutional Court explained that the trial court took into account the fact that the petitioner had announced the event as a public event for the purpose of expressing opinions on public affairs. However, because the general prohibition of assembly regulated at the level of government regulations, the demonstration could not be considered an assembly, and therefore the honking and other violations of traffic rules were considered to be acts outside the scope of fundamental rights protection. The majority opinion of the Constitutional Court stressed that it was not for the body to judge in the emergency situation whether such a general ban on gatherings was necessary to prevent the further spread of the virus, and that the decision on the means of protection to be chosen was a matter for the Government under the constitutional mandate. The Constitutional Court therefore dismissed the constitutional complaints against the decision of the ordinary court.[122]

As regards the Constitutional Court's competence to assess the legal restrictions related to the protection against Covid-19, the Constitutional Court, in a politically sensitive case concerning mining rights, explicitly confirmed the early approach

[121] *Ibid.*

[122] Decision 3152/2022. (IV. 12.) AB.

that its competence was limited to examining whether the legislator had the power to create the contested provision of the regulation in the emergency situation. The examination of whether it was appropriate to create a new rule on the exploitation of mining rights, different from the previous one, was no longer within the competence of the Constitutional Court.

This deferential approach to the review tests in relation to measures against the Government empowered to legislate in emergency situations has been the subject of parallel and dissenting opinions within the Constitutional Court (some of which have become majority opinions in subsequent decisions). Nevertheless, it is a summative observation that when the Constitutional Court has applied more stringent tests, it has still found government decrees and other legislation relating to the pandemic to be constitutional. I illustrate this claim with a few examples below.

Following the launch of the vaccination programme, those who were cured of Covid-19 or received the pandemic vaccine became eligible for an immunity certificate. Persons with an immunity certificate were exempted from certain restrictive measures under a government decree. A total of 823 petitions have been lodged with the Constitutional Court in relation to the decree. According to the petitioners, the contested provisions of the government decree were discriminatory, since the refusal to accept the vaccine could be based on an individual decision for a legitimate reason recognised by the state, such as a medical contradiction due to illness. The Constitutional Court held that, under the Fundamental Law, the exercise of certain fundamental rights may be restricted or even suspended beyond the limits set by the constitution in a state of danger. On this basis, the Constitutional Court accepted the fight against the coronavirus epidemic as a legitimate legislative objective in relation to the restriction of the rights in question. It found that the legislature had fulfilled its obligation by regularly reviewing the need to maintain these restrictive measures. The Court did not examine the classic proportionality of this measure, since it considered that it did not have jurisdiction to assess the necessity of the measures taken in an emergency. As regards discrimination, the Court found that those who are in possession of a certificate of immunity by virtue of vaccination or infection do not form a homogeneous group with those who do not have that status. Therefore, the provisions in question do not infringe the prohibition of discrimination.[123]

There were also a large number of constitutional complaints about the mandatory vaccination of health workers against Covid-19. The Constitutional Court ruled on 3 December 2021, in a fast-track decision, that the contested provisions are not unconstitutional. The Constitutional Court applied the proportionality test of the normal legal order, referring to Article 54 (1) of the Fundamental Law, which can be interpreted as providing an exception to the general limitations on the protection of fundamental rights in the case of Article II on the protection of human dignity

123 Decision 27/2021. (XI. 5.) AB.

in times of danger, i.e. the latter cannot be limited in its entirety or in derogation of the normal proportionality test (i.e. Article I (3) of the Fundamental Law applies).[124]

The introduction of mandatory Covid-19 vaccinations for employees of public and municipal institutions has been challenged in 570 constitutional complaints up to March 2022. The Constitutional Court dismissed the constitutional complaints concerning the unconstitutionality of Government Decree 599/2021. (X. 28.) on the compulsory vaccinations against the coronavirus for employees of public and municipal institutions. Once again, the Constitutional Court applied the standard test for compulsory vaccinations of children, developed in 2007, and referred to the "general scientific world view" that vaccination is effective.[125]

In the case of the constitutional complaints concerning the employer's decision to make the Covid-19 vaccination compulsory for employees, the Constitutional Court dismissed the constitutional complaints on procedural grounds, stating that the employer's decision in these cases could still be challenged before the labour courts, and therefore the complaint was premature.[126]

If we review the case law of the Constitutional Court in relation to successive government decrees in emergency situations, we can conclude that the role of the Constitutional Court has not changed compared to previous years. It is reasonable to suggest that the exceptional power granted to the Government in an emergency requires particularly close scrutiny, but this close scrutiny was not the case in the emergency triggered by the coronavirus epidemic. Even if some cases did come before the Constitutional Court, in which the AB's discretion was exercised, no significantly restrictive decisions were taken against the Government's action. Even if the Constitutional Court found that the measures introduced by the Government did indeed unnecessarily or disproportionately restrict certain fundamental rights (such as access to information of public interest, the right of assembly or the right to conduct a business) or infringed certain constitutional principles (for example, by regulating local government), the Constitutional Court did not find them to be in breach of the Fundamental Law. Rather, and in most significant cases, the Constitutional Court has formulated a constitutional requirement, a mandatory way of interpretation and application of the law, instead of annulling the challenged rule and in many cases, the constitutionality of the restriction of fundamental rights was not examined in the absence of appropriate motions.

So far, we have had little knowledge of the special legal order and the limits of emergency legislation, and fortunately little experience of constitutional law in practice. This period of constitutional jurisprudence, however, has not only not contributed to a significant limitation of governmental power, but has also not provided a consistent contribution to a theoretical or doctrinal understanding of the standards of state action in emergency situations, and in particular of the limitation of rights.

124 Decision 3537/2021. (XII. 22.) AB.
125 Decision 37/2007. (VI. 12.) AB.
126 Decision 3088/2021. (III. 10.) AB.

5.2. The Hungarian Constitutional Court in the European Constitutional Space

5.2.1. Introduction

In 2018, I carried out a survey with Zoltán Szente, of the constitutional courts of ten European countries (France, Italy, Spain, Portugal, Germany, Poland, Hungary, Greece, the United Kingdom, and Croatia) with the help of constitutional law scholars from the countries concerned, paying particular attention to the constitutional context in which the constitutional court decisions were made, i.e. the main constitutional changes that took place after the years of the financial crisis. The methodological problem was whether it was possible to find any analytical criteria for the different European countries that would allow a comparison. In addition to the different constitutional arrangements, different constitutional questions have arisen in the constitutional court practice of the individual states. Although the practice of the ECtHR and the CJEU is influential for most of the European courts, these institutions are not primarily responsible for reviewing legislation. Yet, in response to the difficulties, we sought to compare the functioning and jurisprudence of these courts, asking what role the constitutional courts have played and continue to play in the constitutional resolution of crisis-related problems in socio-economic crisis situations.

It would not have been appropriate to categorise changes in the role of constitutional courts or case law in a simplifying way, since, as the national experts' country reports showed, the range of cases is very diverse and it is difficult to identify an objective basis for comparison. We have seen that three broad categories can be developed to characterise the practice of constitutional courts, and that this is an appropriate analytical framework to show the actual role that European constitutional states give to constitutional review, furthermore, to describe the framework provided by the individual constitutions and, finally, the way in which constitutional courts respond to challenges and respond to petitions in crisis situations.

On the basis of our observations, we have divided the constitutional courts into three categories, the first of which includes those whose practice and role has changed little in the context of the major crises of recent years. This does not mean that certain departures from previous jurisprudence, constitutional concepts or judicial attitudes cannot be identified. In the second group, we have included those bodies whose approach has changed fundamentally on some issues and remained unchanged on others. Here it is difficult to identify judicial attitudes, as it is not clear whether new concepts or doctrines need to be introduced. The third group includes those constitutional courts where a new institutional role or a significant change in jurisprudence can be observed. There is, of course, overlap between the different categories, and constitutional courts could be classified in several groups on the basis of their individual decisions. This grouping of constitutional courts (and other higher courts with similar activities) can be used as a basis for better understanding the Hungarian Constitutional Court, which may help to interpret its changing position and practice.

5.2.2. European constitutional courts' responses to social, economic and political challenges

5.2.2.1. The change

Of the countries we have examined, the practice of the Constitutional Council *(Conseil Constitutionnel)* in France and the Constitutional Tribunal *(Tribunal Constitucional)* in Spain has changed most markedly. The most fundamental changes in the practice of the constitutional courts in these two countries have been mainly in the areas of internal security and social welfare.[127] In these cases, for example, the French Constitutional Court has referred to the need to take account of "reality" and has therefore taken a "pragmatic" approach to answering questions of constitutional law.[128] In fact, in the aftermath of the 2008 global financial crisis, both constitutional courts had to take decisions in the context of an unexpected and serious crisis. The most serious acts of terrorism have also hit these countries. Many aspects of counter-terrorism legislation have been brought before the constitutional review bodies.

In France, the question was whether, in addition to the constitution, whose stability is an absolute value, there was a need to amend the organic laws, which are also considered stable. The latter was the most acute issue when it came to the question of whether it is permissible to deprive a person of his or her nationality as a secondary sanction for a terrorist offence in this exceptional situation, when the Constitution and the organic laws of the State, including the organic law on nationality, do not allow this, on the basis of the principle of equality of citizens.[129] Another example of a change in jurisprudence is the case in which the Constitutional Council had to decide on the constitutionality of a law prohibiting the covering of the face in public buildings, or other forms of religious dress in public institutions to cover the body and face. In these cases, religious freedom had to be weighed against public order considerations and the principle of secularity in times of terrorist threats.[130]

[127] Hourquebie, Fabrice: "Remarks on the case law of the French Constitutional Council in relation to new challenges", in Szente, Zoltán – Gárdos-Orosz, Fruzsina (eds.): *New Challenges to Constitutional Adjudication in Europe*, London, Routledge, 2018, 45–52; Callejón, Francisco Balaguer: "Constitutional Courts under Pressure – New Challenges to Constitutional adjudication: The case of Spain", in *ibid.* 164–185.

[128] Hourquebie, Fabrice: "Remarks on the case law of the French Constitutional Council in relation to new challenges", in Szente, Zoltán – Gárdos-Orosz, Fruzsina (eds.): *New Challenges to Constitutional Adjudication in Europe*, London, Routledge, 2018, 52.

[129] Decision N 2014-439 QPC du 23 Janvier 2015.

[130] Decision N 2010-613 DC du 7 October 2010.

The Spanish Constitutional Tribunal has also developed a specific practice, despite having stated early on that if the legislator wants to preserve the security of the state at all costs, this can easily lead to a crisis of the constitutional state.[131] According to analysts, public opinion must have influenced the Constitutional Court, because it could hardly have come to the conclusion that it would approve differentiated protection of the fundamental rights of people arriving illegally in Spain on dogmatic grounds alone. Although the principle of equality would not have allowed the constitutionality of a law that differentiated between the fundamental rights of legal and illegal residents to be declared, the Constitutional Tribunal approved this provision of the law, basing its reasoning on the crisis situation and deliberately departing from its previous practice. The provision on the right to equal human dignity and the inalienability of the essential content of fundamental rights is part of Spanish constitutional law and was clearly violated by this decision.[132]

In the context of the economic crisis, the Spanish Constitutional Tribunal has approved the government's ambitions. It has developed a doctrine that could be described as a "sensitive economic" interpretation of the Constitution, allowing the constitutionality of the government's crisis management solutions to be approved. As for the cuts to social rights, the Constitutional Tribunal has interpreted them in accordance with the constitutional principle of balanced budget management, thus justifying the budgetary cuts and the fact that the content and level of protection of certain fundamental rights may change.[133] In Spain, one of the main challenges in recent times has been the constitutional treatment of the secessionist aspirations of Catalonia. On this issue, however, the Constitutional Tribunal's practice has not shown any change in standards, with the consequence that it has not supported autonomy aspirations in this case.[134]

5.2.2.2. Continuity and change

As I mentioned above, in recent years, many constitutional review bodies have been characterized by a combination of preserving and changing constitutional principles, doctrinal concepts, and standards of fundamental rights protection; the interpretation of the law has varied from case to case. Greece is a great example of this, because it has been hit very hard by the economic crisis. The practice of the Supreme Court has changed a great deal, and many cases have been brought before it.[135]

---

131 STC 62/2011 of 5 May 2011.

132 Callejón, Francisco Balaguer: "Constitutional Courts under Pressure – New Challenges to Constitutional adjudication: The case of Spain", in Szente, Zoltán – Gárdos-Orosz, Fruzsina (eds.): *New Challenges to Constitutional Adjudication in Europe*, London, Routledge, 2018, 164–185.

133 *Ibid.* 179–181.

134 STC 103/2008. 1 September or STC 31/2010. 28 June.

135 Vlachogiannis, Apostolos: "From submission to reaction: the Greek Courts stance on the financial crisis in challenges", in Szente, Zoltán – Gárdos-Orosz, Fruzsina (eds.): *New Challenges to Constitutional Adjudication in Europe*, London, Routledge, 2018, 72–89.

In Greek constitutional jurisprudence, a "holistic interpretation" emerged, which gave the body the flexibility to interpret the constitutional tests. Constitutionalism was also a general yardstick that was used very intensively by the court in order to adapt the decision in the case to the extreme situation without abandoning the classical yardsticks. Within this framework, the court even introduced the doctrine of "crisis situation" and tried to reconcile it with the requirement of proportionality.[136]

In the first years of the crisis, the Greek Supreme Court was also more lenient on austerity measures, developing interpretations and doctrinal concepts that supported the constitutionality of government legislative acts. One of these allowed the state to increase contributions to the public purse. In other cases, new doctrines were not introduced, but old ones were adapted. The public interest has been invoked to justify the constitutional protection of the budgetary interest defined by the government in a crisis situation. The Greek Supreme Court, which has ruled on constitutionality issues, has had the greatest difficulty in enforcing the right to property and equality in the context of crisis legislation, and has been criticised for failing to do so.[137] There have been times when the general interest or the public has been such an overriding argument that it has seemed to override any individual right. At the height of the crisis, when statehood itself was at stake, any means seemed permissible to avoid disaster.[138]

Greece was not included among the states where the nature of constitutional interpretation has changed significantly because, after the initial leniency, the Supreme Court, as a strict critic of the Government, annulled crisis legislation in a number of cases when it sought to impose severe restrictions on rights on a permanent basis.

This change in the attitude of the court has also involved the reshaping or resetting of some constitutional standards. Increasingly, the proportionality test has been used instead of the simple reasonableness test, and more reference has been made to the more rigorous practice of the past.[139]

Italy is another example of the volatility of constitutional practice. Here, the Constitutional Court has managed to maintain constitutional standards for the protection of fundamental rights, even in the context of the migration crisis, the protection of the rights of immigrants or the threat of terrorism, but the practice of the Italian Constitutional Court *(Corte costituzionale)* has also produced some ingenious solutions.[140]

136 *Ibid.* 80–81.

137 *Ibid.*

138 *Ibid.* 74–78.

139 *Ibid.* 81.

140 Ciolli, Ines: "Global markets, terrorism and immigration: Italy between a troubled economy and a Constitutional crisis", in Szente, Zoltán – Gárdos-Orosz, Fruzsina (eds.): *New Challenges to Constitutional Adjudication in Europe,* London, Routledge, 2018, 111–132.

The Constitutional Court applied tests that were often different from its previous practice and came up with novel results. For example, when it came to the question of increasing the powers of parliament and government, the review focused on the establishment of controllability of public expenditure as a constitutional interest justifying the separation of powers between constitutional institutions, in particular parliament and government.[141]

However, they also introduced the doctrine of the "balanced budget", which is a constitutional idea that allowed the constitutionality of certain austerity measures to be confirmed, and even retroactive legislation was found to be constitutional in some glaring cases, given the crisis situation.[142] The Constitutional Court in Italy has also been in a politically sensitive position, having had to find a balancing decision between the legislature and the executive in the tense situation of the last decade. It has accepted the strengthening of the executive, a move towards presidentialisation. The Constitutional Court also had no objection to the central government increasing its powers vis-à-vis the regions, although in the end nothing in the provisions of the constitution changed, so it was in fact a reinterpretation of the vertical division of powers. The instability of constitutional democracy was most noticeable during the financial crisis. Concentration of powers between the regions and the centre seemed necessary, and the government was given a freer hand in fiscal management. The new interpretation of the constitution that emerged in the wake of the crisis has been applied by the Italian Constitutional Court in several cases.[143] The reason why it is possible to speak of maintaining standards is that the Constitutional Court has stressed that special concessions can only be accepted on a temporary basis, and specifically in the light of the crisis situation.[144]

Portugal is also included in this group in our book. The Portuguese state has also been severely affected by the financial crisis, which has led to several petitions to the Constitutional Court in relation to international lending and Portuguese stability programmes.[145] The Portuguese constitutional practice is specific in two respects. Firstly, in the Portuguese Constitution, social and economic rights are protected by fundamental rights, and are therefore not just objectives of the State, which are merely a state aspiration, but not a subjective right in the Constitution. The second is that Portugal also needed a loan to deal with the crisis, the terms of which were set by the 'troika' (the International Monetary Fund, the European Central Bank and the European Commission). These measures involved cuts in

141 *Ibid.* 117.

142 10/2015. CC.

143 Ciolli, Ines: "Global markets, terrorism and immigration: Italy between a troubled economy and a Constitutional crisis", in Szente, Zoltán – Gárdos-Orosz, Fruzsina (eds.): *New Challenges to Constitutional Adjudication in Europe,* London, Routledge, 2018, 121–122.

144 275/2016. CC.

145 Canotilho, Mariana: "Constitutional law and crisis: The Portuguese Constitutional Court under pressure?", in Szente, Zoltán – Gárdos-Orosz, Fruzsina (eds.): *New Challenges to Constitutional Adjudication in Europe,* London, Routledge, 2018, 144–164.

the public sector, radical reductions in salaries and other benefits and cuts in other social benefits.[146]

The Portuguese Constitutional Court *(Tribunal Constitucional),* like the Hungarian one, has been criticised for its activism, for example for overstepping its powers in resolving certain fundamental rights conflicts, only invoking equality or *legitimate expectation* in cases in which it wanted to support its own position in the absence of a constitutional context, i.e. in the absence of precise relevant constitutional provisions. In fact, however, the Constitutional Court has in several cases found a compromise between the crisis situation and the protection of constitutional rights.[147] For example, it annulled a rule that would have meant a further reduction in the salaries of public sector workers, but it did so *ex nunc,* which meant that the state budget could still benefit from the revenue for a certain period of time.[148] In other cases, this half-hearted, compromise jurisprudence has taken the form of upholding the constitutionality of certain pieces of legislation, freshly enacted in response to the crisis, by recognising their validity only in this exceptional situation; otherwise they would be unconstitutional.[149]

It was also a compromise solution to change the content of some traditional tests and yardsticks, such as the protection of legitimate expectations, the proportionality yardstick, or the substance of fundamental rights in the case of social rights. In many cases, the Constitutional Court has thus given way to government measures to deal with the crisis, but has also stressed the importance of protecting fundamental rights and the need to declare certain unconstitutional government measures in order to protect the fundamental rights. On the whole, therefore, the classic principles and doctrines of constitutional court practice have been preserved.[150]

5.2.2.3. Stability and continuity

Of course, understanding constitutional review is often not a question of whether or not the practice of the constitutional court has changed, but rather of the principles and objectives behind the decisions have changed. We can also see change in the states that we have included in this last category, but these constitutional courts are less inclined to change their practice. It has also been stressed that, within the legal model, as I have shown above in the first part of this book, constitutional courts may of course take into account certain social or natural factors when deciding a case, but that this has a predetermined place and role in the doctrinal argumentation. It should be thought of as a provision for a special legal order in constitutions. If the constituent power predetermines that in certain situations the

146 *Ibid.* 147–156.

147 *Ibid.* 158–159.

148 Portuguese Constitutional Court 353/12; 187/13; 413/2014; 574/2014; 396/11.

149 Portuguese Constitutional Court 574/2014.

150 Canotilho, Mariana: "Constitutional law and crisis: The Portuguese Constitutional Court under pressure?", in Szente, Zoltán – Gárdos-Orosz, Fruzsina (eds.): *New Challenges to Constitutional Adjudication in Europe,* London, Routledge, 2018, 157–160.

general order of lawmaking and law enforcement may change and also determines the way in which this may happen, then this is acceptable within the framework of constitutional democracy.

The constitutional courts of the countries that belong to this group have approached the petitions they received and brought their judgments in a certain way, in order to decide which legislative solutions can be considered constitutional in the case of a financial crisis, a migration crisis or other massive and serious socio-economic problems by preserving constitutionalism.

The constitutional courts in the last group have thus adopted the starting point that constitutional democracy is an elaborate concept capable of providing an answer to any constitutional question arising in the context of a crisis. This does not mean, therefore, that the constitutional solution is exactly the same in times of crisis as in peaceful everyday life, but only that the system of constitutional principles and standards is the same, with different weight given to different aspects in the balancing exercise, depending on the circumstances.

Croatian Constitutional Court practice, for example, has not changed much in this sense. In Croatia, the central issue in the development of the law over the last fifteen years has been how to enforce the rights enshrined in the Constitution. In this country, this may be so because the war period of the early 1990s is a living memory, when severe restrictions on rights were left without state limits. The Constitutional Court has therefore applied a very strict approach to the protection of fundamental rights in matters of internal security.[151]

For example, the Croatian Constitutional Court *(Ustavni sud)* has maintained the standard proportionality test for assessing the constitutionality of legislation aimed at preventing and combating terrorism. In this case, the challenged law would have imposed disproportionate restrictions on the right of assembly, but the Constitutional Court found this unconstitutional and annulled the law.[152] However, it is analysed that the practice of the Croatian Constitutional Court is far from consistent in legislative matters concerning internal security, as very many legislative acts have not been challenged, and thus most of the restrictions have not been subject to constitutional review. It would therefore be very difficult to predict from one or two cases what the Croatian Constitutional Court would and would not consider constitutional in a serious crisis situation. It can be concluded that it places great emphasis on procedural issues, i.e. it primarily examines them when assessing the constitutionality of legislative acts in the field of internal security.[153]

---

151 Gardasevic, Djordje: "Croatian constitutional adjudication in times of stress", in Szente, Zoltán – Gárdos-Orosz, Fruzsina (eds.): *New Challenges to Constitutional Adjudication in Europe*, London, Routledge, 2018, 27–45.

152 Croatian Constitutional Court U-448/2009; U-8113/2009; U-2871/2011.

153 Gardasevic, Djordje: "Croatian constitutional adjudication in times of stress", in Szente, Zoltán – Gárdos-Orosz, Fruzsina (eds.): *New Challenges to Constitutional Adjudication in Europe*, London, Routledge, 2018, 29.

In cases related to the financial crisis, the Croatian Constitutional Court has underlined that the protection of the social state, social justice and social rights is rather a state objective in the Constitution, and does not imply any constitutional obligation. In Croatia, practice in this respect did not need to change much, because social rights were not strongly protected under optimal circumstances, they were not previously considered a fundamental right, and because of the constitutionalisation of the state after the Yugoslav wars in the 1990s, all of which meant that constitutional court practice was already permissive towards government measures in the context of crisis management.[154]

Of the countries covered in the book, Germany has seen the least change in constitutional court practice. The German Federal Constitutional Court *(Bundesverfassungsgericht)* is known to have a very rich practice and has faced many challenges in its decades of operation, so responding to a major wave of migration or terrorist attacks is not a new problem. In the context of the financial crisis, the German Constitutional Court has also had to face constitutional problems of crisis management, albeit in a different way than the Greek or Portuguese Constitutional Courts.[155]

In one case, the German Federal Constitutional Court had to rule on the constitutionality of a financial package put together to rescue EU Member States in difficulty. Despite the fact that Germany was on the creditor side in the EU when the financial crisis was resolved, the constitutionality issue arose here too, but in a different context. One of the problems was to define the limits of sovereignty, the others related to the democratic system and the functioning of representative democracy. The basic dilemma was the extent to which democratic procedures can be modified to ensure effective decision-making in crisis. The Constitutional Court in this case ruled that the *Bundestag* can only agree to a commitment at international or EU level if Germany has the possibility to influence its content, i.e. if it is made through a democratic procedure where Germany participates. However, the relevant case-law of the Constitutional Court has not indicated that a specific, exceptional situation, such as the financial crisis, requires different constitutional standards.[156] The German decisions in these matters are dogmatically follow-ups to the 1993 Maastricht Decision, and it was already confirmed there that the Constitutional Court cannot depart from the basic standards of constitutionality.[157]

The German Constitutional Court also applied the necessity-proportionality test when it had to judge the constitutionality of the anti-terrorism data collection

154 *Ibid.* 35–36, 41.

155 Mehde, Veith: "Beware of Disruption: Bundesverfassungsgericht as supporter of change and anchor of stability", in Szente, Zoltán – Gárdos-Orosz, Fruzsina (eds.): *New Challenges to Constitutional Adjudication in Europe,* London, Routledge, 2018, 53–72.

156 BVerGE 129, 124. 12 June 2016.

157 Mehde, Veith: "Beware of Disruption: Bundesverfassungsgericht as supporter of change and anchor of stability", in Szente, Zoltán – Gárdos-Orosz, Fruzsina (eds.): *New Challenges to Constitutional Adjudication in Europe,* London, Routledge, 2018, 66–67.

system legislation. Perhaps the only surprising decision in the case law of recent years was that the Constitutional Court referred the matter to the CJEU for a preliminary ruling, which it had never done before. However, this in itself cannot be considered as a significant change that would push the boundaries of the category of "unchangeability".[158]

5.2.3. The exceptions

5.2.3.1. Specific routes

Poland, Hungary and the UK are included in this category in the volume.

The UK appears to fall into the second group, i.e. it has changed its practice on some issues but not on others. Yet the courts seem to rely on the legislature's professional competence in cases involving internal security regulation and to refrain from examining substantive issues. When the legislator invokes the general public interest, the courts do not examine its validity but accept it as a regulatory ground. In so doing, the courts give up their traditional position of control over national security issues and instead give the government free rein to judge the necessity of certain restrictions on national security issues, despite the fact that judicial protection of privacy has traditionally been strong, for example in Britain against secret data collection.[159] While practice in the area of homeland security regulation is constantly evolving, it is unchanged that the European Convention on Human Rights and the practice of the CJEU have been the subject of considerable scepticism among British judges since the *Human Rights Act* came into force. It is not only the mandatory application of the Council of Europe's system of legal protection that has been contentious, but EU law as a whole has failed to fit into the British public law order. The primacy of EU law has, according to many members of the English legal profession, raised issues that were incompatible with traditional parliamentary sovereignty. Some argue that this perception may also have contributed to Brexit, the UK's exit from the European Union.[160] However, in the pre-pandemic crisis situations, the *Human Rights Act* and directly applicable EU law also played a role in the ruling.[161] The UK case is therefore specific because the practice of constitutional review was influenced by external constraints, which took the form of legislation and were easier for continental states to deal with than in the UK.

158 2 BvR 27/28/2013. 14 January 2014.

159 Birkinshaw, Patrick: "National security and the limits of judicial protection", in Szente, Zoltán – Gárdos-Orosz, Fruzsina (eds.): *New Challenges to Constitutional Adjudication in Europe*, London, Routledge, 2018, 185–214.

160 McEldowney, John: "The UK Supreme Court and Parliament: Judicial and political dialogues", in Szente, Zoltán – Gárdos-Orosz, Fruzsina (eds.): *New Challenges to Constitutional Adjudication in Europe*, London, Routledge, 2018, 214–232.

161 *Ibid.* 230.

The Hungarian and Polish examples are also special. The positions of the Hungarian Constitutional Court and the Polish Constitutional Council *(Trybunał Konstytucyjny)* were very similar to those of other courts on many issues, but interestingly these decisions had no roots in domestic law, so they developed constitutional concepts that were often completely new.[162] The Polish and Hungarian Constitutional Courts have had experience in dealing with special situations, if we consider that these are institutions that were established after the change of regime and that have developed their functioning in an exceptional situation. Of course, these decisions were often not embedded in a previously established doctrinal system in the same way as similar decisions of long-standing constitutional courts. Furthermore, in the cases related to the financial crisis, it was an important consideration that the Hungarian Constitutional Court's jurisdiction was limited, i.e. it could only examine central budget laws in exceptional cases. Certain issues therefore automatically fall within the competence of the parliamentary majority or the Government under the Fundamental Law. As I have shown earlier, in the 1990s in Hungary, there were a few cases of constitutional review of the budgetary activity of the Parliament, but this practice has been discontinued after 2010.[163]

In both countries, the principle of balanced budget management has played a major role, defining the practice of the Constitutional Court as a constitutional requirement and providing grounds for justifying the constitutionality of governmental and legislative measures, especially in areas such as property rights or the regulation of social and economic rights.[164] In politically sensitive matters, the Hungarian Constitutional Court, in line with this approach, tended to reinforce the political will with constitutional arguments, even if it could only do so by means of a constitutional requirement that led to the development of novel dogmatic elements, standards and concepts in constitutional law.[165] The Fundamental Law, especially the text following the Seventh Amendment, has already provided a positive legal basis for the elaboration of these, although in many cases – and here I would refer back to the first part of this volume – only in such a way that the Constitutional Court also applied the elements of the Preamble, the National Avowal, which has a special legal status, to the development of the legal content in accordance with Article R) of the Fundamental Law. Thus, the position of the Hungarian Constitutional Court has changed fundamentally and, as I have shown above, the former President of the Constitutional Court made this clear in the context of the crisis situations. The cur-

162 Granat, Miroslaw: "Constitutional judiciary in crisis: The case of Poland", in Szente, Zoltán – Gárdos-Orosz, Fruzsina (eds.): *New Challenges to Constitutional Adjudication in Europe,* London, Routledge, 2018, 132–143.

163 Szente, Zoltán – Gárdos-Orosz, Fruzsina: "Judicial deference or political loyalty? The Hungarian Constitutional Court's role in tackling crisis situation", in Szente, Zoltán – Gárdos-Orosz, Fruzsina (eds.): *New Challenges to Constitutional Adjudication in Europe,* London, Routledge, 2018, 89–110.

164 *Ibid.* 89–110.

165 See above, in the discussion of Constitutional Court decisions on foreign currency loans.

rent President of the Constitutional Court has not made a similarly clear statement of belief, but the decisions of the Constitutional Court in response to crisis situations show that the role of the Court has changed, and that on politically sensitive issues or those fundamentally affecting the constitutional order, it endorses the position of the two-thirds majority of the government, seeking arguments to confirm it.

The situation of the Polish Constitutional Council is even more special, because it has been a situation in which the legitimacy of the court has been called into question, and this has determined the discourse on its practice in recent years, which has resulted in some ordinary courts preferring to take upon themselves the task of constitutional review.[166]

5.2.3.2. The Court of Justice of the European Union and the European Court of Human Rights

The situation of the European courts is special because the CJEU has tended to have a greater role in dealing with the financial crisis, while the ECtHR has dealt with individual human rights complaints in the context of crisis situations. The practice of the European Courts is also interesting because their decisions have often served as a reference point for the operation of constitutional courts in the Member States.[167]

The practice of the ECtHR has not changed much in recent years. For example, it has been clearly confirmed that the prohibition of torture is absolute, and the importance of the right to a remedy and to a fair trial remains fundamental, also in the case of persons accused of terrorism or illegal border crossers.[168] In the case in which the Hungarian legislation on secret information gathering was found to be constitutional by the Constitutional Court, the Strasbourg Court held that it constituted an unnecessary restriction on privacy.[169] The ECtHR has found it more difficult to ensure the legal protection of those affected by the financial crisis. The European Convention on Human Rights does not recognise economic and social rights as fundamental rights. However, in some cases it has sought to improve the situation of persons through activist interpretations of civil and political rights. In other cases, the protection of the right to property has been the basis for the ECtHR's finding that restrictive measures by governments are incompatible with

[166] Granat, Miroslaw: "Constitutional judiciary in crisis: The case of Poland", in Szente, Zoltán – Gárdos-Orosz, Fruzsina (eds.): *New Challenges to Constitutional Adjudication in Europe*, London, Routledge, 2018, 138–142.

[167] Szente, Zoltán – Gárdos-Orosz, Fruzsina: "Constitutional courts under pressure – An assessment", in Szente, Zoltán – Gárdos-Orosz, Fruzsina (eds.): *New Challenges to Constitutional Adjudication in Europe*, London, Routledge, 2018, 291–312.

[168] Delzangles, Beatrice: "The negotiating function of the European Court of Human Rights: Reconciling diverging interests born from new European challenges", in Szente, Zoltán – Gárdos-Orosz, Fruzsina (eds.): *New Challenges to Constitutional Adjudication in Europe*, London, Routledge, 2018, 259–273.

[169] Szabó and Vissy v. Hungary, no. 37138/14, 12 January 2016.

the Convention. In the context of the financial crisis, the protection of rights such as the right to a fair trial or the right to a judge according to law has been strengthened. In cases where these rights were not involved, the Strasbourg Court could not, or did not wish to, reduce the discretion of states to take social and economic austerity measures in times of crisis. The Court reflected on the financial crisis by stating that it was an exceptional situation without precedent, which could justify exceptional standards. This was also the approach taken by the CJEU in some areas of case law when it came to the reduction of social benefits that would be granted in a given state to a national of another member state or a third country.[170]

Overall, the number of cases involving fundamental rights before the CJEU was quite small, and in these cases the court mainly referred to the practice of the ECtHR. The practice of the ECtHR and the CJEU has therefore not fundamentally changed in terms of the content of rights, or the standards or the margin of appreciation towards the Member States, but it has also not been able to have a significant impact on the management of crises. The ECtHR has succeeded in enforcing Convention rights in a few blatantly serious cases, but its high-volume position has prevented it from determining the constitutional policy of states.

The ECtHR has ruled, for example, that the threat of terrorism is an extremely serious situation which, since the terrorist attacks of 11 September 2001, has been recognised as a threat to the existence of nations and therefore legitimately affects the practice of law and the scope of protection of certain rights. Despite the Court's rejection that the capacity of States to fulfil their obligations could be a reason for a practice in breach of the Convention, or despite the fact that it considered that there was no concession for certain rights even in the event of a terrorist threat (for example, the prohibition of torture), it accepted the exceptional and unexpected financial crisis as a ground for reviewing the State's restriction of certain rights.[171] In many of these cases, the invocation of proportionality or the examination of the legitimate legislative purpose was only a formality, with little impact on the *ratio decidendi*. Thus, by not applying these yardsticks explicitly, the ECtHR ended up simply not interfering with government policies. This approach can be described as a cooperative negotiating stance, whereby the court is constantly in contact with the member states and their courts in order to reach a position that is acceptable to all.[172] The CJEU is

---

170 For summary, see Delzangles, Beatrice: "The negotiating function of the European Court of Human Rights: Reconciling diverging interests born from new European challenges", in Szente, Zoltán – Gárdos-Orosz, Fruzsina (eds.): *New Challenges to Constitutional Adjudication in Europe*, London, Routledge, 2018, 264–269.

171 Varju, Márton: "The crisis, judicial power and EU law: Could it have been managed differently by the EU Court of Justice?", in Szente, Zoltán – Gárdos-Orosz, Fruzsina (eds.): *New Challenges to Constitutional Adjudication in Europe*, London, Routledge, 2018, 174–288.

172 See Delzangles, Beatrice: "The negotiating function of the European Court of Human Rights: Reconciling diverging interests born from new European challenges", in Szente, Zoltán – Gárdos-Orosz, Fruzsina (eds.): *New Challenges to Constitutional Adjudication in Europe*, London, Routledge, 2018, 180–181.

also increasingly inclined to accept the legislative position of the Member States,[173] especially in crisis situations. According to the ECJ, the Court of Justice has little role to play in deciding on properly designed legislative procedures, and this is even more true when the legislation under scrutiny is detailed. This is generally the case in the area of fiscal and monetary policy, which is why there is little justification for intervention in the case of a review of an elaborate policy decision. What can be observed is that the CJEU has been mindful of the enforcement of EU policies in crisis-related cases and has simply sought to enforce the unconditional application of EU law.[174]

5.2.4. Main constitutional strategies to address social and economic challenges

5.2.4.1. General solutions

Although each case is different and each country has its own constitutional set-up, after reviewing the case law analyses in our book we have been able to identify interpretative methods and substantive constitutional concepts that have appeared in the practice of several constitutional review bodies.[175] First, we had to establish that responding to social problems raises complex legislative issues, most of which are not subject to constitutional review in different European countries, furthermore, not all social problems reach the courts in the same form. Yet comparisons can be made, since the most serious social problems, such as the financial crisis, migration or the threat of terrorism, have developed in almost all European countries into problems which the States have dealt with by legislation, some of which have been subject to constitutional review in the light of the rule adopted, albeit in different procedures (ex ante, ex post, constitutional complaint) and possibly in the form of different questions, but in a very abstractly comparable way. In each case, the fundamental question underlying the detailed questions was the extent to which the body conducting the constitutional review can and does intervene in the shaping of constitutional policy in the event of a serious crisis and allow to examine how its ambitions affect constitutional interpretation.

The financial crisis has also generated a library of literature because it was such a major problem that it raised a number of constitutional questions in all countries in relation to budgetary and fiscal issues, or even fundamental rights (property rights,

---

173 Várnay, Ernő: "Judicial Passivism at the European Court of Justice?", *Hungarian Journal of Legal Studies*, 2019/2, 127–154; Várnay, Ernő: "Tagállami érdekek, tagállami kötelezettségek és az Európai Unió joga", *Jogtudományi Közlöny*, 2022/7–8, 324–326.

174 Varju, Márton: "The crisis, judicial power and EU law: Could it have been managed differently by the EU Court of Justice?", in Szente, Zoltán – Gárdos-Orosz, Fruzsina (eds.): *New Challenges to Constitutional Adjudication in Europe*, London, Routledge, 2018, 286–88.

175 Szente, Zoltán – Gárdos-Orosz, Fruzsina: "Constitutional courts under pressure – An assessment", in Szente, Zoltán – Gárdos-Orosz, Fruzsina (eds.): *New Challenges to Constitutional Adjudication in Europe*, London, Routledge, 2018, 304–310.

social rights, general equality, freedom of enterprise). It is interesting to note that, in the context of the examination of the constitutionality of certain budgetary issues, panels of elected lawyers have been involved in the decision-making process, so that the operation and dilemmas of legal constitutionality could be analysed in a lively situation. However, the decisions show that, despite their constitutional position, the constitutional courts have not intervened strongly in the resolution of legal issues related e.g. to the financial crisis, but have tended to be rather abstentive *(deference)*.[176] It can also be noted that they have been rather accepting the new financial-economic regulatory efforts.[177]

The example of Greece shows that the constitutional review body, for the first time, was more permissive towards policy makers, even when the crisis management measures were subject to legal constraints, in the hope of quickly dealing with the shock of the crisis. But as the crisis dragged on, the court became increasingly strict, and less and less willing to allow temporary restrictions that were acceptable for short periods to become permanent. In cases, such as Portugal, where the constitutional court has accepted the constitutionality of government action, these measures have not become permanent, but rather general, short-term restrictions. It can be seen that there is still a significant role for constitutional courts in Europe, which have not rejected petitions in a crisis situation on the grounds of lack of competence, the courts did not develop doctrines – such as the *political question doctrine* – that might have relieved them of the burden of decision. The constitutional courts have tended to be restrained in substance, intervening with constitutional arguments in political decision-making only in cases of severe and persistent or blatantly unequal restrictions of rights. They preferred intermediate, temporary solutions. What these intermediate solutions looked like depended largely on the constitutional set-up of the state and the political power structure.[178]

We obtained similar findings when we examined the practice of the constitutional courts in relation to national security and terrorism. It is true that no Member State in Europe has taken certain measures, such as the abolition of the ban on torture or the adoption of mass expulsions, but the courts have been lenient in the face of certain restrictions on privacy or data protection in a crisis situation, as the example of the UK has shown.[179]

Mass migration is the issue which has probably had the lowest number of constitutional court proceedings in Europe, which is also due to the fact that the processes that started in 2015 were very fast and the problems mainly took the form of individual court cases; and the constitutional complaints procedure is very lim-

[176] *Ibid.*

[177] Fabbrini, Federico: *Economic Governance in Europe: Comparative Paradoxes and Constitutional Challenges,* Oxford, Oxford University Press, 2016, 100–101.

[178] Szente, Zoltán – Gárdos-Orosz, Fruzsina: "Constitutional courts under pressure – An assessment", in Szente, Zoltán – Gárdos-Orosz, Fruzsina (eds.): *New Challenges to Constitutional Adjudication in Europe,* London, Routledge, 2018, 301–303.

[179] *Ibid.* 302.

ited in Europe and, where it exists, the conditions for admission are strict. The question of what, if any, distinctions can be made between people entering the territory of a country and what rights they enjoy is one of the issues, also linked to the constitutional concept of equality, that has been decided by the constitutional courts. The other major issue in Europe was the question of social rights and social benefits: this too has been the subject of great controversy, even in states with a high economic performance. The fact that a common European solution was certainly needed in this area also influenced the way this issue was viewed, and therefore the constitutional courts could be even more reluctant to take individual positions. There was also a constitutional court – the Hungarian one – for which this crisis situation gave reason to attempt to establish a dogmatic basis for constitutional identity.

Despite the fact that there have been comparable constitutional court decisions on some issues, it is also important to note that before the Covid-19 pandemic, there have been large differences in what caused the most serious crises and difficulties in the procedures for reaching a decision. While in Spain the focus of the pre-Covid-19 period under review was on separatist aspirations, in Italy the constitutional crisis arose from the strengthening of the executive and, in addition, from issues of vertical separation of powers, in the UK the main constitutional problem was the influence of external legal systems, international law and EU law on domestic law, and in Hungary the Constitutional Court was most concerned with issues related to the rule of law and legal certainty in the populist legal change.[180]

5.2.4.2. New interpretative methods and substantive concepts in constitutional law

In examining the practice of European constitutional courts and supreme courts conducting judicial review, we have observed[181] that there has been no trend to set aside classic standards such as the necessity-proportionality test, the requirement of a legitimate legislative purpose or the reasonableness test. Furthermore, the principles that the essential content of fundamental rights cannot be removed and arbitrary legislation is unacceptable have also remained in place. Within this broad framework, however, there has been a slight shift in the practice of constitutional interpretation, with constitutional courts taking greater account of political, economic and social circumstances. Since the legal model of constitutional adjudication allows for these to be taken into account according to a predetermined methodology, the courts have made use of this possibility, often without remaining in their ivory towers. However, as the doctrine of how and how much weight to give to the social, economic or political challenges to be assessed in a particular case is not well developed in the legal system, the assessment has often caused great difficulties in the reasoning. New theoretical approaches, concepts and yardsticks have

180 *Ibid.* 302–303.

181 *Ibid.* 304–305.

therefore been developed in the course of constitutional jurisprudence in order to respond to issues considered to be of exceptional importance within the existing framework, while at the same time positioning the institutions themselves in such a way as to preserve their relevance in order to safeguard constitutionality.

Constitutional courts have sometimes discovered the importance of constitutional provisions that have not previously played a major role in constitutional interpretation (see for example the constitutional identity based on the achievements of the historical constitution in Hungary). Another option that some courts have used is to draw a general "constitutional interpretation veil" over ordinary constitutional interpretation, saying that in the specific situation they are interpreting from a "holistic" (Greece) or "economic" (Spain) perspective. The reference to the public interest or general interest has also been reinforced in the practice of constitutional courts in the context of major social and economic problems. In many cases, it has simply been a case of existing concepts taking on new meanings. Proportionality or necessity, for example, which had previously been regarded as rather abstract criteria, have become capable of supporting interpretations that might not have been acceptable in other situations. It is therefore possible to consider as proportionate what would not have been proportionate in another situation.[182]

It is also possible that a parliamentary majority will introduce new institutions (such as the Finance Council in Italy)[183] which will have powers on certain issues that reduce the possibility of effective constitutional review. If the creation of such institutions, or indeed new procedures, is not unconstitutional, it may be possible simply to outsource certain review powers. This has not only happened in Italy with the establishment of the Financial Council, but also in Hungary, where the Fiscal Council, in limitation of the scope of the Constitutional Court, also oversees the constitutionality of the budget and its implementation.

In some cases the states decided not to declare a special legal order where the standards of constitutional rights restrictions are not clearly set but rather to give special authorization the Governments by a more deferential application of the standard proportionality test. However it has also been argued – most notably in the case of Greece – that short-term restrictions on certain fundamental rights can lead to greater constitutional balance in the longer term. This kind of reflection is a fundamental influence on constitutional policy, which can lead to a lack of a legal model in a given state, even if it is precisely the legal protection of fundamental rights that it seeks to secure.[184]

182 *Ibid.* 303–304.

183 Ciolli, Ines: "Global markets, terrorism and immigration: Italy between a troubled economy and a Constitutional crisis", in Szente, Zoltán – Gárdos-Orosz, Fruzsina (eds.): *New Challenges to Constitutional Adjudication in Europe,* London, Routledge, 2018, 111–132.

184 Szente, Zoltán – Gárdos-Orosz, Fruzsina: "Constitutional courts under pressure – An assessment", in Szente, Zoltán – Gárdos-Orosz, Fruzsina (eds.): *New Challenges to Constitutional Adjudication in Europe,* London, Routledge, 2018, 304.

We have also found an argument in the practice of European constitutional courts that it is necessary to approve fiscal austerity measures in order to safeguard fundamental rights in the long term, as this is essential to restore balanced budget management.

In some cases, we also found arguments that the definition of the public interest is a matter for the elected political majority, and that the public interest is therefore an external factor legitimizing legislation that cannot be reviewed by the Constitutional Court. In addition, the argument can be observed, particularly in British practice, that the court is not even competent to judge certain technical issues, such as security, and that in such situations the decision should be left to the political decision-making bodies with expertise.

In some cases, it was also stated in the reasoning of some decisions that the Constitutional Court cannot make a political type of decision, so if it itself considers a decision to be political, it can declare that it lacks jurisdiction in the case. This is similar to the US *political question* doctrine, except that in European practice it is not such a clear and sharp conceptual decision, rather the opposite; in Europe the constitutional court classifies decisions in the context of a crisis situation, which takes legal form, and delimits its own jurisdiction on the basis of its classification. Finally, some Constitutional Courts have argued that special situations require special standards and solutions, arguing that in non-special situations it is possible to return to the familiar path, to the conceptual framework previously adopted.

Overall, it can be concluded that in crisis situations, constitutional law arguments run a very wide gamut: at one end of the scale is the German Federal Constitutional Court, and at the other end is the Hungarian Constitutional Court, due to the new constitutional environment, i.e. the entry into force of the Fundamental Law. To some extent, all courts of judicial review have been creative in finding ways not to take the lead in determining constitutional policy issues in crisis.

5.3. Possible reasons for changes in case law

5.3.1. European trends

We can learn about the practice of the Constitutional Court from its decisions, and separate opinion, from dissenting or concurring reasoning. In some cases, institutional and jurisdictional changes have been settled at constitutional level.[185] For example, several countries have introduced debt limitation provisions. The principle of balanced and transparent budget management appeared in some European constitutions has also often been relevant in the practice of the constitutional courts.

[185] For a detailed analysis, see Contiades, Xenophon – Fotiaou, Alkmene: "How Constitutions Reacted to the Financial Crisis", in Contiades, Xenophon (ed.): *Constitutions in the Global Financial Crisis. A Comparative Analysis*, Farnham, Ashgate, 2013.

The provisions of the French, Italian, Hungarian and Spanish constitutions have been applied by the courts. In many cases, recent constitutional changes in this respect have in themselves provided grounds for a change in constitutional court practice, as in Hungary. The interpretation of new provisions may open the way to new approaches, and the interpretation of the content of each new provision itself leaves room for the transformation of constitutional practice.[186] The integrated European action on migration has led to an increasing number of decisions in the practice of national constitutional courts which have emphasised the constitutional identity of the Member States in order to make the particular national position acceptable in the face of certain unifying trends.

There are constitutional courts that have changed their practice even when there has been no constitutional amendment, or no provision in the constitution that could be the basis for a different constitutional argument. In such cases, for example in the case of the Polish Constitutional Council, the body has developed the requirement of balanced budget management by interpretation. It can be concluded, therefore, that changes in the nature of constitutional jurisprudence and constitutional reasoning cannot be linked solely to the will of the constitutional authority, i.e. changes do not only occur when the constitution is amended or when changes in jurisprudence are encouraged by changes in the legislative environment. Constitutional texts can only have an impact on jurisprudence, for example when a provision originally included in the constitution is 'found' by the constitutional court and applied. As constitutional courts have not developed ad hoc doctrines of constitutional interpretation to deal with politically sensitive cases involving serious social and economic problems, in most cases there is no doctrinal basis for subsequent changes. Another case is when we talk about a special legal order in a state, although it is obvious that even in such cases the constitutional protection standards are not clear.

We have attempted with Zoltán Szente to examine the evolution of constitutional court practice in Europe. We have looked at whether the constitution has changed in a given country, what the constitutional traditions are (a classic democracy or a newer one), where the state is located on the map of Europe (more in the centre or more on the periphery), whether the state has a constitutional court or whether constitutional review is carried out by another body, and how deeply the state has been affected by crises in recent years. We have examined how and to what extent these independent variables have affected constitutional justice in each country.

We have found that there have been significant changes in constitutional governance in both old and new democracies, as in the cases of France and Hungary. There is relative stability in both old and new democracies, such as Germany and Croatia. The degree of change in constitutional review has also not been influenced by whether a state is at the centre or the periphery of the European political map. We

186 Tuori, Kaarlo – Tuori, Klaus: *The Eurozone Crisis. A Constitutional Analysis,* Cambridge, Cambridge University Press, 2014, 204.

concluded that, since there is no close correlation between the rate of change and the facts and circumstances that we hypothesise to influence it, the change or persistence of jurisprudence can only be explained by the particular legal and political set-up of each state. The degree of change depends on the role of the constitutional institutions in the country concerned and, on the other hand, on the role and powers of the institution conducting the constitutional review and its legitimacy and acceptability in political science terms vis-à-vis other institutions. In some state practices, how the state is affected by the crisis can also make a difference. There are different pressures on the constitutional review institution when examining legislation to deal with a terrorist threat in Hungary, where fortunately there have been no terrorist attacks, and in France, for example following the Nice terrorist attacks. In some cases, the court's reasoning was independent of these external circumstances, while in others it was fundamentally influenced by them. In this situation, many are calling for a new role for the constitutional court in Europe, a new role for political constitutionalism and parliamentary constitutionalism, rather than legal constitutionalism and judicial constitutionalism. According to some authors, the failure of the original form of constitutional review is obvious, and constitutional courts are also engaged in political activity in these situations, without democratic legitimacy.[187] In France, it has been suggested that the Constitutional Council has become politicised, but the same has also been suggested in Portugal and Spain.

The context of the criticisms is still the classic system of requirements expected of constitutional review, a legal type of decision-making based on legal reasoning and respecting legal dogmatic. This is the expectation of the European constitutional courts, even if a number of studies have analysed the disconnection between normative expectations and the actual experience of decision-making. The political character of constitutional court decisions is particularly strong when the crisis situation is very serious, as in Greece during the financial crisis or in France and the United Kingdom after the terrorist attacks. A politically heated and expectant public mood is less receptive to the forward-looking, normative details of the legal reasoning, and more interested in the outcome, which either supports or opposes the political decision. The extent to which bodies adhere to constitutional traditions in their reasoning also varies greatly from country to country. In the case of Britain, the dilemma of EU law versus international law is presumably so important because the preservation of domestic law dogmatic is seen as a struggle to preserve a constitutional tradition that has been in place for many centuries. In other countries, such as Hungary, as I have shown above, we can hardly speak of a living constitutional tradition like the British, since the constitutional order has been built on different traditions in almost every decade in the second half of the 20th century. Countries with a long tradition presumably find it more difficult to fundamentally

[187] Tomkins, Adam: "In Defence of the Political Constitution", *Oxford Journal of Legal Studies*, 2012/1, 157–175; Bellamy, Richard: *Political Constitutionalism. A Republican Defence of the Constitutionality of Democracy*, Cambridge, Cambridge University Press, 2007.

change their perception of constitutionalism, while in other countries it is easier, because the habits and customs are not so strong.

We have concluded that neither continuity nor change can be seen as a negative or positive phenomenon in itself, from the point of view of constitutional democracy. The European constitutional courts have been present in the European constitutional space through their decisions, and have either changed previous constitutional interpretative principles and dogmatic concepts, notions or standards, or have reinforced them through their actions. We have also shown that the Hungarian Constitutional Court has been in a special position even in this highly diverse and politically charged European space.

5.3.2. Explanation of Hungarian Constitutional Court practice – in a crisis situation

For many years after the democratic change of regime (1989), the Constitutional Court was the supreme guardian of constitutionality in Hungary, both against the legislature and the executive.[188] The new constitution was defended by the institutionalised involvement of the legal elite in order to help the political majority find a way to align with Western trends in constitutional democracy, in order to create the conditions for the separation of powers, the primacy of human rights protection and a prosperous market economy. It has often been said that the Hungarian Constitutional Court is one of the most prominent and active constitutional courts in the region.[189] One would have thought that the Constitutional Court would have played a prominent role in scrutinising the legislative response to the serious social, economic, health and other challenges of the last ten years. However, our expert perception is that the Constitutional Court has not played a significant role in the development of constitutional politics and constitutional law, neither in the constitutional management of the financial crisis, nor of migration, nor of the pandemic. Of course, the few decisions that have dealt with substantive constitutional issues in recent years have been very exciting for constitutional lawyers, but we have to admit that these have been rather constitutional titbits that have not had a significant impact on the functioning of our legal system. Thus, while academic legal scholarship played a major role in the development of the legal system in the 1990s, following

188 Schwartz, Herman: *The Struggle for Constitutional Justice in Post-Communist Europe,* Chicago, University of Chicago Press, 2000, 87–108; Sólyom, László – Brunner, Georg: *Constitutional Judiciary in a New Democracy: The Hungarian Constitutional Court,* Ann Arbor, University of Michigan Press, 2000; Halmai, Gábor: "The Hungarian Approach to Constitutional Review: The End of Activism? The First Decade of the Hungarian Constitutional Court", in Sadurski, Wojciech (ed.): *Constitutional Justice, East and West. Democratic Legitimacy and Constitutional Courts in Post-Communist Europe in a Comparative Perspective,* Hague – London, Kluwer Law International, 2002, 189–211.

189 See the critique and analysis of Pócza, Kálmán (ed.): *Constitutional Politics and the Judiciary: Decision-making in Central and Eastern Europe,* London – New York, Routledge, 2018.

the democratic regime change, in the new regime change, which the Prime Minister called illiberal, the constituent power did not intend to give a major role for the Constitutional Court.

We also address the sub-optimal situation for constitutional democracy, based on the non-division of power, caused by the continued politically homogeneous constitutional majority in Parliament since 2010. It is in this situation that Hungary has been hit by the major crises: the global economic crisis, the migration crisis, the pandemic and other crises.[190]

The Prime Minister said back in 2010 that we were at the end of the economic crisis, and when the deficit procedure against Hungary was lifted in 2013, it was again a sign that we were out of the crisis. The decisions I have described above were all taken after 2014. In the same way, in the case of the migration crisis, the legislative and constitutional interpretation decisions analysed earlier were taken well after the crisis phenomena of autumn 2015, when the crisis had essentially ended and the threat of terrorism in Europe had also decreased. Accordingly, the reference to the crisis in the practice of the Constitutional Court was rather a basis of reference, which was not, however, proven in a professional manner. The Constitutional Court has simply accepted the necessities of governance and that it is in this situation that the Constitutional Court must operate. Barnabás Lenkovics, former President of the Constitutional Court, also pointed out that constitutional doctrines should not become dogmas, and that their rigidity should not be allowed to hinder the rule of law or effective governance.[191]

In its decisions, the Constitutional Court has not examined whether the social or economic crisis underlying the legislation is real. It is true that the Constitutional Court is not a court of fact, so the question of evaluation raises serious doctrinal problems, but in extreme cases this fundamental question is still very much present in the context of whether the regulation had a legitimate legislative purpose.

Thus, whether the regulation has a legitimate legislative purpose, whether the chosen instrument is suitable to achieve it, and whether the regulation is necessary to achieve the legislative purpose, can be assessed not only under the general fundamental rights test, but is a basic measure of the actions of the limited government. State legislation is always linked to the achievement of a public objective, and the Constitutional Court must always review this criterion as a first step, but neither the constitution-making process, nor constitutional amendments, nor constitutional court practice have focused on this argument.

Another argument that Hungary's constitutional system and the corresponding constitutional court practice have not been transformed by the need to respond to socio-economic challenges is that there have been constitutional and legal changes

---

190 See Chronowski, Nóra – Varju, Márton: "Constitutional backsliding in Hungary", *Tijdschrift voor Constitutioneel Recht,* 2015/3, 296–310; Chronowski, Nóra – Vincze, Attila: "Alkotmánybíráskodás (gazdasági) válságban", *Alkotmánybírósági Szemle,* 2014/2, 104–112.

191 Interview with Barnabás Lenkovics in *Jogi Fórum,* http://www.jogiforum.hu/interju/122

in a number of issues that are not even supposedly related to the post-2010 regulatory challenges.[192] Much of the criticism of the constitutional system[193] cannot be explained by the fact that the country had to be governed in a crisis situation. The prime minister's view in 2014, which he later reiterated, was that a different, illiberal constitutional settlement could be more fruitful for Hungary.[194] In my view, a Constitutional Court is still needed in the new constitutional regime, but not with a jurisprudence based on the values of liberal constitutional democracy, as was the case in the two decades after 1990, but with a jurisprudence based on illiberal democracy, on the basis of the Fundamental Law.

The constituent power has created a difficult situation for constitutional democracy based on the separation of powers, because the constitutional limit of the majority has become a body elected by that majority, with changes in powers that have made clear the removal of the main role previously assumed in control of the legislation and the government. This is also a difficult situation because, as explained in the introduction of this volume, the essential criterion of the legal model of constitutional review is that the institution imposes a limitation of power by enforcing a constitutional framework and enforcing individual entitlements against public power.

As I have shown above, right after 2010, the Constitutional Court tried to arrive at a constitutional interpretation which was contrary to the express intention of the drafter, instead of a textual interpretation of positive law, by applying contextual, historical and other methods of interpretation, while annulling a legal provision. Later, in 2012–2013, the Court clearly argued that it would rely on its previous prac-

---

192 Vörös, Imre: "The constitutional landscape after the fourth and fifth amendments of Hungarian Fundamental Law", *Acta Juridica Hungarica,* 2014/1, 1–20; Zeller, Judit: "Nichts ist so beständig… Die jüngsten Novellen des Grundgesetzes Ungarns im Kontext der Entscheidungen des Verfassungsgerichts", *Osteuropa-Recht,* 2013/3, 307–325; Vincze, Attila: "Wrestling with Constitutionalism: the Supermajority and the Hungarian Constitutional Court", *ICL Journal – Vienna Journal on International Constitutional Law,* 2013/4, 86–97.

193 For a detailed description of the process, see Kovács, Kriszta – Tóth, Gábor Attila: "Hungary's Constitutional Transformation", *European Constitutional Law Review,* 2011/2, 183–203; Bánkuti, Miklós – Halmai, Gábor – Scheppele, Kim Lane: "Disabling the Constitution", *Journal of Democracy,* 2012/3, 138–146; Pogány, István: "The Crisis of Democracy in East Central Europe: The »New Constitutionalism«", *European Public Law,* 2013/2, 341–367; Bánkuti, Miklós – Halmai, Gábor – Scheppele, Kim Lane: "From Separation of Powers to a Government without Checks: Hungary's Old and New Constitutions", in Tóth, Gábor Attila (ed.): *Constitution for a Disunited Nation. On Hungary's 2011 Fundamental Law,* New York – Budapest, Central University Press, 2012, 237–268. Among international bodies, the European Parliament and the Venice Commission have issued a number of resolutions and criticisms on the erosion of the rule of law in Hungary. For details see Szente, Zoltán: "Challenging the Basic Values – The Problems of the Rule of Law in Hungary and the Failure of the European Union to Tackle Them", in Jakab, András – Kochenov, Dimitry (eds.): *The Enforcement of EU Law and Values. Ensuring Member States' Compliance,* Oxford, Oxford University Press, 2017.

194 E.g. see "Tusványos speech", in 2014, https://mandiner.hu/cikk/20140728_orban_viktor_a_munkaalapu_allam_korszaka_kovetkezik_beszed_tusvanyos_2014

tice and would represent the continuity of the constitutional court case law, even if the Fourth Amendment to the Fundamental Law ruled otherwise, since the decisions of the Constitutional Court prior to 2012 had been repealed.[195]

After 2010, the two-thirds Government majority in Parliament represented, at the level of political communication, that representative government based on elections and continuous national consultation is the most appropriate form of representation of the majority of the electorate. In a country where the ruling political force has had a constitutional majority for 12 years and more, constitutional review is meaningless in the absence of an explicit governmental demand for it.

This phenomenon is only intensified and becomes more visible in situations of ongoing crisis, as the lack of action against the concentration of power is more pronounced. However, the underlying problem of vulnerability and insecurity of the constitutional order is present in the constitutional situation even in the absence of external threats such as a financial crisis, migration, war, the climate crisis or a pandemic.

In summary, it can be concluded that the constitutional changes in Hungary and the related changes in constitutional court practice after 2010 can hardly be attributed exclusively to social, economic or health emergencies, which have occurred globally and locally in large numbers over the past fifteen years. The new policy objectives, which are also reflected in the Fundamental Law in a specific legal form, better explain the constitutional changes. Although the social, health and economic context of crisis has provided the backdrop for these ideas to unfold, and has undoubtedly served as a good reference for constitutional lawmaking and law enforcement, the will for change has gone beyond crisis management.

In the last chapter of the volume, I will examine to what extent the new constitutional justice developed under the Fundamental Law and the two-thirds constitutional majority fits our classic standards of constitutional justice, i.e. to what extent we have seen the legal institution as regressive in recent years, how it has adapted in the new political system, and whether it has been possible to integrate this change into the Hungarian legal system.

195 Sonnevend, Pál – Jakab, András – Csink, Lóránt: "The Constitution in Everyday's Party Politics: The Basic Law of Hungary", in von Bogdandy, Armin – Sonnevend, Pál (eds.): *Constitutional Crises in the European Constitutional Area. Theory, Law and Politica in Hungary and Romania,* Oxford, Hart, 2015.

6. *QUO VADIS*, HUNGARIAN CONSTITUTIONAL COURT?

6.1. On the benchmarks for evaluating constitutional review[1]

Centralised constitutional review of the Kelsen-type, which entrusted the protection of the constitution to a constitutional court separate from the courts, became widespread when, in the course of democratic transitions in South-Central and Eastern Europe, states decided to introduce the Kelsen model rather than the American-style decentralised constitutional review, which had been in place for some time, when establishing their new constitutional system.[2] Centralised constitutional review of the Kelsen-type has not directly affected the powers of the ordinary court. The decision of the constitutional courts was final on the question of constitutionality under consideration, but it contributed to the judicial resolution of specific disputes only indirectly, by possibly annulling the legislation. A few states, such as Greece, adopted a combination of the two systems of centralized and decentralized constitutional review, but in general, it was typical that states opted for either the American or the Kelsen model, and it was also typical that new democracies tended to see the centralised model as more effective.[3] The horrors of the Second World War must have had a major impact on the considerable effort that states invested in developing constitutional and legal protection.[4]

It is interesting to note that after the First World War, Kelsen warned against the constitutional court being entrusted with the power to protect rights by the constituent power. He saw rights as arising from natural law and thus not suitable for the constitutional court to judge their substance. He warned that if the protection of human rights is entrusted to constitutional courts beyond the protection of the constitutional organisation of the state, then the constitutional court as negative

---

1 See more Gárdos-Orosz, Fruzsina: "Alkotmánybíróság", in Jakab, András – Könczöl, Miklós – Menyhárd, Attila – Sulyok, Gábor (eds.): *Internetes Jogtudományi Enciklopédia* (Constitutional Law column, column editors: Bodnár, Eszter – Jakab, András), 2020, http://ijoten.hu/szocikk/alkotmanybirosag

2 Kelsen, Hans: "Judicial Review of Legislation: A Comparative Study of the Austrian and the American Constitution", *Journal of Politics*, 1942/2, 183–200.

3 de Visser, Maartje: *Constitutional Review in Europe. A Comparative Analysis,* Oxford, Hart, 2014.

4 Stone Sweet, Alec: "Constitutional Court", in Rosenfeld, Michel – Sajó, András (eds.): *Oxford Handbook of Comparative Constitutional Law,* Oxford, Oxford University Press, 2012.

legislator inevitably becomes a positive legislator. In the course of interpretation, the constitutional court, by ruling on certain fundamental rights, supplements the content of the constitution or derives new rights from it, which is tantamount to positive legislation, which a constitutional court in a democratic state cannot have the power to do without infringing democratic principles. This caveat, writes Alec Sweet Stone, is often forgotten these days, when Kelsen-type constitutional adjudication of fundamental rights is so popular. In the case of the ordinary court, the guarantee of jurisdiction to adjudicate on fundamental rights is that the court's activities are bound by the law enacted by the supreme representative body of the people, while the constitutional court is responsible for preserving the constitutional framework for the exercise of state power, but has no articulated democratic mandate to interpret and enforce fundamental rights.[5]

According to Alec Sweet Stone's analysis, three main factors have led to the popularity of centralised, Kelsen-type constitutional review. One was that it was felt that a separate institution that could review the constitutionality of legislation simply fitted in with the parliamentary system that was becoming more prevalent. It did not seem sensible to vest such powers in the courts, and the separate institution seemed to have the advantage that the composition of the constitutional court could be determined by parliament. The Kelsen model favoured a fixed-term mandate, rather than the American lifetime appointment, which allowed the supreme representative bodies to influence the development of practice from time to time.

Another reason for the new popularity may have been that in Europe in the 1970s, with the fall of the dictatorships in Southern Europe, and in the 1990s in Central and Eastern Europe and the Balkans, it was very important that the constituent power emphasised the priority of the protection of rights. The prominent role of the state in the protection of the rights was spectacularly reflected in the powers of the centralised constitutional court.

The third reason for the rapid spread is linked to globalisation. In an era of migration of constitutional ideas, a successful model spreads rapidly. The centralised constitutional court is just such an effective instrument for consolidating democracy, that it has spread rapidly from Europe to other parts of the world.[6]

There are constitutional courts in nearly 150 countries around the world, and more than 60% of them are Kelsen-type, centralised constitutional courts. In addition to Europe, this model of constitutional adjudication has become popular in Africa and the Middle East, but can also be found in Asia, Southeast Asia and some countries in Latin America. The American model is clearly dominant only in North America and the Caribbean. It is interesting to note that constitutional courts have been established in authoritarian regimes where the ruling power has not otherwise

5 *Ibid.* 820.
6 *Ibid.* 820.

sought to democratise.[7] In Egypt, for example, a constitutional court was set up in the 1980s and 1990s to show the leader's commitment to legal protection and legal certainty, and thus to gain the acceptance of the international community, to attract investment and to boost trade.[8] Constitutional courts have been established in Latin America for similar purposes and in a similar constitutional context.[9]

In the introductory chapter of this volume, the Constitutional Court in Hungary, established in 1989 after the democratic transformation and operating since January 1990, is placed in this framework of expectations according to the Kelsen model of constitutional justice, emphasising that it is also a conception that is adapted to the legal model.

The volume examined how the Hungarian constitutional judiciary fulfilled its original function and how it performed its tasks after 2010; what kind of framework of rules was established by the constituent power, what kind of Constitutional Court Act and Rules of Procedure were adopted, what cases were brought before the Constitutional Court, who initiated the proceedings of the Constitutional Court, in what kind of cases and how the Constitutional Court decided.

My main question was whether the original function of constitutional adjudication and the original constitutional position of the Constitutional Court could still be maintained in the current constitutional structures.[10]

It is important to bear in mind what I stressed at the beginning of these concluding reflections on the establishment, proliferation and popularity of constitutional courts: constitutional courts are not a value in and of themselves, but are ultimately an institution that ensures the preservation of the rights and freedoms enshrined in the constitution, a check on the public power limited by the constitutions.[11] The practice of today's constitutional courts is heavily dependent on the case law of international and EU courts, and there is an important role for the conscious linking of judicial activities (constitutional dialogue[12]).[13] Constitutional courts and international and EU courts have a strong influence on

---

[7] *Ibid.* 821.

[8] Moustafa, Tamir: "Law and Resistance in Authoritarian States: The judicialization in politics in Egypt", in Ginsburg, Tom – Moustafa, Tamir (eds.): *Rule by law: The Politics of Courts in Authoritarian Regimes,* Cambridge, Cambridge University Press, 2008, 132.

[9] Dargent, Eduardo: "Determinants of Judicial Independence: Lessons from Three Cases Constitutional Courts in Peru", *Journal of Latin American Studies,* 2009/2, 251–278.

[10] See, e.g., Paris, Marie-Luce: "Setting the Scene: Elements of Constitutional Theory and Methodology of the Research", in Bell, John – Paris, Marie-Luce (eds.): *Rights-Based Constitutional Review. Constitutional Courts in a Changing Landscape,* Cheltenham, Edward Elgar, 2016, 2.

[11] Sajó, András – Uitz, Renáta: *A szabadság alkotmánya. Bevezetés a jogi alkotmányosságba,* Budapest, HVG-ORAC, 2019.

[12] Drinóczi, Tímea: *Alkotmányos párbeszéd. A többszintű alkotmányosság alkotmánytana és gyakorlata a 21. században,* Budapest, MTA TK Jogtudományi Intézet, 2017.

[13] Groppi, Tania – Ponthoreau, Marie Claire (eds.): *The Use of Foreign Precedents by Constitutional Judges,* Oxford, Hart, 2013; Halmai Gábor: "In memoriam magyar alkotmánybíráskodás. A pártos alkotmánybíráskodás első éve", *Fundamentum,* 2014/1–2, 56–57.

each other.[14] While the historical perspective of the development of the form of government or the functioning of parliaments has led to a variety of solutions, constitutional courts have taken their current form in the world of globalised constitutional law. This has meant that the level of standardisation of this constitutional institution has become one of the highest, and the constitutional court – often referred to as the fourth branch – is now certainly the constitutional institution with the greatest influence on the shaping of the legal system, alongside the three classic branches of power.

In constitutional moments so politically diverse, learning from previous excesses of state power, wars and conflicts and ultimately mass violations of human rights, decision-makers set up constitutional courts, called the guardians of the constitution, because they believed (or experience had led them to believe) that power was a temptation to oppress others in order to gain undue advantage. The most effective way of countering this, beyond the creation of the constitution, is to enforce it. Constitutional courts have been given the task of ensuring that the new constitutions that have been created are protected, i.e. that the legislature and sometimes the law enforcement bodies are compelled not to exceed the constitutional framework in the exercise of their powers. Constitutional review has become the instrument and the institutional framework has become the ordinary court or the constitutional court.

In many countries around the world, constitutional review is an important component of constitutionalism and one of the most important guarantees of the democratic exercise of power. I have presented in a nutshell the development and models of constitutional justice and constitutional courts, discussed the jurisdictional, organisational and procedural issues related to constitutional institutions, and the theoretical justification and implementation of constitutional justice in Hungary after the democratic regime change and the entry into force of the Fundamental Law. Understanding the basic benchmarks for constitutional adjudication, the question is how the functioning of the Hungarian Constitutional Court compares with the basic expectations that have evolved throughout the history of the institution.

[14] Bodnár, Eszter: "Vigyázó szemetek Strasbourgra vessétek? Az Emberi Jogok Európai Bírósága és az Alkotmánybíróság alapjogvédelmi tevékenységének kapcsolódási pontjai", in Menyhárd, Attila – Varga, István (eds.): *350 éves az Eötvös Loránd Tudományegyetem Állam- és Jogtudományi Kara – a jubileumi év konferenciasorozatának tanulmányai II.*, Budapest, ELTE Eötvös, 2018, 639–654.

6.2. Not everything is what it appears to be

The "clientelism, the capture of the state and the *Gleichschaltung* (direct political control of certain institutions), which is also characteristic of populist governments, requires the use of legal instruments", Zoltán Szente states, describing one of the characteristics of populist constitutionalism identified by populism literature.[15] In Hungarian jurisprudence, there are views that after 2010, the Constitutional Court was taken over by a political majority with a constitution making majority through the nomination and election of new constitutional judges (court packing), which, by transforming the legal system, seek to implement only their own principled and/or pragmatic ideas with the full range of legal instruments at their disposal by the enforcement of the Fundamental Law.[16] We have shown that, certainly, the restructuring of the composition of the Constitutional Court and also the constitutional and legal system has had a fundamental impact on the interpretation of the constitution.[17]

Although the rules governing the Constitutional Court and the composition of judges have changed fundamentally, the constitutional institution has remained formally independent in Hungary. Some elements of the legislation (for example, the fact that members are elected by Parliament for a twelve-year term and cannot be re-elected) could seem to point towards an even stronger independence than before. However, the changes in the Fundamental Law and the Act on the Constitutional Court described above clearly indicate the intention of the constitutional majority to create a new constitutional judiciary, weakened and distanced from the politically relevant legislative issues decided by the governing majority.[18] Although the *de facto* reduction of the Constitutional Court's independence is very difficult to prove, the changes analysed above undoubtedly make it more difficult to preserve this independence prescribed by the Fundamental Law. It is a test for the Constitutional Court if that is given precise constitutional rules for interpreting the Fundamental Law and that it cannot freely and openly draw on the achievements of constitutional development since 1989. It is under pressure if the annulled le-

15 Szente, Zoltán – Gárdos-Orosz, Fruzsina: "Constitutional effects of populism on EU Member States", in Andreu, Josep Maria Castellà – Simonelli, Marco Antonio (eds.): *Populism and Contemporary Democracy in Europe. Old Problems and New Challenges*, Cham, Palgrave Macmillan, 2022, 116.

16 Halmai, Gábor: "In memoriam magyar alkotmánybíráskodás. A pártos alkotmánybíráskodás első éve", *Fundamentum*, 2014/1–2, 56–57.

17 Gárdos-Orosz, Fruzsina: "Challenges to Constitutional Adjudication in Hungary since 2010", in Belov, Martin (ed.): *The Role of Courts in Contemporary Legal Orders*, The Hague, Eleven Publishing, 2019, 321.

18 On the different models of constitutional courts, see Pócza, Kálmán: "Többségi demokrácia és gyenge alkotmánybíráskodás: egy elszalasztott lehetőség", in Gárdos-Orosz, Fruzsina – Szente, Zoltán (eds.): *Jog és politika határán. Alkotmánybíráskodás Magyarországon 2010 után*, Budapest, HVG-ORAC, 2015, 185–212.

gislation would be incorporated into the Fundamental Law the next day by constitutional amendment, or if a constitutional decision that differs from the position of the majority is followed by legislative 'sanctions' on the Court's competencies, organisation or functioning. It is difficult to act as an effective counterweight if the rules of standing are tightened while the number of petitioners is radically reduced, or if the provisions on the admissibility of constitutional complaints might block most important procedures. But more importantly, the de-emphasis of the abstract ex-post scope of review leads to the Constitutional Court being confronted with older legislation even in the context of review procedures. The constitutional complaint under Article 27 of the Constitutional Court Act, which is aimed at reviewing judicial decisions, distracts the Constitutional Court even more strongly from reviewing current legislation, which is often of increased public policy relevance.

The introduction of the new constitutional complaints procedure was a step forward, because an analysis of judicial practice showed that the quality of fundamental rights adjudication is often inadequate.[19] However, by this reasoning, the Fundamental Law implicitly sought to justify the abolition of the possibility for anyone to initiate ex-post abstract review of the constitutionality of legislation. The circle of petitioners in the case of abstract review of norms has been excessively narrowed, and dedicated petitioners unfortunately appear to be very passive in initiating the constitutional court procedure. Constitutional complaints and *actio popularis* can therefore not be alternatives to each other in constitutional adjudication from a theoretical point of view, but have not become alternatives in practice, either. Therefore, the participation of individuals in the operation of the forum for constitutional review should be ensured by means of the petition, while appropriate procedural rules should be drawn up. The two competencies could in theory be viable in several forms at the same time. The remedy of individual rights violations by the constitutional review of decisions of the ordinary courts should not exclude the enforcement of general constitutional protection aspects and the enforcement of constitutional limits on public policy decisions in the form of legislation.[20] The primary form of this letter is the ex-post abstract norm control in the Kelsen-type constitutional jurisprudence.

"The reform has created the opportunity to establish a new balance, in which greater emphasis can be placed on the protection of individual rights and the effective enforcement of fundamental rights," said the President of the Constitutional Court in 2012.[21] The desired "new balance" has not been achieved, as the new Pres-

---

19 For a summary of previous court practice, see GÁRDOS-OROSZ, Fruzsina: *Alkotmányos polgári jog? Az alapvető jogok alkalmazása a magánjogi jogvitákban*, Budapest – Pécs, Dialóg Campus, 2011; SOMODY, Bernadette (ed.): *Alapjogi bíráskodás – alapjogok az ítélkezésben*, Budapest, L'Harmattan, 2013.

20 GÁRDOS-OROSZ, Fruzsina: "Fórum. Az alkotmánybíráskodás jelene: az Alaptörvény és az alkotmányosság legfőbb őrének »feladat- és hatásköre«", *Fundamentum*, 2014/1–2, 85–90.

21 The speech of President Péter Paczolay, https://www.alkotmanybirosag.hu/sajtomegjelenes/az-alkotmanybirosag-a-jovoben-is-kontrollja-lesz-a-torvenyhozasna

ident of the Constitutional Court said in a conference presentation in 2021.[22] While a few rights-enhancing decisions (often with very divided decisions) are taken each year on certain fundamental rights issues, notably on the personal freedoms of natural persons, a new, rights-reducing understanding of the right to property or social rights is more clearly emerging from the practice of constitutional complaints. In addition, in the absence of a petition, the Constitutional Court is often unable to examine legislative or organisational issues, for example, which do not directly affect fundamental rights. It can also be observed that some judges leave the decision on state organisation issues to the legislator, while on fundamental rights issues they tend to think in a more "fundamental rights activist" way as regards the scope of constitutional review. In fact, in important fundamental rights decisions, the votes of judges have also supported the annulment of a legislative provision, while the very same judges, in other types of constitutional matters (non-human rights matters), tend to accept the position of the legislator with deference without any particular constitutional reservations.[23]

On the basis of the articles by Béla Pokol, member of the Constitutional Court, and Gábor Halmai, constitutional lawyer and university professor, a debate has emerged in the practice of the Constitutional Court and in Hungarian public law on the role of constitutional judges in a constitutional democracy, and the extent to which the decisions of the Constitutional Court may justifiably restrict the democratic majority. The debate also delves into questions of political constitutionalism-legal constitutionalism, and ultimately revisits the justifiability of constitutional adjudication as it currently operates.[24] The course of the study also gives a good sense of the need to account with regard to the Hungarian constitutional review, for the loss of ground and the search for new paths, both in terms of content and competence. The constitutional judges who advocate for preserving the original, former content of a constitutional provision, have already thrown down the gauntlet – this is striking in the debate on the citation of pre-2012 constitutional court decisions. The time is gone, the change can not be hindered any more.

The position of the Constitutional Court and the actual enforcement of constitutional control can probably not be assessed only by examining in their complexity the issues of competence, composition, organisation, procedure, state organisation and division of powers, but as the practice stabilises, an intensive analysis

22 Sulyok, Tamás: Az alkotmányos önazonosság az Alkotmánybíróság döntéseiben, https://alkotmanybirosag.hu/kozlemeny/az-alkotmanyos-onazonossag-az-alkotmanybirosag-donteseiben

23 Decision 32/2014. (XI. 3.) AB.

24 The latest in the debate: "Jurisztokrácia-vita", *Jogelméleti Szemle,* 2015/4, http://jesz.ajk.elte.hu/2015_4.pdf; "Politikai konstitucionalizmus vita", *Fundamentum,* 2015/2–3. The debate is about whether it is justifiable for an "elitist" jurist constitutional court to review and possibly annul the decisions of parliament in a participatory democracy. To what extent should the Hungarian Constitutional Court be aligned with the constitutional understanding of the constitutional majority and of the parliamentary majority in general, can the Constitutional Court decide on fundamentally contentious constitutional issues, or is its role much narrower than that?

of the persuasiveness and legal-dogmatic clarity of individual decisions will come to the forefront of research. The long-term survival of the Constitutional Court, of the Hungarian constitutional judiciary, can only be justified if the body carries out legal and constitutional review based on professional expertise and professional autonomy in order to protect constitutionality. (Otherwise, we should be talking about another type of institution, such as an upper house or some kind of governmental or parliamentary advisory body.)

The first results of the academic study of the jurisprudence of recent years have reported changes or modifications in practice in many areas. This shift can hardly be described in terms of new doctrines, but rather by analyses of the inconsistency and variability of practice.[25] The many dissenting opinions, the weakness of the reasoning and the fragility of the decisions are illustrated by the many scholarly works, the decisions were often the results of serious compromises.[26]

According to the Fundamental Law, the role of the Constitutional Court today would still be to give an independent and justified judgment on the rule of law within the limits of its jurisdiction. The rules on the constitutional judiciary are freely determined by the states, and international fora have only set minimum requirements for the development of the legislative acts on the Constitutional Court.[27] In recent years, the rules governing the Constitutional Court and constitutional adjudication have frequently been changed by the constitution-making and amending authority and the legislator, the same two-thirds Government majority.[28] There are fundamental professional criticisms to be made of the legal sources issued by both the constituent power and the legislature and the Constitutional Court operating in this constitutional and regulatory environment. The main problem is that, as a result of the reorganisation of the court, its practice of interpretation became legally and dogmatically uncertain and often biased or deferential to the Government majority, based on the use of specific new concepts in the Fundamental Law. This is even more problematic, because this influences the duality jurisprudence of ordinary courts dealing with criminal, civil, administrative, economic, labour and social law cases.

25 See in general Gárdos-Orosz, Fruzsina – Szente, Zoltán (eds.): *Jog és politika határán. Alkotmánybíráskodás Magyarországon 2010 után*, Budapest, HVG-ORAC, 2015.

26 See, e.g., Decision 19/2015. (VI. 15.) AB; Decision 23/2014. (VII. 15.) AB.

27 Venice Commission, Opinion on three legal questions arising in the process of drafting the new constitution of Hungary, no. 614/2011, Strasbourg, 28 March 2011; Venice Commission, Opinion on the New Constitution of Hungary, no. 720/2013, Strasbourg, 17 June 2013; Venice Commission, Opinion on the Fourth Amendment of the Fundamental Law of Hungary, no. 665/2012, Strasbourg, 19 June 2012; Venice Commission, Opinion on Act CLI of 2011 on the Constitutional Court of Hungary, no. 665/2012, Strasbourg, 9 May 2012.

28 Chronowski, Nóra: "Az alkotmánybíráskodás sarkalatos átalakítása", *MTA Law Working Papers,* 2014/8, 8–9, https://jog.tk.mta.hu/uploads/files/mtalwp/2014_08_Chronowski.pdf; Jakab, András – Szilágyi, Emese: "Sarkalatos törvények a magyar jogrendben", *MTA Law Working Papers,* 2015/32, https://jog.tk.mta.hu/uploads/files/mtalwp/2015_32_Jakab.pdf. As regards the ideal system for a constitutional complaint Szalbot, Balázs: "Az alkotmányjogi panasz legújabb kérdései – A közvetlen panasz", *De iurisprudentia et iure publico,* 2013/2, 1–31.

The Constitutional Court had a difficult time in the period 2010–2014. The applicable constitution changed, the composition of the Court changed, the relevant Constitutional Court legislation changed, and the ground and the legislative environment of the Fundamental Law was constantly shifted by the parliamentary Government majority. At the level of legal technique and at the level of constitutional principles and the rules enshrined in the Fundamental Law, there were inconsistencies in the legislation, and this phenomenon, i.e. the uncertainty, was compounded by the debate on the principle of the 'old and the new' and the uncertainty of the continuity of the constitutional democracy or the change of regime. In the period 2014–2022, much was decided and by 2022 many issues had become clear.

By now, the question of whether a Constitutional Court which can be described as I have done above, can be suitable for performing the classic functions of constitutional adjudication and constitutional protection in the Hungarian public law system defined by the Fundamental Law, seems to have been settled. In my opinion, it certainly cannot, since experience has shown that it can only fulfil its legal and constitutional protection function if the constituent power, the legislative and/or executive power, does not oppose it. If the Constitutional Court can only act effectively if the constitutional and legislative parliamentary majorities agree on the need to protect the right or the institutions, then it may be sufficient for the Constitutional Court to operate as a constitutional advisory body. In this framework, the legislator could correct unconstitutional norms and, accordingly, erroneous judicial practice on the basis of simple constitutional signalling, on the other hand it does not agree than even a constitutional amendment could be adopted on the debated issue. Instead of annulling the pieces of legislation, the proliferation of constitutional requirements in the practice of Constitutional Court points precisely to this direction.[29] In addition, the constitutional complaint procedure is only complementary, since the courts are essentially responsible for the adjudication of fundamental rights, and the Constitutional Court can only have a minor corrective function in relation to individual legal protection. The real weight of a constitutional complaint lies in the defence of the Fundamental Law, the objective defence of the new legal order.

Why do we insist on having the Hungarian Constitutional Court in this form? It makes one wonder why, if the constitutional judiciary, operating according to the Kelsen model, does not fully perform its legal function,[30] the institution has still remained largely unchanged in the legal and institutional system established by

[29] Zakariás, Kinga: "Az alkotmányos követelmény mint hivatalos elvi tétel a Magyar Alkotmánybíróság gyakorlatában", *Jog – Állam – Politika. Ünnepi különszám a 70 éves Kukorelli István tiszteletére,* 2022/2.

[30] Kelsen, Hans: *Wer soll Hüter der Verfassung sein?* Berlin, W. Rothschild, 1931; Kelsen, Hans: *Wer soll der Hüter der Verfassung sein? Abhandlungen zur Theorie der Verfassungsgerichtsbarkeit in der pluralistischen, parlamentarischen Demokratie,* Tübingen, Mohr Siebeck, 2008, XXIII; Kelsen, Hans: "La garantie juridictionnelle de la Constitution (La Justice constitutionnelle)", *Revue du droit public,* 1928, 197–257.

the Fundamental Law. The Constitutional Court has enjoyed a high level of public confidence over the past decades, and its professional credibility and standing have been very high. It has functioned as an institution capable of engaging in constitutional dialogue, defending and explaining the new democratic constitutional order in the European arena. Although its legal function has been weakened by the above features, its political usefulness has increased for the populist's new constitutional system, which the European Parliament referred to in 2022 as a hybrid electoral democracy. The problem is that this political gain, according to Ran Hirschl's theory,[31] only benefits the political force in power and contributes to weakening competition between parties, especially in a state where the ruling party has a two-thirds constituent majority in Parliament. Allied cooperation between constitutional institutions leads to the unity of state power, and with unity of state power, human freedom goes from being an enforceable right to a mere given. It is the task of the Hungarian Constitutional Court to recognise the threat posed by the current political and constitutional situation and to carry out the classic tasks of defending constitutional democracy within this matrix.

The question is whether this is possible in the defence of the Fundamental Law, or whether the Constitutional Court will become an institution within the system of the Fundamental Law that has little of the classic characteristics of constitutional courts, and will rather be an advisory body orienting the practice of courts in the interpretation of the law and providing institutional security for the two-thirds Government majority led by Prime Minister Viktor Orbán.

[31] Hirschl, Ran: *Towards Juristocracy. The Origins and Consequences of New Constitutionalism*, Cambridge, Harvard University Press, 2007.

BIBLIOGRAPHY

ABLONCZY, Bálint: *Az alkotmány nyomában. Beszélgetések Szájer Józseffel és Gulyás Gergellyel,* Budapest, Elektromédia, 2011.

AKHGAR, Babak – BREWSTER, Ben (eds.): *Combatting Cybercrime and Cyberterrorism,* Cham, Springer, 2016.

ALBERT, Richard – ODER, Bertil Emrah: *Unamendability,* Cham, Springer, 2018.

ALEXY, Robert: *Theorie der juristischen Argumentation,* Frankfurt am Main, Suhrkamp, 1991.

AMBRUS, István – GÁRDOS-OROSZ, Fruzsina: "Rémhírterjesztés", in GÁRDOS-OROSZ, Fruzsina – ZAKARIÁS, Kinga (eds.): *Az alkotmánybírósági gyakorlat. Az Alkotmánybíróság 100 elvi jelentőségű határozata 1990–2020,* Budapest, Társadalomtudományi Kutatóközpont Jogtudományi Intézet – HVG-ORAC, 2021, 1013–1034.

ANSELMI, Manuel: *Populism. An Introduction,* Oxfordshire, Routledge, 2018.

ARATO, Andrew: "How We Got Here? Transition Failures, Their Causes and the Populist Interest in the Constitution", *Philosophy and Social Criticism,* 2019/9–10.

"»A történeti alkotmányunk is jogforrás!« Horváth Attila a Mandinernek", *Mandiner,* 15 December 2016, https://jog.mandiner.hu/cikk/20161214_a_torteneti_alkotmanyunk_is_jogforras_horvath_attila_a_mandinernek

"A »valódi alkotmányjogi panasz« és elbírálásának főbb jellemzői – nemzetközi kitekintés", *Alkotmánybírósági Szemle,* 2011/2, 64–74.

Az Alaptörvény érvényesülése a bírói gyakorlatban III. Alkotmányjogi panasz: az alapjog-érvényesítés gyakorlata, Budapest, HVG-ORAC, 2019.

Az Alaptörvény érvényesülése a bírói gyakorlatban IV. A bírói kezdeményezések gyakorlati tapasztalata, Budapest, HVG-ORAC, 2019.

BALAGUER CALLEJÓN, Francisco: "Constitutional Interpretation and Populism in Contemporary Spain", in SZENTE, Zoltán – GÁRDOS-OROSZ, Fruzsina (eds.): *Populist Challenges to Constitutional Interpretation in Europe and Beyond,* London, Routledge, 2021, 217–232.

BALAGUER CALLEJÓN, Francisco: "Interpretación constitucional y populismo", *Revista de Derecho Constitucional Europeo,* 2020, https://www.ugr.es/~redce/REDCE33/articulos/04_BALAGUER.htm

BALÁZS, István – HOFFMAN, István: "A közigazgatási jog rezilienciája – koronavírus idején", in GÁRDOS-OROSZ, Fruzsina – LŐRINCZ, Viktor Olivér (eds.): *Jogi diagnózisok. A COVID-19-világjárvány hatásai a jogrendszerre,* Budapest, L'Harmattan – Társadalomtudományi Kutatóközpont Jogtudományi Intézet, 2020, 45–66.

Balázs, Zoltán: "A közérdek az alkotmánybíráskodásban (2012–2014)", in Gárdos-Orosz, Fruzsina – Szente, Zoltán (eds.): *Jog és politika határán. Alkotmánybíráskodás Magyarországon 2010 után,* Budapest, HVG-ORAC, 2015, 75–104.

Balogh, Zsolt – Holló, András (eds.): *Az értelmezett Alkotmány,* Budapest, Magyar Hivatalos Közlönykiadó, 2005.

Bánkuti, Miklós – Halmai, Gábor – Scheppele, Kim Lane: "Disabling the Constitution", *Journal of Democracy,* 2012/3, 138–146.

Bánkuti, Miklós – Halmai, Gábor – Scheppele, Kim Lane: "From Separation of Powers to a Government without Checks: Hungary's Old and New Constitutions", in Tóth, Gábor Attila (ed.): *Constitution for a Disunited Nation. On Hungary's 2011 Fundamental Law,* New York – Budapest, Central University Press, 2012, 237–268.

Bánkuti, Miklós et al.: "Vélemény Magyarország új alkotmányos rendjéről", *Fundamentum,* 2012/1, 5–34.

Baranger, Denis: "The language of Eternity: Judicial Review of the Amending Power in France (or the Absence Thereof)", *Israel Law Review,* 2011/3, 389–428.

Barber, Sotirios A. – George, Robert P. (eds.): *Constitutional Politics,* Princeton, Princeton University Press, 2002.

Batt, John: "American Legal Populism: A Jurisprudential and Historical Narrative, Including Reflections on Critical Legal Studies", *Northern Kentucky Law Review,* 1995, 651–762.

Bell, John – Paris, Marie-Luce (eds.): *Rights-Based Constitutional Review. Constitutional Courts in a Changing Landscape,* Cheltenham, Edward Elgar, 2016.

Bellamy, Richard: *Political Constitutionalism. A Republican Defence of the Constitutionality of Democracy,* Cambridge, Cambridge University Press, 2007.

Belov, Martin (ed.): *The Role of Courts in Contemporary Legal Orders,* The Hague, Eleven Publishing, 2019.

Bencze, Mátyás: "Az Alapjogok bíróság előtti érvényesülésének szociológiai háttere", in Somody, Bernadette (ed.): *Alapjogi bíráskodás – alapjogok az ítélkezésben,* Budapest, L'Harmattan, 2013, 95–117.

Bickel, Alexander: *The Least Dangerous Branch: The Supreme Court at the Bar of American Politics,* New Haven, Yale University Press, 1986.

Bilgic, Ali: *Rethinking Security in the Age of Migration: Trust and Emancipation in Europe,* London, Routledge, 2013.

Birkinshaw, Patrick: "National security and the limits of judicial protection", in Szente, Zoltán – Gárdos-Orosz, Fruzsina (eds.): *New Challenges to Constitutional Adjudication in Europe,* London, Routledge, 2018, 185–214.

Bitskey, Botond – Fröhlich, Johanna – Gárdos-Orosz, Fruzsina – Rajos, Krisztina: "Az alkotmányjogi panaszeljárás általános szabályai", in Bitskey, Botond – Török, Bernát (eds.): *Az alkotmányjogi panasz kézikönyve,* Budapest, HVG-ORAC, 2015.

Bitskey, Botond – Fröhlich, Johanna – Gárdos-Orosz, Fruzsina – Rajos, Krisztina: "Az alkotmányjogi panaszeljárások tapasztalatai az indítvány beérkezésétől az érdemi elbírálásig", in Bitskey, Botond – Török, Bernát (eds.): *Az alkotmányjogi panasz kézikönyve,* Budapest, HVG-ORAC, 2015.

Bitskey, Botond – Fröhlich, Johanna – Gárdos-Orosz, Fruzsina – Rajos, Krisztina: "Az egyes alkotmányjogi panaszeljárások különös szabályai. Az Abtv. 27. §-a szerinti panasz", in Bitskey, Botond – Török, Bernát (eds.): *Az alkotmányjogi panasz kézikönyve,* Budapest, HVG-ORAC, 2015.

Bitskey, Botond – Török, Bernát (eds.): *Az alkotmányjogi panasz kézikönyve,* Budapest, HVG-ORAC, 2015.

Blokker, Paul: "Populism as a constitutional project", *International Journal of Constitutional Law,* 2019/2.

Blutman, László: "A nemzetközi jog joghatásai az alkotmánybírósági eljárásokban", *Jogelméleti Szemle,* 2013/4, 2–32.

Bobbitt, Philip: "Methods of Constitutional Argument", *University of British Columbia Law Review,* 1989/3, 449–458.

Bodnár Eszter: "Vigyázó szemetek Strasbourgra vessétek? Az Emberi Jogok Európai Bírósága és az Alkotmánybíróság alapjogvédelmi tevékenységének kapcsolódási pontjai", in Menyhárd Attila – Varga István (eds.): *350 éves az Eötvös Loránd Tudományegyetem Állam- és Jogtudományi Kara – a jubileumi* év *konferenciasorozatának tanulmányai II.*, Budapest, ELTE Eötvös, 2018, 639–654.

Bodnár, Eszter – Gárdos-Orosz, Fruzsina – Pozsár-Szentmiklósy, Zoltán: "Developments in Hungarian Constitutional Law", in Albert, Richard – Landau, David – Faraguna, Pietro – Drugda, Šimon (eds.): *2016 Global Review of Constitutional Law,* Boston, ICONnect-Clough Center, 2017, 77–81.

Bragyova, András: "Demokrácia és alkotmánybíráskodás", in Tóth, Károly (ed.): *Emlékkönyv dr. Szentpéteri István egyetemi tanár születésének 70.* évfordulójára, Szeged, JATE ÁJK Tudományos Bizottság, 1996, 135–159.

Bragyova, András: *Az alkotmánybíráskodás elmélete,* Budapest, Közgazdasági és Jogi Könyvkiadó – MTA Állam- és Jogtudományi Intézet, 1994.

Bragyova, András: *Az* új *alkotmány egy koncepciója,* Budapest, Közgazdasági és Jogi Könyvkiadó – MTA Állam- és Jogtudományi Intézet, 1995.

Brewer-Carías, Allan R. (ed.): *Constitutional Courts as Positive Legislators. A Comparative Law Study,* Cambridge, Cambridge University Press, 2011.

Bugarič, Bojan – Kuhelj, Alenka: "Varieties of Populism in Europe: Is the Rule of Law in Danger?", *Hague Journal on the Rule of Law,* 2018 March, 22.

Bugarič, Bojan: "The Two Faces of Populism: Between Authoritarian and Democratic Populism", *German Law Journal,* 2019/3, 390–400.

Callejón, Francisco Balaguer: "Constitutional Courts under Pressure – New Challenges to Constitutional adjudication: The case of Spain", in Szente, Zoltán – Gárdos-Orosz, Fruzsina (eds.): *New Challenges to Constitutional Adjudication in Europe,* London, Routledge, 2018, 164–185.

Canon, Bradley C.: "Defining The Dimensions Of Judicial Activism", *Judicature,* 1983/6, 236.

Canotilho, Mariana: "Constitutional law and crisis: The Portuguese Constitutional Court under pressure?", in Szente, Zoltán – Gárdos-Orosz, Fruzsina (eds.): *New Challenges to Constitutional Adjudication in Europe,* London, Routledge, 2018, 144–164.

Cappelletti, Mauro – Adams, John Clarke: "Judicial Review of Legislation: European Antecedents and Adaptations", *Harvard Law Review,* 1966/6, 1207–1224.

Castellà Andreu, Josep Maria – Simonelli, Marco Antonio (eds.): *Populism and Contemporary Democracy in Europe. Old Problems and New Challenges,* Cham, Palgrave Macmillan, 2022.

Chronowski, Nóra – Drinóczi, Tímea – Kocsis, Miklós: "Mozaikok, azaz milyen értelmezési kérdéseket vethet fel az alaptörvény?", in Drinóczi, Tímea (ed.): *Magyarország új alkotmányossága,* Pécs, PTE ÁJK, 2011.

Chronowski, Nóra – Drinóczi, Tímea – Zeller, Judit: "Túl az Alkotmányon", *Közjogi Szemle,* 2010/4, 1–12.

Chronowski, Nóra – Drinóczi, Tímea: "Alkotmánybírói függetlenség Európában és Magyarországon?", *Közjogi Szemle,* 2010/3, 26–32.

Chronowski, Nóra – Varju, Márton: "Constitutional backsliding in Hungary", *Tijdschrift voor Constitutioneel Recht,* 2015/3, 296–310.

Chronowski, Nóra – Vincze, Attila: "Alkotmánybíráskodás (gazdasági) válságban", *Alkotmánybírósági Szemle,* 2014/2, 104–112.

Chronowski, Nóra – Vincze, Attila: "Önazonosság és európai integráció", *Jogtudományi Közlöny,* 2017/3, 117–132.

Chronowski, Nóra – Vincze, Attila: "Two Eras of Hungarian Constitutionalism: From the Rule of Law to Rule by Law", *Hague Journal on the Rule of Law,* 2016/2, 271–289.

Chronowski, Nóra: "Alkotmányjogi panasz és alkotmányvédelem", *Fundamentum,* 2014/1–2, 91–95.

Chronowski, Nóra: "Az alkotmánybíráskodás sarkalatos átalakítása", *MTA Law Working Papers,* 2014/8, 4, 1–16, https://jog.tk.mta.hu/uploads/files/mtalwp/2014_08_Chronowski.pdf

Chronowski, Nóra: "Az alkotmánykonform értelmezés és az Alaptörvény", *Közjogi Szemle,* 2017/4, 7–15.

Ciolli, Ines: "Global markets, terrorism and immigration: Italy between a troubled economy and a Constitutional crisis", in Szente, Zoltán – Gárdos-Orosz, Fruzsina (eds.): *New Challenges to Constitutional Adjudication in Europe,* London, Routledge, 2018, 111–132.

Claus, Laurence P. – Kay, Richard S.: "Constitutional Courts as »Positive Legislators«, in the United States", *American Journal of Comparative Law,* 2010/1, 479–504.

Comella, Víctor Ferreres: *Constitutional Courts and Democratic Values,* New Haven – London, Yale University Press, 2009.

Contiades, Xenophon – Fotiaou, Alkmene: "How Constitutions Reacted to the Financial Crisis", in Contiades, Xenophon (ed.): *Constitutions in the Global Financial Crisis. A Comparative Analysis,* Farnham, Ashgate, 2013.

Contiades, Xenophon (ed.): *Constitutions in the Global Financial Crisis. A Comparative Analysis,* Farnham, Ashgate, 2013.

Cover, Robert: "The Supreme Court 1982 Term. Foreword: Nomos and Narrative", *Harvard Law Review,* 1982, 4–68.

Csehi, Zoltán: "A német alkotmányjogi panasz hatása – biztató kezdetek a magyar gyakorlatban", *Acta Universitatis Szegediensis – Acta Iuvenum,* 2016/2, 17–32.

Csehi, Zoltán: "A valódi alkotmányjogi panasz és a magánjog lehetséges jövőjéről", *Alkotmánybírósági Szemle,* 2012/2, 126–130.

Cservák, Csaba – Horváth, Attila (eds.): *Az adekvát alapjogvédelem,* Budapest, Porta Historica, 2017.

Currie, David P.: *The Constitution of the Federal Republic of Germany,* University of Chicago Press, 1994.

D. Tóth, Balázs – Enyedi, Krisztián – Halmai, Gábor – Németh, Attila – Polgár, Eszter – Sólyom, Péter: "Alkotmányos és nemzetközi emberi jogi követelmények a rendes bíróságok gyakorlatában", in Fleck, Zoltán (ed.): *Bíróságok a mérlegen II.,* Budapest, Pallas, 2008, 75–88.

De Visser, Maartje: *Constitutional Review in Europe. A Comparative Analysis,* Oxford, Hart, 2014.

Dahl, Robert A.: "Decision-Making in a Democracy: The Supreme Court as a National Policy-Maker", *Journal of Public Law,* 1957, 279–295.

Dargent, Eduardo: "Determinants of Judicial Independence: Lessons from Three Cases Constitutional Courts in Peru", *Journal of Latin American Studies,* 2009/2, 251–278.

Deli, Gergely – Kukorelli, István: "Az emberi méltóság alapjoga Magyarországon", *Jogtudományi Közlöny,* 2015/7–8, 337–347.

Deli, Gergely: "Az emberi méltóság alapjoga Magyarországon", in Kukorelli, István (ed.): *Hány* éves *az Alaptörvény? A régi-új kérdése az Alaptörvényben,* Budapest, Gondolat, 2017, 121–152.

Delzangles, Beatrice: "The negotiating function of the European Court of Human Rights: Reconciling diverging interests born from new European challenges", in Szente, Zoltán – Gárdos-Orosz, Fruzsina (eds.): *New Challenges to Constitutional Adjudication in Europe,* London, Routledge, 2018, 259–273.

Drinóczi, Tímea – Chronowski, Nóra – Kocsis, Miklós: "What Questions of Interpretation may be Raised by the New Hungarian Constitution?", *Vienna Journal on International Constitutional Law,* 2012, 41–64.

Drinóczi, Tímea – Gárdos-Orosz, Fruzsina – Pozsár-Szentmiklósy, Zoltán: "Formal and Informal Constitutional Amendment in Hungary", *MTA Law Working Papers,* 2019/18, https://jog.tk.hu/mtalwp/formal-and-informal-constitutional-amendment-in-hungary

Drinóczi, Tímea (ed.): *Magyarország új alkotmányossága,* Pécs, PTE ÁJK, 2011.

Drinóczi, Tímea: "A 22/2016. (XII. 5.) AB határozat: mit (nem) tartalmaz, és mi következik belőle. Az identitásvizsgálat és az ultra vires közös hatáskörgyakorlás összehasonlító elemzésben", *MTA Law Working Papers,* 2017/1, https://jog.tk.hu/mtalwp/a-222016-xii-5-ab-hatarozat-mit-nem-tartalmaz-es-mi-kovetkezik-belole-az-identitas-vizsgalat-es-az-ultra-vires-kozos-hataskorgyakorlas-osszehasonlito-elemzesben

Drinóczi, Tímea: "A tagállami identitás védelme", in Jakab, András – Fekete, Balázs (eds.): *Internetes Jogtudományi Enciklopédia* (EU law column, column editors: Varju, Márton – Horváthy, Balázs), 2018, http://ijoten.hu/szocikk/a-tagallami-identitas-vedelme

Drinóczi, Tímea: "A tulajdonhoz való alapjog értelmezésének eltérései a rendes bírósági és az alkotmánybírósági gyakorlatban: a bírói kezdeményezések és az alkotmányjogi panaszok tapasztalatai", in *Az Alaptörvény érvényesülése a bírói gyakorlatban III. Alkotmányjogi panasz: az alapjog-érvényesítés gyakorlata,* Budapest, HVG-ORAC, 2019, 277–312.

Drinóczi, Tímea: "Az Alkotmánybíróság határozata a devizahitelekről. A szerződési szabadság régi-új korlátai", *Jogesetek Magyarázata,* 2014/2, 3–12.

Drinóczi, Tímea: "Gondolatok az Alkotmánybíróság 61/2011. (VII. 12.) AB határozatával kapcsolatban", *Jura,* 2012/1, 37–46.

Drinóczi, Tímea: "Loyalty, Opportunism and Fear, The forced privatisation of Hungarian universities", *Verfassungsblog,* 5 February, 2021, https://verfassungsblog.de/loyalty-opportunism-and-fear

Drinóczi, Tímea: *Alkotmányos párbeszéd. A többszintű alkotmányosság alkotmánytana és gyakorlata a 21. században,* Budapest, MTA TK Jogtudományi Intézet, 2017.

Dupré, Catherine: *The Age of Dignity: Human Rights and Constitutionalism in Europe*, Oxford, Hart, 2015.

Dworkin, Ronald: *Taking Rights Seriously: With a New Appendix, a Response to Critics*, Duckworth, 1977.

Dworkin, Ronald: "Objectivity and truth: You'd better believe it", *Philosophy and Public Affairs*, 1996/2, 87–139.

Dworkin, Ronald: "The Forum of Principle", *New York University Law Review*, 1981/56, 469–518.

Dworkin, Ronald: *A Matter of Principle*, Cambridge, Harvard University Press, 1985.

Eatwell, Roger – Goodwin, Matthew: *National Populism: The Revolt against Liberal Democracy*, London, Pelican, 2018.

Eckhart, Ferenc: "Jog és alkotmánytörténet", in Hóman, Bálint (ed.): *A magyar történetírás új útjai*, Budapest, Magyar Szemle Társaság, 1932.

Ely, John Hart: *Democracy and Distrust: A Theory of Judicial Review*, Cambridge – London, Harvard University Press, 1980.

Erdős, Csaba: "Az 1989-es Alkotmányon nyugvó alkotmánybírósági határozatok hatályon kívül helyezésének egyes aspektusai", in Gárdos-Orosz, Fruzsina – Szente, Zoltán (eds.): *Alkotmányozás és alkotmányjogi változások Európában és Magyarországon*, Budapest, Nemzeti Közszolgálati és Tankönyv Kiadó Zrt., 2014, 297–315.

Erdős, Csaba: "Az Alkotmánybíróság gyakorlata az alkotmánymódosítások felülvizsgálatának és alkotmányi szabályok közti kollízió feloldásának területein", in Gárdos-Orosz, Fruzsina – Szente, Zoltán (eds.): *Jog és politika határán. Alkotmánybíráskodás Magyarországon 2010 után*, Budapest, HVG-ORAC, 2015, 317–348.

Erdős, Csaba: "Az alkotmánybíróság kontrollmechanizmusainak változásai", in Kecskés, Gábor (ed.): *Doktori műhelytanulmányok*, Győr, Széchenyi István Egyetem Állam- és Jogtudományi Doktori Iskola, 2013, 137–141.

Erdős, Csaba: "Gondolatok a különleges jogrendi alapjogkorlátozás alkotmánybírósági gyakorlatáról" *Jog* – Állam – *Politika. Ünnepi különszám a 70 éves Kukorelli István tiszteletére*, 2022/2, 103–120.

Erdős, Csaba: *Az Országgyűlés döntési autonómiájának aktustani megközelítése*, Győr, Széchenyi István Egyetem Állam- és Jogtudományi Doktori Iskola, 2014.

Fabbrini, Federico: *Economic Governance in Europe: Comparative Paradoxes and Constitutional Challenges*, Oxford, Oxford University Press, 2016.

Farkas, Zoltán: "Az intézmény fogalma, fedezete és funkcionalitása", *Miskolci Jogi Szemle*, 2007/2.

Favoreu, Louis: *Les Cours Constitutionnelles*, Paris, Presses Universitaires de France, 1986.

Fazekas, Flóra: "EU Law and Hungarian Constitutional Court", in Varju, Márton – Várnay, Ernő (eds.): *European Union Law in Hungary: Institutions, Processes and the Law*, Budapest: HVG-ORAC, 2014.

Fekete, Balázs: "Történeti elemek az EU-tagállamok alkotmány-preambulumaiban", in Lamm Vanda – Majtényi Balázs – Pap András László (eds.): *Preambulum az alkotmányokban*, Budapest, Complex, 2011, 33–45.

Fleck, Zoltán (ed.): *Bíróságok a mérlegen II.*, Budapest, Pallas, 2008.

Gadó, Gábor: "Alapjogok védelme és korlátozása az Alkotmánybíróság döntéseinek tükrében", *Gazdaság és Jog*, 1994/9.

GARDASEVIC, Djordje: "Croatian constitutional adjudication in times of stress", in SZENTE, Zoltán - GÁRDOS-OROSZ, Fruzsina (eds.): *New Challenges to Constitutional Adjudication in Europe*, London, Routledge, 2018, 27–45.

GARDBAUM, Stephen: "What is judicial supremacy?", in JACOBSOHN, Gary - SCHOR, Miguel (eds.): *Comparative Constitutional Theory*, Cheltenham, Edward Elgar, 2018, 21–44.

GARDBAUM, Stephen: *The New Commonwealth Model of Constitutionalism: Theory and Practice*, Cambridge, Cambridge University Press, 2013.

GÁRDOS-OROSZ Fruzsina: "Újabb áttekintés az uniós jog alkalmazásának magyarországi alkotmányos kereteiről", *Közjogi Szemle*, 2013/4, 44–53.

GÁRDOS-OROSZ, Fruzsina - BEDŐ, Renáta: "Az alapvető jogok érvényesítése a magánjogi jogviták során", *Alkotmánybírósági Szemle*, 2018/1, 3-15.

GÁRDOS-OROSZ, Fruzsina - GÁRDOS, Péter: "Az Alkotmánybíróság első határozata a pénzügyi intézmények fogyasztói kölcsönszerződéseiben alkalmazott egyoldalú szerződésmódosítási jogra vonatkozó törvényi szabályozásról", *Jogesetek Magyarázata*, 2015/2, 3-15.

GÁRDOS-OROSZ, Fruzsina - GÁRDOS, Péter: "Az Alkotmánybíróság második határozata a pénzügyi intézmények fogyasztói kölcsönszerződéseiben alkalmazott egyoldalú szerződésmódosítási jogra vonatkozó törvényi szabályozásról", *Jogesetek Magyarázata*, 2016/3, 21-32.

GÁRDOS-OROSZ, Fruzsina - FLORCZAK, Monika - WATOR, Jan Malir - STEUER, Max (eds.): *Emergencies and human rights protection in the Visegrad countries*, Routledge, 2024 (forthcoming).

GÁRDOS-OROSZ, Fruzsina - LŐRINCZ, Viktor Olivér - ZŐDI, Zsolt: "Egy új alkotmányjogi panaszeljárás (Abtv. 27. §) jelentőségének mérhetősége a bírósági és az alkotmánybírósági alapjogvédelem rendszerében", in *Az Alaptörvény érvényesülése a bírói gyakorlatban II. Alkotmányjogi panasz - a hatáskörrel kapcsolatos kérdések*, Budapest, HVG-ORAC, 2019, 363–385.

GÁRDOS-OROSZ, Fruzsina - LŐRINCZ, Viktor Olivér (eds.): *Jogi diagnózisok. A COVID-19-világjárvány hatásai a jogrendszerre*, Budapest, L'Harmattan - Társadalomtudományi Kutatóközpont Jogtudományi Intézet, 2020.

GÁRDOS-OROSZ, Fruzsina - SZENTE, Zoltán (eds.): *Alkotmányozás és alkotmányjogi változások Európában és Magyarországon*, Budapest, Nemzeti Közszolgálati és Tankönyv Kiadó Zrt., 2014.

GÁRDOS-OROSZ, Fruzsina - SZENTE, Zoltán (eds.): *Jog és politika határán. Alkotmánybíráskodás Magyarországon 2010 után*, Budapest, HVG-ORAC, 2015.

GÁRDOS-OROSZ, Fruzsina - ZAKARIÁS, Kinga (eds.): *Az alkotmánybírósági gyakorlat. Az Alkotmánybíróság 100 elvi jelentőségű határozata 1990–2020*, Budapest, Társadalomtudományi Kutatóközpont Jogtudományi Intézet - HVG-ORAC, 2021.

GÁRDOS-OROSZ, Fruzsina: "A bírói döntések ellen benyújtott alkotmányjogi panaszok befogadhatósága I. Az Abtv. 26. § (1) bekezdése", *Alkotmánybírósági Szemle*, 2013/4, 74–81.

GÁRDOS-OROSZ, Fruzsina: "A bírói döntések ellen benyújtott alkotmányjogi panaszok befogadhatósága II. Az Abtv. 27. §-a", *Alkotmánybírósági Szemle*, 2014/1, 82–89.

GÁRDOS-OROSZ, Fruzsina: "A rendes bíróságok és az Alkotmánybíróság kapcsolata az alapjog-érvényesítésben", in *Az Alaptörvény érvényesülése a bírói gyakorlatban III. Alkotmányjogi panasz: az alapjog-érvényesítés gyakorlata*, Budapest, HVG-ORAC, 2019, 11–18.

GÁRDOS-OROSZ, Fruzsina: "Alkotmánybíróság 2010–2015", in JAKAB, András – GAJDUSCHEK, György (eds.): *A magyar jogrendszer állapota 2010–2015,* Budapest, MTA TK Jogtudományi Intézet, 2016, 442–479.

GÁRDOS-OROSZ, Fruzsina: "Alkotmánybíróság", in JAKAB, András – KÖNCZÖL, Miklós – MENYHÁRD, Attila – SULYOK, Gábor (eds.): *Internetes Jogtudományi Enciklopédia* (Constitutional Law column, column editors: BODNÁR, Eszter – JAKAB, András), 2020, http://ijoten.hu/szocikk/alkotmanybirosag

GÁRDOS-OROSZ, Fruzsina: "Az actio popularistól az alkotmányjogi panaszig: a magyar Alkotmánybíróság új hatáskörei", in BOÓC, Ádám – FEKETE, Balázs (eds.): *Il me semblait que j'étais moi-même ce dont parlait l'ouvrage. Liber amicorum Endre Ferenczy,* Budapest, Patrocinium, 2012, 118–133.

GÁRDOS-OROSZ, Fruzsina: "Az alapjogok korlátozása", in JAKAB, András – KÖNCZÖL, Miklós – MENYHÁRD, Attila – SULYOK, Gábor (eds.): *Internetes Jogtudományi Enciklopédia* (Constitutional Law column, column editors: BODNÁR, Eszter – JAKAB, András), 2020, http://ijoten.hu/szocikk/az-alapjogok-korlatozasa

GÁRDOS-OROSZ, Fruzsina: "Az alapvető jogok korlátozása", in JAKAB, András (ed.): *Az Alkotmány kommentárja,* Budapest, Századvég, 2009.

GÁRDOS-OROSZ, Fruzsina: "Az alkotmánymódosítások alkotmányossági felülvizsgálata: elméleti koncepciók, nemzetközi trendek és magyar kérdések", in GÁRDOS-OROSZ, Fruzsina – SZENTE, Zoltán (eds.): *Alkotmányozás és alkotmányjogi változások Európában és Magyarországon,* Budapest, Nemzeti Közszolgálati és Tankönyv Kiadó Zrt., 2014. 167-184.

GÁRDOS-OROSZ, Fruzsina: "Challenges to Constitutional Adjudication in Hungary since 2010", in BELOV, Martin (ed.): *The Role of Courts in Contemporary Legal Orders,* The Hague, Eleven Publishing, 2019. 321–340.

GÁRDOS-OROSZ, Fruzsina: "Constitutional interpretation in Hungary", in GÁRDOS-OROSZ, Fruzsina – SZENTE, Zoltán (eds.): *Constitutional interpretation in the Populist Regimes in Europe and Beyond,* Routledge, 2021.

GÁRDOS-OROSZ, Fruzsina: "Constitutional interpretation under the Fundamental Law of Hungary", in SZENTE, Zoltán – GÁRDOS-OROSZ, Fruzsina (eds.): *Populist Challenges to Constitutional Interpretation in Europe and Beyond,* London, Routledge, 2021, 143–159.

GÁRDOS-OROSZ, Fruzsina: "Constitutional Justice in Credit Crisis. The Hungarian Case", *Südosteuropa,* 2018/1.

GÁRDOS-OROSZ, Fruzsina: "Fórum. Az alkotmánybíráskodás jelene: az Alaptörvény és az alkotmányosság legfőbb őrének »feladat- és hatásköre«", *Fundamentum,* 2014/1–2, 85–90.

GÁRDOS-OROSZ, FRUZSINA: "Reference to constitutional traditions in populist constitutionalism – the case of Hungary", *Acta Juridica Hungarica,* 2020/1, 23–51.

GÁRDOS-OROSZ, Fruzsina: "Rendhagyó alkotmányossági mércék az Alkotmánybíróság »devizahiteles« határozataiban", in GÁRDOS-OROSZ, Fruzsina – SZENTE, Zoltán (eds.): *Jog és politika határán. Alkotmánybíráskodás Magyarországon 2010 után,* Budapest, HVG-ORAC, 2015 373-409.

GÁRDOS-OROSZ, Fruzsina: "The Constitutional and statutory framework of the application of EU law in Hungary", *Acta Universitas Carolinae,* 2013, 315–337.

GÁRDOS-OROSZ, Fruzsina: "The Hungarian constitutional court in transition: from actio popularis to constitutional complaint", *Acta Juridica Hungarica,* 2012/4, 302–315.

GÁRDOS-OROSZ, Fruzsina: "Unamendability as a judicial discovery", in ALBERT, Richard –ODER, Bertil Emrah (eds.): *Unamendability,* Cham, Springer, 2018, 231–258.

GÁRDOS-OROSZ, Fruzsina: *Alkotmányos polgári jog? Az alapvető jogok alkalmazása a magánjogi jogvitákban,* Budapest – Pécs, Dialóg Campus, 2011.

GERA, Anna: "Dsuang Dszi álma az alkotmánybíróságról", *MTA Law Working Papers,* 2021/6, https://jog.tk.hu/mtalwp/torteneti-alkotmanyunk-vivmanyai-az-alaptorveny-specialis-alkotmanyos-rendszereben

GINSBURG, Tom – MOUSTAFA, Tamir (eds.): *Rule by law: The Politics of Courts in Authoritarian Regimes,* Cambridge, Cambridge University Press, 2008.

GINSBURG, Tom: *Judicial Review in New Democracies. Constitutional Courts in Asian Cases,* Cambridge, Cambridge University Press, 2003.

GÖZLER, Kemal: *A judicial review of constitutional amendments: a comparative study,* Bursa, Ekin, 2008.

GRANAT, Miroslaw: "Constitutional judiciary in crisis: The case of Poland", in SZENTE, Zoltán – GÁRDOS-OROSZ, Fruzsina (eds.): *New Challenges to Constitutional Adjudication in Europe,* London, Routledge, 2018, 132–143.

GROPPI, Tania – PONTHOREAU, Marie Claire (eds.): *The Use of Foreign Precedents by Constitutional Judges,* Oxford, Hart, 2013.

GYŐRFI Tamás: *Az alkotmánybíráskodás politikai karaktere. Értekezés a magyar alkotmánybíráskodás első tíz ę́véről,* Budapest, INDOK, 2001.

GYŐRFI, Tamás – KAZAI, Viktor Zoltán – ORBÁN, Endre: *Kontextus által világosan. A Sólyom-bíróság antiformalista elemzése,* Budapest, L'Harmattan, 2022.

GYORFI, Tamas: *Against the New Constitutionalism,* Cheltenham, Edward Elgar, 2016.

GYŐRFI, Tamás: *Az Alkotmánybíráskodás politikai karaktere. Értekezés a magyar Alkotmánybíróság első tíz évéről,* Budapest, INDOK, 2001.

HALÁSZ, Iván: "Alkotmányos identitás", in GÁRDOS-OROSZ, Fruzsina – HALÁSZ, Iván (eds.): *Alkotmányjogi alapok,* Budapest, Dialóg Campus, 2019.

HALMAI, Gábor – TÓTH, Gábor Attila (eds.): *Emberi jogok,* Budapest, Osiris, 2003.

HALMAI, Gábor: "Abuse of Constitutional Identity. The Hungarian Constitutional Court on Interpretation of Article E) (2) of the Fundamental Law", *Review of Central and East European Law,* 2018, 23–42.

HALMAI, Gábor: "Az alkotmányjogi panasz – jelen és jövendő?", *Bírák Lapja,* 1994/3–4, 63–74.

HALMAI, Gábor: "Hans Kelsen és a magyar Alkotmánybíróság", *Világosság,* 2005/II, 3–14.

HALMAI, Gábor: "In memoriam magyar alkotmánybíráskodás. A pártos alkotmánybíráskodás első éve", *Fundamentum,* 2014/1–2, 56–57.

HALMAI, Gábor: "Pártos alkotmánybíráskodás (2010–2014)", in GÁRDOS-OROSZ, Fruzsina – SZENTE, Zoltán (eds.): *Jog és politika határán. Alkotmánybíráskodás Magyarországon 2010 után,* Budapest, HVG-ORAC, 2015, 105–150.

HALMAI, Gábor: "The Hungarian Approach to Constitutional Review: The End of Activism? The First Decade of the Hungarian Constitutional Court", in SADURSKI, Wojciech (ed.): *Constitutional Justice, East and West. Democratic Legitimacy and Constitutional Courts in Post-Communist Europe in a Comparative Perspective,* Hague – London, Kluwer Law International, 2002, 189–211.

HALMAI, Gábor: "The Invalid Anti-Migrant Referendum in Hungary", *Verfassungsblog,* 04 Oktober 2016, https://verfassungsblog.de/hungarys-anti-european-immigration-laws

HALMAI, Gábor: *Alkotmányjog, emberi jogok, globalizáció: az alkotmányos eszmék migrációja*, Budapest, L'Harmattan, 2013.

HARDING, Andrew – LEYLAND, Peter (eds.): *Constitutional Courts: A Comparative Study*, London, Wildy, Simmonds & Hill, 2009.

HENKIN, Louis: "Is There a »Political Question« Doctrine?", *The Yale Law Journal*, 1976/5, 597–625.

HIRSCHL, Ran: *Comparative Matters – The Renaissance of Comparative Constitutional Law*, Oxford, Oxford University Press, 2013.

HIRSCHL, Ran: *Towards Juristocracy. The Origins and Consequences of New Constitutionalism*, Cambridge, Harvard University Press, 2007.

HOLLÁN, Miklós: "Büntetőbírói döntések az Alkotmánybíróság ítélőszéke előtt a *nullum crimen et nulla poena sine lege* elv tükrében", in *Az Alaptörvény érvényesülése a bírói gyakorlatban III. Alkotmányjogi panasz: az alapjog-érvényesítés gyakorlata*, Budapest, HVG-ORAC, 2019, 64–97.

HOLLÓ, András: *Az alkotmányjognak asztalánál*, Budapest, HVG-ORAC, 2015.

HOLLÓ, ANDRÁS: *Az alkotmányvédelem kialakulása Magyarországon*, Miskolc, Bíbor, 1997.

HÖNNIGE, Cristoph: *Verfassungsgericht, Regierung, und Opposition – Die vergleichende Analyse eines Spannungsdreiecks*, Wiesbaden, VS Verlag, 2007.

HOURQUEBIE, Fabrice: "Remarks on the case law of the French Constitutional Council in relation to new challenges", in SZENTE, Zoltán – GÁRDOS-OROSZ, Fruzsina (eds.): *New Challenges to Constitutional Adjudication in Europe*, London, Routledge, 2018, 45–52.

HÜBNER MENDES, Conrado: *Constitutional Courts and Deliberative Democracy*, Oxford, Oxford University Press, 2013.

IGLESIAS-RODRIGUEZ, Pablo – TRIANDAFYLLIDOU, Anna – GROPAS, Ruby (eds.): *After the Financial Crisis. Shifting Legal, Economic and Political Paradigms*, London, Palgrave Macmillan, 2016.

ISMAYR, Wolfgang (ed.): *Die politischen Systeme Osteuropas*, Opladen, Leske und Budrich, 2002.

ISMAYR, Wolfgang: "Die politischen Systeme Osteuropas im Vergleich", in ISMAYR, Wolfgang (ed.): *Die politischen Systeme Osteuropas*, Opladen, Leske und Budrich, 2002, 15–19.

JACOBSOHN, Gary – SCHOR, Miguel (eds.): *Comparative Constitutional Theory*, Cheltenham, Edward Elgar, 2018.

JAKAB, András – DYEVREA, Arthur – ITZCOVICH, Giulio (eds.): *Comparative Constitutional Reasoning*, Cambridge, Cambridge University Press, 2017.

JAKAB, András – FRÖHLICH, Johanna: "The Constitutional Court of Hungary", in JAKAB, András – DYEVREA, Arthur – ITZCOVICH, Giulio (eds.): *Comparative Constitutional Reasoning*, Cambridge, Cambridge University Press, 2017.

JAKAB, András – GAJDUSCHEK, György (eds.): *A magyar jogrendszer állapota 2010–2015*, Budapest, MTA TK Jogtudományi Intézet, 2016.

JAKAB, András – SZILÁGYI, Emese: "Sarkalatos törvények a magyar jogrendben", *MTA Law Working Papers*, 2015/32, https://jog.tk.mta.hu/uploads/files/mtalwp/2015_32_Jakab.pdf

JAKAB, András (ed.): *Az Alkotmány kommentárja I–II.*, Budapest, Századvég, 2009.

JAKAB, András: "A bírói jogértelmezés az Alaptörvény tükrében", *Jogesetek Magyarázata*, 2011/4.

Jakab, András: "A szocializmus dogmatikai hagyatéka", *Jogelméleti Szemle,* 2003/4, http://jesz.ajk.elte.hu/jakab15.html

Jakab, András: "A szocializmus jogdogmatikai hagyatékának néhány eleméről", *Iustum Aequum Salutare,* 2007.

Jakab, András: *Az új Alaptörvény keletkezése és gyakorlati következményei,* Budapest, HVG-ORAC, 2011.

"Jurisztokrácia-vita", *Jogelméleti Szemle,* 2015/4, http://jesz.ajk.elte.hu/2015_4.pdf

Kádár, Pál – Hoffmann, István: "A különleges jogrend és a válságkezelés közigazgatási jogi kihívásai: a kvázi különleges jogrendek helye és szerepe a magyar közigazgatásban", *Közjogi Szemle,* 2021/3, 1–11.

Kadlót, Erzsébet: "Az indítványok szűréséről", *Alkotmánybírósági Szemle,* 2012/1, 96–105.

Kapiszewski, Diana – Silverstein, Gordon – Kagan, Robert A. (eds.): *Consequential Courts: Judicial Roles in Global Perspective,* Cambridge, Cambridge University Press, 2013.

Karsai, Dániel – Mihály, Eszter: "Elefántsirató – a sikeres alkotmányjogi panaszok utóélete", *MTA Law Working Papers,* 2017/21, 1–31, https://jog.tk.mta.hu/uploads/files/2017_21_Karsai_Mihalyi.pdf

Kaunert, Christian – Léonard, Sarah (eds.): *European Security, Terrorism and Intelligence. Tackling New Security Challenges in Europe*, London, Palgrave Macmillan, 2013.

Kelemen, Katalin: *Judicial dissent in European constitutional courts: A comparative and legal perspective,* Routledge, 2018.

Kelemen, Katalin – Steuer, Max: "Constitutional Court of Hungary", in Grote, Rainer – Lachenmann, Frauke – Wolfrum, Rüdiger (eds.): *Max Planck Encyclopedia of Comparative Constitutional Law,* Oxford University Press, 2019.

Kelsen, Hans: "Judicial Review of Legislation: A Comparative Study of the Austrian and the American Constitution", *Journal of Politics,* 1942/2, 183–200.

Kelsen, Hans: "La garantie juridictionnelle de la Constitution (La Justice constitutionnelle)", *Revue du droit public,* 1928, 197–257.

Kelsen, Hans: "Wesen und Entwicklung der Staatsgerichtsbarkeit", in Häberle, Peter (ed.): *Verfassungsgerichtsbarkeit,* Darmstadt, Wissenschaftliche Buchgesellschaft, 1976, 98–144.

Kelsen, Hans: „Ki legyen az alkotmány őre?" in Takács Péter (ed.): *Államtan. Írások a XX. századi általános államtudomány köréből,* Budapest, Szent István Társulat, 2003, 289–332.

Kelsen, Hans: *Tiszta jogtan,* Budapest, ELTE Állam- és Jogtudományi Kar – Bibó István Szakkollégium, 1988.

Kelsen, Hans: *Wer soll der Hüter der Verfassung sein? Abhandlungen zur Theorie der Verfassungsgerichtsbarkeit in der pluralistischen, parlamentarischen Demokratie,* Tübingen, Mohr Siebeck, 2008.

Kelsen, Hans: *Wer soll Hüter der Verfassung sein?* Berlin, W. Rothschild, 1931.

Kis, János: *Alkotmányos demokrácia. Három tanulmány,* Budapest, INDOK, 2000.

Kiss, Barnabás: "Az alapjogok alkotmányi szabályozásának általános kérdései", in Ádám, Antal (ed.): *Alkotmányfejlődés és jogállami gyakorlat,* Budapest, Hanns Seidel Alapítvány, 1994.

Kiss, Tibor: „Pillanatfelvétel a képmás védelméhez fűződő jog bírói gyakorlatáról 2. rész", *Debreceni Jogi Műhely,* 2017/3–4, http://www.debrecenijogimuhely.hu/archivum/3_4_2017/pillanatfelvetel_a_kepmas_vedelmehez_fuzodo_jog_biroi_gyakorlatarol

KLEIN, Eckhart: "Az alapjogok meghatározása az alkotmányban" in ÁDÁM, Antal (ed.): *Alkotmányfejlődés és jogállami gyakorlat,* Budapest, Hanns Seidel Alapítvány, 1994.

KOLTAY, András – NYAKAS, Levente (eds.): *Magyar és európai médiajog,* Budapest, Wolters Kluwer, 2015.

KOLTAY, András – TÖRÖK, Bernát (eds.): *Sajtószabadság és médiajog a 21. század elején 4.,* Budapest, Wolters Kluwer, 2017.

KOLTAY, András: "A becsület, a jóhírnév és az emberi méltóság fogalmi elhatárolása a magyar magánjogban", in KOLTAY, András – DARÁK, Péter (eds.): *Ad astra per aspera.* Ünnepi *kötet Solt Pál* 80. *születésnapja alkalmából,* Budapest, Pázmány Press, 2017, 435–458.

KOLTAY, András: „A jó hírnév és a becsület védelme, különös tekintettel a közéleti szereplőkre és a közügyek vitáira", in KOLTAY, András – NYAKAS, Levente (eds.): *Magyar és európai médiajog,* Budapest, Wolters Kluwer, 2015, 309–347.

KOLTAY, András: „Az »általános személyiségi jog« azonosítása felé. Alkotmányjogi, magánjogi és büntetőjogi vizsgálódás", in KOLTAY, András – TÖRÖK, Bernát (eds.): *Sajtószabadság és médiajog a 21. század elején 4.,* Budapest, Wolters Kluwer, 2017, 267–296.

KÖRÖSSÉNYI, András (ed.): *A magyar politikai rendszer – negyedszázad után,* Budapest, Osiris, 2014.

KOVÁCS, Ágnes: "New trend in the debate on justifying judicial review: Considering the benefits of judicial reasoning", in CSERNE, Péter – KÖNCZÖL, Miklós – SONIEWICKA, Marta (eds.): *The Rule of Law and Challenges to Jurisprudence,* Frankfurt am Main, PL Academic Research – Peter Lang, 2014.

KOVÁCS, Kriszta – TÓTH, Gábor Attila: "Hungary's Constitutional Transformation", *European Constitutional Law Review,* 2011/2, 183–203.

KOVÁCS, Péter: "Az Emberi Jogok Európai Bírósága ítéletére való hivatkozás újabb formulái és technikái a magyar Alkotmánybíróság, valamint néhány más európai alkotmánybíróság mai gyakorlatában", *Alkotmánybírósági Szemle,* 2013/2, 84.

KOVÁCS, Virág: "A ki nem hirdetett törvények Alaptörvénnyel való összhangjának vizsgálatáról", *Alkotmánybírósági Szemle,* 2012/2, 78–91.

KUKORELLI, István (ed.): *Alkotmányjog I.,* Budapest, Osiris, 2007.

KUKORELLI, István (ed.): *Hány éves az Alaptörvény? A régi-új kérdése az Alaptörvényben,* Budapest, Gondolat, 2017.

KUKORELLI, István: "A magyar alkotmánybíráskodás előzményei, létrejötte és jellemzői", in KUKORELLI, István – TÓTH, Károly: *A rendszerváltoztatás államszervezeti kompromisszumai. Antológia,* Lakitelek, 2016, 398–407.

LÁBADY, Tamás: "Sérelemdíj *versus* nem vagyoni kártérítés", *Állam- és Jogtudomány,* 2016/1, 40–45.

LAMM, Vanda – MAJTÉNYI, Balázs – PAP, András László (eds.): *Preambulum az alkotmányokban,* Budapest, Complex, 2011.

LAMPRECHT, Rolf – MALANOWSKI, Wolfgang: *Richter machen Politik,* Frankfurt am Main, Fischer, 1979.

LANDAU, David E.: "Political institutions and judicial role in comparative constitutional law", *Harvard International Law Journal,* 2010/51, 319–378.

LÁPOSSY, Attila – SZAJBÉLY, Katalin: "Egy nem lovagias ügy", *Szuverén,* 4 December 2013, http://szuveren.hu/jog/egy-nem-lovagias-ugy

Lápüssy, Attila: "Közvetve és közvetlenül: az alapvető jogok biztosának indítványozási jogköre az alkotmánybíráskodás és alapjogvédelem szemszögéből", *Kodifikáció és Közigazgatás,* 2012/2, 39-52.

Lápossy, Attila: "Populáris akcióból ombudsmani akciók?", *Magyar Közigazgatás,* 2011/3, 120-131.

Law, David - Versteeg, Mila: "The Evolution and Ideology of Global Constitutionalism", *California Law Review,* 2011, 1163.

Lemieux, Scott E. - Watkins, David J.: *Judicial Review and Contemporary Democratic Theory: Power, Domination, and the Courts,* New York - London, Routledge, 2018.

Marcic, René: *Verfassung und Verfassungsgericht,* Wien, Springer Verlag, 1963.

Marcic, René: *Vom Gesetzesstaat zum Richterstaat. Recht als Mass der Macht / Gedanken über den demokratischen Rechts- und Sozialstaat. Der Weg zwischen Sicherheit und Freiheit,* Wien, Springer, 1957.

Marshall, William P.: "Constitutional Law as Political Spoils", *Cardozo Law Review,* 2005.

Mazmanyan, Armen: "Majoritarianism, Deliberation and Accountability as Institutional Instincts of Constitutional Courts", in Popelier, Patricia - Mazmanyan, Armen -Vandenbruwaene, Werner (eds.): *The Role of Constitutional Courts in Multilevel Governance,* Cambridge - Antwerp - Portland, Intersentia, 2013.

McEldowney, John: "The UK Supreme Court and Parliament: Judicial and political dialogues", in Szente, Zoltán - Gárdos-Orosz, Fruzsina (eds.): *New Challenges to Constitutional Adjudication in Europe,* London, Routledge, 2018, 214-232.

Mehde, Veith: "Beware of Disruption: Bundesverfassungsgericht as supporter of change and anchor of stability", in Szente, Zoltán - Gárdos-Orosz, Fruzsina (eds.): *New Challenges to Constitutional Adjudication in Europe,* London, Routledge, 2018, 53-72.

Möllers, Christoph: "Scope and Legitimacy of Judicial Review in German Constitutional Law - the Court versus the Political Process", in Pünder, Hermann - Waldhoff, Christian (eds.): *Debates in German Public Law,* Oxford - Portland, Hart, 2014.

Montesquieu: *A törvények szelleméről,* Bukarest, Kriterion, 1987.

Morrison, Fred L. (ed.): *Fiscal Rules - Limits on Governmental Deficits and Debt,* Berlin, Springer, 2016.

Moustafa, Tamir: "Law and Resistance in Authoritarian States: The judicialization in politics in Egypt", in Ginsburg, Tom - Moustafa, Tamir (eds.): *Rule by law: The Politics of Courts in Authoritarian Regimes,* Cambridge, Cambridge University Press, 2008.

Mudde, Cas - Kaltwasser, Cristóbal Rovira: *Populism. A Very Short Introduction,* Oxford, Oxford University Press, 2017, 10-11.

Müller, Jan-Werner: *Contesting Democracy: Political Ideas in Twentieth-Century Europe,* New Haven, Yale University Press, 2013.

Naszladi, Georgina: "A német alkotmányjogi panasz hatása a hazai szabályozásra és az alkotmánybírósági joggyakorlatra", *Jura,* 2014/1, 235-240.

Naszladi, Georgina: "Alkotmánymódosítások alkotmányosságáról döntött az Alkotmánybíróság", *Közjogi Szemle,* 2011/3, 65-66.

Naszladi, Georgina: "Az alkotmányjogi panasz első fél éve", *Közjogi Szemle,* 2012/4, 41-42.

Nishihara, Hiroshi: *Constitutional Meaning of the Proportionality Principle in the Face of "Surveillance State",* www.enelsyn.gr/en/workshops/workshop15(en).htm

Noonan, Norma - Nadkarni, Vidya (eds.): *Challenge and Change. Global Threats and the State in Twenty-first Century International Politics,* London, Palgrave Macmillan, 2016.

Orbán, Endre: "A bírói döntések ellen benyújtott alkotmányjogi panaszok tapasztalatai", *Magyar Jog,* 2016/10, 577–588.

Orbán, Endre: "Quo vadis, »alkotmányos identitás»?", *Közjogi Szemle,* 2018/3, 1–13.

Orbán, Endre: "Teczár-ügy reloaded", *Arsboni,* 12 October 2016, https://arsboni.hu/teczar-ugy-reloaded

Pacelle, Richard L., Jr. - Curry, Brett W. - Marshall, Bryan W.: *Decision Making by the Modern Supreme Court,* New York, Cambridge University Press, 2011.

Paczolay, Péter (ed.): *Alkotmánybíráskodás és alkotmányértelmezés,* Budapest, ELTE ÁJK, 1995.

Paczolay, Péter: "A történeti alkotmány és a konzervatív jogi gondolkodás", in Tőkéczki, László (ed.): *Magyar konzervatizmus. Hagyomány és jelenkor,* Budapest, Batthyány Lajos Alapítvány 1994, 29–36.

Paczolay, Péter: "Hans Kelsen és az alkotmánybíráskodás európai modelljének fejlődése", in Cs. Kiss, Lajos (ed.): *Hans Kelsen jogtudománya,* Budapest, Gondolat, 2007, 447–155.

Pap, András László: *Democratic Decline in Hungary. Law and Society in an Illiberal Democracy,* London, Routledge, 2018.

Papp, Imre: "A jogbiztonság formai eleme: a kellő felkészülési idő követelménye", *Kodifikáció,* 2013/1, 5–60.

Paris, Marie-Luce: "Setting the Scene: Elements of Constitutional Theory and Methodology of the Research", in Bell, John - Paris, Marie-Luce (eds.): *Rights-Based Constitutional Review. Constitutional Courts in a Changing Landscape,* Cheltenham, Edward Elgar, 2016.

Peretti, Terri Jennings: *In Defense of a Political Court,* Princeton, Princeton University Press, 1999.

Perry, Michael J.: "An Originalist Understanding of Minimalism", *Northwestern University Law Review,* 1993/88, 84–164.

Perry, Michael J.: *The Constitution, the courts, and human right: an inquiry in the legitimacy of constitutional policymaking by the judiciary,* New Haven, Yale University Press, 1982.

Petrétei, József: *Az alkotmányos demokrácia alapintézményei,* Budapest - Pécs, Dialóg Campus, 2009.

Pfersmann, Otto: "Unconstitutional constitutional amendments: a normativist approach", *Zeitschrift für öffentliches Recht,* 2012/1, 98–103.

Pikler, Kornél: *A bourzsoá alkotmánybíráskodás,* Budapest, Közgazdasági és Jogi Könyvkiadó, 1965.

Pócza, Kálmán (ed.): *Constitutional Politics and the Judiciary: Decision-making in Central and Eastern Europe,* London - New York, Routledge, 2018.

Pócza, Kálmán: "Az Alkotmánybíróság", in Körössényi, András (ed.): *A magyar politikai rendszer - negyedszázad után,* Budapest, Osiris, 2014, 161–184.

Pócza, Kálmán: "Politika és Alkotmánybíróság: a Bundesverfassungsgericht létrejötte", *Külügyi Szemle,* 2014/1, 111–131.

Pócza, Kálmán: "Többségi demokrácia és gyenge alkotmánybíráskodás: egy elszalasztott lehetőség", in Gárdos-Orosz, Fruzsina - Szente, Zoltán (eds.): *Jog és politika határán. Alkotmánybíráskodás Magyarországon 2010 után,* Budapest, HVG-ORAC, 2015, 185–212.

Pogány, István: "The Crisis of Democracy in East Central Europe: The »New Constitutionalism«", *European Public Law,* 2013/2, 341–367.

Pokol, Béla: "Aktivista alapjogász vagy parlamenti törvénybarát? A magyar alkotmánybíráskodásról", *Társadalmi Szemle,* 1992/5, 67–78.

Pokol, Béla: "Az alapjogok és az »alapjogi« bíráskodás", *Társadalmi Szemle,* 1991/5, 55–64.

Pokol, Béla: *A magyar parlamentarizmus,* Budapest, Cserépfalvi, 1994.

Pongrácz, Alex: „Gondolatok a tulajdon(jog)ról, figyelemmel az Alaptörvény szabályozására", in Deli, Gergely - Szoboszlay-Kiss, Katalin (eds.): *Tanulmányok a 70 éves Bihari Mihály tiszteletére,* Győr, Universitas, 2013.

Popelier, Patricia - Mazmanyan, Armen - Vandenbruwaene, Werner (eds.): *The Role of Constitutional Courts in Multilevel Governance,* Cambridge - Antwerp - Portland, Intersentia, 2013.

Pozsár-Szentmiklósy, Zoltán: "Az arányossági teszt a jogalkalmazásban", *Alkotmánybírósági Szemle,* 2016/2, 97–107.

Pozsár-Szentmiklósy, Zoltán: *Alapjogok mérlegen. Az általános alapjogi tesztek dogmatikája,* Budapest, HVG-Orac, 2016.

Pritchett, Herman C.: "The Development of Judicial Research", in Grossman, Joel B. - Tanenhaus, Joseph (eds.): *Frontiers of Judicial Research,* New York, Wiley, 1969.

"Politikai konstitucionalizmus - jogi konstitucionalizmus vita", *Fundamentum,* 2015/2–3, https://fundamentum.hu/politikai-alkotmanyossag

Redish, Martin H.: "Judicial Review and the »Political Question«", *Northwestern University Law Review,* 1985, 1031-1061.

Reiner, Roland: "Védett nők?", *Republikon blog,* 28 November 2013, http://republikon.blog.hu/2013/11/28/vedett_nok_589

Richards, Anthony: *Conceptualizing Terrorism,* Oxford, Oxford University Press, 2015.

Rixer, Ádám: "Hungary's Fundamental Law and the concept of the historical constitution", *European Journal of European History of Law,* 2013/4, 116–123.

Rixer, Ádám: *A vívmány-teszt,* Budapest, Ludovika Egyetemi Kiadó, 2018.

Rixer, Ádám: *Features of the Hungarian Legal System after 2010,* Budapest, Patrocinium, 2012.

Rosenfeld, Michel: *The Identity of the Constitutional Subject: Selfhood, Citizenship and Community,* London, Routledge, 2009.

Rousseau, Dominique: *La justice constitutionnelle en Europe,* Paris, Montchrestien, 1998.

Sadurski, Wojciech (ed.): *Constitutional Justice, East and West. Democratic Legitimacy and Constitutional Courts in Post-Communist Europe in a Comparative Perspective,* Hague - London, Kluwer Law International, 2002.

Sajó, András - Uitz, Renáta: *A szabadság alkotmánya. Bevezetés a jogi alkotmányosságba,* Budapest, HVG-ORAC, 2019.

Sajó, András - Uitz, Renáta: *The Constitution in Private Relations,* Eleventh Publishing, 2006.

Sajó, András (ed.): *Alkotmányosság a magánjogban,* Complex, 2006.

Sajó, András: "A »láthatatlan alkotmány« apróbetűi. A magyar Alkotmánybíróság első ezerkétszáz napja", *Állam- és Jogtudomány,* 1993/1-2, 37–96.

Sajó, András: *Az önkorlátozó hatalom,* Budapest, Közgazdasági és Jogi Könyvkiadó - MTA Állam- és Jogtudományi Intézet, 1995.

Sári, János: *Alkotmányjog II. Alapjogok,* Budapest, Osiris, 2004.

Scharpf, Fritz Wilhelm: "A Functional Analysis", *The Yale Law Journal,* 1966/4, 517–597.

Scharpf, Fritz Wilhelm: *Die Grenzen der richterlichen Verantwortung. Die political-question-Doktrin in der Rechtsprechung des amerikanischen Supreme Court,* Karlsruhe, C. F. Müller, 1965.

SCHEPPELE, Kim Lane: "Autocratic Legalism", *University of Chicago Law Review,* 2018/2.

SCHWARTZ, Herman: *The Struggle for Constitutional Justice in Post-Communist Europe,* Chicago, University of Chicago Press, 2000.

SCHWARZE, Jürgen: *Verfassungsrecht und Verfassungsgerichtsbarkeit im Zeichen Europas,* Baden-Baden, Nomos, 1998.

SCHWEITZER, Gábor: *A magyar királyi köztársaságtól a magyar köztársaságig,* Budapest, Publikon, 2017.

SEBŐK, Miklós – GÁRDOS-OROSZ, Fruzsina – KISS, Rebeka – JÁRAY, István: *How to quantify constitutional reasoning – a text mining approach* (forthcoming).

SEPSI, Tibor: "Az Alaptörvény személyes adatok védelméhez való joggal összefüggő rendelkezéseinek érvényesülése – az alkotmánybírósági gyakorlat a rendes bíróságok eljárásában az Alaptörvény hatálybalépése óta", in *Az Alaptörvény érvényesülése a bírói gyakorlatban III. Alkotmányjogi panasz: az alapjog-érvényesítés gyakorlata,* Budapest, HVG-ORAC, 2019, 260–276.

SÓLYOM, László – BRUNNER, Georg: *Constitutional Judiciary in a New Democracy: The Hungarian Constitutional Court,* Ann Arbor, University of Michigan Press, 2000.

SÓLYOM, László: "A magyar Alkotmánybíróság önértelmezése és Hans Kelsen", in Cs. KISS, Lajos (ed.): *Hans Kelsen jogtudománya,* Budapest, Gondolat, 2007.

SÓLYOM, László: "Az Alkotmány emberi jogi generálklauzulájához vezető út", *Iustum Aequum Salutare,* 2005.

SÓLYOM, László: "Az alkotmány őrei", in SÓLYOM, László: *Documenta, Alkotmányjog,* Budapest, HVG-ORAC, 2019.

SÓLYOM, László: "Ezen a lejtőn nehéz lesz megállni!", *Iustum Aequum Salutare,* 2010/4, 5–9.

SÓLYOM, László: *A személyiségi jogok elmélete,* Budapest, Közigazgatási és Jogi Könyvkiadó, 1983.

SÓLYOM, László: *Az alkotmánybíráskodás kezdetei Magyarországon,* Budapest, Osiris, 2001.

SÓLYOM, Péter: "Kelsen köpönyegéből. A magyar Alkotmánybíróság keletkezéstörténetéhez", *Közjogi Szemle,* 2021/2, 1–17.

SOMODY, Bernadette – SZABÓ, Máté – SZIGETI, Tamás – VISSY Beatrix: "Alapjogi igények, alapjogi szabályok: az alapjogi ítélkezés egy koncepciója", in SOMODY Bernadette (ed.): *Alapjogi bíráskodás – alapjogok az ítélkezésben,* Budapest, L'Harmattan, 2013.

SOMODY, Bernadette – SZABÓ, Máté Dániel – VISSY, Beatrix: *Az alapjogi bíráskodás kézikönyve,* Budapest, HVG-ORAC, 2013.

SOMODY, Bernadette (ed.): *Alapjogi bíráskodás – alapjogok az ítélkezésben,* Budapest, L'Harmattan, 2013.

SOMODY, Bernadette: "A rendőrarcképmás-ügy mint az alapjogi ítélkezés próbája", *Fundamentum,* 2016/1, 103–112.

SONNEVEND, Pál – JAKAB, András – CSINK, Lóránt: "The constitution as an instrument of everyday party politics: the basic law of Hungary: The Basic Law of Hungary", in VON BOGDANDY, Armin – SONNEVEND, Pál (eds.): *Constitutional Crisis in the European Constitutional Area. Theory, Law and Politics in Hungary and Romania,* Oxford, Hart, 2015, 46–123.

STERN, Klaus: *Verfassungsgerichtsbarkeit zwischen Recht und Politik,* Düsseldorf, Westdeutscher, 1979.

STONE SWEET, Alec – MATHEWS, Jud: "Proportionality Balancing and Global Constitutionalism", *Columbia Journal of Transnational Law,* 2008, 68–149.

Stone Sweet, Alec: "Constitutional Court", in Rosenfeld, Michel – Sajó, András (eds.): *Oxford Handbook of Comparative Constitutional Law,* Oxford, Oxford University Press, 2012.

Stone Sweet, Alec: *Governing with Judges. Constitutional Politics in Europe,* Oxford, Oxford University Press, 2000.

Stumpf, István: "Rule of Law, Division of Powers, Constitutionalism", *Acta Juridica Hungarica,* 2014/4, 299–317.

Stumpf, István: *A tulajdonhoz való jog* (lecture, Győr, 3 March 2016).

Sulyok, Gábor: "Újabb visszatérés a nemzetközi jog és a belső jog viszonyának alaptörvényi szabályozásához", in Fekete, Balázs – Horváthy, Balázs – Kreisz, Brigitta (eds.): *A világ mi magunk vagyunk... Liber Amicorum Imre Vörös,* Budapest, HVG-ORAC, 2014.

Sulyok, Tamás – Deli, Gergely: „A magyar nemzeti identitás az Alkotmánybíróság gyakorlatában", *Alkotmánybírósági Szemle,* 2019/1, 57–59.

SULYOK, Tamás: *Az alkotmányos önazonosság az Alkotmánybíróság döntéseiben,* https://alkotmanybirosag.hu/kozlemeny/az-alkotmanyos-onazonossag-az-alkotmanybirosag-donteseiben

Sunstein, Cass S.: *One Case at a Time: Judicial Minimalism on the Supreme Court,* Cambridge, Harvard University Press, 2001.

Szabó I., László: "Az intézményi, szervezeti bizalom helyzete Magyarországon 2014 elején", *Nemzet és Biztonság,* 2014/3, 133–139.

Szakály, Zsuzsa: "A történeti alkotmány és az alkotmányos identitás az Alaptörvény tükrében", *Pro Publico Bono – Magyar Közigazgatás,* 2015/3, http://uni-nke.hu/uploads/media_items/szakaly-zsuzsaa-torteneti-alkotmany-es-az-alkotmanyos-identitas-az-alaptorveny-tukreben.original.pdf

Szalbot, Balázs Mihály: "A közvetlen alkotmányjogi panasszal támadható normák körének meghatározása", *Magyar Jog,* 2017/6, 347–361.

Szalbot, Balázs: "Az alkotmányjogi panasz legújabb kérdései – A közvetlen panasz", *De iurisprudentia et iure publico,* 2013/2, 1–31.

Szeghalmi, Veronika – Papp, János Tamás: "A rendőr képmásának védelme – a vita jelenlegi állása", *Iustum Aequum Salutare,* 2015/4, 95–110.

Szente, Zoltán – Gárdos-Orosz, Fruzsina (eds.): *New Challenges to Constitutional Adjudication in Europe,* London, Routledge, 2018.

Szente, Zoltán – Gárdos-Orosz, Fruzsina (eds.): *Populist Challenges to Constitutional Interpretation in Europe and Beyond,* London, Routledge, 2021.

Szente, Zoltán – Gárdos-Orosz, Fruzsina: "Constitutional courts under pressure – An assessment", in Szente, Zoltán – Gárdos-Orosz, Fruzsina (eds.): *New Challenges to Constitutional Adjudication in Europe,* London, Routledge, 2018, 291–312.

Szente, Zoltán – Gárdos-Orosz, Fruzsina: "Constitutional effects of populism on EU Member States", in Castellà Andreu, Josep Maria – Simonelli, Marco Antonio (eds.): *Populism and Contemporary Democracy in Europe. Old Problems and New Challenges,* Cham, Palgrave Macmillan, 2022, 113–135.

Szente, Zoltán – Gárdos-Orosz, Fruzsina: "Judicial deference or political loyalty?", in Szente, Zoltán – Gárdos-Orosz, Fruzsina (eds.): *New Challenges to Constitutional Adjudication in Europe,* London, Routledge, 2018, 89–110.

Szente, Zoltán: "A 2011. évi Alaptörvény és a történeti alkotmány összekapcsolásának mítosza", *Közjogi Szemle,* 2019/1, 1–8.

SZENTE, Zoltán: "A 2020. március 11-én kihirdetett veszélyhelyzet alkotmányossági problémái", *Állam- és Jogtudomány,* 2020/3, 115–139.

SZENTE, Zoltán: "Az alkotmánybírák politikai orientációi Magyarországon 2010 és 2014 között", in GÁRDOS-OROSZ, Fruzsina – SZENTE, Zoltán (eds.): *Jog és politika határán. Alkotmánybíráskodás Magyarországon 2010 után,* Budapest, HVG-ORAC, 2015.

SZENTE, Zoltán: "Az alkotmánybírák politikai orientációi Magyarországon 2010 és 2014 között", *Politikatudományi Szemle,* 2015/1, 31–57.

SZENTE, Zoltán: "Az Alkotmánybíróság értelmezési gyakorlata 1990–2010", in DELI Gergely – SZOBOSZLAY-KISS Katalin (eds.): *Tanulmányok a 70 éves Bihari Mihály tiszteletére,* Győr, Universitas, 2013.

SZENTE, Zoltán: "Az angol és a magyar párhuzamos alkotmányfejlődés mítosza", *Közjogi Szemle,* 2016/2, 23–32.

SZENTE, Zoltán: "Breaking and Making Constitutional Rules – The Constitutional Effects of Financial Crisis in Hungary", in CONTIADES, Xenophon (ed.): *Constitutions in the Global Financial Crisis. A Comparative Analysis,* Farnham, Ashgate, 2013.

SZENTE, Zoltán: "Challenging the Basic Values – The Problems of the Rule of Law in Hungary and the Failure of the European Union to Tackle Them", in JAKAB, András –KOCHENOV, Dimitry (eds.): *The Enforcement of EU Law and Values. Ensuring Member States' Compliance,* Oxford, Oxford University Press, 2017.

SZENTE, Zoltán: "Jog és politika határán: az alkotmánybíróságok és az alkotmánybíráskodás jellegéről", in GÁRDOS-OROSZ, Fruzsina – SZENTE, Zoltán (eds.): *Jog és politika határán. Alkotmánybíráskodás Magyarországon 2010 után,* Budapest, HVG-ORAC, 2015.

SZENTE, Zoltán: "Populism and populist constitutionalism", in SZENTE, Zoltán – GÁRDOS-OROSZ, Fruzsina (eds.): *Populist Challenges to Constitutional Interpretation in Europe and Beyond,* London, Routledge, 2021, 3–28.

SZENTE, Zoltán: "The Controversial Anti-Migrant Referendum in Hungary is Invalid", 2016, http://constitutional-change.com/the-controversial-anti-migrant-referendum-in-hungary-is-invalid

SZENTE, Zoltán: "The Doctrine of the Holy Crown in the Hungarian Historical Constitution", *Journal of the History of Law,* 2013/4, 109–115.

SZENTE, Zoltán: „Az Alkotmánybíróság döntése Magyarország Alaptörvényének Átmeneti rendelkezései alkotmányosságáról: az Alaptörvény integritása és az alkotmányozó hatalom korlátai", *Jogesetek Magyarázata,* 2013/2, 11–21. www.jema.hu/article.php?c=231

SZENTE, Zoltán: "Populist Constitutionalism in Populist challenges to Constitutional Interpretation in Europe and Beyond", in SZENTE, Zoltán – GÁRDOS-OROSZ, Fruzsina (eds.): *Populist Challenges to Constitutional Interpretation in Europe and Beyond,* London, Routledge, 2021.

SZENTE, Zoltán: "The Interpretive Practice of the Hungarian Constitutional Court: A Critical View", *German Law Journal,* 2013, 1591–1614.

SZENTE, Zoltán: *Érvelés és értelmezés az alkotmányjogban,* Budapest, Dialóg Campus, 2013.

SZILÁGYI, Emese: "A kommunikációs alapjogok általános értelmezése és alkalmazása a rendes bírósági és az alkotmánybírósági gyakorlatban – a bírói kezdeményezések és az alkotmányjogi panaszos ügyek tapasztalatai", in *Az Alaptörvény érvényesülése a bírói gyakorlatban III. Alkotmányjogi panasz: az alapjog-érvényesítés gyakorlata,* Budapest, HVG-ORAC, 2019, 98–121.

SZILÁGYI, Emese: "Az Alkotmánybíróság az alkotmánykonform bírói jogértelmezésről – terítéken az Alaptörvény 28. cikke", *Közjogi Szemle,* 2015/1, 66–68.

SZILÁGYI, Emese: "Homályos kép. Alkotmánybírósági határozat a rendőrök arcának kötelező kitakarásáról", *Közjogi Szemle,* 2014/4, 59–60.

SZOMORA, Zsolt: "Az alkotmányos követelmények hivatkozási tipológiája becsületsértési és rágalmazási ügyekben hozott büntetőítéletekben", *Jogtudományi Közlöny,* 2014/10, 469–476.

TAKÁCS, Albert: "Az alkotmányosság dilemmái és az Alkotmánybíróság ítéletei", *Acta Humana,* 1990/1, 38–56.

TAKÁCS, Albert: "Magyarország alkotmánybírósága tegnap és holnap között", in ÁDÁM, Antal (ed.): *Alkotmányfejlődés és jogállami gyakorlat,* Budapest, Hanns Seidel Alapítvány, 1994.

TÉGLÁSI, András: "A devizahitelezés problémája és kezelésének alkotmányos kérdései az Alkotmánybíróság gyakorlatának fényében", in LENTER Csaba (ed.): *A devizahitelezés nagy kézikönyve,* Budapest, Nemzeti Közszolgálati és Tankönyvkiadó, 2015, 315–334.

TÉGLÁSI, András: "A szociális jogok (alap)jogvédelmi szintjének csökkenése a gazdasági válság hatására. Avagy a jogrendszerek versenye „rückwärts"-ben (?)", *Justum Aequum Salutare,* 2016/2, 141–170.

TÉGLÁSI, András: "A tulajdonhoz való jog védelme az Alkotmánybíróság gyakorlatában az Alaptörvény hatálybalépését követően", in CSERVÁK, Csaba – HORVÁTH, Attila (eds.): *Az adekvát alapjogvédelem,* Budapest, Porta Historica, 2017.

TÉGLÁSI, András: "Az alapjogok hatása a magánjogi viszonyokban az Alkotmánybíróság gyakorlatában az Alaptörvény hatálybalépését követő első három évben, különös tekintettel a tulajdonhoz való jog alkotmányos védelmére", *Jogtudományi Közlöny,* 2015/3, 148–157.

TILK, Péter – NASZLADI, Georgina: "Az Alkotmánybíróságra vonatkozó szabályozás átalakulása 2010 után", in GÁRDOS-OROSZ, Fruzsina – SZENTE, Zoltán (eds.): *Jog és politika határán. Alkotmánybíráskodás Magyarországon 2010 után,* Budapest, HVG-ORAC, 2015, 41–74.

TILK, Péter: "Gondolatok az Alkotmánybíróság vizsgálati lehetőségeinek szűkítéséről", in TRÓCSÁNYI, László (ed.): *Dikaiosz Logosz. Tanulmányok Kovács István emlékére,* Szeged, Pólay Elemér Alapítvány, 2012, 145–153.

TOMKINS, Adam: "In Defence of the Political Constitution", *Oxford Journal of Legal Studies,* 2012/1, 157–175.

TORDAI, Csaba: "Az alkotmánybírósági esetjog hatása a rendes bírói ítéletekre az információszabadság és a képmáshoz való jog területén", in *Az Alaptörvény érvényesülése a bírói gyakorlatban III. Alkotmányjogi panasz: az alapjog-érvényesítés gyakorlata,* Budapest, HVG-ORAC, 2019, 245–259.

TORDAI, Csaba: "Az első év tapasztalatairól", *Alkotmánybírósági Szemle,* 2012/2, 131–133.

TÖRÖK, Bernát: "A közügyek vitájának körvonalai a véleményszabadság magyar doktrínájában", in KOLTAY, András – TÖRÖK, Bernát (eds.): *Sajtószabadság és médiajog a 21. század elején 4.,* Budapest, Wolters Kluwer, 2017, 425–460.

TÖRÖK, Bernát: "A szólásszabadság hatóköre és az általa nyújtott védelem", *Magyar Jog,* 2015/7–8, 385–393.

TÖRÖK, Bernát: "A szólásszabadság védelmének dinamikája", *Magyar Jog,* 2017/12, 721–733.

Török, Bernát: "Alkotmányjogi tesztek hálójában: a sajtószabadság esete a tőkepiaccal", in Fejes, Zsuzsanna – Török, Bernát (eds.): *Suum cuique. Ünnepi tanulmányok Paczolay Péter 60. születésnapja tiszteletére,* Szeged, Pólay Elemér Alapítvány, 2016, 671–684.

Tóth J., Zoltán – Térey, Vilmos: „A bírói döntésekre is kiható alkotmánybírósági jogvédelem tapasztalatai (2012–2017)", *Alkotmánybírósági Szemle,* 2017/2, 102–107.

Tóth J., Zoltán: "A »valódi« alkotmányjogi panasz használatba vétele: az Abtv. 27. §-a szerinti panasz első két éve az Alkotmánybíróság gyakorlatában", *Jogtudományi Közlöny,* 2014/5, 224–238.

Tóth J., Zoltán: "Az egyéni alapjogvédelem az Alkotmányban és az Alaptörvényben I–II.", *Közjogi Szemle,* 2012/3–4, 11–19.

Tóth J., Zoltán: *A büntetőjogi rágalmazás és becsületsértés. A defamatorikus bűncselekmények elméleti és gyakorlati megítélése a véleménynyilvánítási szabadság és az emberi méltósághoz való jog kontextusában,* Budapest, Médiatudományi Intézet, 2017.

Tóth, Attila Gábor: "Az eljárási alkotmányosság tartalma", *Fundamentum,* 2004/3, 5–33.

Tóth, Gábor Attila (ed.): *Constitution for a Disunited Nation. On Hungary's 2011 Fundamental Law,* New York – Budapest, Central University Press, 2012.

Tóth, Gábor Attila: "Historicism or Art Nouveau in Constitutional Interpretation? A comment on Zoltán Szente's *The Interpretive Practice of the Hungarian Constitutional Court—A Critical View*", *German Law Journal,* 2013/8, 1615–1626.

Tóth, Gábor Attila: "Mi van és mi legyen a magyar alkotmányjogban?", *Közjogi Szemle,* 2011/2, 2–3.

Tóth, Gábor Attila: *Életfogytig szabadláb. Alkotmányjogi karcolatok*, Budapest, Élet- és Irodalom, 2011.

Tóth, Péter – Molnár, Benedek – Németh, Márton (eds.): *Mérlegen az Alaptörvény. Interjúkötet hazánk új alkotmányáról,* Budapest, HVG-ORAC, 2013.

Troper, Michael: "The logic of justification of judicial review", *International Journal of Constitutional Law,* 2003/1, 105–107.

Tuori, Kaarlo – Tuori, Klaus: *The Eurozone Crisis. A Constitutional Analysis,* Cambridge, Cambridge University Press, 2014.

Tushnet, Mark – Bugaric, Bojan: "Populism and Constitutionalism: An Essay on Definitions and Their Implications", *Cardozo Law Review,* 2020/6.

Tushnet, Mark: "Authoritarian Constitutionalism", *Cornell Law Review,* 2015, 391–462.

Tushnet, Mark: *Advanced Introduction to Comparative Constitutional Law,* Cheltenham, Edward Elgar, 2014.

Uitz, Renáta: "Egyéni jogsérelmek és az Alkotmánybíróság", *Fundamentum,* 1999/2, 39–52.

Uitz, Renáta: "The Illusion of a Constitution in Europe: the Hungarian Constitutional Court after the Fifth Amendment of the Fundamental Law", in Bell, John – Paris, Marie-Luce (eds.): *Rights-Based Constitutional Review. Constitutional Courts in a Changing Landscape,* Cheltenham, Edward Elgar, 2016, 374–405.

Vadász, Vanda – Gárdos-Orosz, Fruzsina: "Alkotmányértelmezés a rendes bíróságok és az alkotmánybíróság gyakorlatában a bírói kezdeményezések tükrében", in *Az Alaptörvény érvényesülése a bírói gyakorlatban IV. A bírói kezdeményezések gyakorlati tapasztalata,* Budapest, HVG-ORAC, 2019, 237–318.

Vanberg, Georg: *The Politics of Constitutional Review in Germany,* Cambridge, Cambridge University Press, 2005.

VARGA Zs., András: "Történeti alkotmányunk vívmányai az Alaptörvény kógens rendelkezésében", *Iustum Aequum Salutare,* 2016/4, 83–89.

VARJU, Márton – VÁRNAY, Ernő (eds.): *European Union Law in Hungary: Institutions, Processes and the Law,* Budapest: HVG-ORAC, 2014.

VARJU, Márton: "The crisis, judicial power and EU law: Could it have been managed differently by the EU Court of Justice?", in SZENTE, Zoltán – GÁRDOS-OROSZ, Fruzsina (eds.): *New Challenges to Constitutional Adjudication in Europe,* London, Routledge, 2018, 174–288.

VÁRNAY, Ernő: "Judicial Passivism at the European Court of Justice?", *Hungarian Journal of Legal Studies,* 2019/2, 127–154.

VÁRNAY, Ernő: "Tagállami érdekek, tagállami kötelezettségek és az Európai Unió joga", *Jogtudományi Közlöny,* 2022/7–8, 324–326.

VERSCHRAEGEN, Gert: "Hybrid Constitutionalism, Fundamental Rights and the State", *Rechtsfilosofie en Rechtstheorie,* 2011, 216–229.

VINCZE, Attila – CSUHÁNY, Péter – SONNEVEND, Pál – JAKAB, András: "Az Alkotmánybíróság", in JAKAB, András (ed.): *Az Alkotmány kommentárja I–II.*, Budapest, Századvég, 2009, 1099–1172.

VINCZE, Attila: "Az Alkotmánybíróság határozata az Alaptörvény negyedik módosításáról. Az alkotmánymódosítás alkotmánybírósági kontrollja", *Jogesetek Magyarázata,* 2013/3.

VINCZE, Attila: "Wrestling with Constitutionalism: the Supermajority and the Hungarian Constitutional Court", *ICL Journal – Vienna Journal on International Constitutional Law,* 2013/4, 86–97.

VISSER, Maartje de: *Constitutional Review in Europe. A Comparative Analysis,* Oxford, Hart, 2014.

VISSY, Beatrix: "A bírói döntések alkotmánybírósági felülvizsgálata mint a politikai hatalom korlátozásának eszköze?", in GÁRDOS-OROSZ, Fruzsina – SZENTE, Zoltán (eds.): *Jog és politika határán. Alkotmánybíráskodás Magyarországon 2010 után,* Budapest, HVG-ORAC, 2015, 349–374.

VISSY, Beatrix: "A valódi alkotmányjogi panasz legitimitása Hans Kelsen szemszögéből", *Közjogi Szemle,* 2015/3, 35–41.

VISSY, Beatrix: "Az individuális alapjogvédelem kilátásai az alkotmánybíráskodásban. Merre mutat az alkotmányjogi panasz iránytűje?", *Magyar Közigazgatás,* 2012/2, 199–211.

VISSY, Beatrix: "Támpontok a valódi alkotmányjogi panasz hatókörének megállapításához", *Közjogi Szemle,* 2014/2, 40–46.

VÍZKELETY, Mariann (editor-in-chief): 5 éves *az Alaptörvény. Válogatás az ünnepi konferenciasorozat beszédeiből,* Budapest, Magyar Közlöny Lap- és Könyvkiadó, 2017.

VLACHOGIANNIS, Apostolos: "From submission to reaction: the Greek Courts stance on the financial crisis in challenges", in SZENTE, Zoltán – GÁRDOS-OROSZ, Fruzsina (eds.): *New Challenges to Constitutional Adjudication in Europe,* London, Routledge, 2018, 72–89.

VON BOGDANDY, Armin – SONNEVEND, Pál (eds.): *Constitutional Crises in the European Constitutional Area. Theory, Law and Politica in Hungary and Romania,* Oxford, Hart, 2015.

VÖRÖS, Imre: "A felhatalmazási törvénytől az egészségügyi válsághelyzetig és tovább", in GÁRDOS-OROSZ, Fruzsina – LŐRINCZ, Viktor Olivér (eds.): *Jogi diagnózisok. A COVID-19-világjárvány hatásai a jogrendszerre,* Budapest, L'Harmattan – Társadalomtudományi Kutatóközpont Jogtudományi Intézet, 2020, 1–28.

VÖRÖS, Imre: "A történeti alkotmány az Alkotmánybíróság gyakorlatában", *Közjogi Szemle,* 2016/4, 44–57.
VÖRÖS, Imre: "The constitutional landscape after the fourth and fifth amendments of Hungarian Fundamental Law", *Acta Juridica Hungarica,* 2014/1, 1–20.
WALDRON, Jeremy: "The core of the case against judicial review", *Yale Law Journal,* 2006/115, 1346–1407.
WECHSLER, Herbert: "Toward Neutral Principles of Constitutional Law", *Harvard Law Review,* 1959, 1–35.
WEINER, Greg: *The Case against Judicial Supremacy,* Lawrence Kansas, University Press of Kansas, 2019.
WHITTINGTON, Keith E.: "The Political Foundations of Judicial Supremacy", in BARBER, Sotirios A. – GEORGE, Robert P. (eds.): *Constitutional Politics,* Princeton, Princeton University Press, 2002, 261–297.
ZAKARIÁS, Kinga: "A bírói döntések alkotmánybírósági felülvizsgálata terjedelmének dogmatikai keretei – a jogalkalmazás közvetlen és közvetett alapjogsértésének kontrollja a német és magyar gyakorlat tükrében", *Állam- és Jogtudomány,* 2021/4, 101–127.
ZAKARIÁS, Kinga: "A bírósági határozatok ellen irányuló alkotmányjogi panasz a Német Szövetségi Alkotmánybíróság Esra-határozatának tükrében", *Alkotmánybírósági Szemle,* 2011/2, 92–100.
ZAKARIÁS, Kinga: "A képmáshoz való alapjog. A bírói döntések alkotmánybírósági felülvizsgálatának terjedelme a rendőr képmás ügyekben", *Alkotmánybírósági Szemle,* 2017/2, 108–114.
ZAKARIÁS, Kinga: "A rendes bíróságok határozatainak felülvizsgálata a Német Szövetségi Alkotmánybíróság gyakorlatában", *Jogtudományi Közlöny,* 2010/2, 98–104.
ZAKARIÁS, Kinga: "Az alkotmányos követelmény mint hivatalos elvi tétel a magyar Alkotmánybíróság gyakorlatában", *Jog – Állam – Politika. Ünnepi különszám a 70 éves Kukorelli István tiszteletére,* 2022/2, 401–414.
ZAKARIÁS, Kinga: "Az alkotmányos követelmény", *Jog – Állam – Politika. Ünnepi különszám a 70 éves Kukorelli István tiszteletére,* 2022/2
ZAKARIÁS, Kinga: *Az emberi méltóság,* Budapest, Pázmány Press, 2019.
ZELLER, JUDIT: "Nichts ist so beständig… Die jüngsten Novellen des Grundgesetzes Ungarns im Kontext der Entscheidungen des Verfassungsgerichts", *Osteuropa-Recht,* 2013/3, 307–325.
ZÉTÉNYI, Zsolt (ed.): *A történeti alkotmány – Magyarország ősi alkotmánya,* Budapest, Magyarországért Kulturális Egyesület, 2010.
ZIPPELIUS, Reinhold: *Juristische Methodenlehre,* München, C. H. Beck, 1994.
ZOLDAN, Evan: "Targeted Judicial Activism", *16 Green Bag,* 2d 465, 2013.
ZUCCA, Lorenzo: *Constitutional Dilemmas,* OUP, 2007.
ZURN, Christopher F.: *Deliberative Democracy and the Institutions of Judicial Review,* Cambridge, Cambridge University Press, 2007.

www.ingramcontent.com/pod-product-compliance
Lightning Source LLC
Chambersburg PA
CBHW071243230926
51849CB00001B/210
* 9 7 8 9 4 0 3 5 2 0 2 8 5 *